Natchez Country

Early American Places is a collaborative project of the
University of Georgia Press, New York University Press,
Northern Illinois University Press, and the University of
Nebraska Press. The series is supported by the Andrew
W. Mellon Foundation. For more information, please visit
www.earlyamericanplaces.com.

ADVISORY BOARD
Vincent Brown, *Duke University*
Cornelia Hughes Dayton, *University of Connecticut*
Nicole Eustace, *New York University*
Amy S. Greenberg, *Pennsylvania State University*
Ramón A. Gutiérrez, *University of Chicago*
Peter Charles Hoffer, *University of Georgia*
Karen Ordahl Kupperman, *New York University*
Mark M. Smith, *University of South Carolina*
Rosemarie Zagarri, *George Mason University*

Natchez Country

Indians, Colonists, and the Landscapes
of Race in French Louisiana

GEORGE EDWARD MILNE

The University of Georgia Press
ATHENS AND LONDON

© 2015 by the University of Georgia Press
Athens, Georgia 30602
www.ugapress.org

All rights reserved

Most University of Georgia Press titles are
available from popular e-book vendors.

Printed digitally

Library of Congress Catalog-in-Publication Data
Milne, George Edward.
Natchez Country : Indians, colonists, and the landscapes of race in French Louisiana /
George Edward Milne.
   pages cm. — (Early American places)
ISBN 978-0-8203-4749-3 (hardback : alkaline paper) —
ISBN 978-0-8203-4750-9 (paperback : alkaline paper) —
ISBN 978-0-8203-4751-6 (e-book)
1. Natchez Indians—First contact with Europeans. 2. Natchez Indians—Government
relations—To 1789. 3. Natchez Indians—Wars, 1729. 4. Natchez Indians—Ethnic identity.
5. French—Louisiana—History. 6. France—Colonies—America—Race relations.
7. Slavery—France—Colonies—History. 8. Indians of North America—Louisiana—
Government relations—To 1789. 9. Indians of North America—Mississippi River Valley
—History. 1 0. Natchez (Miss.)—History.
I. Title.
E99.N2M55 2015
323.1197′9—dc23

2014023168

British Library Cataloging-in-Publication Data available

In memory of my father, George Milne, 1928–2013

Contents

	List of Figures	xi
	Acknowledgments	xiii
	Introduction	1
1	Rising Suns	15
2	Thefts of the Suns	45
3	Impudent Immigrants	79
4	The Many Lands of Natchez Country	120
5	"These Are People Who Named Themselves Red Men"	149
6	Fallen Forts	175
	Legacies	207
	Notes	217
	Bibliography	265
	Index	285

Figures

0.1	Louisiana, circa 1718–1730	xvi
1.1	Mound sites in Natchez Country	34
3.1	Natchez Country, circa 1723–1726	87
3.2	Bouteux's map of Natchez Country	89
3.3	Detail of Bouteux's map: The Apple Village	90
3.4	Dumont de Montigny's Natchez Country	91
3.5	Broutin's map of Natchez Country, 1723	92
3.6	The "inner commons" of Natchez Country	99
3.7	Cabins of the Great Sun	111
4.1	The funeral procession of the Tattooed Serpent	127
4.2	Archaeological excavation of the Temple Mound, circa 1965	129
4.3	The Terre Blanche Concession (detail from Dumont de Montigny)	138
6.1	Cabins of the *femme chef*	179
6.2	The Chouaouchas Village and concessions, circa 1723	184
6.3	Natchez forts, 1730	192

Acknowledgments

This book is the result of a journey that began with words from two great teachers, Joy Jimon Hintz and Geoffrey Shugen Arnold, who told me that each of us could make happen those things we truly want to make happen.

The financial support of Oakland University has been invaluable in bringing this journey to a close. Funds from the Faculty Research Fellowship allowed me to spend a summer in New Orleans. The University's Faculty Research Award gave me a chance to travel to Québec, Paris, and Aix-en-Provence to conduct research at various repositories. Several colleagues at Oakland have also provided intellectual and moral support, among them Karen Miller, Don Matthews, and Sara Chapman. Sara deserves special mention since her work on kinship and patronage within the French nobility furnished a crucial interpretive model for understanding circles of influence among both Louisiana's colonists and the Natchez Indians.

The librarians and archivists at the Archive nationale de France, the Bibliothèque nationale de France, and the Archives nationales d'outre mer rendered valuable assistance, as did those at the Service historique de la defense at the Chateau Vincennes.

My journey took me across the United States as well. Ann Voge at the Center for Louisiana Studies at the University of Southwestern Louisiana was a warm friend who showed me around the archives. Erin Kinchen and Sarah Elizabeth Gundlach provided excellent support at the Louisiana State Museum Historical Collection. The staff members of the Huntington Library in San Marino, California, were exceptionally helpful. Juan Gomez, Chris Addes, and Kate Henningsen made my time there enjoyable as well as productive.

The staff and faculty of the History Department of the University of Oklahoma were invaluable in guiding and sustaining my early investigations of the Natchez and French Louisiana. I would like to thank Professors Robert Griswold and Paul Gilje, and especially Josh Piker. The numerous grants and fellowships from the Department and the University of Oklahoma permitted me to conduct research and attend conferences on two continents. These included several Bea Mantooth Travel Grants, the Anne Hodges Morgan and H. Wayne Morgan Dissertation Fellowship, and the A. K. & Ethel T. Christian Scholarship for Research Travel. The University of Oklahoma Graduate College aided my work with the Robberson Research Travel Grant. The University of Oklahoma's College of Arts and Sciences contributed the Robert E. and Mary B. Sturgis Scholarship. The University also supported my efforts with generous funding in the form of the Hudson and the Alumni Fellowships.

The Huntington Library provided funds in the form of two fellowships as an Andrew Mellon Reader. The American Historical Association supported my work with a Robberson Research Travel Grant, and the American Philosophical Society provided a fellowship from its Philips Fund for Native American Research. The Phi Alpha Theta History Honors Fraternity helped with the John Pine Dissertation Scholarship.

Deserving of thanks are Greg O'Brien and Gregory Waselkov for reading the book manuscript and offering sound advice. Josh Clough was a great help as my proofreader during my writing process. Sophie White has also provided her perspective on my work. Erin Greenwald merits special mention for bringing the Calliot Manuscript to my attention. Her colleagues at the Historic New Orleans Collection were also invaluable in directing me to key documents. Gordon Sayre also played an important role by translating some particularly difficult documents, contributing advice, and directing my attention to the role of Natchez women in intercultural diplomacy. I also wish to acknowledge my *collègue*, Anne-Marie Libério, who has been a constant source of sound advice, frank observations, accurate translations, and friendship. Several other friends lent moral support: Kim Kino and Jimmy Raccioppi the foremost among them.

Without my parents, however, this journey would never have begun. I owe them a debt of gratitude not only for their obvious roles in bringing me into this world, but for also instilling in me a respect for education. My father imparted a love of history from my earliest memories when he would tell me about life in the "olden days." Unfortunately, he did not live to see the publication of this book, but it is dedicated to his memory. My mother spent her holidays with my dad driving up and down the Atlantic Coast with a station wagon full of boys towing a tent-camper. Even though these might not have been ideal vacations for her, she was there every time we stopped at nearly every restored village, abandoned fort, and roadside museum between the Canadian border and the Everglades.

Some passages originally appeared in *Mapping the Mississippian Shatter Zone: The Colonial Indian Slave Trade and Region Instability in the American South*, edited by Robbie Etheridge, and are used by permission of the University of Nebraska Press. Copyright 2009 by the Board of Regents of the University of Nebraska.

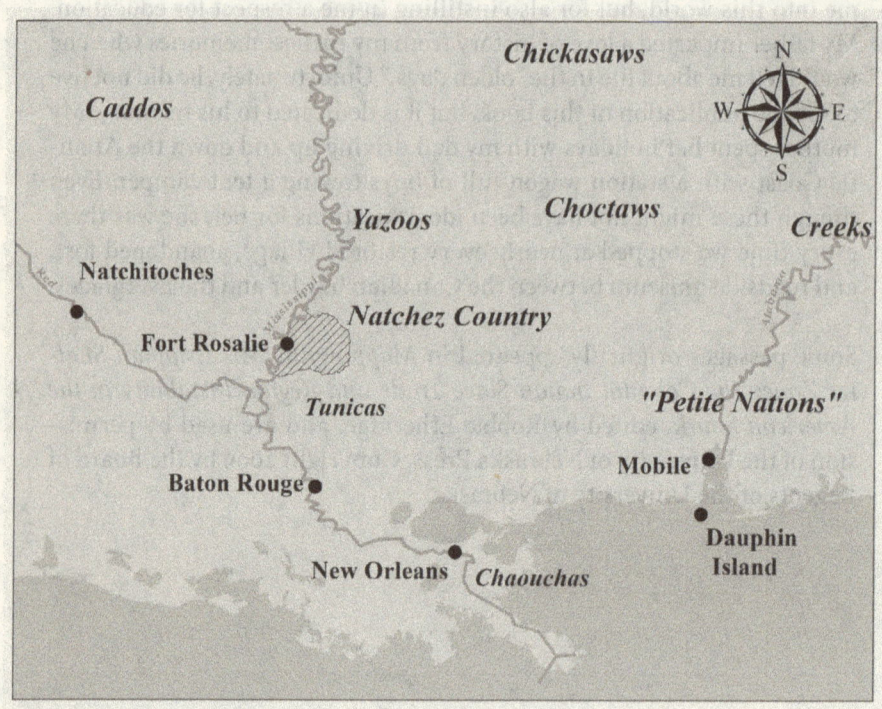

FIGURE 0.1. Lousiana, circa 1718–1730.

Natchez Country

Introduction

A Choctaw leader and his twenty companions stared in horror at the two rows of severed heads set before them. Their hosts, the Natchez Indians, had neatly arranged them outside the smoldering ruins of a plantation known as St. Catherine's Concession. Those in one row belonged to colonial officials, those in the other to ordinary Louisianans. The Great Sun—the hereditary leader of the Natchez peoples—heartily greeted the Choctaw delegation and told them that the former owners of the heads had died because "the French had treated the red men badly."[1] This grisly display was the product of one of the bloodiest confrontations north of the Rio Grande to that date.

The violence began on a morning in late November 1729, when several hundred Natchez warriors entered Fort Rosalie, ostensibly to pay off old debts and to borrow firearms for a great hunt. They positioned themselves throughout the post and among the surrounding homes. Upon a prearranged signal from the Great Sun, each warrior fell on the nearest outsider. In less than an hour, all but a handful of the European men, along with many of their women and children, were dead. Almost as soon as the assault began, the Natchez cornered the fort's commander, Captain de Chépart, in his vegetable garden. The terrified officer whistled in vain for the guards to come to his aid. The high-status men among the attackers thought it beneath their dignity to kill such a craven individual. They called for a lesser person to dispatch the officer, and a low-caste "stinkard chief" soon arrived to club the Frenchman to death.[2] From that day, the tenor of Native American relations with France's subjects in the Lower Mississippi Valley changed forever.

Nearly all historians of colonial Louisiana agree that this event marked a turning point in France's colonial project. Most of them also agree that the destruction of the post and nearby European settlements marked the culmination of friction that had been growing for years between the immigrants and the indigenous peoples.[3] Daniel Usner, however, argued that the breakdown of intercultural relations in Natchez Country "should not be viewed as the inevitable process of conquest by more advanced or more powerful Europeans."[4] The story leading up to fall of Fort Rosalie is far more complex. This book argues that the Indians' coup of November 28, 1729, represents a turning point in American history because of one of the means the Natchez chose to solve their problems: the discourse of racial categories. The rhetoric used by Natchez headmen in the years leading up to the attack constitutes some of the first recorded examples of an indigenous "racial" identity. In the words of one of their holy men, the Natchez were "people who named themselves Red Men."[5] Moreover, the actions that they took following their attack helped to spread the discourse of redness throughout the Southeast.

Nancy Shoemaker, in her groundbreaking article "How Indians Got to Be Red," traced the origins of the term to the Natchez and other southeastern peoples.[6] She concentrated on the development of a specific racial category within the context of diplomatic relations between exogamous political groups: European colonists (and the citizens of the United States who followed in their wake) and American Indians.

The following study expands on Shoemaker's work by exploring why the Indians decided to become "red" in Natchez Country and why they decided to do so in that particular place with such determination. I argue that members in that polity observed that the discourse of race worked well for the "white" Europeans who lived among them, not only as a tool to dominate their "black" slaves, but also as means to unify their heterogeneous population. As Edmund Morgan pointed out in his classic *American Slavery, American Freedom: The Ordeal of Colonial Virginia*, the settlers' upper classes used skin color to ameliorate social unrest and maintain their grip on the reins of political and economic power.[7] Much like their immigrant neighbors in Louisiana, the hierarchs of the Natchez faced challenges to their authority from elements within their linguistically and ethnically diverse chiefdom. Thus, their embrace of an ideology based on biological characteristics had at least as much to do with the establishment of an internal political hegemony as it did with relations with those who came from across the Atlantic.

These Native Americans have intrigued novelists and historians for generations. The Natchez were the subjects of François-René de Chateaubriand's classic romances *Atala* (1801) and *René* (1802). The nineteenth-century author Charles Gayarré, who wrote his histories with the aid of the works of Le Page du Pratz, Dumont de Montigny, and Charlevoix, and included in them in vignettes created by his own fertile imagination, devoted several chapters to the Natchez. Francis Parkman mentioned them briefly in his 1869 monograph on La Salle. Mark Twain echoed Parkman's vision of Natchez "despotism" in his *Life on the Mississippi*. Alcée Fortier's focus on the Natchez was slight in his four-volume *History of Louisiana*. Writing in the early 1900s, he, like several of the previously named authors, blamed the uprising on de Chépart's malfeasance.[8]

From the second until the fourth decade of the twentieth century, the *Louisiana Historical Quarterly* (*LHQ*) published an index to the records of the Superior Court of Louisiana, some of which dealt with Natchez Country. These proved invaluable in locating the physical documents in the Louisiana State Historical Museum in New Orleans. The *LHQ* also set in print a number of translated documents from the Archives nationales de France. The general tenor of the articles on French Louisiana that the journal published during the early 1900s, however, tended to be more celebratory than analytic.

The Jesuit historian Jean Delanglez worked during the 1930s and 1940s. He was far more methodical in his treatment of the colony's inhabitants. His writings on Cadillac and Périer are fine examples of critical inquiry based on archival research.[9] His perspectives informed key aspects of my study, particularly with those relating to an alleged pan-Indian conspiracy. He argued that the "Natchez plot" was a creation of Commandant-General Périer used to obscure his role in the disaster. Delanglez also questioned the veracity of other eighteenth-century memoirs concerning the colony's history. His dissertation on the Jesuits in the French possession stands as one of the better studies of the "Black Robes" in the region.[10]

The Church and State in French Colonial Louisiana, by Father Charles O'Neill, was also an expansive treatment of the colony's ecclesiastical history.[11] O'Neill's work aided my investigation in two ways. First, it laid bare the intricate struggles for authority between the Jesuit and Capuchin orders. The second arose from my good fortune to have been permitted access to Father O'Neill's papers in the Jesuit Archives at Loyola

University in New Orleans soon after his death. These proved invaluable to other areas of my research, particularly in clarifying the nature of the relationships between government officials of colonial Louisiana and the province's clergy.

Marcel Giraud's monumental five-volume *History of French Louisiana* covered the entire colony up to the destruction of the Natchez on the Black River in 1731. He wrote his extensive study between 1953 and 1993. Giraud based his interpretations squarely on exhaustive archival research. In doing so, he highlighted the difficulties the French government experienced in its attempts to enforce its policies in Louisiana. He also focused on the humanitarian impulses of that government as it addressed the complaints and concerns of its ordinary subjects.[12] Giraud's perspectives on imperial control have influenced my approach to the colony's governance and relations with Native Americans. Moreover, his work served as a survey of the French archives that has yet to be equaled. Around the same time that Giraud was writing his books, Mathé Allain also investigated the *métropole*'s frustration with controlling events in Louisiana.[13] Jacob Price's study of the French tobacco trade, and especially his focus on the financier Antoine Crozat and the French Company of the Indies in Louisiana, also furnished valuable insights.[14]

Patricia Dillon Wood's *French-Indian Relations on the Southern Frontier, 1699–1762*, which devoted several chapters to the Natchez, was equally valuable. Wood was the first to suggest that the Natchez viewed the French as another group to incorporate into their polity, a suggestion that I have further developed in the following pages. Daniel Usner's "frontier exchange economy" also informed my work by presenting an alternative to the cultural bifurcation implied by "frontier" interpretations of Louisiana history.[15] Furthermore, it provided a framework for understanding the mechanics of trade in Natchez Country. In a similar manner, Kathleen Duval's study of indigenous control of cross-cultural exchange played a role in reconstructing eighteenth-century life around Fort Rosalie and the Grand Village.[16] Shannon Dawdy's theory of "rogue colonialism" has been especially helpful for comprehending the obstacles that faced Louisiana's officials as they attempted to create their version of "order" in the province.[17]

The chapters that follow also respond to recent analyses of the Natchez political system. They dispute James F. Barnett Jr.'s thesis that the Natchez lacked a central authority and that they used the resultant flexibility to "form alliances and do business simultaneously with both the French and the English."[18] Contemporary European observers frequently commented on the power of the Great Sun and his family, and went so far as to call their commands "absolute." Moreover, several conflicts between Louisiana and the Natchez included instances in which the Suns of the Grand Village co-opted the colonial military to eliminate those who disputed their control of the chiefdom. Certain Natchez leaders were therefore extremely interested in creating and maintaining centralized power. Their appeal to a shared identity became another effective device to achieve those ends.

Arnaud Balvay's recent *La Révolte des Natchez* did an excellent job demythologizing the Natchez for a French readership whose knowledge of the era arises from Chateaubriand's famous romantic accounts of the Natchez "Revolt" of 1729.[19] His rejection of anthropologists' names for the conflicts of the 1710s and 1720s, the "First, Second, and Third Natchez Wars," exemplified his fresh approach to the subject. I have followed suit and used descriptive titles for hostilities that often resulted in a few handfuls of casualties. Balvay, however, blamed the "revolt" on the colonists' encroachment on Indian territory as they created and expanded their tobacco plantations. While Louisianans' greed for more farmland definitely played a role in the tensions that led to the destruction of Fort Rosalie and the surrounding *habitations*, the amount of acreage they had acquired by 1729 was relatively small. The Natchez had several other reasons to eliminate their impudent neighbors.

Their motivations to attack the Europeans led to several questions not addressed by Balvay, Shoemaker, and others, and that serve to inform my investigation of the Natchez case. First, why did the indigenous peoples of Natchez Country embrace the discourse of race as a means to internal hegemony? Other Native American groups that had contact with similar racialized colonial projects did not do so. Why did the Natchez adoption of a "red" identity lead directly to violence with outsiders? Other Native Americans used the term "red men" to avoid conflict with Europeans and their colonists. What role did chattel slavery play in the development of these mounting tensions? How did the relatively small size of Natchez Country contribute to these tensions? In short: What made Natchez Country different?

The answers to several of these questions can be found within the unique spatial conditions in the region. In the words of Henri Lefebvre, "social space is a social product." Space is more than a void through which actors move: it is an integrative and generative component of human interaction. To put it another way, the Natchez created the spatial aspects of Natchez Country, and those aspects, in turn, fashioned and authorized their social structures.

The Natchez lived in a complex chiefdom: an agglomeration of towns and villages centered on a primary headman's settlement. For centuries before Europeans arrived, communities like these dotted the Mississippi basin from Wisconsin to Alabama, and from the eastern fringe of the Great Plains to the western slopes of the Appalachians. The elites of these polities drew their authority from key sites within their constructed landscape, namely their mounds and adjacent plazas. These locales served as staging grounds for rituals, as platforms for semi-permanent buildings, and as graves for their leaders. To borrow a term coined by the archeologist Christopher Tilley, their heritage was "sedimented" within the landscape.[20]

These authority-bestowing terrain features were what Michel Foucault called "heterotopias." Foucault defined heterotopias as "something like counter-sites, a kind of effectively enacted utopia in which the real sites, all the other real sites that can be found within the culture, are simultaneously represented, contested, and inverted."[21] The mounds and plaza of the Grand Village linked living inhabitants to their dead leaders; the headman to the solar deity from which he descended; the lower and the higher status groups; and outsiders with indigenes. These were simultaneously spaces of inclusion and exclusion, spaces in which only the select few could enter but over which the uninitiated many could watch.[22] They were spaces in which the Natchez, or the "People of the Sun," as they called themselves, encountered and reunited with one another and reaffirmed their collective identity.[23] Theirs was a society that was a product of social spaces that created social spaces.

Europeans recognized (however imprecisely) that these spaces were similar to their own power-generating heterotopias: cathedrals, churches, convents, monasteries, courts, and palaces. These sites often contained the bones of their ancestors, but more important, they authorized the policies and reinforced the influence of those qualified to occupy and use them.[24] Indeed, several of the earliest visitors from the Old World thought that these structures anchored these Indians to the terrain in such a way that they would make easy converts to Roman Catholicism. These indigenous sites also served as triggers for the hostilities in Natchez Country. Many Europeans who came later misread their cultural meanings and, eventually, disregarded the spiritual significance of these Indians' landscapes. The newcomers' observational blind spot regarding that significance is perhaps best exemplified by the fact that seventeenth- or eighteenth-century French-language documents do not mention the Natchez name for their homeland.

Another aspect of the unique spatial conditions of the region involved the physical dimensions in which nearly two thousand Africans, Europeans, and Native Americans lived. The part of Natchez Country where the vast majority of the contact took place amounted to fewer than a dozen square miles. The area of the most intense and frequent interaction constituted a rectangle about two miles by three miles. The concentration of this many radically different cultures in such a small space within a span of thirteen years was rare in colonial America.

Yet, an uneasy peace graced the inhabitants of Natchez Country while a "frontier exchange economy" was in operation. Daniel H. Usner characterized such an arrangement as "a regional economy that connected Indian villagers across the lower Mississippi Valley with European settlers along the Gulf Coast and lower banks of the Mississippi. The term *frontier exchange* is meant to capture the form and content of economic interactions among these groups with a view to replacing the notion of frontier as an interracial boundary with that of a cross-cultural network."[25] This system, along with what could be called a case of mutually mistaken identities—the perception held by both Native Americans and people from the Old World that each shared more similarities with the other than they actually did—allowed large numbers of strangers to move into Natchez Country. To the Indians, who had created a sociopolitical system that thrived on the absorption of outsiders, the European newcomers at first appeared to be one more collection of wayfarers like those they had successfully incorporated during the previous centuries.

Aside from their excellent technology, La Salle's 1682 expedition looked and behaved much like the Native American bands that had come to the Grand Village in search of food and protection. The small bands of travel-worn Canadians, Frenchmen, and Italians who moved through the region, almost always accompanied by contingents of American Indians, appeared to differ little from the previous immigrants. The first European who moved to Natchez Country in 1699 might have acted out a role similar to one played by earlier refugees when he consorted with the Great Sun's sister. When Antoine Crozat sponsored the area's first trading post in 1714, the handful of Frenchmen who worked there were too few to be considered anything more than a miniscule coterie of traders with extremely useful and durable goods. These tiny groups presented little threat to the Natchez hierarchy. In fact, as long as the Suns retained control over the distribution of the European merchandise the outsiders provided, these immigrants were welcome additions to their world.[26]

To the newcomers, the Natchez, with their hereditary ruler, social ranks, political offices, permanent temples, and monotheistic beliefs, appeared to have many of the hallmarks of "civilization." Karl G. Lorenz described how many of these perceptions distorted the indigenes' sociopolitical structures.[27] Europeans wrote that these Indians were organized into descending ranks of "suns," "nobles," "honored men," and "stinkards." To the immigrants, this hierarchy resembled the systems of inherited privilege of the Old World, where complex rules determined social rank. Their experiences were similar to those of the English colonists at Jamestown, who, as Karen Kupperman demonstrated, recognized analogous degrees of status among the Powhatans when the colonists first encountered them.[28] The immigrants to Louisiana saw in the Great Sun a monarch who wielded the power of life and death over his subjects.[29] One Catholic missionary described the Natchez leader as possessing "the air of an ancient emperor."[30] Others detected similarities between classical Roman and Egyptian religions and indigenous spirituality and compared the Natchez temple to that of Latin goddess of the hearth, Vesta.[31] These perceptions of similarity—mistaken as they were, temporarily obviated many of the difficulties that plagued other colonial ventures.

For the first two decades of regular contact, these mistaken identities allowed the two groups to coexist despite several violent episodes. The acumen of certain individuals, both native and newcomer, played a role in ameliorating the worst of these clashes. Many of the Europeans who also helped to establish the province often worked outside the boundaries of policies and behaviors prescribed by the homeland. Men like Pierre Le Moyne, sieur d'Iberville, and his brother, Jean-Baptiste Le Moyne, sieur de Bienville, two of the founders of French Louisiana, fit the profiles of these independent-minded operators. Shannon Dawdy has aptly characterized such men as "rogue" colonists who were "often acting on their own initiative and in pursuit of their own interests."[32] The Natchez had their political and diplomatic adepts as well. The Tattooed Serpent and his sister-in-law, the White Woman, helped keep the peace. To some extent, they constructed a "middle ground" where both sides learned enough about the other to use that knowledge to meet their ends without resorting to force.[33]

As in the Great Lakes region described by Richard White, the "middle ground" that was Natchez Country was a world of villages.[34] It was, however, a collection of villages peopled not only by Indians, but also by African, Canadian, French, Swiss, Czech, and German inhabitants.

Unlike the Great Lakes region, Natchez Country attracted large numbers of people from the Old World who employed increasingly forceful means to achieve their ends. The French government's desire to integrate Louisiana into its portion of the Atlantic world brought many of these less pliant immigrants to the Lower Mississippi Valley.

Unfortunately for the Natchez, their preliminary assumptions that these newcomers were candidates for adoption into their polity had lulled them into permitting nearly a thousand of them to move into their homeland. When large numbers of European settlers and African slaves augmented the initial mission station and a handful of traders, the People of the Sun slowly began to realize that these were not just new bands of refugees.[35] This batch of recent immigrants refused to recognize the authority of the Suns; nor did they partake in the old practices that reinforced the Suns' power. Indeed, some of the Indians employed long-standing methods to control the threat that the outsiders represented.

During the early 1720s, some Natchez villagers attempted to bring the most rambunctious settlement of newcomers into compliance by initiating a series of graduated acts of violence. Frederic Gleach and Hal Langfur noted that the Powhatans in Virginia and the Botocudos in Brazil employed similar tactics against their English and Portuguese colonial neighbors.[36] These tactics came into play as two groups of settlers—one indigenous, the other a collection of Europeans and Africans—began to vie for the same swath of land between the Grand Village and Fort Rosalie. Unlike many other struggles between Native Americans and other European colonists, these groups fought for supremacy within a well-established zone of habitation rather than in the borderlands and hunting grounds between the two. They competed for terrain that Allan Greer called the "inner commons": which was both "a place—the village pasture—and . . . a set of access rights, such as gleaning and stubble grazing . . . located within the tillage zone." He contrasted these spaces with the "Outer commons . . . [, which were] collectively owned resources in the surrounding area beyond local croplands."[37]

These actions did not succeed in changing the newcomers' behavior but instead sparked several conflicts with Louisiana. The Suns of the Grand Village, however, were past masters at managing internecine challenges to their authority. They directed the wrath of the colonial forces toward the outlying Natchez towns that were the homes of their political rivals. Bienville recognized the importance of maintaining good relations with key members of the chiefdom who could provide a modicum of stability. Consequently, the commandant-general adhered to the

Suns' judgment regarding who was a threat to intercultural peace. Thus, the diplomatic acumen of senior Native American and colonial negotiators mitigated the worst effects of the violence. These minor conflicts remained struggles between competing settlements, events that were not unusual in the Mississippian world. When these veteran players left the scene, individuals with lesser skills led their peoples into war.

Bienville, the commandant-general of Louisiana, had been one of the most accomplished mediators. His questionable business dealings, however, put him at odds with the French Company of the Indies. This firm, which ran the colony as a commercial venture during the 1720s, sought to rein in the profiteering and graft that thwarted its ability to make a return on its investments. To bring order to a notoriously disorderly province, the Company recalled Bienville to France in response to complaints that he was tyrannical and corrupt. To replace him, it sent Étienne Périer, a naval officer who had amassed an enviable record while serving at the Company's African slaving stations on the Guinean coast. His employers expected him to protect their interests and bring some semblance of order to Louisiana. Moreover, his experience with large numbers of enslaved people and with complex chiefdoms in Africa made him a logical choice to send to New Orleans. His background fit with the Company's scheme to transform the colony into a major tobacco producer. The Company hoped that Louisiana's crop would compete with Virginian leaf on the global market. These plans included the importation of thousands of Africans into the Lower Mississippi Valley to work the fields of its tobacco farms. The land around Fort Rosalie and the Grand Village figured prominently in this arrangement.

At the same time that they were increasing the African population of Louisiana, the French government and its colonial counterparts were transforming the extant slave codes into a mature racial discourse. They followed a process similar to the one that had worked in seventeenth-century Virginia that Winthrop Jordan outlined in his landmark book *White over Black*.[38] Armed with a revised Code Noir that specified skin color as a mark of an inferior legal category, the province's Superior Council pushed the discourse further. It issued a number of decrees that relegated Native Americans to the same inferior category. These changes took place over the course of a few years, and they did not go unnoticed by the original inhabitants of Natchez Country.

One more set of events brought the growing tensions to an explosive culmination. Sometime during the summer of 1729, de Chépart summoned the Sun of the Apple Village and demanded that his people leave their homeland.[39] Thus, in a region in which fertile soil could be found in abundance, the captain attempted to seize one of the most sacred locations in the chiefdom. As the People of the Sun planned their response, they embraced a red racial category. With the most powerful portion of their landscape being threatened, the Natchez started to use the term "red men" to unite those villagers who had previously been reluctant to fight against the colony. They then used the term when they began to cast about for other indigenous allies. For them, it had become a portable source of power when their immobile sources of identity were about to be stolen—a source of power similar to one that apparently worked very well for their European neighbors.

A unique blend of social and political conditions made Natchez Country a matrix for the transformation of an indigenous means of identification into a racial category. The region contained a large and powerful Native American chiefdom. A contingent of European settlers almost as numerous lived within the western portion of the territory, and held in bondage growing numbers of unfree laborers with easily distinguishable physical features. The confined dimensions of the region added to the pressures within this matrix. Next, the newcomers threatened key authority-generating sites inside this small area. They also ignored the indigenous inhabitants' conventions that regulated the use of the inner commons between the settlements in Natchez Country. After a short time, these outsiders began to relegate the People of the Sun to the same inferior legal status as their African slaves. Finally, a rogue like Étienne de Chépart, a man with a notable deficit of integrity and judgment, but who lacked the diplomatic acumen of a rogue like Bienville, took charge of Fort Rosalie.

The following chapters trace these developments as they unfolded among the various peoples who created and then destroyed this matrix. In them, I employ anthropological, documentary, and cartographic material to recover their pasts. The Natchez Mississippian chiefdom survived the ravages of disease and slave raids with a political system that retained many of the practices that had been in use during the preceding centuries. Archaeologists have excavated their mounds and found the graves of the penultimate Great Sun and members of his family. Their finds, combined with data from similar polities, help to shed light on the world entered by La Salle and those who followed in his wake.

Richard White wrote that the middle ground of his study "existed on two distinct levels. It was both a product of everyday life and a product of formal diplomatic relations between distinct peoples. For historians, however, the middle ground is easiest to perceive as it was articulated in formal settings."[40] It is impossible, of course, to reconstruct a complete picture of what it might have been like to make a home in the Grand Village or to live among the tobacco workers at St. Catherine's Concession. Nonetheless, this book makes an attempt to provide some insight into what it meant to live those everyday lives. For three decades, the Natchez, Africans, and Europeans dwelled near one another in a patchwork of settlements and homesteads spread over about a dozen square miles. They planted crops in neighboring fields. Their chickens scratched the same feeding grounds. They bought and sold at the same warehouses. They fell in love and bore children. Together, they built a multiethnic world along the banks of the Mississippi River. In short, it is crucial to understand what went right in Natchez Country to understand what went wrong that November morning in 1729.

The Europeans left behind extensive documentation of their lives in Natchez Country and their experiences with its first inhabitants. Their writings range from field reports, government briefs, business correspondence, military communiqués, and religious missives, to ethnographic memoirs and autobiographic journals. Each of their authors had a unique perspective and agenda. In these pages, I strive to unravel their perspectives and uncover their agendas.

Although European writings about colonial Louisiana often focused on elites and their interactions, many more provided glimpses of that everyday life, of the personal interactions and relations of which human existence is made. As Gordon Sayre has argued, analyses of the texts pertaining to Natchez Country—who produced them and why—is critical in writing the region's history.[41] Whenever possible, I consulted the original French-language documents and placed them in the contexts of their production. The report of an officer whose subordinate had sparked a war reads very differently from the courtroom testimony of an enslaved Natchez youth who chose the gallows over continued bondage. The journal of a colonist that contains the recollections of his wife, who had been held prisoner by the Natchez, sounds a different note than does a plantation manager's encomium about the fertility of the Louisiana countryside.

Aside from written sources, Europeans created an expansive body of cartographic material. These illustrate, in part, their vision of Natchez Country. By cross-referencing these maps and charts with census data and textual sources, it is possible to add depth to that vision. I also place these sources in the context of global statecraft by drawing upon the ideas of historians of cartography such as J. B. Harley, Christine Marie Petto, and David Buisseret, who characterized maps as instruments of imperialism.[42] Geographic Information System software (GIS) has enabled me to generate several representations of the terrain and to plot the locations of homes, mounds, temples, and farms and their relationships to one another. By doing so, the reasons (and the humanity) behind decisions of where to build or plant, where to bury or defend, become intelligible. This methodology also makes it easier to see the manners in which both natives and newcomers inscribed their power upon and drew their authority from the land.

Keeping with Tristam R. Kidder's assertion that Mississippian chiefdoms exhibited a great deal of local and regional variation, this book examines Natchez Country as a discrete unit with unique social, religious, and political practices.[43] Consequently, I have avoided, as much as possible, "upstreaming," a methodology that assumes that social practices change very slowly over time. Its proponents argue that by examining later cultural structures, one can deduce their antecedents. Although this might be a viable approach in some cases, it does not work in this one. The point of this book is to demonstrate that the Natchez were past masters at innovation. Within a few years they rapidly altered their social and diplomatic policies. My reluctance to engage in overgeneralizing is particularly strong in my discussions of the construction of racial categories. Employing "upstreaming" methodology, projecting backward from later periods, can only serve to obscure the origins of the racial appellation of "red men."

A similar reluctance also extends to my analyses of both indigenous and immigrant policies regarding the other. Consequently, I eschew terms such as "pro-British" or "pro-French" as much as possible. Rather, many of the records suggest that local interests animated decision makers among the People of the Sun far more than did their particular villages' alignment with distant western European imperial projects. Similarly, many of those from the Old World operated according to personal agendas at odds with the official policies of the French Crown. Moreover, many of the colonists did not come from France, and of those who did, many held very weak allegiances to the kingdom. Therefore appellations such as "European," "German," "Swiss," or "Canadian" often work better to describe the newcomers to the region. In other words, it was precisely these local variations among its inhabitants that helped to make Natchez

Country such a unique place. Both sets of people brought with them distinct memories of their respective pasts that informed their lifestyles. These pasts also engendered concepts about land, space, time, and other-than-human entities that shaped their daily existence. These concepts arrived in the baggage of the newcomers to encounter, blend, and clash with those of the native peoples of Natchez Country.

1 / Rising Suns

During the early spring of 1700, a small party of European officers, sailors, craftsmen, and laborers, guided by Native Americans, rowed up the Mississippi River. They had come to chart the region for the king of France. After several days of traveling north, they stopped to visit a large town inhabited by a powerful nation of Indians. The brother of the local headman greeted the expedition's commander with a gift of a small white cross. He then escorted the newcomers to the Grand Village to meet the Great Sun.[1] The outsiders had arrived in Natchez Country at a particularly auspicious occasion—around the time of the Deer Moon—when headmen from the chiefdom's outlying towns attended feasts with its leader.[2]

Part of their story was recorded in the log of the *Renommée*, by the ship's commander and the new governor of Louisiana, Pierre le Moyne, sieur d'Iberville. In his entry for March 11, 1700, he described the countryside surrounding the native's town as "very much like France." He called the inhabitants "Nadches," after the name of their principal village, although they used another name for themselves: the Théoloëls—the People of Sun—after their solar deity, Thé.[3] Their ruler attracted the attention of several of the expedition's members. Iberville wrote, "To me he seemed the most tyrannical Indian I have beheld."[4] The Jesuit chaplain Father Du Ru saw the same man in a more favorable light: "The chief's manner impresses me; he has the air of an ancient emperor." The missionary recorded the elaborate courtesies paid to the "Great Chief" by his retainers and by all of the Natchez.[5] Du Ru spent several more days writing about the temples and the society of the Grand Village and the outlying districts.

The accounts of Captain Iberville and his companions provide insights into the ways these eighteenth-century Europeans perceived the people they met. His characterization of the Natchez's chief as a tyrant reveals that he perceived an unusual amount power at the Sun's disposal. Others observed reflections of Old World discourses of authority, dignity, and power in the Mississippi chiefdom—tantalizing hints of "civilization" among a non-European people. The Natchez, in turn, had the opportunity to see much among the newcomers that resonated with their own experiences of power and civility.[6]

This encounter illustrated some of the reasons that the Natchez and the Europeans assumed certain things about the other. The People of the Sun and the subjects of Louis XIV made their assumptions because of the ways that each organized their society, distributed resources, and described their relations with other-than-human powers. In the Sun King's France, most people attributed natural phenomena to the work of supernatural beings: saints and other deities. They ascribed status through kinship, and believed that their ruler held a divine mandate. The Natchez believed that the Great Sun also based his tenure upon a divine appointment. His blood relations supported him in his political activities. These Indians also believed that other-than-human forces intervened in their lives. Thus the first Louisianans and their indigenous hosts' tendency to see parallels among each other were based on cohesive and intelligible perceptions. When the party of René-Robert Cavalier, sieur de La Salle, arrived in 1682, it looked and sounded like a Native American trading or hunting expedition because the majority of them *were* Native Americans. Moreover, those in the party who were not Native Americans often acted like Native Americans. These and other similarities allowed each of these two peoples to fit the other into their respective epistemological categories.[7]

The descriptions of the realms of the Sun King and the Great Sun that follow are by no means exhaustive. They merely outline some of the characteristics that allowed each group to recognize aspects of their own culture in the other's way of life. Many of their suppositions about such resemblances were the result of gross misperceptions—neither group saw the other without distortions. Nonetheless, neither side was staring at empty mirages; each had good reasons for making connections between themselves and the other. These resemblances generated grave consequences as Europeans and Natchez drew upon them to construct polices for dealing with each other.

The Sun King

At the dawn of the eighteenth century, the kingdom of Louis XIV represented perhaps the most refined expression of western European civilization. The colonization of Louisiana was a conscious attempt to extend France's *"gloire"* while improving its strategic footing in the New World. France's political institutions provided some of the conditions for the governance of the new province. The nature of its society determined who would cross the seas to rule at Mobile and New Orleans and, equally important, who would stay at home. Despite the nation's sophisticated urban areas, most of its inhabitants lived in small agricultural hamlets in which the patterns of daily life changed very slowly. The missionaries, settlers, soldiers, and officials who came to the Lower Mississippi Valley often drew upon their experiences of the high culture of the court and church. Many of them, especially the lowborn, also drew upon those culled from the rural villages where they had spent the earlier parts of their lives. The realm of the sacred also played a crucial role in shaping their views of themselves, the world around them, and the world they would soon encounter. These sources of experience informed the ways they perceived and wrote about the Indians they met in Louisiana's forests and prairies.

Louis emblazoned his domain with images of the sun to illustrate the central position of his monarchy. The motto *une foi, une loi, un roi*—one faith, one law, one king—epitomized this unity. France, however, was not a homogeneous polity. Louis XIV faced numerous obstacles to the exercise of his power; his was by no means an "absolute monarchy." Political theorists of the time imagined the king at the center of the state, with his nobles, church, and people in orbit around the throne in the same way the planets revolved around the sun. Louis furthered this imagery when he employed cultural and social patronage to counter centrifugal political forces that threatened to sunder the kingdom. As he did so, he gained leverage to steer the state in some of the directions that he chose. At times he succeeded; in other instances, he accomplished less than he intended.

The king's penchant for centralization played an important role in framing Louisiana's government as well as that of the *métropole*. Although circumstances thwarted Louis's hopes for administrative efficiency at home, the colonies seemed to offer a clean slate. His plan for a strong governor and Superior Council to run Louisiana exemplified the Sun King's penchant for bureaucratic hegemony.[8] The tabula rasa of "le Mississippi" notwithstanding, stability eluded his transplanted subjects: many of France's social and political tensions followed them to the shores of the Gulf of Mexico.

The problems of the New World traced some of their roots back to the numerous obstacles that impeded the Sun King from exerting greater control over France's institutions. Despite his desire for a firm grip on the domestic government, ancient traditions, civil and canon law, foreign distractions, restive nobles, and refractory *parlements* thwarted Louis's designs.[9] He also faced constitutional limitations on his power to levy taxes. The means by which he circumvented some of these obstructions made a lasting impression on the nation's governing structures. Louis's high-level administrative appointments and his efficient use of supervisory officers called *intendants* aided his quest. Louis also marshaled the finer things in life to solve some of his political problems. The celebrated Court of Versailles and the magnificent artistic and literary culture associated with his reign tamed his nobles and won the admiration of the rest of Europe.

For all his political maneuverings, Louis's right to the throne rested on his birth into the royal family. Louis's claim arose from his descent from the Bourbon line of kings that began with his grandfather, Henri IV. In France, as in nearly every other state throughout the globe, kinship played the defining role in determining who held the reins of power. Through blood or marriage, the king was related to many of the ruling families in Europe. The bonds of inherited privilege and authority carried forward into the quotidian practices of governance.

Louis's court was a realm in which kinship, the most elemental and ubiquitous of all human relations, carried enormous weight. Here, Louis's most powerful relatives attempted to influence national policy through their ancient prerogatives. This elite group had exerted far more influence only a few decades earlier, often with violent outcomes such as the series of uprisings known as the Frondes. During the late 1640s and early 1650s, the *parlements*, and then segments of the upper nobility, tried to take advantage of the vacuum created by the death of Louis XIII and the minority of his heir. Throughout these years, Louis XIV lived in the Louvre as little more than a prisoner of the mobs of Paris and princes of the blood. Despite the machinations of sections of the nobility, eventually a respect for the rule of succession won out, and Louis ascended to the throne.

His youthful experiences as a virtual hostage during the Frondes, coupled with an enduring memory of the chaos that preceded his grandfather's reign, strengthened his determination to concentrate the power of the state in his own hands. In 1661, after the death of Cardinal Mazarin—the man who successfully navigated the young king through the turbulent politics of his early life—Louis began to rule his kingdom directly. To achieve this end, the king began to restructure aspects of his government. Essential to these reforms was the further development of a corps of professional bureaucrats. These were men dependent upon the king's favor rather than upon high birth for their authority. These minions gradually circumvented the ancient prerogatives of the upper nobility by performing the necessary but monotonous work that kept the wheels of government turning. The career of Jean-Baptiste Colbert, who headed many of the government's ministries during Louis's reign, personified this trend. In a society in which kinship legitimized control, his family's relatively recent ennoblement and its consequent lack of prestige precluded his co-option of the king's influence.

Low birth notwithstanding, Colbert realized that the efficient management of the state's resources was crucial to maximizing France's (and his own) influence. The colonies felt the impact of Colbert's policies when he embraced a mercantilist agenda in his efforts to channel the wealth of France's overseas possessions into the coffers of the motherland. To accomplish this end, he standardized colonial commercial and legal practices through a series of edicts. The Code Noir, although published two years after Colbert died, exemplified the minister's proclivity for organization and attention to detail.[10] Besides regulating slavery, the Code excluded non-Catholics from the colonies and standardized judicial proceedings. These reforms would have an enormous impact on Louisiana's government, society, and economy. The racial aspects of the Code Noir would play an especially significant role in the colonists' relationship with the Natchez.

Louis's and Colbert's centralizing impulses required men to implement them on a local level. *Intendants*, officials with fiduciary authority, administered the day-to-day functions of the government. Since the king drew them from his household staff and paid them directly, the *intendants* executed royal policy without depending on external sources for their salaries.[11] Because they often reported on state business in the provinces and audited the account books of those who oversaw it, these independent bureaucrats often found themselves at odds with nobles who had inherited or purchased their offices.[12]

Some of these administrative practices of Old France made their way to the New World, albeit with certain modifications. In Louisiana, the governor acted as chief executive and mirrored to some extent the authority of the monarch. Assisting him was a *commissaire-ordonnateur*, who managed the fiscal affairs of the colony.[13] Both held seats on the Superior Council, an advisory board of six or seven important men of the colony. This body mimicked some aspects of the *parlements*. It first served as a court of last resort; however, soon after its creation, the Superior Council exceeded its Old World model when it acquired legislative powers.[14] Despite the apparent simplicity of this arrangement, Louisiana's records are strewn with conflicts over the civil and military affairs of the colony. The historian Donald Lemieux observed: "The reason for this conflict lies not within French Louisiana, but rather in Versailles."[15] The imprecision with which the king defined their powers led to constant bickering between the *ordonnateur* and the governor. These disputes routinely intruded upon relations with Louisiana's neighbors. Parsimonious administrators frequently sent the colony's negotiators to American Indians' council fires with an insufficient number of the customary gifts, which earned them the derision of their indigenous hosts.

The political divisions in Louisiana reflected larger problems in the domestic French government. Louis found it difficult to increase the state's revenue because of statutory restraints. He could impose few new nationwide taxes without the consent of the États Générales, a legislative body that had not been convened since 1613. This problem was compounded by the byzantine revenue system. Payments were frequently interrupted because the Crown often granted certain provinces tax exemptions in exchange for advance payments, further throttling the state's revenue. In other cases, certain regions like Provence negotiated reduced rates for supplying the king's troops guarding the borders.[16] The nobles and people of these regions jealously clung to these "liberties" for generations after they obtained them. In many instances, the king leased his collections rights to tax farms—essentially granting private individuals and companies the right to gather the nation's revenues in return for a profit.[17]

The king also raised part of the money that he needed through the creation of venal offices. These saleable positions came with inheritable titles that admitted their purchasers into the "nobility of the robe." Such offices permitted their holders to charge fees for their services. Aside from the promise of steady, if small, returns, Louis's sale of offices catered to the aspirations of wealthy merchants who wanted to improve their social rank. The use of venality was not new; connections between "public authority and private property" dated back to the Frankish kingdoms of the seventh century. Henry IV increased the number of these saleable positions in the late sixteenth century.[18] His grandson Louis XIV sold still more of these offices to pay for his palaces, his enormous fêtes, his art collections, and, most of all, his wars.

Yet, this solution had its limits. Venal offices were property and could not be recouped by the Crown without compensation and thus passed beyond the reach of the king. This led to the creation of even more titles. During the 1690s alone, Louis issued nearly a thousand blank letters of ennoblement that he marketed through his *intendants* for the sum of 6,000 livres apiece.[19] In total he raised between 2.3 and 2.4 billion livres through the sale of venal offices during his reign, a figure that does not include funds collected from the *paulette*, the annual tax that maintained the heritability of the offices.[20]

The sale of these posts generated several negative consequences for Louisiana. First, the practice diverted capital away from investment in risky ventures like colonization. Second, these offices siphoned off talented men from commercial vocations—the law generally prohibited new nobles from engaging in mercantile activities.[21] The Crown enforced this provision with the threat of derogation. Consequently, the most ambitious and successful men of the realm bought their way out of commerce and into the *noblesse de robe*. Candidates with poor management skills like Antoine de le Mothe, sieur de Cadillac, held positions of authority in Louisiana partly because the best men were safely ensconced in venal positions at home. Third, it expanded the state bureaucracy and created layers of overlapping jurisdictions and redundant functionalities that took a revolution to untangle. Finally, the sale of venal offices pitted the parvenus against the ancient "nobility of the sword," who had inherited their status from the medieval warrior class. Louisianans struggled over this rift when relatively highborn officials from the mother country and lowborn Canadians wrestled for control of the financial and military affairs of the colony.[22]

Colonial problems aside, Louis found other ways besides administrative reform to consolidate his power. The arts and the theater of state proved to be among his most effective tools. These came together at the Versailles, a hunting lodge a few miles outside of Paris, which Louis built into the most opulent residence in Europe. With grand diversions, Louis drew France's restive nobility to its halls and reduced them to dandified courtiers. There he selectively dispensed perquisites, gifts, and pensions to those in regular attendance. Through these emollients, he demonstrated his respect for the rank of the nation's most important families that chose to make the palace their de facto residence. To attract Louis's attention, some of the most important men of the kingdom became little more than lackeys during certain times of the day. The king's *lever* (rising) was one of the rituals that provided the Sun King with a daily reminder of exactly who resided within his orbit. The men who handed Louis articles of clothing, carried his candle, and brought his "pierced chair" gained opportunities to make their requests. Princes of the blood, dukes, and counts from families that had once directly competed for power with earlier monarchs willingly took roles in the spectacle and dissipated their time and their resources doing the work of stagehands in the theater of state. Courtly life diverted members of the nobility and their money from other endeavors.

In contrast to the seventeenth-century English colonial project, few of France's highborn nobles concerned themselves with its overseas provinces, leaving their development to the *noblesse de robe*. Unlike the grandees of the kingdom's ancient houses, these second-tier elites lacked the social and political capital to effectively advocate for distant outposts like Louisiana.[23] There were no French equivalents of the Earl of Shaftsbury or Baronet George Carteret—men who made up the driving forces behind England's burgeoning Atlantic colonies.

Although the monarchs of Europe looked on the opulence of Versailles with envy, they also feared its master's territorial ambitions. Louis sought to consolidate the patchwork of duchies, bishoprics, and principalities that made up France's marchlands. These semi-autonomous remnants of medieval kingdoms and city-states within the heartland of the nation clung to ancient "liberties" that conflicted with the king's sovereignty. Worse, the Hapsburgs' domains on the Spanish frontier and along the Rhine pinned France between lands held by its traditional enemies. To remedy these conditions, Louis XIV engaged in five major wars during his reign. His victories brought large numbers of Germans, Walloons, and Flemings under Bourbon rule. Consequently, state and church functionaries sought ways to acculturate these newcomers.

Other aspects of France's society were as complex as the contours of its marchlands. The hierarchy in place during the seventeenth and eighteenth centuries allowed every Frenchman, from beggar to monarch, to know his or her place. Over the course of several hundred years, jurists had worked out the intricacies of this system in a discourse that reached its most refined state under the Bourbons. Innumerable charters, decrees *parlementaires*, royal dispensations, municipal prerogatives, heraldic law, and local customs dictated most aspects of everyday social interactions. What appears to present-day sensibilities to have been trivial considerations—the marching order of a procession, the seating arrangements in a church or at a dinner, the removal of hats—denoted an individual's rank. However, cracks in the foundation of this apparently stable structure were developing beneath its ornate veneer. Stresses such as war or the uncertainty inherent in the early stages of colonization often uncovered these fractures.

The experiences of Louisiana's first years revealed these fissures when lowborn men gained positions of power by virtue of their military prowess or their linguistic and diplomatic skills. The colony's governing house, the Le Moynes, exemplified this trend. They lacked ancient titles; consequently, their social capital at Versailles would have been negligible compared to that of the grand families at court. Nonetheless, they wielded considerable power in the New World through their successes in battle and at the council fires of North America. Their successes in the New World did not always translate into the political gravitas necessary to lobby the king for a more robust colonial policy.

The ascension of the Le Moyne family also illustrated a fundamental characteristic of French society: the family was the primary source of identity and status. From the highest to the lowest orders of the kingdom, the family was the elemental social unit. Moreover, biological relationships with other families—kinship—dictated where a particular family stood within the social hierarchy and thus determined the amount of power at its disposal. The first among this order were princes of the blood who were directly related to the king but far enough removed to exclude them from the line of succession. Louis bridled their political ambitions when he invited them to live amid the splendors of Versailles as his guests.[24] The highest nobility inhabited the next tier, often literally, at the palace. The lessons culled from the uprisings of early years of his reign taught the king to keep these lesser families entertained and under his supervision. After these ancient houses came the *noblesse de robe*. They furnished members for the *parlements*, who constituted the most prestigious group in this order. These households also fed the pools of candidates from which Louis drew his *intendants*. Behind the *parlementaires* followed an array of middle- and low-ranking nobles that trailed off into obscurity among the common folk.

It was from the middle and lower ranks of the nobility that Louis selected promising men to staff his expansive government. Colbert owed his rise to this policy, as did his son and grandson, who replaced him as minister of marine. Hence, seventeenth-century France presented opportunities for social mobility over the course of several generations. This era witnessed the rise of few self-made men, but it saw the slow ascension of many self-made merchant families. Some of the most dynamic of these households originated in the Netherlands. Italians, Germans, Swiss, and Spaniards played an important role in the commerce of Marseilles, while Scots, Irishmen, and Jews were prominent merchants in Bordeaux.[25] As discussed earlier, some of these men (at least those who maintained the appearance of being Catholics) became petty bureaucrats by purchasing one of Louis's many venal offices.[26] A few rose quite high in French society. For instance, the financier Antoine Crozat, through a series of judicious loans to the king, rose from peasant to marquis. Crozat's experience was an anomaly; most officials contented themselves with comfortable, if undistinguished, positions among the *noblesse de robe*. Few men of ability abandoned such security for a dangerous and uncertain future in Louisiana.[27]

Some members of these rising houses cemented their place within the political networks through carefully considered marriages. Wealthy merchants bought their way into the nobility and then took wives from more prestigious lines. Such unions provided parvenus with powerful connections within the upper reaches of society. In turn, this gave elite women important roles as negotiators and advocates for their husbands at court and with other prominent families. As the historian Sara Chapman demonstrated, the Pontchartrains, whose sons directed the Ministry of Marine, the section of government that controlled the colonies, exemplified this trend of ascension through marriage.[28]

Not all businesspeople managed to purchase titles; most spent their lives as commoners. Like most of the human race during early modern times, the vast majority of Europeans lived in small agricultural villages. After the family, the village was the primary social unit of France. Many of Louis's subjects identified themselves as *habitants* of their county or *payes* rather than as French. The bulk of the aristocracy and nearly all of the peasantry lived out their lives in rural hamlets and towns grouped around a parish church. The ties that bound people together seldom extended beyond the jurisdiction of the local noble and priest. Shopkeepers and craftsmen exercised some control over their condition through guild associations. Together with religious fraternities, they provided a buffer against bad economic times. These tradesmen also housed and trained generations of apprentices, many of whom married the master's daughters and entered into his kinship network. These arrangements provided a modicum of security—at least enough that few French people willingly left their farms or workshops. Although some men sought seasonal employment in Spain or the Low Countries, most returned to their native towns at the end of the year.[29] New France and Louisiana offered bleak prospects for a promising plowman or apprentice, particularly after stories from repatriated colonists circulated throughout the countryside during the 1720s. The village, although crucial, was not the only institution around which French society organized itself.

Like many governmental and social institutions, religion often provided an element of stability for both those who remained in the motherland and for the emigrants to the Mississippi.[30] Whether peasant, noble, or king, nearly everyone in France looked toward the Catholic Church for spiritual guidance and an intelligible cosmology. Its rituals and pedagogy provided a common set of experiences for all but a few. Louis's kingdom was widely known as the *"fille aînée de l'Eglise"*—the eldest daughter of the Church—because of its role in the spread of Christianity in the fourth century, and later for its support of religious scholarship. For many, the Church afforded a sense of order through its elaborate administrative apparatus on earth and through its representations of the afterlife as a hierarchy. This predilection for organization and rank made Catholicism understandable not only for the European immigrants to the Mississippi, but also for the indigenous people of the New World. Certain aspects of clerical offices and church hagiography resonated with American Indian spiritual practices, particularly those of the Natchez.

Catholic theologians portrayed heaven as a kingdom, with God the Father as the ruler, with Christ at his right hand. The Holy Spirit completed the tripartite godhead. Mary, the mother of Jesus, took the penultimate place in Catholic hagiography, just below the Trinity. By the high Middle Ages, she represented a feminine component in Catholic mythology absent from most Protestant denominations. The "communion of saints" dwelled in the next level of existence. According to Church doctrine, saints were deceased humans whose faith and good works allowed them proximity to the Almighty. Consequently, saints could intercede with God on behalf of the living. Moreover, many saints looked after certain groups and occupations or took up particular causes. For instance, Saint Eustachius protected huntsmen, Saint Benedict of Narsia attended to farmers, Saint Joseph served as the patron saint of carpenters, and Saint Michael watched over soldiers.[31] Those afflicted with throat disorders could invoke the intervention of Saint Blaise.[32]

As Mary's and the saints' status implied, the Almighty did not inhabit heaven alone. In Catholic eschatology, the soul lives on after death. Those who lived immoral lives would find themselves in hell, and those who lived good ones found their reward in heaven. Most believers, however, spent time expiating their sins in the middle realm of Purgatory. The denizens of that place could gain merit from prayers, Masses, and other rituals performed on their behalf by those on earth, which shortened the length of their penance. The location of cemeteries on church grounds within town limits served as a constant reminder of the brevity of life. Thus, the dead remained part of the routines of the living.[33]

Other aspects of the church became part of their routine as well. The celebration of the Mass allowed Catholics to re-create and participate in Christ's sacrifice. The consecration of the host was the point of the service that the Eucharist became body and blood of Christ and therefore an object of adoration. The Church granted the authority to administer this and other sacraments only to the ordained.[34] The most auspicious place to perform this rite was over a church altar that contained the relics of a saint, usually a bone or other preserved part of his or her body. The monopoly priests possessed over the dispensation of this and other grace-bestowing rituals gave them tremendous power over the believers in their communities—they held the keys to the kingdom of heaven.[35]

This spectacular nature of Catholicism played an important role in the Church's missions in the Western Hemisphere. The Mass permitted American Indians to observe this theology as a communal performance complete with talismans, transformational utterances, sacred smoke, and specialized ceremonial equipment. Many other aspects of Catholicism's practices and items resembled those of Native Americans. The historian James Axtell pointed out that these resemblances gave its missionaries a significant advantage over Protestant clerics whose emphasis on the written word and didactic sermons had little in common with indigenous spirituality.[36]

Catholic priests acted as intermediaries between the earthbound and the spirit world, a role also played by Indian holy men. The unique vestments of these clergymen set them apart not only from the Indians, but from the French laity as well. These clerics also took vows of chastity that theoretically removed them from the competition for wives among the people whom they served. This practice relieved them from kinship obligations in Native American societies, allowing them to mediate disputes among their Indian hosts without favoritism. Most Catholic priests in colonial Louisiana eschewed commercial activities. Hence, they posed little economic threat to their Native American charges beyond the cost of their food and lodging, for which their sponsors in Europe provided partial funding.

The Catholic Church in France, however, was not of one mind on doctrinal issues; it, too, suffered from factionalism. Some disputes traveled across the Atlantic to the shores of the Gulf Coast. The effects of such disagreements played out in the affairs of the first Catholic clerics in the Lower Mississippi Valley. Priests from the seminary of the Société des Missions Étrangères ventured into the region at the close of the seventeenth century. These men reported to their headquarters in Québec, where their superiors enjoyed frequent contact with the only bishop north of Mexico. Disputes in Paris over the "Chinese Rites"—the Jesuits' toleration of the veneration of ancestors by their converts in China—carried across the Atlantic. Because of his disdain for the Jesuit Order's tolerance of this and other non-Christian cultural practices, Jean-Baptiste de la Croix de Chevrière de St. Vallier, the bishop of Quebec, consistently ruled against the Jesuits' attempts to expand southward from the Great Lakes. Instead, during the 1690s he permitted the Société des Missions Étrangères to open a post among the Tomoroas in Illinois despite the fact that the Jesuits had been laboring at nearby Kaskaskia since 1682. The issue roiled for several years until it was finally settled in 1701. That year a commission of three bishops appointed by Louis XIV ruled in favor of the Sociéte.[37] Over the course of the following decade, the Jesuits withdrew from Louisiana. However, their dwindling numbers and general lack of converts led the Compagnie des Indes to replace the Missions Étrangères' men with the Capuchins in 1722.[38] It was also during the 1720s that the Society of Jesus once again vied for the right to harvest souls in the Lower Mississippi Valley. After 1726, the Jesuits extended their authority over a region that stretched from the Great Lakes to Fort Rosalie on the Mississippi River.[39] Their presence bought further ecclesiastical rows in the years that followed, some of which were felt by the inhabitants of Natchez Country.

The battle to win souls in the New World was part of a larger struggle for the "Church militant." Its search for proselytes in North America constituted part of a broad drive that began at home and, to a large extent, stayed there. The bulk of France's spiritual outreach took place within the realm. For instance, at the height of their power in the seventeenth century, a third of Jesuits resided within the Province of Paris, and of the 3,000 in France; only 180 worked in its overseas possessions.[40]

This reforming impulse arose after the end of the Wars of Religion (1562–98), when members of the clergy began to address what they believed to be a decline of conventional religious observance among the peasantry.[41] Folk traditions had diluted orthodox practice in the countryside. In 1610, one priest in Brittany wrote that he had witnessed peasants entering their chapels to threaten the statues of saints with punishment if their prayers went unanswered. He also saw women collect the dust from their local churches and toss it in the air to create a fair breeze for their men who had gone to sea.[42] Clerics of the seventeenth century drew comparisons between the spiritual heterodoxy of the countryside and the outright "ignorance" of the indigenous peoples of the New World.

In response, various clerical organizations conducted catechizing missions that traveled through the provinces with the object of reinvigorating lay observance. At the forefront of this peripatetic work were Vincent de Paul and his Prêtes de la Mission. The Capuchins who conducted missions drew the warmest responses with their popular oratories, while the Jesuits staged their theatrical performances at strategic locations with impressive logistical support. The typical internal mission lasted about three weeks, during which time lapsed parishioners, Jews, and Protestants were admonished to repent and join the Church.[43] The same proportions held for the other religious houses of the realm. The Catholic Church, Gallican or otherwise, devoted nearly all of its resources to European endeavors, as the poverty of the clerics in the eighteenth-century Southeast attests.[44] The acts of Louisiana's missionaries, and more important, what they wrote about Native Americans in general, and the Natchez peoples in particular, were often conditioned by domestic considerations. American Indians and their spiritual practices often served as convenient foils for theological disputes at home as much as they represented potential converts abroad.

The most intriguing questions regarding religious exchange in Natchez Country were almost certainly the most ubiquitous and perhaps the most important. Moreover, the answers will most likely never be known. For instance, how did an average Natchez and European share their beliefs and spiritual practices? There were never more than one or two Catholic priests at one time among the hundreds of Europeans and Africans who lived around the Grand Village between 1716 and 1729. The majority of these *habitants* and slaves could not read or write. Their concepts of Christian dogma were probably far more heterodox than those of their pastors, or of the other educated men who left their impressions of religious life in Natchez Country. Rites to ensure good harvests or to gain protection from enemies and illness probably dominated the spiritual practices of both the native and immigrant men and women who worked in its fields. One can only imagine the topics of the innumerable unrecorded conversations that indigenous and European farmers and hunters had during those years. How did an illiterate day laborer explain the significance of his rosary to his Natchez neighbor? Did they draw parallels between the Virgin Mary and the Natchez's female deity, the White Woman? How did Europeans convey their conceptions of the Trinity? What ideas did women from the slums of Paris and the forests of the Mississippi trade regarding the other-than-human beings that protected their children or watched over their births? To whom did hunters pray before the chase? In contrast, what aspects of missionaries' accounts of Natchez spirituality were informed by their desire to drive the "pagan" and "superstitious" elements from their parishioners' religiosity?[45] Finally, how did African theology play out in Natchez country? What did Bambaras tell Théoloëls about Islam or about the other-than-human beings that inhabited their world? The priests and educated laity who left records had a vested interest in ignoring the nonelites' answers to such questions.

Despite their internal tensions, the opulence and rich traditions of the Church and the court of the Sun King provided a modicum of stability. France's social system ascribed status to the wellborn; men from the nobility staffed positions in both institutions. Although this system sometimes hindered the rise of natural talent, it provided a place for all of the king's subjects. Catholicism offered a set of shared experiences and an intelligible cosmology that provided solace to the lowly and underwrote the power of the mighty. Many characteristics of western European societies survived the journey across the Atlantic to become part of France's colonial project. Moreover, some of these characteristics arrived in a form that suggested to the Natchez some similarities with their own social structures and religious ideas.

The Land of the Great Sun

In much the same way that a veneer of unity cloaked the divisiveness that troubled France during the seventeenth and eighteenth centuries, the Great Sun's prestige obscured divisions within the Natchez polity.[46] The two "Suns" faced the challenge of consolidating their authority in the face of political rivals. Both men had to deal with acculturating foreigners who dwelt in their marchlands. Despite frequent charges of despotism, the Great Sun's power often depended on his ability to forge consensus among his people. The Sun King, despite the discourse of absolutism attributed to him, spent much of his time and money garnering the support of his nobles. These similarities, as ephemeral as some of them were, explain why the newcomers thought that they had found an American Indian "kingdom" that shared many of the social and political characteristics that they had left behind in the Old World.

To the Frenchmen and Canadians, the Natchez appeared to be most advanced society that they had encountered in North America. Although most of the Great Lakes and Laurentian peoples familiar to them engaged in farming, none cultivated fields as large as those that Iberville saw near the Grand Village. Likewise, the temple mounds the Natchez built had no equals among the Indians of the North.

Of all the characteristics that seemed to fulfill the legends of a powerful native kingdom, the image of an Indian potentate loomed large in the minds of those who encountered the Natchez. In some ways, the Théoloëls' centralized political structure resembled those of the powerful empires of South and Central America that fell to the Spanish. Europeans often remarked upon the regal status of the Great Sun. Iberville's description of the Indian's authority as "tyrannical" drew upon imagery from the ancient history he had studied as a youth at the Jesuit college in Montreal.[47] The Sun's quotidian routines also resembled more contemporary monarchical theater. André Penicault, a ship's carpenter who sojourned at the Grand Village for the year 1704, observed:

> This grand chief commands all other chiefs of the eight other villages. He sends them his orders through two of his lackeys, of which he has as many as thirty that can be called his hirelings. . . . [H]e also has many servants . . . this grand chief is as absolute as a King. His people, out of respect do not approach him, When they speak with him they do so from a distance of four paces. . . . [W]hen distinguished old men approach his bed they raise their arms aloft making frightful howls; this is how they salute him though he does not even look them at them.[48]

Nor was Penicault alone in his perceptions regarding the Indian leader's power. Antoine Le Page du Pratz, a *concessionnaire* who lived among the Natchez for several years during the 1720s, wrote:

> In effect, these Peoples are raised in perfect submission to their Sovereign, that authority they [the Great Sun and his retinue] exercise on them is a veritable despotism which can perhaps be compared to that of the first Ottoman Emperors. He is like them,

absolute master of the goods and lives of his Subjects; he disposes of them as he pleases, his will is his reason; and by an advantage that the Ottomans never enjoyed; he has no need to fear seditious movements nor an attack upon his person. When he ordains that a man who merits it be put to death, the unfortunate neither begs, nor makes intercession for his life, nor looks to escape, the order of the Sovereign is executed on the spot and not a person there murmurs. The parents of the Great Sun participate more or less in this authority, according to their proximity of their bloodline.[49]

Nor was Le Page du Pratz's analogy to the potentates of the Mediterranean world completely strained. Like many monarchs of the Old World, the indigenous retainers carried their leader on a shoulder-born conveyance. The most accomplished Natchez warriors carried the Great Sun on a litter made of painted deerskins and wooden poles, a sort of North American sedan chair.[50]

When Father Pierre-Francois-Xavier de Charlevoix passed through the Grand Village in December 1721 on his survey of the Mississippi, he, too, noted the status of the Great Sun and his mate:

> The great chief of the Natchez bears the name of the Sun. . . . The rank of Female Chief is accorded to his Wife; and although she does not ordinarily meddle with the Government, they render to her great honors. She, as well as the Sun, has the power over life and death. As soon as somebody has had the misfortune to displease one or the other, they order their Guards, whom they call Allouez [lackey], to kill him. "Rid me of that dog," say they; and they are obeyed on the spot. Their Subjects, and even the Chiefs of the Villages, never approach them unless they salute them three times, letting loose a cry, which is a type of howl. They do the same upon leaving, and retire by backing away. When they encounter them, they must stop and get off the road and make the same cries that I spoke of, until they have passed. One is also obliged to carry them the best of their Harvest, and products of their hunts and of their fishing trips. Last but not least, even their closet relatives, who make up the Noble Families, while they have the honor to dine with them, [they] do not have the right to drink from the same cup [as the Sun and his wife] nor put a hand on their plates.[51]

In this passage, Charlevoix referred to protocols familiar to his European readership. For instance, one never turned one's back to royalty.

More important, the Jesuit's narrative provides a stark contrast to earlier accounts of Native Americans' egalitarianism and clemency.[52]

An anonymous description published in 1758 reiterated the Suns' control over the economic resources of the nation: "The veneration which these savages have for their great chief and for his family goes so far that whether he speaks good or evil, they thank him by genuflections and reverences marked by howls. All these Suns have many savages who have become their slaves voluntarily, and who hunt and work for them.... All these relatives of the Sun regard the other savages as dirt."[53] These observations suggest parallels between Natchez and European social ranks. European peasants endured similar treatment at the hands of those with more status. They owed their labor to the lord of their manor, a nobleman who also administered justice in their *seigneury*. Commoners also had to show proper respect by removing their hats, bowing, and averting their eyes when they encountered nobles or senior clerics.[54]

The parallels between the two Suns did not end with the treatment of their subjects; both leaders faced domestic unrest. George R. Milner and Sissel Schroeder noted an inherent predilection for divisive political rivalries within complex chiefdoms.[55] The Great Sun's problems arose from the recent changes within the Natchez polity. In the years just before Iberville arrived, the Théoloëls had shifted their paramount town from a site to the north to the Grand Village. This displacement generated tension with the outlying communities whose leaders consequently had less access to the nation's decision-making apparatus. The early Bourbons faced a similar problem when they began to concentrate the power of the state in the monarchy—a policy that provoked unrest among sections of the French nobility. Moreover, the Great Sun and his entourage, like Louis, faced the trials of acculturating the waves of immigrants that had moved into the Natchez Country. This influx of newcomers fit in with the cyclical nature of Mississippian chiefdoms.

A number of anthropologists have described the rise and fall of Mississippian chiefdoms. Most follow a general pattern set out by Patricia Galloway in her book *Choctaw Genesis, 1500–1700*. She argued that cycle began with segmented tribes led by "big men" who used their persuasive skills to lead their people. The next phase came about as the segmented tribes joined together as "simple chiefdoms." During this stage, the chiefs redistributed agricultural surpluses in public ceremonies or to acquire exotic goods to enhance their prestige. These groups of villages then consolidated into centralized complex chiefdoms led by men who used rituals to increase their influence over their peoples. The successes of these chiefdoms contained the makings of their downfall. According to Galloway, this final stage collapsed when the population outstripped the fertility of the soil and the technology the people used to collect food. Overburdened by demands for tribute, subordinate communities revolted, breaking into segmented tribes to begin the process anew.[56]

The anthropologist Karl Lorenz suggested that the Natchez were assembling into a complex chiefdom when Iberville arrived at the turn of the eighteenth century.[57] In the last decades of the 1600s, refugee communities, already weakened by pandemics, sought asylum from what the anthropologist Robbie Ethridge called "militaristic Native slaving societies" by moving into Natchez Country.[58] The opulence of the Natchez's culture and the prospect of safety provided by their strength attracted disparate groups to settle around the Grand Village as subordinate members of a Mississippian chiefdom. As Milner and Schroeder pointed out, the growing population and power of polities like these made it easy for them to coerce their neighbors to join them.[59] European observers reported that the towns southeast of that town contained the Tunican-speaking Grigras and Tioux. Members of La Salle's party described the Koroas as one of the more powerful communities in the region that also enjoyed a close relationship with the People of the Sun.[60]

European observers often wrote about the Grand Village as if it was a kind of capital of the Théoloël polity, but it had acquired whatever preeminence that it enjoyed only shortly before the founding of Louisiana. The "Emerald Site," the name twentieth-century archaeologists gave to a much larger settlement to the north, previously held a central position in the region's political structure. During the Emerald Site's predominance, the Grand Village operated as its tributary. In turn, the Grand Village had its own satellite communities scattered across the lands near St. Catherine's Creek. Excavations undertaken during the 1940s revealed that the Emerald Site had been abandoned by the turn of the eighteenth century. The reason for this desertion remains unclear. Perhaps, like their Tunican neighbors to the north, its inhabitants were escaping from Chickasaw raiders.[61] Written sources corroborate the archaeological data regarding the previous center of the Natchez polity. Several eighteenth-century authors related stories about a great temple that once stood at the northern edge of the Indians' homeland.[62]

Not all of the surrounding towns supported the Grand Village as it took on the leading role vacated by the deserted settlement. The headmen of several outlying Natchez communities competed with the Great Sun and his supporters for control over relations with the arrivistes from

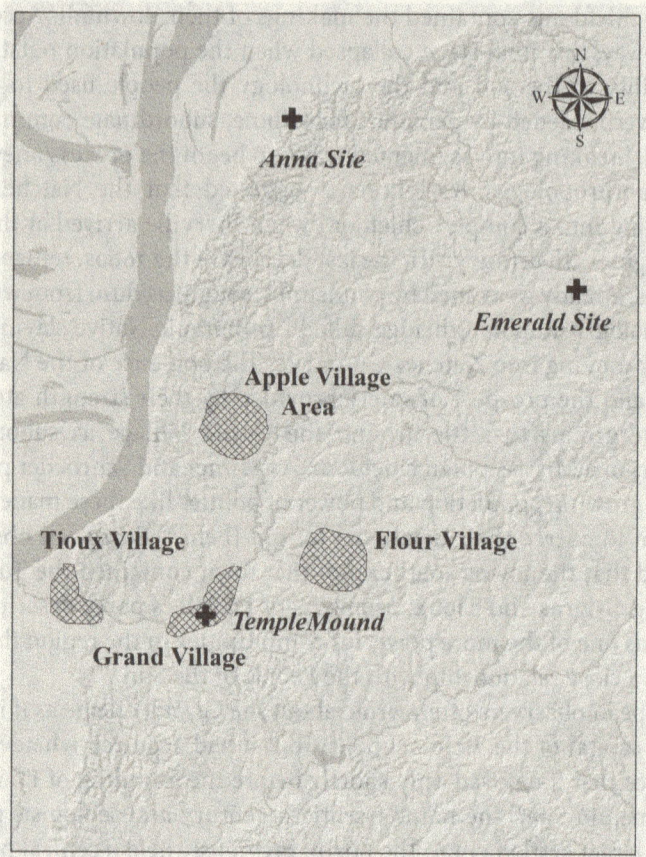

FIGURE 1.1. Mound sites in Natchez Country.

Europe. The most determined challenges came from the Apple and Jenazaque Villages.[63] These people lived near the old Emerald Mound; perhaps they were trying to regain the leadership by virtue of their proximity to the former "capital." Conversely, as Milner and Schroeder contended, outlying settlements in complex chiefdoms were inherently difficult for the paramount chiefs to control as a direct function of their distance from the core of the polity.[64] Perhaps as important, by the turn of the eighteenth century, some of these outliers were closer to the Chickasaws, who had access to British traders. During the 1710s and 1720s, "big men," who built consensus by means of persuasion and by their ability to access prestigious manufactured goods, led these marchland towns. These headmen gained enough political capital to demand a voice in the

Natchez polity's decision making. In doing so, they contested the rule of the Great Sun and his family. Several of these refractory leaders were at the forefront of the anti-Louisianan faction that played an increasingly prominent role in Natchez diplomacy. After his surrender at the close of the Last Natchez War, the last Great Sun reported that one of his chief rivals, "the Sun of the Apple Village was a usurper, who, although he was not a noble, had seized the place which rendered him the third most powerful person in the nation."[65]

The archaeologist Ned Jenkins suggested another source of tension closer to the chiefdom's ruling families. He theorized that all of the sons of the chief's sister possessed claims to lead their people. Only one of them, however, could take control of the chiefdom. Those who lost out in the competition for power started new outlying towns or communities beyond the immediate supervision of the paramount chief in a process Jenkins called "budding." The leaders of these new settlements might have been able to call upon the parent chiefdom for support during difficult times, but they also had the potential to act as rivals to the paramount chief.[66] The documentary evidence lists similar rivals to the Great Sun. Although these second-tier elites lived quite differently than Louis's contentious relatives, the princes of the blood, they occupied a similar niche within the Natchez kinship network.

The Natchez "ancien regime" sought to counteract such centrifugal forces with ritual grandeur and monumental architecture. Between the mound that supported the Great Sun's home and the temple mound was a ceremonial plaza. This built environment formed a heterotopic location where he and other elites acted as mediators with the unseen powers, met with outsiders, and buried their dead. The anthropologist Cameron Wesson characterized these spaces as "cosmograms . . . where a culture translates abstract notions of social, political, and historical order into physical forms."[67] Much like Versailles, this ground served as a stage for Natchez spectacles, evoking awe from both natives and newcomers. In a manner similar to the French palace, it also served as a discursive space that generated social and political power. Both the Great Sun and the Sun King used their respective *axes mundos* to help validate their rule.

Another classic Mississippian tool of statecraft—political theater— attracted the attention of the French chroniclers.[68] Like nobles who attended the *enlever* of Louis, the nation's elders greeted the waking Great Sun. The Indian leader spent the rest of his day surrounded by retainers who supplied him with sustenance and protection.

The Natchez hierarchy shared other traits with its European counterparts: several types of workers and officials served the Great Sun. The Sun's brother acted as his community's chief diplomat. In 1682, he welcomed La Salle to Natchez Country and escorted him to the main village. During the second and third decade of the eighteenth century, this envoy's job became increasingly important as the Natchez Louisianan policy developed. This trend was evident in the career of the Tattooed Serpent, the penultimate Great Sun's brother, when he negotiated several agreements with Iberville's sibling, Jean-Baptiste Le Moyne, sieur de Bienville.

Other Natchez people served the Great Sun in less distinguished capacities. As mentioned earlier, the diarist Penicault made his cursory reference to thirty "lackeys."[69] These individuals appeared to perform at least one bureaucratic role in the transmission of the "great chief's" orders. In addition to this group, an entourage of warriors hunted and acted as an armed escort for the Great Sun. According to Le Page du Pratz, these men did their work on a purely voluntary basis.[70] Finally, male and female field laborers tilled the soil for the Suns. The exact nature of these workers' relationship to the Suns is unclear despite Europeans' characterization of these individuals. Charlevoix hinted that some form of coercion forced the populace to turn over "the best of their harvests, the products of their hunts and fishing."[71] B.A. Luxembourg, the author of the *Memoire sur Louisiane* characterized these workers as "voluntary slaves."[72] As the historian Christine Snyder pointed out, "Western concepts of personal freedom and dependence had little meaning in a society in which kinship played a fundamental role."[73] Nonetheless, to the outsiders from overseas, the roles of "slaves," "stinkards," "guards," and "lackeys" bore a striking resemblance to the social hierarchy they had left behind in the Old World. In both cases, the vast majority of the population lacked prestige and had little power over the fruits of their labor.

Like Europeans, the Natchez had something that looked like a hereditary upper class. The indigenes' system, however, defied simple analysis. In the early twentieth century, the anthropologist John R. Swanton characterized it as a four-tiered system that began with commoners (the elites referred to them as *puants* or stinkards), honored men, nobles, and Suns. European observers recorded what they saw as an intricate scheme. According to several of them, commoners could marry any member of the nation. In contrast, the upper ranks had to choose a mate from among the commoners.[74] Accordingly, the Great Sun was the offspring of a stinkard father and a Sun mother. Complicating the matter further, the Natchez class structure possessed a regressive element; half of the children from these marriages lost status according to a pattern. The male child of a male Sun lost one rank and became a noble although his daughter remained a Sun. Thus, a noble could have been the child either of a Sun father and a stinkard mother or of a stinkard father and a noble mother. Honored people could come from an honored father and a stinkard mother or from a noble mother and a stinkard father.

Problems with Swanton's analysis gave rise to the "Natchez Paradox," a series of anthropological debates that continued for sixty years after he introduced his theory. Some scholars reasoned that if Swanton's explanation was correct, the People of the Sun would have run out of eligible commoner mates within a few generations.[75] A number of solutions to the "paradox" were put forth over the years. Among these was George I. Quimby's suggestion that the Natchez system perpetuated itself through the long-standing convention of absorbing foreign elements through intermarriage. This practice would have increased the number of potential wives and husbands for the upper classes. Derogation of the offspring would also help return some people to the lower, marriageable ranks. These unions would also spread members of recently adopted groups throughout the entire polity, giving them a sense of acceptance. Jeffrey Brain agreed with the assimilation model but disputed Quimby's assertion that the Natchez had employed it for very long by the time the French arrived.[76] Moreover, the presence of several non-Natchez towns that were politically dependent on the Grand Village helps to substantiate Quimby's theory.

The anthropologist Vernon Knight proposed a much less complex theory. He argued that the Natchez used an exogamous clan system similar to those employed by neighboring Native communities. The reduction in the males' status kept the upper ranks small in comparison to the rest of the population. Patricia Galloway and Jason Baird Jackson offered an even simpler explanation: that the Natchez divided themselves into moieties, and that promotions into the ranks of the honored peoples and nobles were attained through personal achievements.[77]

Archaeological and historical evidence also supports Brain's corollary that by the time of European contact, the People of the Sun had only recently adopted intermarriage as a means of acculturation. They had little need for it until the Grand Village became the locus for the region's politics and thus had to integrate outsiders into its population. Lorenz's and Jenkin's ideas about the struggle for authority between the Suns of the Grand Village and the outlying towns during the 1710s and 1720s also lend credence to Brain's argument.[78] The ruling family may have been in the process of consolidating its position when Iberville, Penicault, and other Europeans encountered the Natchez. The reaction of the marginalized leaders from the outer villages during that time to the policies of the Grand Village leaders suggests that their authority had limits. More important, the Natchez's internecine rivalries casts doubt upon the Europeans' characterizations of the Great Sun as an "absolute" monarch. Rather, as Lorenz argued, observers from the Old World and Canada were projecting early-modern concepts of sovereignty and authority onto the People of the Sun.[79] The Natchez were in certain ways different from other Native American polities whom newcomers had encountered, but their political institutions were nowhere near as stable or as "absolute" as the outsiders imagined. Nonetheless, these characterizations were to prove useful for both immigrants and indigenes during the first few decades of Louisianans' efforts to settle in the region.

As in Europe, religious practices also helped to ameliorate dissension among the Indians' disparate communities. For instance, Le Page du Pratz wrote that the Natchez worshiped a unitary creator.[80] Several other Europeans corroborated the Dutchman when they wrote that the Natchez venerated the sun as a representation of this Supreme Being. According to the Jesuit Father Le Petit, who had visited with the Natchez, the temple mound's height allowed the nation's leaders to converse more easily with the solar deity.[81] In the afterlife, the good were rewarded and the evil punished in places that resembled the Catholics' heaven and hell. "Those who are virtuous in life go to a delicious land after death," and those who "lived in the opposite manner go to a barren land . . . where they no longer eat meat and they will eat no other food except [the flesh of] crocodiles."[82]

The Natchez had a moral code that was not unlike that of the Christian Old Testament; it prohibited theft, murder, and adultery. This last proscription must have especially pleased Catholic missionaries in light of their criticisms of the "debauchery" that they had so often perceived among other indigenous communities. The People of the Sun also had priests who conducted ceremonies and provided access to the powers of the unseen world and did so in dedicated spatial frameworks. Consequently, the Natchez belief system gave some of the French hope that they might make easy converts among the Natchez since their faith seemed to be so similar to their own.[83]

The Natchez leadership based their authority upon this belief system.[84] Their origin story stated that sometime in the distant past, a being named

Thé and his wife, White Woman, appeared among their ancestors. The two shone so brightly that they could have come only from the sun itself. Impressed with the authoritative manner with which the shining man spoke, the elders of the Natchez asked him to become their sovereign. At first Thé refused, but he relented on the condition that they follow him to a better land. He then gave them instructions on forming a government. They must agree to marry outside their rank and not allow the sons of the leader to inherit their fathers' status. Rather, these boys would become mere nobles, but the girls were to remain in the ruling family. From that time until 1731, the first son born to the Great Sun's daughter became the leader of the nation. Thé told them not to kill except in self-defense, to avoid drunkenness, lies, and adultery, and to respect the property of others. He ordered them to share their food and goods with one another without envy. Finally, the Natchez had to promise to build a temple and maintain a sacred fire within it. Thé ignited the first sacred flame by means of his supernatural powers.[85] To fulfill their promise, the Théoloëls constructed a hallowed building in which to conduct their ceremonies atop an earthen mound near the home of the paramount chief. Inside burned a fire of four logs arranged in the shape of a cross. Four men tended the fire at all times, periodically pushing the tree trunks into center of the blaze as the flames consumed them.[86] Although nearby Native American groups maintained similar fires, the Natchez seemed to garner special attention.[87] For some Europeans, these practices evoked comparisons with classical antiquity. A Parisian journal described "a temple... erected from time immemorial, in which a perpetual flame is maintained, much as it was in the Temple of Vesta in Rome."[88]

In his 1724 book, Father Joseph-François Lafitau compared the Natchez's veneration of a solar deity to Greek, Parthian, as well as Latin forms of worship.[89] These comparisons resonated with Father Du Ru's description of the Great Sun's deportment as that of an "ancient emperor." Some of these similarities were not coincidences; the Natchez had shaped some of their stories for the benefit of the newcomers. An example of this willingness to recast their origin myth is evident in the solar deity's admonition to avoid drunkenness since alcohol was a recent import to the New World.

The Great Sun's office included religious duties. Each morning, the chief emerged from the door of his home on the town's highest mound. The height of the low prominence was unimportant; its utility rested in "the visible differential between it and the surrounding elements of the total community design."[90] From that vantage point, with his arms extended, he turned to the east to greet the rising sun. He then bowed three times from the waist and offered tobacco smoke drawn from a sacred calumet. The Great Sun and his wife also took part in daily evening worship services inside the temple. He presided over other celebrations as well, particularly the Green Corn Festival in early autumn and the Deer Moon Festival in the spring.[91]

Other members of the nation besides the Great Sun possessed influence over the unseen forces. Natchez priests employed a combination of medicine and ritual. Although most of his contemporaries doubted these native doctors' capabilities, Le Page du Pratz wrote about his experiences regarding two successful treatments by Théoloël physicians.[92] Father Le Petit, however, characterized them as "indolent old men, who, wishing to avoid the labor which is required in hunting, fishing, and cultivation of the fields, exercise this dangerous trade to gain a support for their families."[93] The cynicism of foreigners notwithstanding, these men must have effected some cures if the Natchez were willing to underwrite their status as full-time practitioners. Doctors in France were only beginning to abandon supernatural explanations for illness at the turn of the eighteenth century. Yet, many French people, particularly those lacking a formal education, still thought that witchcraft or other-than-human beings caused and cured sicknesses.

Many of the more literate European observers referred to these men as *jongleurs*, a word that is often translated into English as "jugglers." The French word, however, implied more than dexterity or prestidigitation. Medieval *jongleurs* sold medicinal herbs and unguents in addition to providing entertainment. One authority wrote that *jongleurs* "were universal artists embracing all branches of human knowledge."[94] When clerics employed the word to describe their opposite numbers in Natchez society, they meant to invoke images of charlatans and tricksters. Yet, the Catholic missionaries' choice of the word revealed that they regarded their indigenous counterparts as men with spiritual power, albeit of a darker sort, in the same way they often regarded the *jongleurs* of France as practitioners of witchcraft. Experts in canon law labeled *jongleurs*, along with magicians and prostitutes, as *infamia*, and excluded them from the sacraments or from bringing suits in ecclesiastical courts. According to these clerics, to give money to a *jongleur* was the moral equivalent of demon worship.[95] These associations with non-Catholic religious and healing practices allowed the European priests who wrote about the Natchez to recast their medical skills, no matter how effective, as challenges to Christian orthodoxy.

The art of healing was only one of the characteristics by which the two societies resembled each other. A hereditary monarch, assisted by attendants and supported by nobility, appeared to rule the chiefdom. They seemed to maintain an elaborate system of inherited privilege. They paid taxes in kind in the form of tribute to the Great Sun. They had a religious tradition with a moral code, standardized rituals, a supreme being, and an afterlife. These attributes made it easy for the upper-class French officials and missionaries who came to Natchez Country to identify with the Théoloëls.

The Peoples of the Suns Meet

In late March 1682, several canoes hove onto the shore of the Mississippi River. They carried a mix of twenty-three Europeans and more than three dozen American Indians. The indigenous contingent included ten women and three children.[96] Leading the group was René-Robert Cavelier de La Salle. The Europeans hailed from France, Italy, Canada, and Flanders. Except for two Chickasaw interpreters and two Koroa slaves, the Indians came from communities along Great Lakes or the St. Lawrence River Valley. Henri Tonti, La Salle's second-in-command, had purchased a young Koroa boy for two knives and a small kettle at a Taensa village a few days earlier. A Loup Indian acquired the second Koroa, a prisoner of war, from a Taensa headman at the same place.[97]

Among this group were the first people from the Old World to record their visits to the People of the Sun since the last of De Soto's conquistadors sailed by in 1542 on their retreat to the Gulf of Mexico. The Natchez's initial contact with the subjects of the Sun King provided the foundation upon which the Natchez and his colonists would build their relationship. It cast into bold relief the characteristics that helped to build the illusion that the two shared parallel social and political practices.

These resemblances began with the timing of the strangers' appearance. The newcomers had appeared at an opportune moment during which the Indians were eager to demonstrate their hospitality. La Salle arrived at the waning of the Deer Moon, the first moon in the Natchez calendar. The Natchez marked their new year with a festival that included sham battles and the presentation of gifts to the Great Sun.[98] It was customary for the headman to invite honored visitors to take a meal with him at the close of these festivities.[99] The brother of the Great Sun escorted La Salle several miles to a village called Natché to be the guest of his people's headmen.[100]

Afterward, the Frenchmen raised the king's flag over the town and gave presents to the Natchez.[101] Sometime during their stay, Tonti's slave slipped away to his home village among nearby Koroas.[102] The party left Natché on Good Friday, March 27. A Koroa leader, who had been summoned by the Great Sun after La Salle arrived, guided them downriver. It is highly likely the Indians had an opportunity to observe the celebration of a Mass before the strangers departed. The expedition's chaplain, Father Membré, wrote that they arrived at another town located on a "beautiful eminence" about twenty miles south of their starting point.[103] After a brief sojourn, they left two bags of corn at the home of the "chief" of the village with the understanding that they would come back to claim the food on their trip upriver.[104] La Salle and his party continued south to the mouth of the Mississippi, which they claimed for the Sun King in the first week of April 1682.[105]

La Salle's visit to the village of Natché marked the beginning of a dialogue between the world of the Sun King and the Great Sun. Although the meeting was brief and the numbers of his party small, certain aspects of the dialogue's syntax were in play. The first of these aspects could be seen in the fact that those who entered Natchez Country did so on Natchez terms. When La Salle's men returned to the village for their sacks of corn a few weeks later, they received a far less hospitable reception; only some fast talk from the Loup's Koroa slave saved them from annihilation by 1,500 Natchez warriors.[106] On his 1690 venture into the Lower Mississippi Valley, Henri Tonti found out that unbidden guests were still unwelcome. The Italian sent two members of his party ahead to the main Natchez village only to find out a few days later that the villagers had killed the pair.[107]

Slavery constituted the second characteristic of the developing conversation between the two worlds. The war chief of the French held a slave taken from a town associated with the Natchez. In the years to come, Europeans would not only demonstrate their willingness to enslave Indian children, but would eventually threaten the Suns with the same treatment.

Finally, the newcomers brought along one of their black-robed shamans on their trip to the Gulf of Mexico. The Natchez saw for the first time the elaborate rituals and heard the colorful stories of the Catholics. It is reasonable to assume that the Indians also viewed images and heard tales of the Europeans' "White Woman"—the Virgin Mary, the patron saint of France. Over the next three decades, French missionaries would return to the land of the Great Sun. When the men of the *Renommée* entered the Grand Village in March 1700, they found a letter waiting for them. The author, Father Montigny, a priest from the Seminary of the Foreign Missions, had departed only a few days earlier and claimed to have baptized 185 Indian children.[108]

The discourse between the French and the Natchez that began with La Salle's visit continued with Iberville's expedition eighteen years later. Despite the jumbled European accounts, certain facts about the peoples of the Great Sun and the Sun King are clear. Both the natives and the newcomers were peoples on the rise. When Iberville landed in the spring of 1700, he encountered a complex chiefdom in the midst of assembling disparate peoples into a defensible union in much the same way that Louis XIV had recently consolidated the marchlands of his realm. Both respected the appearance of order embodied in a single ruler. The Europeans equated such respect with that paid to their kings. Consequently, they assumed that the deference the Natchez accorded the Great Sun reflected similar power. The Natchez had a monarch, a noble class, political offices with standardized responsibilities, and an organized body of religious beliefs and practices that resembled institutions of in the Old World.

At the same time, the Indians saw spiritual practices among the Europeans that probably looked familiar. Catholicism's rites and symbolism resembled many forms of indigenous worship. Its priests' movements and utterances during their complex rituals were not entirely unintelligible to Native Americans. The motions of elevating the Eucharist skyward and making the sign of the cross looked like the gestures of their own shamans and healers. Censers emitted purifying smoke, as did calumets and the temple's sacred fire. Moreover, the idea of a special group of men imbued with the power to influence the spirit world was a familiar concept in Native America. The Natchez priesthood worked closely with the political hierarchy of the Grand Village just as the "Grey Robes" and "Black Robes" worked alongside colonial officers at Mobile, Fort Rosalie, Yazoo, and New Orleans. Both sets of priests enjoyed the deference of their people and did not engage in physical labor. Both wore special garb when officiating at ceremonies.[109] As superficial as these likenesses may have been, they were enough for the Natchez to have permitted the Catholic shamans to operate in their villages for five decades.

Beyond the Natchez's and Europeans' fascination with the "exotic" aspects of the others' society, the most pervasive similarity between their worlds was the social institution of the village. Like the vast majority of the Europeans, the Natchez were village people. Although the main town captured the attention of the outsiders, the Grand Village constituted only one of nine settlements that made up the Natchez polity.

Criticisms that any of these similarities were at best ephemeral are undeniably correct. That is my point; the reason that the Natchez and French often misunderstood each other was because their ways resembled one another on the surface. Once the Natchez realized that they were not dealing with a group seeking to aggregate with the Grand Village, the manner in which they dealt with the outsiders changed. Similarly, when colonial officers started to see the Natchez as just another group of "*sauvages*," the soldiers changed the way that they related to the Indians. Part of the reason that these revelations shocked both the natives and the newcomers arose from their original assumptions of familiarity.

The first permanent European resident in Natchez Country, a Catholic priest, reinforced those assumptions. Strangely, another series of events, often termed the "First Natchez War," also strengthened perceptions of similarity. The manner in which the French and the Théoloëls resolved their problems during that conflict reinforced their misperceptions of the other. It was, however, the impressions garnered during these first contacts that gave both peoples the idea that they were gazing into a mirror that reflected their own world. These impressions smoothed over problems long enough for the Europeans to build farmsteads, forts, and villages in Natchez Country.

2 / Thefts of the Suns

"The Great Sun of the Natchez, who is the chief of the tribe, is the bastard of Father Saint Cosme of Canada."[1] The preceding sentence was the first in an unsigned memoir held in the manuscript collection of the Bibliothèque nationale de France. This document, dated 1728, describes St. Cosme's relationship with the Natchez *femme chef*. During their conversations, she admitted to him that the story of her family's descent from a solar deity was merely a ploy to win control over her people. Moreover, the report told of her attempts to convert St. Cosme to her religion and of her persistent, and ultimately successful, attempts to seduce him.

Father Cosme was the first permanent nonindigenous resident of Natchez Country. As such, he constituted an advance guard for both the French imperial project and the Catholic Church in the Lower Mississippi Valley. He encountered a robust culture that thrived in a region wracked by slave raiders and imported diseases.[2] The Natchez weathered disruptions that destroyed many communities of the Southeast by means of their ability to absorb foreign elements into their chiefdom. The arrival of St. Cosme heralded the advent of another group of outsiders. This new group, however, had originated overseas.

Adrift among the Suns

Jean-François de Buisson de Saint-Cosme was born in Québec in 1667 and entered the priesthood at the age of twenty-three. A few years later his brother Michel also entered a Catholic order as did one of his sisters.

St. Cosme served during the 1690s in the mission at Grand Pré in what is now Nova Scotia and returned to Québec in 1698 after allegedly interfering in local secular affairs. It was in July of that year that the Seminary of the Foreign Missions of Québec sent him on his journey to the heart of the North American continent. He arrived at his new post at a Tamoroas village on the east bank of the Mississippi River a few miles below the mouth of the Missouri.[3]

When he moved from Canada, he faced not only the challenges of preaching to Native Americans, but he also had to overcome the rival Jesuits, who had established a mission among the Kaskaskia two decades earlier. The Society of Jesus had not only gained a dominant role in the mission fields of New France, but they occupied key ecclesiastical offices in the *métropole* as well. Jesuits served as the kings' confessors from 1604 until 1764. They also enjoyed the favor of the Pontchartrain family, which controlled the naval ministry and colonial affairs.[4]

The Jesuits' power and influence inspired opposition from many quarters, including Madame Maintenon, who was secretly married to Louis XIV, and the bishop of Québec, Jean-Baptiste de La Croix de Chevrières de Saint-Vallier. Both backed the efforts of the Seminary of Foreign Missions to evangelize the interior of North America. The Jesuits eventually lost their struggle to have one of their own named as the bishop's vicar in Louisiana, in part because the controversy over the "Chinese Rites." While the Society of Jesus continued to staff their outpost in Illinois, in 1704, they withdrew their bid for ecclesiastical authority over Louisiana and recalled their priests from the province.[5] Nonetheless, before the departure of its missionaries from the Lower Mississippi Valley, the Jesuits played a role in St. Cosme's ministry. One of the members of the order hindered his early efforts to catechize the Tamoroas, while another took care of St. Cosme during an extended illness while he labored among the Natchez.[6]

St. Cosme arrived at his post near the Grand Village sometime after July 1700. He summed up his first impressions in a letter to the bishop: "I know of no place more beautiful than that of the Natchez [for a mission]."[7] During his first months there he managed to translate some simple prayers and a rudimentary catechism. Despite his cheerful outlook for the future, his letter foreshadowed a number of problems that would soon dominate his communiqués. The first of these was a perennial shortage of money. His stipend was too meager to purchase supplies or allow him to trade with his hosts. The second problem was his lack of progress, marked by an inability to baptize children or "people of good sentiment before they died."

By the end of 1701, his letters conveyed his growing disillusionment. He had come to distrust the members of his new flock: "These savages here are all thieves and still regard missionaries as the same as other Frenchmen and these base people are always trying to snatch and make off with some thing." He again complained that money was short and also reported that a Jesuit had established a mission among the Houmas about forty miles from his post. Far worse for his prospects, however, was his admission that learning the Natchez language was much more difficult than he had first realized.[8] Most who traveled through the region employed Mobilian trade jargon, a mix of Muskogean dialects with words borrowed from English, Spanish, and French.[9] Another European who wrote nearly two decades later, Antoine Le Page du Pratz, mentioned that he understood the "vulgar language well enough for matters regarding the needs of life and those concerning trade," but knew that he needed to learn Natchez because few of their women spoke the trade jargon."[10] For the rookie missionary to effectively minister to all the members of his flock, he needed to master their tongue.

St. Cosme also requested that his superior send a lay assistant to hunt and fish for him. The priest further underscored his entreaty by stating the need for assistance in ejecting unwelcome visitors from his home because "one could not use his fists on an impertinent savage because it would not be good for a missionary to be obliged to sometimes strike a savage."[11]

These problems persisted throughout the following year. St. Cosme reported that food was very dear and he was forced to trade for paltry rations. Moreover, he wrote, the language barrier still presented a challenge: "There are different manners for addressing a single person, two people, and many people. When they speak of the Great Spirit, there is still another manner. When I make a mistake, they say that I offend the Great Spirit."[12] In the autumn of 1702, he sent word that the nearby Koroas, a community with close ties to the Natchez, had killed his coreligionist, Father Foucault. St. Cosme wrote that these people "will kill a man to have his knife."[13]

Later correspondence revealed more obstacles to his work. St. Cosme had difficulty with the Natchez use of their living space. Their dispersed settlements allowed them to farm and hunt without overburdening the forest's game or the soil's fertility; to the cleric, the intervening distances made his ministry difficult if not impossible. He provided a glimpse of the breadth of Natchez Country: "It takes four or five days to make a tour of the villages, and babies can die before a missionary can know of them." He included an equally telling observation regarding the conversion process among the native peoples: "It is necessary to make these barbarians men and then one may make them Christians." St. Cosme believed that only the establishment of French settlements among the Natchez would civilize the latter. He also requested that he be allowed to return to Québec.[14]

It was clear by his posts of 1705 that St. Cosme's fortunes had continued to decline. The missionary was living in a world that was coming undone, and he had given up hope. Slave raiders, encouraged by Englishmen residing among the Chickasaws, ravaged the Lower Mississippi Valley. St. Cosme, at this point a defeated man, wrote, "I believe that there is not much point to this undertaking."[15]

In his final letter of January 8, 1706, he laid bare his deep despair. St. Cosme restated his failure to learn the Natchez language and the difficulty of ministering to a dispersed population. As the historian Arnaud Balvay noted, St. Cosme's letter provided the first details on the Natchez social and religious structures: "They regard their chief as a descendant from one of the idols in their temple. They have great respect for this stone statue housed in a box of wood. They say that this is not the Great Spirit, but one sent by him in another time to this place to be master of the land. . . . It is from him that their primary chief has descended from then until the present."[16] The cleric had little chance to write more. In 1706, a band of Chitimacha warriors murdered him and several of his French companions as they camped along the Mississippi River.[17]

The priest's letters did not answer the charge posed by the document mentioned at the beginning of this chapter. The question remains: Was St. Cosme the father of the last Great Sun? Soon after the missionary's death, Father La Vente, chaplain of the settlement on the Mobile River, remarked on "a calumny most black" regarding St. Cosme, "that people of charity are prevented of mentioning to you."[18] The chaplain refrained from further discussion of the charges. Nonetheless, there are several discrepancies in the narrative offered by the manuscript report in the Bibliothèque nationale de France. The first of these involves the age of the headman; later observers wrote that the last chief was eighteen years old in 1728. If they were correct, then he would have been born sometime in 1709 or 1710, too late to be the offspring of St. Cosme. Moreover, Charlevoix and others wrote of a Sun named St. Cosme who aided the Great Sun in his negotiations with the Louisianan army during the 1731 campaign. Charlevoix mentioned that he was the offspring of the *femme chef* and therefore in line to succeed the Great Sun. The missionary might have fathered this "St. Cosme," but that would have meant that an older, rather than a younger, heir followed in his uncle's footsteps.[19] Charlevoix attributed the headman's name to the esteem with which the *femme chef* held St. Cosme because he had won her "good graces."[20] Le Page du Pratz included an account in his history of the colony in which the Tattooed Arm, mother of the last Great Sun, reminded the headman that "everybody has told you, and I tell you too, that you are the son of a Frenchman."[21]

The date of the document does little to resolve the issue. It was written at the height of a dispute between the superior of the Jesuit house in New Orleans, Father Beaubois, and the vicar of the province, Father Raphael. Was the report part of a plot to discredit earlier missionaries and strengthen the Jesuits' bid for control over the region? As we shall see, Father Beaubois was a contentious man who did not shrink from pushing the limits of his authority as the leader of his order.

The document's slender provenance is also problematic. The memoir appears in a bound volume of correspondence from the French navy. From the mid-seventeenth century, the Jesuits had a strong presence in several of the port cities on the west coast of France. The order's inclusion of hydrography in their schools' curriculum had succeeded in attracting the sons of merchant families who hoped for careers in the fleet.[22] Thus there were ready channels for a negative missive to wend its way through the navy's bureaucracy to the desks of the highest officials and possibly that of the king. Of course, these possibilities are speculative; there are no definitive clues to the report's origin or the identity of its author.

There are blatant errors in the document as well. It mentions 1703 as the date of the missionary's arrival in Natchez Country, when he actually reached his new post in 1701, and it describes the priest as "well built, strong and vigorous and between the ages of twenty-eight and thirty years old," even though St. Cosme was thirty-four. Further, it mistakenly lists his death in 1705, a year before his actual demise.

Several historians have wrestled with the question of the last Great Sun's paternity. Céline Dupré dismissed the allegation out of hand because of the missionary's repeated criticisms of the Natchez morals and behaviors, as if one has never had a dim opinion of one's in-laws.[23] James F. Barnett relied on Charlevoix's explanation that the Native American St. Cosme was named in memory of the esteemed priest.[24] In the latest work on the Natchez, Arnaud Balvay, who examined the accusative Bibliothèque nationale document, found the evidence inconclusive.[25]

Indeed, Balvay's reluctance to rush to judgment was prudent; the evidence is not compelling enough to unequivocally name St. Cosme the father of the Great Sun. Despite its problems, this document retains a modicum of historical value because it provides a perspective on the Natchez from the 1720s. As Charlevoix noted, St. Cosme had won the *femme chef*'s esteem. Aside from the unsigned document's sexual implications, it highlights their cross-cultural exchanges. It portrays a high-status woman teaching the priest about her religion in a failed attempt to convert him; in doing so, she outlined aspects of Natchez cosmology that can be corroborated elsewhere. St. Cosme's last letter demonstrated that he knew that the Natchez regarded a solar deity as the mythic ancestor of their leading family. According to the memoir's author, who may have been attempting to avoid openly validating a non-Catholic belief system, the female chief also admitted to the cleric that the Suns' origin story was a ploy to gain control over their chiefdom.

The narrative thread of the Biblothèque nationale account—of an outsider under the instruction of a *femme chef*—conforms to other aspects of Natchez social and political practices. Moreover, St. Cosme's poor language skills and lack of social acumen required remediation if he and his people were to become members of the chiefdom. His grasp of the Natchez world and how to survive in it were weak. He lacked adequate means to feed himself. The priest did not comprehend the expectations of his hosts that he distribute his "prestige" goods in order to curry favor. Instead, St. Cosme frequently referred to the Natchez as thieves who were ready to snatch from him whatever they could. The missionary's letters convey the despair of a stranger adrift in a land that he understood poorly and in which he knew he did not belong. From the indigenes' perspective, he was an important man in need of help.

The obvious choice to render assistance was a prospective mate. If the Natchez were to inculcate St. Cosme into the chiefdom, a high-ranking woman was a logical choice. The historian Theda Perdue detected a great number of similar pairings among British colonists and Native American women during the same period. Men took indigenous brides to gain access to new land, trade networks, linguistic skills, and political power.[26] It is apparent from St. Cosme's final correspondence that he had learned the rudiments of Natchez theology and government, particularly those relating to the origins of the ruling family. The *femme chef* would have also made an ideal mate since, by the rules of succession provided by later observers, a male offspring of the Great Sun's sister would become the primary chief upon his uncle's death. If they had married, their union would have reinforced the illusion that the outsiders had acknowledged the Natchez's political superiority. According to other Europeans, the sister of the Great Sun could only marry a lower-caste man. Several decades later, Le Page du Pratz refused to marry the *femme chef*'s daughter because he thought that the Natchez would perceive him as an underling. When she made her proposal, the Dutchman's first reaction was, "'Do you take me for a Stinkard?' because the female Suns do not marry their own men."[27] The priest's acceptance of *femme chef*'s offer would have implied that he had accepted a lower station for himself and his people.

Additional conclusions regarding St. Cosme are possible. The first is that he failed to convert very many of the Natchez to Catholicism; most of those he managed to baptize were children near death. Second, judging from his frequent requests for an assistant, he was lonely. Third, he never felt competent in his command of the Natchez language, although he did remark on elements of its structure. Fourth, St. Cosme left fragments of information about the breadth of Natchez Country, a land whose settlements required four to five days to visit. Finally, he wanted to return home to Canada. In short, it is likely that if the Indians regarded the priest as the vanguard of a foreign culture, which is one purpose of a missionary, he probably projected an image of an impoverished people who needed guidance and protection. That was very much the sort of people who had been joining the Natchez polity for some time.

Father St. Cosme's experiences among the People of the Sun constituted a pattern that would be replicated in the decade after his death. Subsequent contacts were also marked by accommodations born of perceived resemblances. As had been the case with the missionary, what these newcomers sought and the manner in which they sought them made them appear to blend into the Mississippian order of things.

Strangers among the Suns

The turn of the eighteenth century saw a slow but steady trickle of travelers from the Old World and Canada pass through Natchez Country. The region was a natural waypoint along the Mississippi route from Canada to the new settlements on the Gulf Coast. Its location also facilitated the integration of the region into the Mississippi Valley's economy as a producer of foodstuffs and peltries, and as consumers of European goods. More important, from the perspective of the Natchez, the deportment of outsiders like Father St. Cosme and those who followed him demonstrated the outsiders' continued need for their assistance.

During the autumn of 1700, Father Jacques Gravier, a Jesuit stationed at Kaskaskia, stopped at the Tunica mission to minister to its ailing priest,

Antoine Davion, another missionary sent by the Seminary of the Foreign Missions. St. Cosme arrived a few days later from his post among the Natchez. If St. Cosme and the *femme chef* were involved in a romantic relationship, the Jesuit never mentioned it. Instead, Gravier complained that the Natchez "are polygamous, thievish, and very depraved—the girls and women being even more so than the men and boys, among whom a great reformation must be effected before anything can be expected from them."[28]

Later, in November 1700, Father Gravier traveled to the Grand Village, where he met with the *femme chef*. In his words, "This woman Chief is very intelligent, and enjoys greater influence than one thinks."[29] In contrast, the Jesuit had little respect for the abilities of the headman of the Natchez, writing in his report that "her brother is not a great genius." The priest had arrived in time to witness the autumn harvest ceremonies, when the Great Sun and his sister offered the first fruits of the field to the spirits of their ancestors. Unfortunately, Gravier learned little about the theology behind their acts of worship since the indigenes rebuffed the missionary's inquiries about their rituals. Only later would Gravier's missionary colleague learn more about their beliefs.

The colonists who followed in the priests' wake did little to disabuse the People of the Sun of the idea that they were potential additions to the Natchez order of things. Almost as soon as they established themselves on the Gulf Coast, the colonists revealed their weakness. In July 1701, the first governor of Louisiana, the sieur de Sauvole, asked the Jesuit Father Limoges to purchase corn from the Théoloëls as he made his way north to his mission at Kaskaskia. The governor wanted the priest to have the grain stored in a cabin so that it could be retrieved and shipped by pirogue to Biloxi.[30] By leaving the food behind, Limoges adhered to a pattern set by La Salle's 1682 expedition. The members of that earlier party had left two sacks of grain at the Grand Village for their return voyage up the Mississippi. More important, Limoges's purchase resembled the redistribution system of a complex chiefdom. If so, from the indigenes' point of view, the governor's request for supplies implied his reliance upon the Suns.

During those early years, the leaders of the colony had to deal with storms brewed in other parts of the globe. The War of Spanish Succession broke out in 1702 and involved most of western Europe. In a bid to prevent a union of the French and Spanish Crowns, England formed an alliance with Austria, Prussia, Hanover, and the Netherlands. On the other side stood Louis XIV's France, Spain, Portugal, and Bavaria.[31]

Although Louis fielded large armies on land, his maritime forces were found wanting. The Royal Navy harassed French shipping and effectively cut Louisiana off from the Old World.

English naval superiority, together with the threat of attack by the Alabamas and other Native American groups, kept Louisiana from expanding beyond its shallow beachhead on the Gulf Coast. There were almost no presents for diplomatic initiatives among the nations close to the colony's outposts. For several years, few ships arrived from the homeland and imported provisions and equipment ran out. To prevent famine, Bienville, who had become the colony's de facto governor upon Sauvole's death, billeted his soldiers in nearby Mobilian Indian villages so their hosts could feed them. The commandant's decision to order his men to shelter among the more prosperous indigenous peoples resembled the behavior of previous native refugee groups who had joined larger Mississippian chiefdoms to secure food and protection. One such group of Louisianans moved into Natchez Country in 1704; among them was André Penicault, a ship's carpenter who had accompanied Iberville on his 1700 voyage up the Mississippi.[32]

Their requests for Native American aid placed the colonists in a bad light. One Choctaw leader asked Bienville if there were as many people in France as he had heard. The headman quipped: "You have been here for six years. Instead of increasing you are diminishing. The good men are dying and only children come in their places."[33] Nonetheless, until the War of Spanish Succession ended, Louisianans had too many problems of their own to worry about the impression that they might have been making among their Native American neighbors. The colony's loss of prestige had its effect on some indigenous communities, however, as many southeastern villages began to cooperate with English merchants and diplomats.

Nor were the English slow to use the war to gain leverage among Native Americans. Even before the conflict, as early as 1698, rumors reached Paris that traders from Carolina were lurking south of Illinois. That same year, the Carolinian agent Thomas Welch visited the Quapaws, who lived along the Arkansas River. The appearance of Charles Town merchants in native villages along the Mississippi also provoked French countermeasures during the late seventeenth century. Louis XIV dispatched the Canadian Iberville and his brother in 1699 to thwart Daniel Coxe's well-publicized plans for a settlement in the Lower Mississippi Valley. Their success at English Turn, where Bienville bluffed an English frigate's captain into withdrawing, was transitory. Nonetheless, the Royal Navy's victories during the first decade of the 1700s allowed England's merchants to ship inexpensive cloth, tools, and weapons to the New World.[34]

Throughout the War of Spanish Succession, France's inability to meet the Natchez and other Indian nations' demand for trade goods created an economic vacuum that allowed the English to further their influence in the region. Thomas Nairne traveled among the peoples of the Lower Mississippi Valley to expand the influence of Charles Town in the middle of the continent.[35] Voyageurs traveling between Illinois and Mobile brought word of Nairne's sojourn among the Natchez.[36] Slave raids conducted by the Chickasaws and Creeks on behalf of Charles Town traders disrupted the Choctaws as well as smaller indigenous communities along the Mobile River basin. A short break for these peoples came when the Carolinians and their allies turned their attention toward the rich slaving grounds of Florida's Franciscan missions. After they devastated the Spanish settlements, the English sent more traders into the Southeast, much to the alarm of Mobile's tiny population.[37] To the colonists in that town, the incursions of their enemies into the Mississippi Valley portended the destruction of Louisiana.

The global conflict also had an impact on France's ability to support its new colony. Fighting several European powers for nearly a dozen years had drained the coffers of the Sun King. Louis XIV's limited authority to levy new taxes meant that he needed to find other sources of income. Louis, like those who had ruled before him, relied on "extraordinary affairs," which were excises on commodities and services, for additional revenue. The king often sold the rights to collect these duties to private individuals and associations under a system of tax farms. When they worked well, these institutions gave the government access to funds without the burden of maintaining an administrative apparatus.[38] Moreover, the farmers and monopolists had far better credit than the king, were able to raise large sums quickly at lower costs, and bore the financial risks in these arrangements (a bad harvest, war, or plague could wreck their chances of turning a profit). From 1674, one of the more lucrative sectors of the economy involved the tobacco tax farm monopoly that controlled the importation, processing, distribution, and taxation of the leaf for all of France.[39]

Antoine Crozat stood out among these grandees of the tobacco monopoly. By the 1680s, Crozat had risen from a senior clerk in Languedoc to become one of the wealthiest and most influential figures in French financial circles.[40] The dismal performance of the colony during its first years made it an unlikely place to aid him in his quest for greater riches. Louisiana had yet to show a profit despite the assurances of the Le Moyne brothers of its potential. Strangely enough, the Gulf Coast settlements offered a glimmer of hope for the kingdom's fiscal well-being. The Crown granted Crozat a fifteen-year concession in the colony in September 1712 in return for underwriting Louisiana's administrative and military expenses. As part of the deal, Crozat gained exclusive rights over the colony's commercial life. Despite his connections to the tobacco monopoly, Crozat did not intend to profit by promoting the cultivation of the leaf but rather from the province's fur trade, forest products, and mineral wealth.[41] Unfortunately for Louisianans, the new management did little to alleviate the bleak situation on the shores of the Gulf of Mexico. As part of his quest for a return on his substantial investment, Crozat initiated a 300 percent markup on imported goods, making them prohibitively expensive for Native Americans and colonists alike.[42] Worse, the high price of French goods gave British traders operating in the Southeast an even greater advantage with the region's first inhabitants.

The appointment of Antoine de La Mothe, sieur de la Cadillac, as governor marked another change in Louisiana's governance. The king named him to the post in 1710, but it was nearly three years before the former commandant of Detroit arrived in Mobile to take charge.[43] The historian Charles O'Neill characterized the new governor as a reformer who wished to suppress the licentiousness of his charges. In his quest for an orderly colony, the acerbic Cadillac demonstrated little restraint in his assessment of the settlers:

> According to the proverb "Bad country, bad people" one can say that they are a heap of the dregs of Canada, jailbirds without subordination for religion and for government, addicted to vice principally with Indian women who they prefer to French women. It is very difficult to remedy it when his Majesty desires that they be governed mildly and wishes that a governor conduct himself in such a way that the inhabitants may make no complaints against him.[44]

Not surprisingly, he quickly provoked the antagonism of many colonists.[45]

Almost immediately after Cadillac arrived, provincial politics coalesced into two feuding camps. One side was led by Bienville, who was irked at being passed over for post even though he had ruled Louisiana for several years and goaded by the actions of the new governor. Cadillac's defense of Crozat's interests in the colony, as Cécile Vidal noted, did little to enhance his standing with many of the *habitants* who saw him as a "company man."⁴⁶ Jean-Baptiste du Bois du Clos, the colony's *commissaire-ordonnateur*, or financial officer, was a natural opponent of its chief executive. Du Clos did not mince words when it came to his assessment of the situation: "I am only too well convinced . . . that Mr. De La Mothe Cadillac is both the most selfish and the most cunning man in the world and that it would be in fact very difficult for a man upright enough not to bend to his wishes and at the same time clever enough not to let himself be dominated by him, to remain long in the colony."⁴⁷ On the other side of the divide were Cadillac's supporters, embittered by Bienville's blatant profiteering and favoritism. For the next few years, nearly every policy initiative faced opposition from one faction or the other.⁴⁸

Internal rivalries aside, the existence of English interlopers deep in the interior of the continent demanded a response from the colony's new government. The Louisianans' response had immediate consequences for Natchez Country. As early as 1713, Crozat recognized that the land around the Grand Village would make a superb location for a warehouse to divert the region's pelts into French rather than English hands.⁴⁹ The Ministry of Marine agreed with him and in December 1714 ordered Cadillac to send Bienville to build a fort on the bluffs overlooking the Mississippi River. It was to be named "Rosalie" after the wife of the minister of the navy, Pontchartrain.⁵⁰ The post would ward off interlopers and redirect the commerce of the region into Crozat's hands. To provide economic support and to prepare the foundation for this venture, he sent the La Loire brothers into Natchez Country as his commercial agents in 1714. Among their staff was André Penicault, who had spent time in Natchez Country during the previous decade. He was to serve as a clerk and translator. In his journal, Penicault described his experiences living and working among the People of the Sun.

Although the records are silent on Natchez attitudes toward the Gallic newcomers, several outlying Théoloël towns continued to trade with British merchants.⁵¹ Demographic and political shifts among the Natchez shed light on their interactions with the English. As noted earlier, the Emerald Mound was the indigenes' administrative center when La Salle arrived in 1682. By the early eighteenth century, European observers wrote about the Grand Village on St. Catherine's Creek as the home of the Great Sun, the leader of the Natchez people. The relocation of the Natchez ceremonial and political institutions deprived those still living around the site of the old "capital" of immediate contact with the chiefdom's decision makers. It also deprived them of ready access to prestige goods and foodstuffs, which were redistributed from a location farther south. Nonetheless, such outlying communities were not devoid of strong leadership, as the archaeologist Ned Jenkins noted. He argued that headmen who lost the competition for the chieftainship to a brother often moved to the periphery of their polity, where they would "found a colony or independent chiefdom that retained social, ceremonial, and economic ties while establishing an independent or partially independent local authority structure."[52] Lorenz went even further when he argued that these rivalries were indicative of a far more decentralized polity than some French observers realized.[53] By the middle of the 1710s, certain Natchez villages were beginning to assert their autonomy with the aid of outside forces.

The appearance of English traders helped weaken ties between the Grand Village and its satellite communities. John Worth's study of the Timucuans' complex chiefdoms in Spanish Florida provides some insight on conditions in Natchez Country. Worth argued that officials from St. Augustine used luxury items to reinforce the prestige of local caciques, or headmen, who supported the colony's policies. In this manner the Spanish steered the actions of local leaders to meet imperial ends. In turn, the caciques supplied the missions and garrisons of Florida with food, laborers, and warriors. These chiefs redistributed European-made clothing and tools to their indigenous supporters in conspicuous displays designed to bolster their influence. The proximity of St. Augustine's military strength and a steady supply of goods kept the old order of the Timucuans intact.[54] This arrangement operated among many communities that traced their roots to complex chiefdoms. Groups like the Creeks, who lived closer to Charles Town and farther from St. Augustine, exchanged deer hides and slaves for manufactured goods. Individual warriors or loosely organized bands gathered these commodities for trade. When they exchanged them for textiles, tools, and weapons, these items entered their villages through nonelites. They circumvented the old pattern in which these goods entered their towns as gifts bestowed by hereditary chiefs. Consequently, these increasingly decentralized nations came under the direction of leaders who won battles, captured slaves, or secured favorable trade terms. Consequently, the best fighters and hunters led the men of their villages—but only as long as their prowess and luck held out. In contrast, the political structures of the Timucuans' paramount chiefdoms, which were relatively isolated from Spain's European rivals, persisted well into the eighteenth century.[55]

During the most successful phase of Spain's policy in Florida, the Natchez weathered the protohistoric era in relative isolation. This changed when the English-sponsored slave raiders appeared in the Lower Mississippi Valley at the end of the seventeenth century. The Natchez social and political structures not only survived these incursions, but also profited from the disruption left in their wake. Refugee bands of Koroas, Tioux, and Grigras moved into Natchez Country and took up subordinate positions in the chiefdom. The sporadic visits of Francophone traders during the late 1600s and early 1700s, along with the opening of their first trading post in 1714, helped to strengthen an emerging political order centered on the Grand Village. Crozat's warehouse presented a new and steady source of prestige goods for the Grand Village Suns to channel to their supporters.[56] Conversely, the ruling family's command over food surpluses gave them significant leverage with the newcomers. If the Natchez followed social patterns evident in some earlier Mississippian societies, the Suns exchanged corn and game for manufactured goods used in conspicuous displays or dispensed as gifts to loyal followers. Thus, early economic exchanges with the colonists reinforced the power of the chiefdom's elites in a manner similar to the way Spaniards buttressed Timucuan caciques' influence.

At the same time, there were economic forces at work against both the Suns and their Gallic underwriters. Archaeological data suggest that some of the Natchez purchased European manufactures from English merchants residing among the Chickasaws. This alternate source of goods counteracted the centripetal influence of the Louisianan–Grand Village exchange system. Evidence for this shift can be found in the items retrieved in a series of excavations undertaken during the 1920s and 1930s. These digs identified the Fatherland Site in Natchez, Mississippi, as the Grand Village of the 1700s. Robert Neitzel conducted further archaeological investigations in the early 1960s and again in the early 1970s. His teams found some trade goods from the Old World in the Fatherland mounds. The graves at these locations contained items such as iron axe heads and calumet pipes that Lorenz called "prestige goods" that indicated the political authority of their occupants. These burials also held flintlock pistols, cooking utensils, tailored clothing, clasp knives, iron ornaments, farming tools, and silver jewelry. Later digs, however, uncovered significant caches of glass beads in the Rice Site, the "subordinate" village of the Jenzenaques.[57] The Rice Site also yielded gunflints, musket parts, silver and brass bells, items Lorenz characterized as "wealth goods," as well as iron axe heads and calumet pipes.[58] More important, the quantity of European manufactures was significantly greater in the gravesites closer to Chickasaw Country and, therefore, to British commerce. These goods were also more widely distributed among the burials in the outer districts than those at the Grand Village. The fact that these individuals acquired trade items in significant quantities indicates that the Grand Village was not their only distribution point. From this data, the anthropologist Karl Lorenz extrapolated that peripheral settlements enjoyed some degree of autonomy since they, too, possessed objects that symbolized power, particularly those associated with war and peace. These outliers were also in the process of loosening their economic bonds with the central town as they acquired new sources of "wealth items."[59]

Several of the towns closest to the Chickasaws, allies of Carolina, were also involved in anti-Louisianan activities, supposedly at the behest of English traders. Their undertakings became particularly troublesome by the second decade of the eighteenth century. The Treaty of Utrecht may have officially ended the War of Spanish Succession, but it did little to discourage the English from expanding their influence in the Lower Mississippi Valley. A ready supply of tools and weapons from Charles Town and other British colonies aided the outer Natchez settlements in their quest for autonomy vis-à-vis the Suns of the Grand Village.[60]

Suspicions about British penetration into the region were confirmed when Marc Antoine de la Loire, the eldest of the two brothers stationed near the Grand Village, captured Price Hughes, a Carolina agent. The Welshman had traveled among the Natchez and Yazoos during the winter of 1715, buying deerskins and promising English support. Later that spring, Bienville interrogated Hughes at Fort St. Louis in Mobile. After a stern warning, Bienville sent the interloper back to Carolina.[61] The outbreak of the Yamasee War prevented English colonials from following through on Hughes's plan to settle five hundred families along the Mississippi.[62] Hughes never made it back to the Atlantic seaboard; a Tohome warrior killed him somewhere along the path to Charles Town. Hughes's presence deep in territory claimed by France underscored the urgency of securing the Mississippi River Valley. Pontchartrain had ordered construction of a fort in Natchez Country in 1714, but only after receiving clear evidence of rivals at work there did Cadillac finally make concrete plans to build the post.

The reason for the delay may have been the governor's desire to investigate rumors of silver deposits near the mouth of the Missouri River. His attention to reports of mineral wealth reflected Crozat's goal of recouping his investment in Louisiana from the natural resources there, which left him little time to supervise the construction of forts. Late in the winter of 1715, the governor left Mobile to check on the veracity of the rumors. In his haste to reach the Missouri River, Cadillac managed to anger the Natchez whose territory he passed through by ignoring indigenous diplomatic protocol. In the words of Bienville:

> Mr. de la Motte [sieur de Cadillac] had passed their place when he traveled up and downriver on the voyage he had made to Illinois. He had refused their offer to chant the calumet of peace with them, which is a very great insult among all the savage nations, especially from the grand chief of the French. Mr. de la Motte in this occasion had wanted to save a bit of merchandise [for gifts] that would have cost us very little.[63]

The tensions created by his oversight were not immediately apparent when Cadillac returned in the autumn of 1715. Soon after the governor's junket, however, leaders from Natchez communities to the east of the Grand Village attacked several voyageurs traveling on the Mississippi. Hughes's efforts in the region had given some Théoloëls reason to believe that they might procure more goods from other English merchants. The possibility of a new source of manufactures made a close relationship with Louisiana expendable. Moreover, these items would not have been routed through the Grand Village, which would have allowed even greater autonomy to outlying Natchez settlements. Cadillac's faux pas only reinforced such reasoning. The governor's diplomatic failure eroded the newcomers' position in the Natchez order of things. With Cadillac's snub, the behavior of the Louisianans was beginning to depart from the apparent subordination to the Great Sun that they had adhered to during the previous three decades of contact. It would be up to his second-in-command to remedy the situation.

The Natchez Hostage Crisis of 1716

The next few months represented a milestone in Natchez-French relations. The preliminary phase of the Natchez Hostage Crisis of 1716, commonly called the First Natchez War, began in January of that year. Its initial phase coincided with Cadillac's tardy compliance with Crozat's order to construct Fort Rosalie. The governor directed Bienville, recently commissioned as a *lieutenant du roi*, to take a detachment north to build the installation.[64] To accomplish his mission, Cadillac gave Bienville command of a company of forty soldiers, grossly insufficient to accomplish the task at hand. Desertions and illness at Mobile quickly reduced their numbers to thirty-four, and delays in procuring supplies and boats held up the expedition's departure for a month.[65]

Before leaving for the Mississippi Valley, Cadillac received a message that changed the nature of Bienville's assignment from difficult to suicidal.[66] The communiqué reported that late in 1715 some Théoloëls had robbed and murdered four traders on their way to Illinois. The voyageurs had stopped at the Grand Village to hire several Native American rowers. Four Natchez men had accompanied the traders as far as Petite Gulf. During the night, the rowers killed their employers while they slept and returned home with the dead men's merchandise.[67]

André Penicault, the clerk at the La Loires' warehouse in Natchez Country, had an unobstructed perch from which to observe the beginning of the crisis. His journal recounts his discovery of the murders soon after their commission. Penicault noticed goods belonging to the departed traders among the villagers and warned his employer that he suspected foul play. After hearing the news, the younger La Loire and his staff pretended not to notice the stolen wares among the villagers. A little later the other La Loire brother arrived with a convoy of fourteen men and three pirogues loaded with merchandise bound for Illinois. The traders realized that they were in danger and made plans to leave. To mask their intentions, the senior Frenchmen told the Natchez that Cadillac had ordered all of the warehouse's staff to go north to Kaskaskia. For the next two weeks, the older La Loire and his employees procured supplies and loaded their pirogues. They also hired eight Natchez men to help row the craft against the current. Rumors that were circulating among the villagers that *coureurs* had been murdered confirmed the merchants' suspicions.

The Great Sun aided the colonists in their efforts to secure rowers to reach Illinois. When the outsiders were ready to depart, the headman came to the waterfront to see them off. He charged his native rowers not to stop even if they spotted signals from the riverbank because he feared the convoy might come under attack. The Natchez leader made certain that the colonists overheard his words. The Great Sun probably knew more than he said in front of the foreigners. The facts that he permitted Natchez oarsmen to man the merchants' boats and issued his warning demonstrated the value he placed upon his people's relationship with the Louisianans, particularly with those who supplied his clique with trade goods. Perhaps the Sun wanted his caveat to serve as evidence of the good intentions of the pro-Louisianan faction and to demonstrate that its members still controlled Théoloël policy toward outsiders.[68] Nonetheless, the murders of the voyageurs by warriors from the outer villages and the Sun's open support of the La Loires mark the point at which his struggle with his political rivals intruded upon the conduct of Natchez-Louisianan relations.

The anti-Louisianan plot to which the Great Sun had alluded soon began to unravel. The first night after the convoy left the village, one of the rowers confessed to Penicault that a Natchez leader named the Bearded One (Fr: *le Barbu*) lay in ambush with 150 warriors at Petite Gulf. The other seven rowers confirmed the story when the Frenchmen promised to reward them if they told the truth. The party returned to the warehouse near the Grand Village under the cover of darkness. Penicault slipped into the town and retrieved the younger La Loire, who had been persuaded by his brother to remain at the Grand Village to guard Crozat's goods.[69]

The La Loires and their employees then paddled south to the village of the Tunicas, where they learned more about their former hosts' plans. During their stay, a three-man Natchez delegation arrived to secure the cooperation of their southern neighbors in a war against the French colony. The merchants stayed out of sight while the two groups parleyed. The Théoloël diplomats assured their Tunican listeners that the British would replace the Louisianans as trading partners. They wanted their hosts to help them prevent France from dominating the region. The La Loires' abandonment of their post lent weight to the proposal of the Natchez envoy. The leader of the Tunicas, a staunch ally of the French, was shocked by the speech and wanted to kill the ambassadors. Father Davion, the Seminarian missionary to the Tunicas, restrained the headmen from executing his indigenous guests. The priest then wrote a dispatch to Cadillac informing him of the events he had witnessed and sent it along with the La Loires' convoy. The merchants reached Mobile sometime in early 1716 bearing tales of their experiences.[70]

Despite the news of hostilities to the north, Cadillac refused to amend his orders to Bienville. Instead, he augmented the lieutenant's command with a mere fourteen boatmen to help him navigate the Mississippi. Acting on his own initiative, Bienville later added to these numbers by hiring some Canadian voyageurs en route. Against him the Natchez could muster "800 men capable of bearing arms."[71]

The small force left Mobile on March 15, 1716, in eight pirogues. In a move that exemplified Shannon Dawdy's notion of "rogue colonialism,"

Bienville commandeered a convoy of ten pirogues on Mississippi headed for the Illinois posts. The Canadian sent them ahead of his main force to await his arrival at the Tunicas. To alert northbound travelers of the danger, Father Davion had posted a sign on a tree near the banks of the Mississippi "for the first Frenchman who passes by." On their way upriver, Bienville's men retrieved the priest's notice. It warned that the Natchez and Tunicas had concluded an anti-French alliance, and told of an additional murder by the Natchez of a southbound voyageur named Richard.[72]

On April 23, 1716, Bienville arrived at a spot near the Tunica village at Grand Gulf. He kept most of his men out of sight to conceal their small numbers. The Canadian entered their town, smoked the calumet with the headmen, and notified them that he had encamped nearby due to sickness and fatigue among his men. Father Davion told Bienville that the Natchez were ignorant of the fact that the Louisianans knew of the fate of the five voyaguers and that they believed that they still enjoyed a good relationship with the colonists. The lieutenant also found that the Tunicas had not gone over to the other side. Bienville asked his hosts to send a delegation to inform the Natchez that Cadillac had ordered him to establish a warehouse to purchase their peltries and supply them with all the merchandise that they might need. In the meantime, he wanted the People of the Sun to know that he was at a camp near the Tunicas.[73]

Later that day, Bienville ordered his men to construct a fortified camp on an island in the Mississippi approximately a mile from the main village of the Tunicas. They built three huts, one to house his troops, another to secure their ammunition, and the last to serve as a guardhouse. The lieutenant also ordered as many tents as possible pitched around the camp to create the illusion that his force, which had grown to approximately one hundred men, looked like an army of six hundred.[74]

Four days later, three Natchez ambassadors arrived to smoke the calumet. Bienville told them that they could smoke with some of his soldiers, but that he would only smoke with them when the Suns arrived. Bienville thus claimed a status analogous to that of a Natchez Sun. He also equated his soldiers with their warriors and thereby exploited the notion that the two groups shared parallel institutions. This news initially disturbed the three visitors, but Bienville invited them to dinner and laughed with them as they ate and conversed. He inquired about individual chiefs and hinted that if the Natchez did not want France's business, he would set up a warehouse among the Tunicas. The next morning, the Native American envoys, accompanied by a young Frenchman who spoke their language, returned to the Grand Village carrying the lieutenant's invitation.[75]

On May 4, 1716, while the French waited on their island, six voyageurs arrived from upriver. They had come from the Natchez bearing more news of divisions among the polity's leadership. Unaware that the Théoloëls had assaulted other Frenchmen, the six Canadians made landfall at the Grand Village in late April 1716. Twenty warriors led by the Bearded One robbed and threatened to kill the outsiders. The men reported that the "great chiefs of the people" rescued them. After scolding the perpetrators, the Natchez chiefs restored to the Canadians as much of their stolen property as they could recover. The Suns then sent the voyageurs on their way, informing them that Bienville was with the Tunicas and that the Natchez would soon arrive with their most important men.[76]

Four days after the arrival of the Canadians, sentries sighted pirogues bearing the young French interpreter and many high-status Théoloëls. Among them were the Great Sun, his brothers, the Tattooed Serpent, and the Little Sun. Once they landed, the French commander, following Natchez protocol, invited them to his quarters. The indigenes asked Bienville to smoke the calumet with them and were startled when he refused. The high priest who accompanied the Indian delegation invoked his solar deity's intevention to soften Bienville's attitude. The Canadian brushed the pipe aside when the Indians offered it to him a second time. He told them that he was tired of their rituals and demanded satisfaction for the five murders committed by their people. The revelation that the outsiders knew of the killings stunned his guests. At that point, Bienville signaled to his men to seize the Natchez leaders and take them to the prison hut. Once inside the jail, the brothers refused to eat and sang their death songs.[77]

Over the next two weeks, Bienville and the three hostage Suns conducted several rounds of negotiations. The initial talk took place on the first night of the Natchez Suns' captivity. Bienville met with the three headmen in his quarters. He explained that he meant them no harm; he simply wanted the heads of the murderers.[78] In particular, he demanded that of the Oyelape, the Sun of the Apple Village.[79] Bienville then listed numerous examples of his ability to rally the indigenous peoples of the region to his causes. In each of these instances, native communities that had injured or killed Louisianans had suffered severe consequences. He recounted the vengeance he took upon the Chitimachas for the murder of Father St. Cosme, a man familiar to the prisoners. Bienville recounted several other punitive expeditions against offending communities. To demonstrate that he expected the same order of justice for his own people, the Canadian reminded them that he had executed a colonist who had murdered two Pascagoulas. Bienville promised the same fate would befall the Natchez if they did not cooperate. This initial interview, however, produced no resolution since the Suns refused to speak to their captor.[80]

The next morning, the Great Sun, the Tattooed Serpent, and the Little Sun sought an audience with the lieutenant. They informed Bienville that nobody in their villages had sufficient authority to arrest those responsible for the deaths of the voyageurs. They suggested that he release the Great Sun to return home to capture the culprits. Bienville rejected their terms, but he set free the Little Sun to apprehend the killers. Perhaps he thought that the junior leader might succeed where the Great Sun could not since the latter was too closely identified with the Grand Village faction.

Five days later the Little Sun returned with three heads, two of which belonged to the actual murderers, the third to a man who happened to be in the wrong place at the wrong time. Penicault identified the third victim as the "most simple-minded person who lived in their village."[81] Bienville chided the Natchez for shedding innocent blood to perpetrate a fraud. The young leader replied that his brother, the Great Sun, would rather see the entire village perish than give up his brother, the Sun of the White Earth Village. The Little Sun's refusal lends credence to Ned Jenkins's theory that kinship ties held the outer towns in a loose orbit to the central settlement of a complex chiefdom. It also lends substance to Arnaud Balvay's contention that the fault lines in Natchez foreign policy toward the French and British colonial projects ran along clan lines.[82] The headman also stated that the pro-British faction of his people had obstructed the capture of the offender. To ameliorate the impact of his failure to execute Bienville's instructions, the Little Sun brought along two voyageurs and two Illinis whom he had rescued from the execution rack a few days earlier. Despite having saved those lives, the Little Sun found himself once again clamped in irons by order of the Canadian. On the following day, May 15, Bienville sent two more "chiefs" along with the high priest of the temple to bring back the head of Oyelape.[83]

The Little Sun's attempt to substitute the death of an innocent man for that of a guilty one bespoke a disjuncture that lurked close to the surface of the Natchez-Louisianan relations. The indigenous leaders may have hoped to trick the lieutenant with the bogus head, but they also may have hoped that the death of one of their people, although blameless, would compensate for the death of one of Bienville's countrymen. If that were the case, perhaps perceptions of similarity had misled the Sun to assume that the practice of reciprocal killing that functioned among the Native Americans of the region also operated among the Europeans. Bienville quickly, but only temporarily, disabused him of that notion.

Over the subsequent weeks, several factors began to work against the Canadian officer's plans. During the next ten days, spring floods pushed the Mississippi over its banks, inundating the encampment with six inches of water. Dysentery broke out on the island, afflicting both the Natchez and the colonial forces. The Tattooed Serpent also came down with a high fever. In the meantime, Bienville moved to a wooden hut to keep dry. The lieutenant also released the Tattooed Serpent and invited the headman to share his personal quarters.[84]

Bienville and the Tattooed Serpent apparently gained each other's trust during this time. The latter revealed that the colonial army already held four of the offenders in their guardhouse. These included the Bearded One and Alahofléchia, both high-status men, and two warriors. The Natchez headman also confessed that the British agents had been operating among his people during the preceding year (a fact that Bienville knew). The war leader said that the Natchez had ejected the Anglo merchants when the foreigners suggested that they kill the Louisianans living in the village and make war on the French colony. The other captive Suns corroborated the Tattooed Serpent's story. They claimed that they never attended any of the councils that ordered the murders of the *coureurs de bois* and that they heard of the crimes only after their commission. According to them, Jenzenaque, White Earth, and Grigras villagers, all outliers from the main town, were behind the unrest.[85] The Suns of these settlements had consorted with British operatives and had ordered the deaths of the Canadian travelers. Bienville expressed his satisfaction with the three Suns' revelations.

On May 25, 1716, two of the Natchez leaders dispatched by Bienville a few days earlier returned without the head of Oleyape. They reported that he had fled and could not be found. The two chiefs, however, brought with them with a number of slaves and possessions that had belonged to the slain Frenchmen. The return of this valuable chattel appears to have further assuaged Bienville.[86]

Although the main culprit had not yet been punished, the Louisianan commander began to revise his strategy. With disease wasting his men, it became apparent to Bienville that to linger on the island waiting for the Natchez to capture Oleyape might cost him more than it was worth: the inadvertent death of one of his hostages threatened to upset the emerging rapport. Bienville brought most of the prisoners to his lodgings to join the three Suns. Only the four accused of murder remained in irons. When all of his Natchez captives were assembled, the lieutenant dictated his peace terms. Those who were guilty of murder would die for their crimes. If Oyelape turned up, his head was to be sent to Bienville to show that he had paid for his misdeeds. The Natchez were to restore all of the merchandise that they had stolen from Crozat's warehouse or from French subjects. Finally, the People of the Sun were to provide the materials and labor to build Fort Rosalie. The hostages agreed to these terms and pledged to live in peace with Louisiana. They also thanked the lieutenant for removing members of a faction that had undermined their power among the borderland Natchez towns. In a few short weeks, the Suns watched as Bienville eliminated a set of dangerous rivals for them. They also secured a steady supply of prestige goods and recruited a new immigrant group to their polity.[87]

After the parley, the Tattooed Serpent quietly asked for one modification of the terms. At this point, the special status of the Natchez Suns came into play. The Tattooed Serpent feared that a public execution of the high-ranking prisoners would provoke negative reactions among his countrymen, so he requested that the four be sent to Mobile for the governor to determine their punishment. Bienville agreed.[88]

Bienville's change of tactics soon bore fruit. On June 3, 1716, the lieutenant sent *aide-major* Pailloux and two soldiers to escort three of the Suns and the other hostages back home; only the Tattooed Serpent and the Little Sun remained behind at the camp. Pailloux arrived at the Grand Village and wrote back that the Natchez had accepted all of the peace terms. An enlisted man, accompanied by nine elders of the nation, carried the *aide-major*'s letter to Bienville. The note described a small hillock near the village that would make a good site for the new post. Upon reading that the Natchez response had been favorable, the lieutenant finally smoked the calumet, this time proffered by the nine Natchez diplomats. The Little Sun then returned home accompanied by a detachment of soldiers assigned to bring tools and materials to construct Fort Rosalie. The Tattooed Serpent stayed on the island along with the four murderers.[89]

Bienville discharged his Canadian irregulars in the second week of June. He ordered them to take the condemned Natchez some distance away from the camp and "smash their heads." As the Bearded One marched toward the boat that was to take him to his end, he chanted his death song. Just before his execution, he switched to a war song, during which he listed the five Frenchmen whose lives he had taken. The Bearded One died saying that he only wished he could have killed more. Upon hearing this news, the Tattooed Serpent responded, "he is my brother, but I no longer regret [his death]. You are freeing us of a wicked man."[90]

Reading the Natchez Hostage Crisis of 1716

The Natchez Hostage Crises hardly merits the name "the First Natchez War," which was coined by John Swanton.[91] It was a short-lived affair that cost both sides only a handful of lives. The speedy resolution of the conflict helped to mitigate its negative impact on relations between the Théoloëls and Louisiana. Its violence was muted; no European soldiers met Natchez warriors in open combat, and only Canadian traders and their murderers died. Moreover, these men perished beyond the sight of their countrymen, while the voyageurs met their fate in Natchez Country without European witnesses. The Natchez had already killed several low-status murderers themselves and brought their heads downriver. Bienville took care that no Théoloëls saw their leaders die at the hands of French subjects. One of the Suns expressed little regret for the passing of men who had challenged their authority in their homeland. Thus, one of the most traumatic aspects of combat, the witnessing of an enemy killing one's fellows, was absent from this struggle. More important, the fact that the social and political structures of the two peoples had facilitated negotiations further reinforced perceptions of similarity. The leaders of both sides supported the police action against wrongdoers who had violated the terms upon which the two peoples interacted.

The words spoken by the Tattooed Serpent—"You are releasing us from a wicked man"—provide clues to the manner in which he perceived his captor.[92] The Natchez leader's choice of pronouns hinted that he perceived Bienville's rank as not very different from his own. The Tattooed Serpent's identification with Bienville was indicated by his use of the familiar *tu*. The texts do not reveal whether he uttered that pronoun in French or in his own tongue. It is clear, however, that the author of the passage, in this case most likely Bienville's colleague Captain Chavagne de Richebourg, wished to convey that a close relationship had developed between the Tattooed Serpent and the king's lieutenant.[93] The Tattooed

Serpent's willingness to treat Bienville as an equal was in line with other parallels that the Natchez saw in the Louisianans.

One of the more subtle parallels was that of inherited status. Although European societies traced succession through the father's side, the career of Bienville implied a system of authority that was derived from matrilineal descent. The Great Sun, the Tattooed Serpent, the Little Sun, and the Sun of the White Earth Village were all "brothers." The Tattooed Serpent also told Bienville that the Bearded One was his mother's son. Although it is uncertain that all of these leaders shared the same father (they might have been half brothers), both Richebourg and Penicault recorded the Indians as using the word *frères* to describe their relationship. They had inherited their ranks through their mother according to the Natchez kinship system.[94]

Detecting parallel among the Europeans is difficult if one relies upon the rules of patrilineal succession. Viewed through the lens of matrilineal succession, however, a Natchez observer might have concluded that Bienville inherited his rank through his mother, like the Great Sun. Pierre Le Moyne, sieur d'Iberville, had established France's colonial presence in the region, and served as the first governor of Louisiana. Although Jean-Baptiste Le Moyne, sieur de Bienville, possessed obvious leadership abilities, his older brother had launched his career. Iberville commissioned his brother as a midshipman sometime during the 1690s. For the Natchez, the practice of delegating authority to the Great Sun's younger brother dated back at least to the 1680s, when one such man greeted La Salle and escorted him to the polity's administrative center. Upon the Iberville's death, the Natchez system of descent would not have named Bienville his people's leader. Instead, his relationship would have already made him their senior war leader, much like the Tattooed Serpent. Although the Great Sun theoretically commanded his people's military, the actual fighting and peacemaking were the provinces of second-tier elites. In French practice, a *lieutenant du roi* directed a city or region's military affairs and was the governor's second-in-command.[95] Thus, both Bienville and the Tattooed Serpent played prominent military and diplomatic roles among their people, but they did not take over the positions of their brothers. Bienville's decision to share his lodgings with the Tattooed Serpent and later with the other Suns reinforced the illusion of similarity between the upper ranks of the colonists and those of the Natchez. As if to further that illusion, two other Le Moyne siblings, Antoine Le Moyne de Châteaguay and Joseph Le Moyne de Sérigny et Loire, served as officers and de facto governors of the colony at different times over the course of the first three decades of the eighteenth century. Several other important Louisianans were also related to the Le Moynes through marriage to female members of the family.

In contrast, the fact that Cadillac was not related by blood to the founder of the colony, Iberville (or more accurately, to Iberville's mother, Catherine Thierry), may have weakened his prestige. According to Natchez rules of descent, he would have been outside the line of succession to rule Louisiana. Regardless of what they might have thought of Cadillac's biological credentials, the Natchez realized that Bienville was not the ultimate political power in the colony despite his claims to have been the "chief of the French." The Tattooed Serpent's request that the Canadian remand the indigenous murder suspects to the governor in Mobile, a man that the Natchez leader called *le chef du françois*; demonstrated that he understood that Cadillac held final authority. Nonetheless, the region's native peoples also knew that Iberville's brother, Jean Baptiste Le Moyne, sieur de Bienville, still lived and commanded great respect as a war leader and diplomat.

The Suns and Bienville shared another trait: they both held slaves. Canadian and European witnesses frequently mentioned that the Suns commanded the labor of Natchez commoners without remuneration.[96] Their status, and indeed the status of those that French-language sources characterize as "*esclaves*," was not analogous to that of the human chattel of the antebellum South, however. The historian Christine Snyder argued that the Native American forms of bondage differed greatly from the European colonists' increasingly binary categories of voluntary and involuntary labor: "Indians, like other people in early America, found themselves locked in a web of hierarchy and interdependence and saw no stark divide between slavery and freedom."[97] Snyder observed that slavery was not "a static institution" among Native Americans; rather, indigenous peoples over time adapted it to meet their changing needs.[98] Generally, the term in French-language documents referred to captives taken in war. Several fates awaited many of these prisoners: their captors either adopted them into their community, gave them to outsiders as diplomatic gifts, exchanged them in trade, or ritually executed them in public spectacles.[99] The voyageurs that turned up at Bienville's Mississippi River camp in late May 1716 reported that during their brief captivity, the anti-Louisianan Natchez headmen told them "that they were now their *esclave*s."

From their first contacts with Francophones in the late seventeenth century, the Natchez could see that the newcomers treated humans as property. La Salle's party brought several captive laborers with them when they visited Natchez Country. One of them escaped to his home among the Koroas, providing direct testimony regarding Europeans' treatment of slaves. Eighteenth-century observers also wrote that slaves of the Natchez Suns worked in the fields as agricultural laborers in the same way the slaves from Africa toiled on the farms of Louisiana.[100] While serving as commandant of Fort Louis in Mobile, Bienville held seventeen Indian slaves as well as four Africans.[101] Bienville's captives included important individuals such as Framboise, the "chief" of the Chitimachas.[102]

The manpower shortage that afflicted Bienville's small army during the Natchez Hostage Crisis required him to mobilize every available worker or soldier. Although the records of his expedition of 1716 do not mention whether slaves made up part of the contingent, some probably accompanied the expedition as camp servants, laborers, and rowers. During their captivity, it is highly likely that the Suns watched unfree men wait upon Bienville and his fellow officers in much the same way that low-status Théoloëls attended them in the Grand Village. The fact that Bienville relaxed some of his demands when the two Natchez war leaders arrived with slaves belonging to the dead voyageurs suggests that he placed a high value on human property.[103]

On the little island in the Mississippi, the leaders of the two warring parties may have recognized a commonality in terms of status and slaveholding, but their respective societies enjoyed less cohesion. Factionalism plagued both Louisianan and Natchez politics. Leaders from the chiefdom's marchlands challenged the authority of the Grand Village Suns, while Louisiana was rent by similar tensions. In other words, both sets of leaders were familiar with problems among their own peoples that were generated by internal rivalries.

The split between the Bienville and Cadillac parties filled pages of correspondence to and from the Ministry of Marine. Both men clamored for the other's ouster, and both had solid reasons behind their entreaties. Cadillac's diplomatic and administrative incompetence brought war to the colony according to many witnesses. Bienville's insolence, together with his influence among Native Americans and many colonists, exasperated the governor. Moreover, Bienville's commercial dealings had already aroused the suspicions of Pontchartrain and the *intendants* in charge of Louisiana's account books. After a lengthy investigation during the first decade of the 1700s, the king's commissioner failed to prove anything, but it appeared that Bienville had tampered with the witnesses.[104]

Bienville's long tenure as the de facto leader of Louisiana made for a difficult situation when Cadillac arrived in 1713. The new governor's dyspeptic remarks equating this "bad country" with "bad people" did not help his reputation among his charges.[105] Relations between Cadillac and his second-in-command deteriorated quickly. In the words of Captain Bénard de La Harpe: "The arrival of M. de Lamothe Cadillac could have produced a good effect on the settlement of Louisiana had he wished to act in harmony with M. de Bienville; but, jealous of the affection which the troops and Indian tribes had for M. de Bienville, M. de Lamothe tried to hinder him on every occasion. Altercations arose between them which give rise to two factions in the colony that have persisted until this day."[106] Colonists rallied around these two strong personalities. Arguments over the colony's commercial assets, Indian policy, and ceremonial prerogatives fueled the schism. By the time news of the murders of the five voyageurs reached Mobile in the winter of 1716, the rift between the two men had widened significantly.

With the frequent travel along the Mississippi by native and European soldiers, merchants, and river men, word of the disputes among the provincial leaders probably reached the Grand Village, particularly after the La Loire brothers set up their post. Le Page du Pratz noted that "all of the voyageurs who passed and stopped at this place came to see the Natchez Naturals, the road, a league in length, was so beautiful and the countryside so good, the Naturals were so helpful and so familiar, the women there were so amiable that they never grew tired of praising the Canton and the Naturals who lived there."[107] Some of the Canadians roaming along the river also would have known about Cadillac's checkered career in the Great Lakes region. It is not unreasonable to suppose that these wayfarers shared information with the staff of Crozat's warehouse. These visitors from the North who frequented Natchez Country may have also gossiped about Cadillac and Bienville.

The Suns who lived in the Grand Village also endured challenges to their rule during this time period. Much like their counterparts in France and Louisiana, the headmen of the town sought to maintain hegemony over the margins of their polity. Nonetheless, Anglo traders had made inroads with the Natchez who lived in the outlying villages. Those settlements farthest from the Mississippi, often under the direction of the brothers of the Great Sun, treated with Carolinians and Virginians. Some of these refractory outliers sat astride the route that led from the Grand Village northeast through Chickasaw Country.

Archaeological excavations performed at one of these villages uncovered graves filled with items of European origin. These objects were similar in quality to those found during excavations of the Grand Village temple mound, but the graves in the outlying villages contained larger quantities of overseas manufactures than did the main town's burial sites. The bulk of these finds were what Lorenz called "wealth goods," which did not confer status on their owners.[108] From the presence and quantities of overseas manufactures, it appears that the Jenzenaque and White Earth towns profited handsomely from their relationships with traders connected to the English colonies. Consequently, if word of the long-running dispute between Bienville and the arriviste governor reached the Grand Village, it may have resonated with the Indian leadership's experiences with its own domestic rivals.

The manner in which the dispute between the Europeans and the Native Americans unfolded also echoed indigenous practices. Bienville's capture of the Great Sun followed a pattern familiar to the Natchez. Le Page du Pratz wrote that during one of their annual festivals the Théoloëls reenacted a legend in the life of Thé, the first Great Sun. They staged an episode in which their mythic ancestor was seized by an enemy and then rescued by the Natchez. This sham battle took place in early spring, during the Deer Moon in the month of March. Much like the conflict with the French, the "battle" ended with the leader's return to the Grand Village.[109]

The fête began with the men of the village dividing into two groups. The one that represented the "enemy" wore red plumes, and those who played the Sun's warriors wore white feathers. The intruders, led by the Natchez war chief, approached the cabin of the leader, who emerged acting as if he had just awoken. The red faction seized the Great Sun and attempted to carry him off. The chief defended himself with a "war club of the old design" in mock combat while his men rallied to drive off the insurgents.[110] The triumphant Natchez then brought their leader back to his home on the temple mound while the entire population shouted with joy. Restored to his cabin, the leader "recuperated" for a short time and then reappeared to conclude this phase of the display with a series of invocations. During the finale, he stood motionless facing the temple with his arms extended in the shape of a cross. The Sun then donned his finest robes and officiated at the feast that terminated the proceedings.

The precise religious function of the Deer Moon Festival remains a mystery. It may have celebrated the arrival of spring; Le Page du Pratz offered no explanation in his account. It is apparent that the ritual reminded the people of their common origin and clearly reinforced the authority of the Natchez primary chief. If this was the case, the "teams" of warriors on either side represented competitors who battled for control of the polity, a contest that always ended with the victory of the Great Sun. The contest also might have served to ameliorate social and political tensions that beset complex chiefdoms by reminding the Théoloëls that struggles for power were part of the political routine of their polity. The war chief, though unnamed, would have been the Tattooed Serpent, the Great Sun's brother. During the Natchez Hostage Crisis of 1716, the Suns of the Grand Village found themselves at odds with not only Louisiana, but several of the siblings of their leader. Finally, the Deer Moon Festival's theatrics included factions dressed in red and white. Again, Le Page du Pratz's memoir is silent on the meaning of these colors in Natchez cosmology, but it is apparent that the "red" group, captained by the war chief, took the most aggressive role in the ritual's mock violence.

On a May morning in 1716, French warriors seized the Great Sun in a manner similar to what the participants in the sham battle had done during the Deer Moon Festival. Some aspects of events surrounding the Sun's imprisonment by Bienville mimicked the spring ritual. Nonetheless, the leader's capture by the Europeans was not an act; nor were the results foreordained. Although the Natchez contemplated an outright assault on the island prison, they relented and yielded to the majority of Bienville's demands. The records do not reveal the People of the Sun's reasons for rejecting a military solution despite their overwhelming numbers—perhaps they feared for the lives of the hostages. They also might have recognized the parallels between their festival and the state of affairs downriver and hoped that the Sun would be released unharmed. If the Natchez acted on the belief that their ruler would be set free if they waited, they were not disappointed. In this scenario, Bienville and his men unwittingly played the role of the "red" faction, and they played it according to the script even as far as their hesitation to harm the Suns or their retainers.[111]

The actual violence that occurred during the war—the execution of the Bearded One and his coconspirators—solved problems for those on both sides of the conflict. The advantages for the colonists were obvious: it avenged the death of their countrymen and demonstrated their military power in the region. The Natchez of the Grand Village profited when Bienville took action against the leaders of the outer settlements. The Canadian eliminated several of their domestic rivals for them. Moreover, he did so without any of the captive Suns having to shed the blood of their kinsmen. The heads that the Little Sun brought to the Louisianan encampment were those of two culprits and an innocent victim, none of whom were described as high-status men. The latter was a substitute for that of Oyelape, whom the junior headmen refused to harm. Nonetheless, all of the refractory Suns died except for the leader of the White Earth Village; they met their ends at the hands of Canadian *coureurs de bois* and at the behest of the king's lieutenant.

Another aspect of the conflict that reinforced the illusion of similarity also concerned the fate of the murderers of the voyageurs. Their deaths suggested that the Bienville had accepted indigenous justice in the form of retaliatory killings. In June 1716, the Canadian lieutenant appeared to be satisfied with a rough parity between the number of Europeans murdered and the indigenous men executed. This suggests that that was an opening of what Richard White characterized as "middle ground," a space of cross-cultural exchange that accommodated Native American notions of blood debt.[112] Six of those who died had played a direct role in the murders—the Bearded One, Alahofléchia, the two warriors on the island, and the two culprits brought in by the Little Sun—although one of the dead had not been involved in the killings. Although Bienville publicly refused to accept the head of an innocent man as a substitute for Oyelape, his ardor slackened when the number of dead Natchez surpassed that of the five murdered Canadians.

This apparent adoption of "native justice" was reinforced by the termination of hostilities. The Tattooed Serpent and Bienville negotiated the terms of peace after the French had lost five men. Up until the evacuation of the Mississippi island fort, the Natchez had lost only three warriors—the individuals brought in by the Little Sun. The other four culprits, including the Bearded One, would die soon enough. This would happen, however, beyond public view. When the Natchez leaders returned to the Grand Village, they too could claim a double victory: they had gained the release of the Great Sun and his cohort and had inflicted more casualties than they had suffered. This outcome depended on the Canadians actually escorting the four suspects to Mobile to face the governor. The Tattooed Serpent was the only Théoloël who knew about his kinsmen's fates, and the records are silent about whether he told any of his countrymen. If he kept the murderers' executions secret, his fellow villagers could celebrate their triumph over the French ignorant of the real score.

Regardless of the ways that each side perceived the conflict, the Canadian officer inserted a provision into the peace agreement of June 1716 that the Natchez bring back Oyelape, dead or alive. The Natchez heartily agreed to the conditions and promised to look for the fugitive Sun. He may have escaped permanently since no records after that date mention his capture. His intentions notwithstanding, Bienville's actions were consistent with indigenous practices of reciprocal killings.

What was Bienville's motive to release his hostages before the Théoloëls handed over all of the leaders responsible for the murders? Did the lieutenant expect the Natchez to honor the Oyelape clause of the treaty? Captain Richebourg wrote that the spring floods triggered an epidemic that deprived Bienville of all but a handful of soldiers. Perhaps the Canadian no longer commanded the resources to force the issue. With dysentery depleting his small army and with his base of operations underwater, he decided it was time to "bring an end to this little war."[113] The Natchez commitment to turn over the last suspect allowed him to save face. When the Louisianans returned to Mobile, they could congratulate themselves for punishing the Natchez. They, too, could boast that had inflicted more casualties than they had sustained: seven Natchez compared to five Canadians. To force the indigenes to track down Oyelape would require them to kill a Sun, a serious problem for the Natchez, who held their leaders in special reverence. The death of one of these leaders was a major loss for the Natchez that required them to sacrifice his spouses and retainers as well as several infants.[114] Consequently, the execution of this last Sun might have upset the illusion of parity.

Whatever his thoughts may have been regarding the escape of one of the culprits, Bienville appeared content with the outcome of the war. He traveled to Natchez Country after leaving his island fortress and passed the summer of 1716 there. During his stay, his hosts complied with one of the treaty's provisions by providing wooden pilings and bark planks for Fort Rosalie's construction. The building of the post also played into the rubric of similarities: the newcomers required the assistance of the hosts. This resembled the pattern established by La Salle in 1682 and Limoges in 1701 that the newcomers needed help from the People of the Sun. More important, the outsiders were building something in Natchez Country that resembled a village. Perhaps the men who garrisoned the post would soon marry local women and thereby enter into the Natchez order of things as the newest influx of "stinkards."

The Natchez Hostage Crisis brought together two sets of warriors and diplomats. Their interaction, although often hostile, reinforced the illusion of similarity between the colonists and the Natchez. It also provided continuity with established practices of intercultural relations. At first glance, the collection of Canadian backwoodsmen, French conscripts, and impressed oarsmen amounted to little more than a strong war party by the standards of southeastern nations. Indeed, they organized themselves in ways analogous to a Théoloël war party; the Louisianan army's hierarchy included a "war chief," officers, soldiers, and slaves. The

Natchez ranked themselves as "chiefs," "true warriors," "ordinary warriors," and "apprentice warriors." They also divided the French into "true warriors" and "youngsters."[115] Thus, in some ways, the European expedition resembled previous bands that had entered the Great Sun's realm, especially after they stayed to build a permanent settlement.

Bienville's success earned him accolades from everybody except the colony's governor. In his report to the Minister of Marine, Cadillac wrote, simply, "The sieur de Bienville has made peace with the Natchez and has been established among them."[116] The governor's popularity had declined further when he attempted to court-martial Captain Richebourg, one of Bienville's officers, for insubordination. In response to these charges, Richebourg submitted a detailed report of the conflict that only served to glorify his commander.[117] Bienville forwarded his account of the skirmish to the governor in June 1716. It began with a mention of the thirty-four "small new soldiers" assigned to him. The Canadian wrote that he had recovered the merchandise pillaged from Crozat's warehouse and from the dead voyageurs. He also told of his success in getting several other indigenous communities to "chant the calumet" and live in peace. Comments in the margin of the document filed with the Ministry of Marine, possibly by Pontchartrain, laud Bienville's accomplishments and call into question Cadillac's behavior in the affair.[118]

After Fort Rosalie was finished, Bienville returned to Mobile. He arrived there in the autumn of 1716 to discover that Versailles had ordered Cadillac's recall. The Natchez and the small garrison that he left behind enjoyed several years of tranquility.

Events under way in France were about to cause momentous changes in the governance of Louisiana. Over the course of a few years, Crozat discovered that the costs of maintaining his concession far exceeded his projections.[119] He had spent more than 1 million livres on the colony with no profit in sight.[120] Moreover, the Crown had assessed him for 6.6 million livres. Crozat requested to be released from his obligations to his Louisiana franchise and that the funds that he had spent on the colony be deducted from his tax bill.[121] Paris complied with his request for divestiture the following year and eventually repaid his investments.[122]

Regardless of the situation in France, who controlled Natchez Country remained an open question. Arnaud Balvay posited that the disputes between Cadillac and Bienville "slowed the affirmation of the sovereignty of France over the area occupied by the Natchez."[123] Concerns regarding the extension of sovereignty in Natchez Country were not the monopoly colonial officials in Mobile; the Suns of the Grand Village also had trouble exerting authority over settlements just a few miles away. Natchez Country remained a fractious land of semi-autonomous towns populated by independent-minded peoples. The next few years witnessed the establishment of a few more villages built by peoples nearly as intractable as those that lived in the Apple or Jenzenaque Villages. The salient difference was that these newcomers came from Europe and Africa.

3 / Impudent Immigrants

Late in October 1722, two Native American ambassadors shuttled between the Apple Village, St. Catherine's Concession, and Fort Rosalie on a series of peace missions. Several Natchez, slaves, and colonists were already dead or wounded from a round of shooting incidents. The war chief of the Flour Village and his unnamed companion attempted to bring an end to the conflict that had broken out between the concession and the Apple Village. The former was a rambling commercial plantation that was home to nearly two hundred Africans, Europeans, and Indians. The latter was a relatively new town built in the scrub oak and pine prairie north of the band of colonial homesteads between the Mississippi River and St. Catherine's Creek. Their violent exchanges threatened to spiral out of control into a full-blown war between the People of the Sun and the subjects of Louis XV.

Strangers in the Land

Some of the troubles that plagued Natchez Country during the early 1720s had roots deep in European politics. The end of the War of Spanish Succession in 1713 produced a number of consequences, some anticipated, others not. First, the war left the monarchy mired in debt. Louis XIV found himself at the end of his financial tether with little hope of wringing more revenue from his overburdened subjects. As mentioned earlier, the French government frequently used extraordinary measures to meet the enormous costs of war.¹ Crozat's concession in Louisiana in 1712 was one of these expediencies.

Another, less foreseeable outcome of the war was a growth in the demand for Virginia tobacco. During the seventeenth century, the French populace consumed a fraction of the tobacco used by its neighbor across the Channel. France acquired a taste for Virginian leaf, however, over the course of the Nine Years' War (1689–97). This came about because privateers based in the motherland captured ships on their way from the New World; the historian Jacob M. Price calculated that the seizure of just one-tenth of the vessels sailing from the Chesapeake would have dumped more tobacco on the French market than had been legally imported before the war. Moreover, Virginia tobacco became more popular in France than the inferior grades grown in Saint Domingue.² Plantation owners on the island had already begun to shift toward sugar production. The transition was nearly complete by the second decade of the eighteenth century. Consequently, France had few colonial sources for smoking tobacco. Whatever leaf that was still shipped from Saint Domingue was more suited for chewing.³ Tobacco grown domestically in the Garonne River Valley was turned into snuff.⁴ Nonetheless, a tax on French smokers' addiction seemed to offer a way to pay down the Crown's war debts, but the bulk of the tobacco would have to come from overseas. The end of the Sun King's reign opened a window of opportunity for those who would pursue that option.

Louis XIV's death on September 1, 1715, lifted his five-year-old great-grandson, Louis XV, onto the throne. During the boy's minority, the Council of the Regency, a group of fourteen nobles led by Philippe, Duc d'Orléans, governed France. This group remained in control until André-Hercule de Fleury became chief minister to the king in 1726. Until its replacement, the Council, in search of ways to pay down the kingdom's debt, became intrigued with the financial theories of a Scottish émigré named John Law. One of Law's solutions to the debt crisis included an overhaul of the French colonial project in Louisiana. His schemes propelled a wave of settlers across the ocean to the Gulf of Mexico region.

This wave gained size and force as the Council recognized that Britain's trans-Atlantic possessions underwrote the island kingdom's growing prosperity.⁵ The French government wanted to expand the empire, but it also recognized that it had to increase the merchant fleet and thereby lower its shipping costs. The shortage of ships also rendered uncompetitive the old commercial system of extracting forest products from New France and Louisiana. The expense of transporting manufactured goods drove up their prices for the Native Americans who gathered the animal skins. By the end of the war, indigenous fur gatherers were turning to British merchants, who could offer better deals. In response to these conditions, French officials drew up plans to transform Louisiana into an agricultural colony like Virginia or South Carolina. The financial policies of John Law appeared to fit that objective quite well.

The Scot looked to the English and Dutch financial systems as models for righting France's fiscal affairs.[6] In 1716, the government opened the Banque Générale under Law's direction to issue paper currency backed by the state's gold and silver reserves. He intended for the infusion of banknotes to stimulate the kingdom's stagnant economy. Law then drew up a plan to direct Louisianan and Canadian commercial activities through a single administrative institution. He would then sell that institution's bonds and guarantee a return of 4 percent per annum. Receipts from the Tax Stamp Farm, one of the private companies that had purchased the right to collect a portion of the kingdom's revenue, were to be used to pay the dividends on the notes.[7] Law also counted on Louisiana furnishing the entire domestic market tobacco of the same quality as Virginia's. He boldly predicted that Louisiana would furnish the kingdom with its entire demand for the leaf by 1721.[8] To make this boast a reality, and to further strengthen the French economy, Law organized the Compagnie d'Occident, which he merged in 1719 with several other financial institutions under the name of the Compagnie des Indes.[9] Some of France's most influential subjects bought into the company, initially providing it with a solid base.[10] This conglomerate soon controlled all of France's commerce outside of Europe, which included the kingdom's business with East Asia and the African slave trade.[11] The paper that he floated on the rue Quincampoix, Paris's open-air stock exchange, traded briskly and soon became the darling of speculators. According to Arnaud Balvay, its price rose from 500 to 18,000 livres by 1719.[12] Encouraged by the initial success of his policies, the Regency Council turned over control of France's overseas trade to Law and appointed him minister of finance.[13]

Law's triumphs were short-lived, however. He began to issue new paper to pay the interest on his companies' initial offerings. As each subsequent payment came due, he sold more bonds. The economic historian Charles Kindleberger summed up the situation: "The stock rose to giddy heights, with profits available to anyone, especially insiders, who bought early and sold in time—the same sort of chain letter operation that characterized the South Sea Bubble by which it was infected—but no possibility for all to win."[14] The first rumblings of trouble sounded in April 1720, after the pool of investors dried up and rumors of fiscal improprieties had begun to circulate among the public. In response, shareholders dumped their stocks onto the market. By September 1720, the notes of the "Mississippi Company" had sunk below their original value, ruining the fortunes of hundreds. The collapse left 2.22 billion livres in unpaid debt.[15] In December 1720, Law slipped across the border into the Austrian Netherlands and exile.[16] As Kindleberger characterized the lasting imprint on French popular imagination: "French experience with John Law was such that there was hesitation in even pronouncing the word bank for 150 years—a classic case of collective financial memory—banking institutions were typically called *caisse*, *crédit*, *société*, or *comptoir*, and not bank."[17]

Despite Law's downfall, his "system" also made a lasting impression on the French colonial project in Louisiana. In the words of the historians Gilles Havard and Cécile Vidal, "When the financier [Crozat] resigned there were only 550 people in the colony, 300 of them soldiers. Everything changed with the creation of the *Compagnie d'Occident*, which was to transform Louisiana into a colony of settlements."[18] At first, Law focused his attention on the Gulf Coast as an ideal location for development. Then the Compagnie, after evaluating the glowing reports of the fertile soils of the interior, sold concessions, or land grants, to investors who pledged to send settlers. To meet the demand for workers, Law's operatives combed through the kingdom's *hôpitaux* and prisons and assembled a collection of orphans and prostitutes, as well as petty thieves, salt smugglers, and other criminals for transport. The low character of the forced emigrants, tales of the hot climate and the incidence of disease, coupled with Louisiana's high mortality rate dissuaded more promising candidates for colonization from leaving home.

To overcome the reluctance of the king's subjects, Law mobilized the Archers of the Treasury, a special police force that enforced certain tax statutes. The public despised these "bandoliers," whose name came about because of the ammunition belts that they wore over their shoulders. In 1719, the Archers rounded up more unemployed and undesirable types and brought them to the Atlantic ports. Riots broke out as overzealous constables hauled in not only the dregs of society, but ordinary folk going about their daily business, for resettlement in "le Mississippi." The resulting disorder reached a fevered pitch when stories circulated that the bandoliers were kidnapping innocent children. When a few of the émigrés who survived the colonial ordeal returned to France, they brought back accounts of disease and starvation. Because of their stories,

Louisiana quickly entered the French popular imagination as a place of sorrow and exile, typified by the Abbé Prevost's novel *Manon Lescaut*.[19]

The province's miserable reputation was not unwarranted. Between 1718 and 1721, the immigrant population climbed to 7,020. Their numbers included 2,462 indentured laborers, many of whom had been impressed by the bandoliers, and 1,278 convicts.[20] Many of the newcomers were stuck on Dauphin Island, Louisiana's main port. Officials on either side of the ocean had made few arrangements for these immigrants, however. A lack of small boats prevented the new colonists from traveling inland to the concessions.[21] Lieutenant Jean-François Benjamin Dumont de Montigny recounted the resulting disaster: "At last, the famine was so severe that a great number died, some from eating herbs they did not know, and which, instead of prolonging life, produced death, and others from eating oysters, which they went and gathered on the seashore."[22]

New Neighbors

The elites of the colony fared poorly, too, although in different ways. Marc-Antoine Hubert, *commissaire-ordannateur*, arrived in 1717 with Governor L'epinay. In a lengthy memoir, Hubert gave his first impressions of the colony, which include a particularly scathing assessment of its inhabitants:

> The colonists of the present time will never be satisfied with this infallible resource [the fertility of the soil], accustomed as they are to trade with the Indians the easy profit which supports them, giving them what they need day by day like the Indians who find their happiness in an idle and lazy life. Lacking nothing in case of need on account of the abundance of fish game which never fails them, their lives flow along without ambitions tormenting them.[23]

By virtue of his position as *commissaire-ordannateur*, Hubert controlled the purse strings of the colony, which made him few friends among either military personnel or civilians. Soldiers accused him of withholding their pay, while established colonists regarded him as a meddlesome arriviste intent on throttling their ambitions.[24] He also ran afoul of Bienville, who, as the de facto head of the colony, found a natural nemesis in whoever held the *commissaire*'s office. Hubert did not restrain himself when it came to criticizing Bienville. Their rivalry ground on until, Hubert, tired of the thankless burdens of his office, took up residence in Natchez Country in late 1719.[25]

Hubert brought his spouse and two children with him to help build a plantation astride the "River of the Natchez," about a mile upstream from the Grand Village. He traveled up the Mississippi River in eight boats filled with personal effects and merchandise for trade. Hubert also took with him sixty "*domestiques*," thirty of whom were African and Native American slaves.[26] He temporarily took up residence at the home of La Loire des Ursins, the director of the trading post near Fort Rosalie.[27] Soon after settling in, he examined the land chosen for him by his agent, Antoine Le Page du Pratz, a Dutchman who had arrived in the colony in 1718.[28] Hubert renamed the River of the Natchez "St. Catherine's Creek" in honor of his wife's baptismal name.[29]

The newly installed concession holder and his workers took up the task of building a viable enterprise. His carpenters began to construct a large home for the concessionaire's family. They also erected a water mill and installed the millstones that Hubert had shipped from France. He put a young miller in charge of its operation. The installation attracted soldiers from Fort Rosalie, as well as Natchez from the nearby villages, who wished to have their grain ground into flour. According to Penicault, the work of the mill alone "made this concession very rich."[30] Hubert's men began to reshape the landscape as well. Within a year his employees had cleared 160 arpents (roughly 135 acres) of brush and trees, opening up new vistas previously unavailable.[31] The concession also boasted a forge operated by a blacksmith who repaired tools and weapons and was particularly useful in fashioning plowshares.

At first, Hubert was astute in his relationship with his indigenous neighbors. He welcomed the Suns of the Natchez when they came to chant the calumet. He also managed to convince Bienville to pardon Oleyape, a Sun of the Apple Village, for his role in the deaths of the voyageurs during the Hostage Crisis of 1716. The Great Sun of the Grand Village marked this diplomatic coup with an eight-day festival. St. Catherine's Concession hosted several more calumet ceremonies for envoys of the Yazoos, Chackchiumas, Arkansas, Choctaws, and Chickasaws. Hubert made certain that he distributed presents in accord with established peacemaking practices, but this last aspect of his diplomacy drew the ire of Bienville. The fact that a private colonist gave gifts as part of a ceremony of friendship undercut the Canadian's influence among the Native Americans of the Lower Mississippi Valley.[32]

This first incarnation of St. Catherine's Concession, if not completely analogous to a Natchez village's social structure, had enough elements to be intelligible to its indigenous neighbors. Its European "headman," together with his mate, commanded a significant number of subordinate workers. Hubert also took care to observe long-standing practices of intercultural relations. He respected the authority of the Suns and employed his influence to spare one of their own from a death sentence. Some negative qualities of the concession also resembled those found in the communities of their indigenous neighbors. This immigrant "chief" was embroiled in a conflict with a powerful leader of the colony: Bienville. In this regard, the settlement was indeed an outlier from the colony's new capital in New Orleans. This competition for authority in the colonists' corner of Natchez Country mirrored some aspects of rivalries between the Grand Village Suns and the leaders of the towns they claimed to rule. Relations between the concessionaires and the People of the Sun also showed signs of deterioration. De La Loire wrote that some of "the Natchez had gone to the habitation of Hubert to cut the throats of his family," but their plans had been averted by the "firmness of Sieur Hubert."[33] Tired of the constant struggles, he sold his interest in St. Catherine's Concession fifteen months after he bought it and departed for New Orleans.

In the same convoy that brought Hubert upriver was a contingent of thirty tobacco workers led by the sieur de Montplaisir de la Guchay. This group had come from Clairac in the Garonne River Valley in southwestern France. They settled downstream of the Grand Village on St. Catherine's Creek on a site also chosen by Le Page du Pratz. It quickly acquired the name Terre Blanche, or the White Earth Concession.[34] Consequently, two immigrant villages had sprung up on either side of the Grand Village of the Natchez in less than two years. The new managers of the estate had arrived in Mobile in late 1720. These arrivistes had few contacts among the previously established Francophone colonists, and none with the indigenous inhabitants of Natchez Country.

The change of ownership of St. Catherine's Concession was part of an initiative by an Alsatian banker named Jean Deucher and his partners, Jean-Daniel Kolly of Fribourg, Switzerland, and Abbé Charles-Elisabeth de Coëtlogon. These three men were already deeply involved with France's financial institutions through their association with John Law. In the autumn of 1719, the three formed the Associates of the Concession of St. Catherine.[35] They negotiated with the Compagnie d'Occident for an agricultural concession in Louisiana. A few months later, the Associates petitioned that parent corporation for permission to purchase 1,500 slaves in Africa for shipment to the colony. They also requested that they be allowed to import livestock from St. Domingue. The directors responded favorably by dispatching ships to the coast of Guinea to trade for slaves.[36]

The two principles of the Associates of St. Catherine's, Kolly and Duecher, sent Jean-Baptiste Fauçon, sieur Dumanoir, to oversee the establishment of their enterprise. Deucher and Kolly gave him authority over the plantation and its workers and granted him power of attorney over its affairs. His contract provided for an annual salary of 3,000 livres as well as a twenty-first of the concession's profits.[37] Through the winter of 1719–20, Dumanoir scoured France's Atlantic ports for recruits. The bursars listed carpenters, masons, cooks, vintners, and bakers among them, but day laborers far outnumbered them all.[38] In August 1720, 198 emigrants departed Lorient bound for Natchez territory aboard the Compagnie ship *La Loire*. They landed in Biloxi that autumn only to languish at the port due to a lack of small craft to transport them up the Mississippi. During that time, disease had winnowed their numbers. Eventually, Dumanoir's workers made it to their destination, but more than a year had passed since their departure from France.

Before his party reached Natchez Country, Dumanoir had arranged to buy Hubert's farm as a site for the new concession. By doing so, he spared his depleted staff the trouble of clearing land. The manager estimated that he had saved "fifteen months of work without the cost of the workers' salaries or their food." Among his retinue he counted thirty Africans and seventy-nine "whites." He also boasted that within the next year the plantation would produce 100,000 pounds of tobacco with the help of the technicians from Clairac "who know how to twist [the leaves into cords]."[39]

The Jesuit Father Charlevoix passed through the region in the fall of 1722 and visited St. Catherine's and the Terre Blanche plantation. He called the former "the Concession des Maloins" because St. Malo in Normandy was the birthplace of several of its officers. He remarked that the distances between St. Catherine's, Fort Rosalie, and the Terre Blanche Concession made a perfect triangle in which each angle was a league in length (about two-and-a-half miles). The priest also noted the use of slaves and indentured servants by both enterprises.[40]

Throughout his letters, Dumanoir inserted brief mentions of other purchases that he had made on credit during his stay on the coast and his journey upriver. Aside from slaves and the land, the director bought provisions for the journey and secured the services of four boatmen. His expenditures are noteworthy because they revealed a shortage of

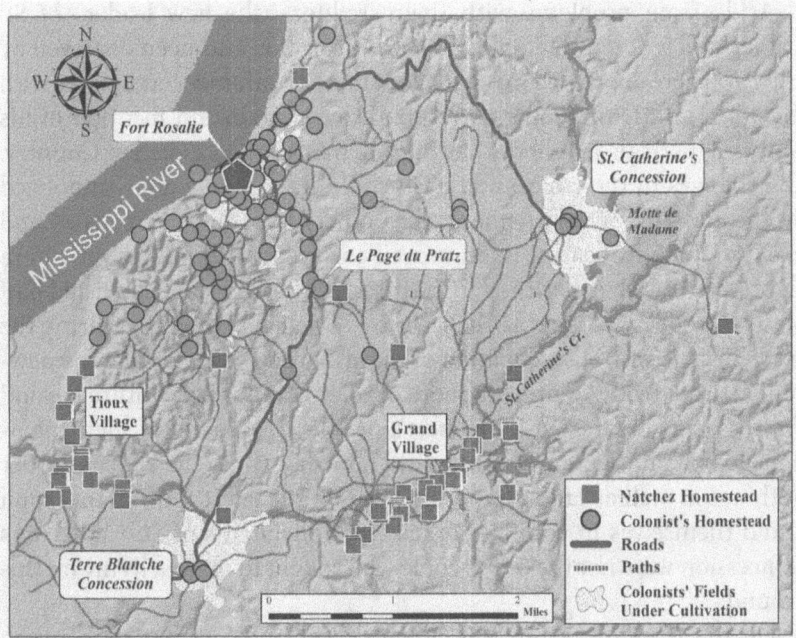

FIGURE 3.1. Natchez Country, circa 1723–1726.

ready capital at his disposal. The investors began in 1719 with roughly 90,000 livres in liquid assets to support not only St. Catherine's Concession but the Concession of Saint Reine near Pointe Coupée as well. The property in Natchez Country alone cost the Association 50,000 livres. By August 1723, St. Catherine's Concession owed 91,500 livres, of which it had retired 6,500 livres.[41] The lack of ready cash, combined with the debt racked up by the concession's management, led to friction not only with Native American farmers who supplied the settlement with corn, but also with his own workers. The plantation's poor finances triggered a steady stream of lawsuits against Dumanoir for the next decade. These legal actions culminated in a full investigation of St. Catherine's accounts in 1731. This was when the Compagnie des Indes attempted to ascertain its losses after the Natchez destroyed the concession. It was precisely these disputes over unpaid wages and expenses that helped to frame the plantation as a weak and troublesome neighbor for the People of the Sun. These problems also left the concession in the hands of its second-in-command, Pierre Guenot de Tréfontaine, because Dumanoir was busy downriver in New Orleans answering writs against him and his employers.

Aside from problems with their creditors, the new leaders of St. Catherine's ignored the diplomatic protocols that had been observed by Hubert. There are no records of negotiations or calumet ceremonies with the Suns, and Dumanoir's correspondence contains no mention of his Native American neighbors during his first year in Natchez Country. The changes in the concession itself could have hardly gone unnoticed by the Indians. By 1722, there were ninety-two European males and twenty-four European women as well as seventy-nine slaves, of whom eight were Native Americans.[42] The directors of the plantation listed half of the European workers as "*dèfricheurs*"—men tasked with clearing the land. The specialized occupation of the last group suggests that the newcomers were ready to prepare more of their land for agriculture beyond the 135 acres deforested by Hubert's people. Regardless of their intentions to expand, these newcomers did not conform to the Natchez order of things as well as Hubert and his settlers. The latest immigrants soon found themselves in conflict because the inhabitants of St. Catherine's Concession were not the only people who sought to make a living on this ground.

During the early 1700s, the broken scrubland and prairie between Fort Rosalie and the Grand Village attracted the attention of Native Americans as well as Europeans. After the decades of violence generated by the slave trade, that land must have looked like a safe haven to the Apple People. The pardon Hubert arranged for Oyelape also made the Europeans look like good neighbors. The attention that the concession's first leader paid to the calumet ceremonies most likely reinforced that assumption. Sometime between 1716 and 1722, the Apple Villagers built a new town close to the European immigrants.[43] Jean Baptiste Michel Le Bouteux, an engineer who had arrived in the colony in the 1710s, drew a map of Natchez Country in which he placed the Apple Village (Village de la Pome [sic]) to the north of the cart track that led to the concession. The latest set of Native American immigrants, however, proved to be far less tractable in reality. Among the leaders of these indigenous settlers were some of the same men who were behind the deaths of the voyageurs in the winter of 1716.

The concessionaires' farming techniques also marked significant departures from indigenous uses of the land. Plows tore up the ground more rapidly and deeply than the fragile bone hoes of the first inhabitants. This enabled the newcomers to cultivate far more acreage than their Native American neighbors. Equally destructive were the horses, cattle, and hogs that roamed the scrublands between the Grand Village

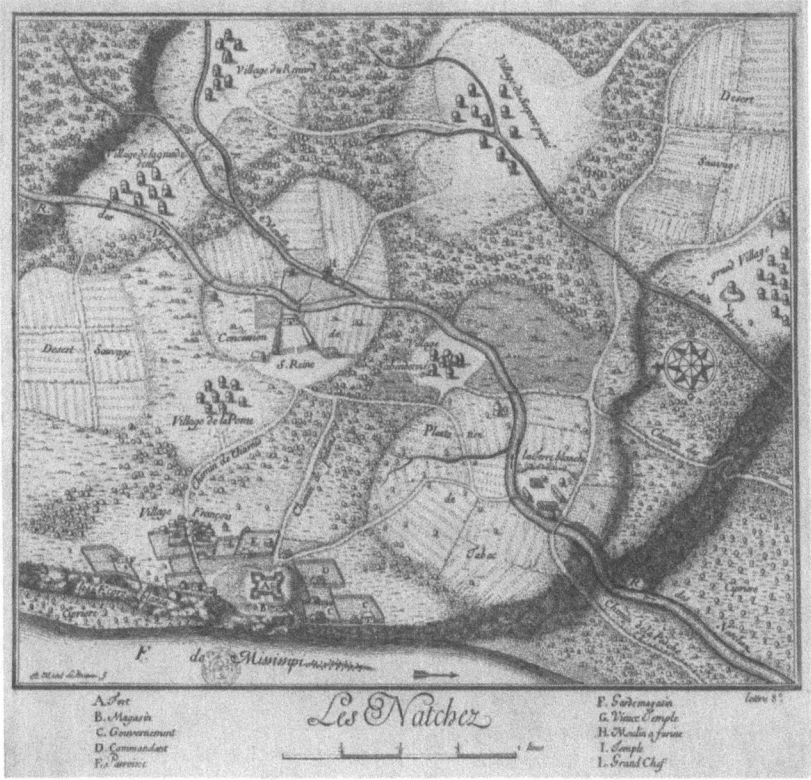

FIGURE 3.2. Bouteux's map of Natchez Country (Les Natchez [Material cartográfico/B. Michel Le Bouteux] Biblioteca Nacional, C.C. 55 P2, Lisbon por Le Bouteux, J. B. Michel, fl. 1748).

and Fort Rosalie, trampling Natchez planting grounds as they foraged for food. They also provided muscle power for the immigrants' iron machines that clawed the earth. Virginia DeJohn Anderson noted that the same creatures were responsible for similar tensions in the colonial Chesapeake and New England regions. In those colonies, the introduction of draft animals rapidly improved the productivity of English farms that allowed their inhabitants to become self-sufficient in food production while threatening indigenous supplies.[44]

Dumanoir's people were no exception; they devoted a good portion of their acreage to food production, particularly to maize. His concessionaires also used the Motte de Madame to grow corn. If the colonists succeeded in harvesting in autumn the crops that they planted in the spring of 1722, the Natchez farmers would face serious competition when it

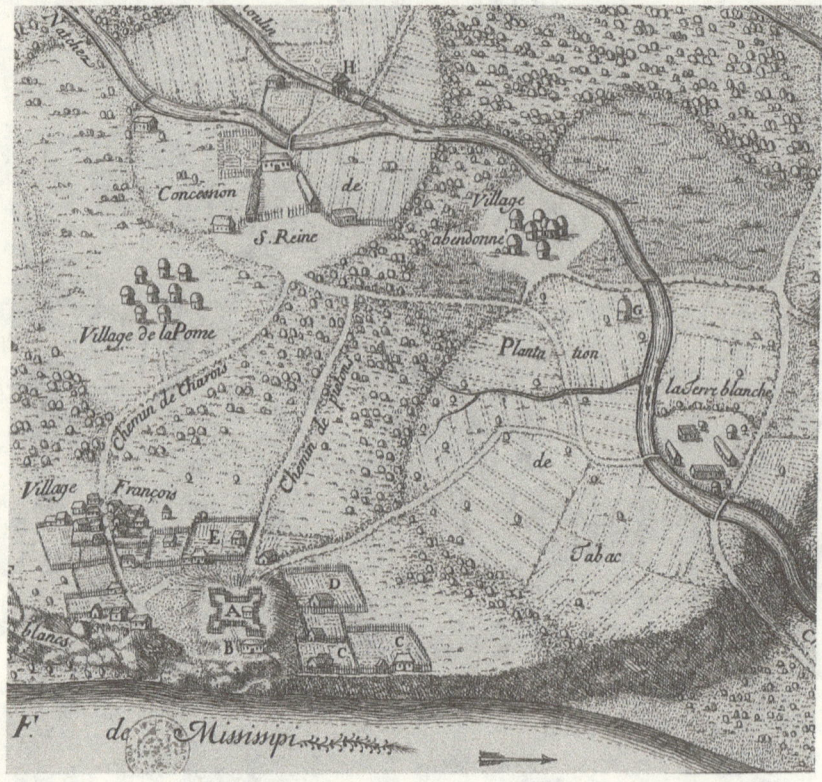

FIGURE 3.3. Detail of Bouteux's map: The Apple Village (Village de la Pome [*sic*]).

came time to supply the garrison at Fort Rosalie and the *coureurs de bois* who stopped to trade.

The problems the People of the Sun faced were not limited to market rivalries. The Europeans' conceptualizations and representations of the space also began to play a role in intercultural relations. The newcomers embraced a system of private property that excluded others from their newly fashioned landscape. Their plows, paths, cart tracks, and fences inscribed their spatial practices on the land in a process described by Henri Lefebvre: "The spatial practice of a society secretes that society's space.... [I]t produces it slowly and surely as it masters and appropriates it."[45] St. Catherine's concessionaires, first under Hubert and then under Dumanoir, began a process of refashioning the terrain of Natchez Country as they appropriated its fields, cypress groves, as well as the towns and the trails that connected them. They turned them into strange new

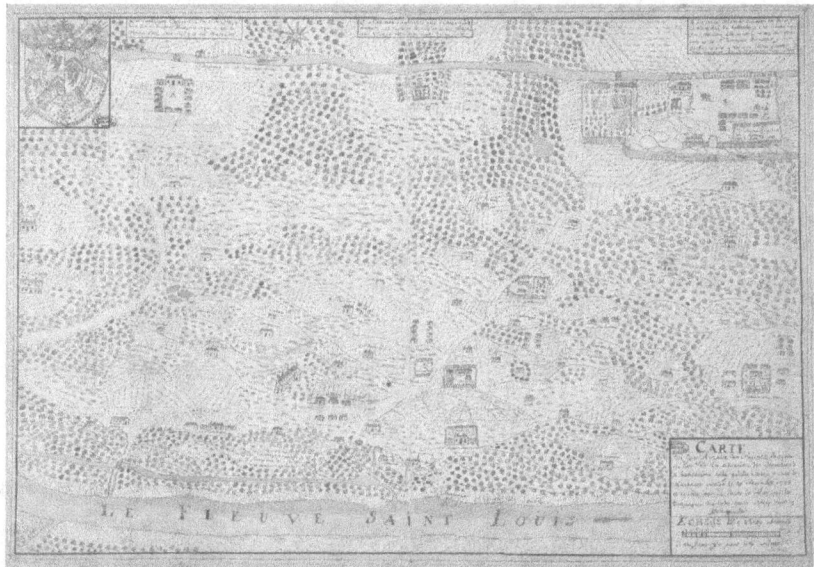

FIGURE 3.4. Dumont de Montigny's Natchez Country (Archives nationales de France [Paris] Cartes et Plans, N III Louisiane 1/2).

spaces of production. Although economic planners in France placed their hopes in tobacco, the concession failed to export more than five hundred pounds of the leaf during its first year. Food crops were far more valuable in a colony where starvation had stalked its most recent immigrants.

The colonists found other ways to convey their domination of Natchez Country, albeit in an ideological sense. During the early and mid-eighteenth century, cartographers and illustrators drafted images that reinforced Europeans' claims on the homeland of the Natchez. Many of these representations were little more than schematics that showed the approximate locations of the major landmarks such as Fort Rosalie, the two concessions, and a few key dwellings. These depictions provide insights into how newcomers perceived the terrain. Dumont de Montigny placed the Mississippi River (Fleuve Saint Louis) at the bottom of his map. This orientation turned the region on its side by situating the western edge, rather than the southern edge, at the foot of the chart. Most of the other cartographers of Natchez Country also introduced their viewers to the region from the west via the river. For Dumont de Montigny and his European colleagues, the Mississippi represented the key to exploiting the region, and their images made this connection abundantly clear.

FIGURE 3.5. Broutin's map of Natchez Country (Bibliothèque nationale de France, Département des cartes et plans, Ge DD 2987 [8834 B]).

Perhaps the most revealing of all the extant representations is Ignace François Broutin's map, *Carte des environs du Fort Rosalie aux Natchez*, drafted in 1723. He surveyed the region between the fort and the Grand Village that he used to produce an extremely detailed picture of the landscape.[46] Broutin's representation, like more rudimentary depictions by Dumont de Montigny and Bouteux, depicted Natchez Country on its side, with the north on the left side of the map.[47]

The Apple Villagers and the Jenzenaques lived closer to the Chickasaws than to the other Natchez towns.[48] Although these locations rendered them vulnerable to slavers, it also placed them in favorable positions to trade with the English merchants to the northeast. Once the Apple People built their new town close to St. Catherine's Concession, they attempted to maintain control of the high ground of the Motte de Madame because the road to Chickasaw Country led over this small promontory. (It also gave them an excellent perch from which to observe St. Catherine's Concession.) The supply of trade goods from Britain undermined the established patterns of redistribution that bolstered the prestige of the Great Sun and his cohort. Consequently, the Apple Villagers, by virtue of their location, had the connections to steer a course independent of the Grand Village its allies from France. When the Apple Natchez chose to expand, they took on yet another set of problems; the place they selected to build their new town put them in direct competition with the colonists. It was not very long before violence erupted.

The Village Crisis of 1722

This new crisis centered on the means by which two towns, the Apple Village and St. Catherine's Concession, would construct and use the space around them. The spaces inhabited by natives and newcomers, simultaneously shared and contested, were not merely backdrops upon which the crisis played out. They generated the violence as they were simultaneously shaped by the conflict. The proximity of European, African, and Native habitats made this patch of ground unique. Only a few regions in North America, perhaps places like the Cherry Valley of New York; short stretches of the St. Lawrence River Valley; or some of the Pueblo communities had similar concentrations of radically different cultures. It was in this small section of Natchez Country—a few square kilometers at most—that France's strategic plans for Louisiana began to unravel.

The concessionaires' troubles with the Apple Villagers began a few months after Dumanoir's people arrived. The Indians stole fifteen horses from the fields, only one of which was recovered. The directors of St. Catherine's notified Berneval, the commander of Fort Rosalie, but he took no action. According to Dumanoir, this lack of initiative only encouraged further "insults" from the Apple Villagers. Warriors from the town followed up by killing two of the settlement's horses.[49]

Although Dumanoir and his assistants interpreted these undertakings to be wanton acts of violence, the incidents followed a pattern that represented a series of graduated warnings. The historian Frederic Gleach recognized comparable warnings in the Powhatans' selective attacks on the English settlements in Virginia during the first half of the seventeenth century. He argued that the Powhatan complex chiefdom attempted to "educate" the colonists to conform to the role of a subordinate people within their indigenous polity. Unlike the Apple Villagers, however, the Powhatans first had tried removing themselves from the area. The English followed in their wake, and failed to heed their messages. The Virginians struck back against the Indians' warnings with increasing fury that culminated in the Powhatan War of 1644–46. In a similar fashion, warriors from the Apple Village first targeted livestock, then low-status concessionaires, and finally colonial leaders in an effort to persuade the latest inhabitants of Natchez Country to conform to their station as a subordinate community within the chiefdom.[50]

When Apple Villager "messages" went unheeded, violence against colonists escalated, as events on the night of February 9, 1722, indicated. According to the account of one concessionaire, a number of "*sauvages* of the environs of the concession gathered and came armed with the design to defeat the French of this concession."[51] The Indians approached under the cover of darkness and fired several musket shots into the gardener's cabin, which was occupied by four workers. None were hurt, but the director of the plantation considered the incident to be a declaration of war. The same document mentioned a "savage chief who had desired to kill the French for a long time." Dumanoir wrote that several Natchez told him that "Old Hair led the party to avenge the death of his brother." When or where the headman's sibling died remains a mystery. He might have been one of those from the Apple Village executed by Bienville at the conclusion of the Hostage Crisis of 1716. The concession's manager insisted that the incident merited a "decisive response."[52] In the meantime, Captain Berneval stationed half of his troops at the concession to keep the peace. The Superior Council, which included Bienville, responded to Dumanoir's request by authorizing officials at the fort and surrounding settlements to arrest the headman responsible and bring him to justice. The orders were not carried out, however, and Old Hair of the Apple Village remained at large. Fortunately for the *habitants*, the situation around the settlement calmed down during the spring and summer; Louisianan records barely mention St. Catherine's Concession during that time.

Dumanoir's rhetoric reveals a pattern. He singled out Old Hair, the Sun of the nearest Natchez town, as the instigator of the unrest. At first glance, the European's accusations against the leader of an anticolonist conspiracy seem quite plausible. According to Dumanoir, the concession was simply the target of a Native American headman and his followers who sought to avenge the death of a kinsman. In his version, the concessionaires had furnished no provocation for the incident. He even went as far as to suggest that Bienville had encouraged the attacks. Nor did communications penned by other Europeans at the concession suggest that the Apple Villagers had more immediate reasons for the attacks. Nonetheless, Natchez tactics suggest a discrete strategy that operated against the Europeans in a selective manner. In the next round of the violence, Apple Villagers carefully singled out their opposite numbers from among the concessionaries.

This selectivity became evident in the hostilities that began at the gates of Fort Rosalie on October 21, 1722. According to Louis Auguste de La Loire de Flaucourt, the Compagnie's chief clerk at the Natchez post, two warriors approached the fort "without a doubt searching for some pretext for a dispute as they were accustomed."[53] A sergeant named La Fontaine, who had sold the Indians merchandise that belonged to the ensign of the garrison, challenged them. The sergeant demanded to know when the two warriors would pay for the goods. The men merely smiled and then began to mock the French soldier, who repeated his demand for compensation. The Natchez continued to verbally abuse him, apparently in a manner loud enough to attract the attention of Madame Berneval, the commandant's wife. Although Captain Berneval himself was not present, his spouse came to the gate to investigate. With cane in hand, she attempted to drive off the two warriors. They responded by menacing her with their hatchets. Madame Berneval, badly shaken, called out the guard "without thinking of what might happen next." Several soldiers poured out of their barracks, shot one of the Natchez and bayonetted the other. A number of Théoloëls witnessed the fracas and carried the two wounded men back to their village.[54]

Antoine Le Page du Pratz, who published his three-volume *Histoire de la Louisiane* nearly two decades after he left the colony, described the incident with Sargent La Fontaine quite differently:

A young soldier of Fort Rosalie had advanced some things to an old Warrior of a Village of the Natchez. [the footnote reads: "This Village was of White Apple: each Village had its particular name"] who owed him grain in return at the beginning of the Winter of 1723. This Soldier lodged near the Fort and he saw the old Warrior there. The Soldier demanded his grain. The Natural responded softly that the grain was not dry enough to shell and besides, his wife was sick, and he would as soon as it was possible. The young man, not content with this response, menaced the elder with a stick. This happened within the soldier's cabin. The old man became indignant at this threat and said that he would see him outside and see who was the stronger. At this defiance, the Soldier cried "assassin" and called the Guard to come to his aid. The Guard came running and the young man pressed upon them to fire on the warrior as he was returning to his Village at an ordinary gait, a Soldier was imprudent enough to do so. The old man fell. Soon the Commandant was advised of these happenings and came to the place where there were witnesses…who instructed him about the deed. Justice and prudence would have submitted the Soldier to exemplary punishment, but he let him off with a reprimand, after the Naturals made a litter and carried off their Warrior who died the following night.[55]

Le Page du Pratz's perspective, of this and other events, is crucial for several reasons. The Dutchman left the most extensive and cohesive account of the Natchez. The Seven Years' War was raging around the globe when Le Page du Pratz published his history. By casting the Natchez as victims in this instance and in other examples of intercultural tensions, he affirmed the viability of the French colonial project. The province of Louisiana still possessed significant potential for the kingdom if managed correctly. It was only the actions of a few corrupt soldiers and officials that kept the province from reaching it. Despite the fact that Le Page du Pratz did not claim to have witnessed the struggle between the guards and the warriors, his has become the standard account of the cause of the crisis, often characterized as the "Second Natchez War."[56]

On the same day that the two warriors were wounded, Pierre Guenot de Trefontaine, one of the assistant directors of St. Catherine's, rode from Fort Rosalie to the concession. An Apple Villager hidden in the canes alongside the cart track put a bullet in the Frenchman's right shoulder. Guenot clung to his saddle and spurred his horse to the plantation to raise an alarm. The *habitants* spent the night on their guard against further attacks. Several of the besieged concessionaires kept a combined journal for several weeks in which they documented subsequent assaults.[57]

The day after Guenot's shooting, a detachment of six concessionaires escorted a cart to the fort to pick up ammunition and clothing. On the return journey, a Natchez man stepped out of the brush to warn them of an ambush on the road ahead. The cart and its guard hurried back to the fort. In another incident that morning, Natchez warriors fired upon six African slaves belonging to St. Catherine's. One of the slaves, an African man named Bougou, died, and his brother suffered a wound to the leg. The attackers made off with "five axes and six iron wedges."[58]

The Natchez's removal of axes from the site where the African slave died demonstrates some continuity with an established discourse of power. Axes, as noted by the anthropologist Karl Lorenz, denoted political authority in Natchez material culture. Indeed, their significance in Mississippian societies dated back to the halcyon days of Cahokia in the eleventh century.[59] One of these implements along with several calumets was unearthed at the Rice Site, a place that Lorenz connected with the fractious Jenzenaques. If their allies had axes and were employing them as symbols of political power, perhaps the Apple Villagers were confiscating items they associated with the concessionaires' authority. They might also have been attempting to obtain their own accoutrements of status that would allow them a greater degree of autonomy within the Natchez polity.[60] The autonomy that individual European *habitants* had also enjoyed now worked against them. Throughout that day La Loire watched as settlers took refuge at the Compagnie warehouse near the fort. Their homes were too dispersed throughout the countryside to provide mutual support if attacked.

That night, concessionaires heard several gunshots "in the area halfway to the fort." They discovered the next day that twenty men from the Apple Village had decapitated a man named La Rochelle "who had the temerity to remain in his house alone" after the troubles began.[61]

The target of the attack suggests the Apple Villagers' motive. Farmsteads "dependent on St. Catherine's" named Le chaudron d'or, or the Golden Cauldron, were situated squarely in the disputed territory on the trail that ran from Fort Rosalie to the concession. It was here that La Rochelle had made his home. The scene of the killing might serve to explain La Rochelle's murder by the Théoloëls since he lived in the area both groups wanted to use for their expanding communities. Another clue comes from a map drafted by Michel Le Bouteux. This chart showed the Apple Village in a location northwest of St. Catherine's and suggests that it was built after Broutin drafted his map. If this was the case, both the Apple Village and St. Catherine's Concession claimed the same space. To Apple Villagers determined to enlarge their holdings, La Rochelle and his fellow Europeans represented unwelcome squatters on land too close for comfort.

The historian Allan Greer characterized such terrain as an "inner commons"—areas "located within the tillage zone of a given community" that provided access to certain resources of those areas.[62] He argued that Native Americans as well as Old World Europeans recognized that specific groups possessed communal privileges over specific acreage. If one considers Natchez Country—a collection of agricultural towns and homesteads—in its totality, the space between St. Catherine's and the Apple Village fits Greer's criteria for an inner commons. The model is all the more compelling in light of the Natchez perception of the newcomers as candidates for absorption into the chiefdom. It would have been highly impractical for residents of any these towns and homesteads, most of whom were agriculturalists, to conduct trade at either the Grand Village or the magazine near Fort Rosalie without traversing this inner commons. It also provided fertile plots for crops as well as the water to make them grow. The commons also furnished cover for small game and wild plants for human foragers. Thus the place where La Rochelle lost his life and the concessionaires lost their livestock constituted a geographic core of Natchez Country. It was perhaps the most valuable real estate in the region, far too valuable for the Suns of the Grand Village to allow it to fall under the exclusive control of a single group that might challenge their authority.

La Rochelle's death did not mark an end to the violence. Natchez warriors continued sniping at the concession's inhabitants throughout October 23. Colonial records note that the indigenous marksmen used the Motte de Madame, a flat-topped hill to the east of St. Catherine's Creek, as their vantage point.[63] Once again, they chose African slaves as their targets, shooting at them as they worked in the garden inside the farmstead. The Apple Villagers also attacked the concession's livestock as the animals grazed in the scrubland between the farm and the Mississippi River. Their gunmen atop the *motte* taunted the concessionaires, telling them "to send bread because they already had enough meat," from slaughtered cattle and pigs. One of the Europeans shouted back, "Come here and look for it."[64]

On the afternoon of the same day, the Apple Village warriors launched their strongest assaults. Approximately eighty men poured more than

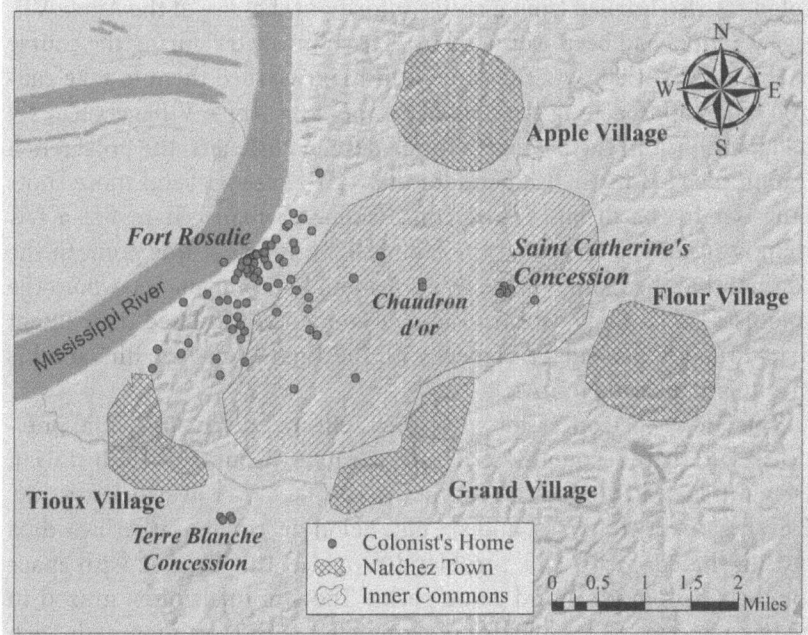

FIGURE 3.6. The "inner commons" of Natchez Country.

150 rounds into the concession. The besieged settlers fired off three rounds from a small cannon to signal the garrison at Fort Rosalie that they needed help. The soldiers replied with a single blast from one of their artillery pieces.

Berneval employed an even more effective means of communication. He enlisted the aid of the war chief of the Flour Village, another Natchez town. The headman, along with one of his townsmen, volunteered their services to the colonists. The two carried a letter from the officer to St. Catherine's. Berneval also sent a detachment of six soldiers and thirteen colonists. The two Native Americans returned that evening with a letter from Martin Des Longrais, one of the "sub-directors" of the concession.[65]

During the night, the concessionaires of St. Catherine's heard more gunshots coming from the direction of the pastures, and the morning light revealed four livestock carcasses left by raiders from the Apple Village. Warriors subsequently launched three separate assaults in which one soldier died and an indentured worker was wounded.[66] The colonists managed to beat back the assailants until a relief force of sixteen armed *habitants* arrived under the command of Antoine Le Page du Pratz.[67] The colonists also learned from a native informant that five of the Apple Village warriors had been wounded by French musketry during the course of the fighting that day. The same informant warned them to take caution when approaching the concession because Apple Villagers had set up an ambush in the pastures. To reassure his listeners, the pro-French Indian pledged his own town's loyalty.[68] At sunset, several more shots rang out in the distance. The concessionaires managed to fire a few rounds at fleeting targets in the fading light. It was at this point in the conflict that the Flour Village war chief and his companions, whom the colonists called their two *"sauvages de confiance,"* declared their intent to go to the Apple Village to meet with the Sun to convince him and his men to put away their arms.[69]

The fate of the concession's livestock reflected divergent spatial practices related to the economic structure of Natchez Country.[70] The historian Daniel Usner attributed the conflict to disputes over livestock grazing. Eleven cattle, two horses, and six pigs belonging to St. Catherine's died during the conflict.[71] This scrubland provided the Natchez with space for their garden plots and game parks. These animals often grazed in Native Americans' cornfields and competed with large mammals such as deer and elk. Consequently, the livestock literally became fair game for indigenous hunters.[72] Virginia Anderson described similar attacks in New England and Chesapeake during the seventeenth century. There, too, the Europeans' creatures vied with indigenous species for fodder. The owners' willingness to allow them free range turned them into targets for Native American hunters.[73] Unlike the more random attacks in the English colonies, the discrimination exhibited by the Apple Villagers marked a different strategy. Their actions resembled the cattle maiming and rick burning of rural Britain rather than the killings in Virginia and Massachusetts. During the eighteenth century, it was not uncommon for dissatisfied English tenants to cripple or kill cattle and horses belonging to their landlords to send a warning.[74] The Indians in Natchez Country selected their targets for much the same reason as Britons: their neighbors had violated an unstated moral economy through an overuse of the commons.[75] The fact that they chose to kill specific cows, horses, and pigs reveals the village-versus-village aspect of the conflict (the records mention no attacks on livestock owned by any other French settlement in the region). The warriors killed only animals that belonged to the offending concession. In short, the social space had generated social practice.

The raids on livestock also indicated that at least some of the Natchez were beginning to abandon the idea that every aspect of Louisianan colonial society mirrored their own. Four-footed animals, unlike chickens, had not yet become part of indigenous husbandry. The concessionaires did not mention the theft of poultry in their detailed inventory of losses.[76] Chickens would have been easy to absorb into the Apple Village economy and would have been difficult to identify as stolen property by colonists intent on recovering them. Why, then, did the Natchez fail to target these small birds in their raids? It is possible that they took action against horses, cattle, and pigs because they were a part of the newcomers' world and alien to their own. In this manner, the Natchez struck at the markers of difference between themselves and the Europeans. Both Virginia Anderson and Jill Lepore argued that the seventeenth-century Wampanoags employed similar tactics against the English in Massachusetts.[77]

Animals were not the only "possessions" held by the French that were foreign to the Natchez way of life. African slaves, although "owned" by European "headmen" who held ranks analogous to their own Suns, belonged to a social category unlike those found among the Indians. The Suns commanded the uncompensated labor of others, but the Europeans recorded this system as a voluntary arrangement. Moreover, as Christina Snyder noted, among Native Americans one often saw was "no stark divide between slavery and freedom."[78] The People of the Sun, through their marriage practices, gradually absorbed indigenous non-Natchez groups rather than condemning them to heritable enslavement. In Louisianan society, however, Africans remained a permanently marginalized people. They seldom gained their freedom or anything that resembled political or social equality. While two enslaved Africans died in the October 1722 violence, none of the seven Native American slaves at St. Catherine's suffered harm during the war. The historian Hal Langfur noted similar tactics used by indigenous Brazilians: "Indians were cognizant of the variations in skin color, labor, and caste that structured colonial society and could single out slaves, the most valuable and vulnerable of assets."[79] Although Langfur's work focuses on a Portuguese colony, there are parallels between the strategies of the Botocudos of Minas Gerais and the Natchez of the Mississippi Valley. Both were indigenous peoples who found themselves under increasing pressure from European slaveholding colonial projects that threatened to transform their landscapes by means of Western agricultural practices, deforestation, and overhunting. Like the Botocudos, the Apple Villagers targeted men trapped in an institution, chattel slavery, which they did not share with the Europeans.[80] Both groups used graduated levels of violence toward slaves to communicate warnings to their neighbors.

The narrow focus of the hostilities, which included only St. Catherine's Concession and the Apple Village, underscored the limited nature of this crisis. Its narrow scope permitted some of the old relationships among other European settlements and Natchez towns to persist. The colonists were able to use people from other Théoloël communities to collect information and act as go-betweens. The mediation of the war chief of the Flour Village and his unnamed companion exemplified the persistence of older diplomatic practices.[81]

The reports of the two-man peace mission from the Flour Village also highlight some of the strains within the Natchez chiefdom. When they left, Longrais reported that the diplomats had said that they would tell Old Hair that if his men did not stop their attacks, their people would join the side of the colonists. When they returned to St. Catherine's on the evening of October 26, they disclosed to the concessionaires the results of their talks with Old Hair. They told him "if they killed the French ... they would kill [the Apple Villagers] also and [it] would be good if his village died with the French."[82] Old Hair denied that he had played any role in the troubles; instead, he blamed "mutineers" among his warriors. He complained that the two men who had been wounded by the fort's guard on October 21 had lingered in agony in the sight of his townspeople. The spectacle of their suffering had spurred the attacks. The diplomats reported to the colonists that this was a ruse on the part of Old Hair because "he had enough authority over his people" to stop the violence. In the opinion of the Flour Village war chief, "this was a case of repaying an injury with blood."[83]

On October 27, a delegation from the Tioux, one of the subordinate communities within the Natchez polity, arrived at the fort to chant the calumet with Berneval. They offered their assistance against the Sun of the Apple Village. The lieutenant rewarded them with gifts of powder and clothing. Their sincerity quickly came into question when one of the colonists recognized a warrior who had been involved in the attacks on St. Catherine's Concession. Then another settler reported that he had heard from an Offagoula woman who lived in their village that the Tioux should play this role as long as they could to get as much merchandise as possible.[84]

The Flour Villagers appeared to have been more consistent in their support of the Louisianans. The "two *sauvages* of confidence" visited the Fort Rosalie and told of their encounter the previous night with twenty-three Apple Village warriors at the burned-out cabin of La Rochelle. The war chief and his companion dissuaded them from attacking the concession. They also reported that Old Hair wished to treat with the colonists. He requested that Berneval send a colonist who could speak on the officer's behalf. The captain found it difficult to find a man willing to risk going to the village alone. He finally located a settler named Dumenil who volunteered despite having been unjustly imprisoned by Berneval.[85] Dumenil led a relief detachment from Fort Rosalie to the concession. From St. Catherine's, the two men of the Flour Village escorted him to Apple Village.[86]

On October 28, Dumenil returned and made his report. Old Hair asked for peace and said that he had only the best wishes for the Louisianans. Dumenil replied that he, too, wanted peace and did not want the colonists "to be obliged to destroy his village." He continued, stating that "the French who were in this colony had come to live a better life." Again the Sun of the Apple Village denied complicity and repeated his desire for peace. He then asked about the health of Mr. Guenot, because he feared that the subdirector was dead. Dumenil replied that Guenot was doing well. Old Hair seemed to be pleased with the news.[87]

Additional pro-Louisiana factions among the Natchez were also at work formulating a peaceful solution. This group included other Natchez communities that desired an end to the Apple Village's war against St. Catherine's Concession. On October 29, 1722, a delegation from several towns brought word to the plantation that the Sun of the Apple Village wished to make peace, corroborating Dumenil's report. The diplomats who carried the news included the Sun of the Flour Village, the "female chief," and the wife of the Tattooed Serpent. One of the delegates from the Apple Village offered to smoke the calumet with Le Page du Pratz. The Dutchman refused the pipe, telling the Indian that he lacked the authority to negotiate. Le Page du Pratz told the villager to present the pipe to the commandant at Fort Rosalie, the leader of the French. Unbeknownst to the concessionaire, the Tattooed Serpent had already chanted the calumet with Berneval. Within a few days, the Tattooed Serpent and his entourage came to St. Catherine's to sing the calumet. The Sun of the Grigras also accompanied the group and offered his people's assurances to the officials at the concession. These rituals concluded the war on the evening of November 4, 1722.[88]

The composition of the Natchez peace delegation demonstrated another aspect of continuity in their diplomatic practices. Longrais mentioned women playing a role in these negotiations.[89] The reference to these women's participation in his account raises a number of questions. First, the author failed to give details on the services rendered by these women. Were they active negotiators? Did they formulate policy or were they substitutes for their husbands, acting as couriers or consorts rather than diplomats? Second, the term "*femme chef*" is imprecise. Was she the wife of the Great Sun? Was she the spouse of a leader from a subordinate village? Was she the Tattooed Arm? Longrais failed to elaborate. If the White Woman did take part in the peace negotiations, her presence in the delegation discredits Father Charlevoix's statement that the Great Sun's wife "ordinarily . . . does not meddle with the government."[90]

The part played by the Great Sun's brother is less obscure. As in the previous conflict, the Tattooed Serpent took an important role in assuaging the French when the violence threatened to get out of control. During the war, Old Hair directed his efforts against his opposite number, Guenot, and his hometown's chief rival, the Concession of St. Catherine. To end the war, the Tattooed Serpent first sought out the nearest European "Sun"—Captain Berneval—at the most prestigious colonial settlement, Fort Rosalie, before he sent delegates to the directors of the concession. Meanwhile, the Sun of the Flour Village and his wife took the calumet to St. Catherine's and treated with the concessionaires. Le Page du Pratz reinforced this diplomatic convention when, on October 29, he told the peace delegation that had come to the plantation to bring their calumet to the "commander-in-chief," meaning Berneval.

The efforts to limit the effects of the conflict were not limited to the environs of Fort Rosalie and St. Catherine's Concession. The Tattooed Serpent must have recognized the seriousness of open war with the Louisianans. He also knew that word was traveling downriver to New Orleans. Time was not on his side, and he moved quickly to meet with the colony's acting governor, Bienville. Indeed, Captain Dutisné and his wife had left on October 23, a week before he chanted the calumet with the commandant of the fort.[91] D'Artiguiette Diron, at his concession "Baton Rouge," wrote that Dutisné had passed by on his way to the colonial capital. The captain gave his report on October 29. A few days later, word arrived that the Tattooed Serpent and his brother were at the Houmas, about sixty miles north of New Orleans.[92] Bienville commissioned Jacques Barbazant de Pailloux, the man who helped negotiate the end to the Hostage Crisis of 1716, now a major general of the colonial troops, to go upriver to escort the Tattooed Serpent to his meeting with Bienville. By the time the Natchez delegation arrived on November 4, Bienville had fallen ill and was unable to receive them.[93] The Tattooed Serpent's delegation finally chanted the calumet with Bienville present on November 6, 1722.

The Natchez agreed to make reparations to St. Catherine's Concession with regular payments of chickens.

In a short speech, the Canadian recalled the threatening behavior of the two warriors at the gates of Fort Rosalie. "The guards would have never fired on them if they hadn't seen them ready to kill the French." To show that he was willing to "forget that which had happened," Bienville handed over 800 livres' worth of presents and munitions to the Tattooed Serpent. He related that he had heard that Old Hair had made overtures to the Chackchiumas, which proved the leader had a "bad heart." The Canadian warned the Natchez that he would not hesitate to use force if they returned to their insolence. To drive his point home, he told his guests that he had sent five hundred Frenchmen (a gross exaggeration) to the Choctaws so the combined force could destroy the Chickasaws. He expressed his wish that the two peoples could live together, which would gladden his heart.[94] Pailloux left soon after with sixty recruits to reinforce the garrison at Fort Rosalie.[95]

The willingness of several Indian leaders to resolve the crisis with the French also reveals some of the factionalism that persisted within the Natchez polity. Obviously, the Suns of the Grand Village did not support Old Hair's harassment of the French. The Tattooed Serpent secured the assistance of the Flour Village, and possibly the Tioux, to bring about Old Hair's compliance.[96] The goods sent by Bienville would allow the Suns to reward those who supported them in their efforts to rein in the refractory villages.

The end of hostilities between the two settlements did not end St. Catherine's fiscal problems. At the end of their "Relation of the war that the Natchez had made," the principals of the concession provided a detailed report of their losses at the end. Nearly three tons of beans went to feed the livestock that could not be turned out to pasture during the fighting. The decision by concessionaires to cut down their cornfields to deny the Apple Village musketeers cover deprived the plantation of four tons of maize. The attacks destroyed the second tobacco crop of 500 pounds, a far cry from the 100,000 pounds Dumanoir had promised his employers the previous year. The Apple Villagers managed to make off with nearly five tons of potatoes, and left the flourmill at the concession in need of extensive repairs. One slave died, another was wounded, while an *engagé* could no longer work due to a shattered arm.[97] The crop and livestock losses demonstrated that the concessionaires had been well on the way to becoming self-sufficient in the production of food prior to the hostilities; had they been able to reap all that they had sown, they would have had little need to barter with their indigenous neighbors. That had all changed. St. Catherine's Concession, poorly capitalized from the onset, was slipping into deep financial trouble.

Bienville's War

The accord worked out in November 1722 did not last long.

Despite the arrival of Pailloux and his troops, the Apple Villagers resumed their harassment of St. Catherine's Concession. By early December, Longrais reported several thefts and attacks on the concession's animals. The plantation manager complained that Apple warriors had stolen a horse and led it to their town. This time, the culprits demonstrated a brazenness that disturbed the concession's directors; the thieves did not attempt to conceal the location of the animal. They injured the beast so badly that it could no longer work. In a more ominous gesture, they displayed the head of La Rochelle in their temple. In other instances, some Indians mutilated the concession's livestock while they grazed within sight of the settlement's cabins. They left distinctive wounds, such as scarring the animals' cheeks and cutting off their tails, to identify themselves as the assailants.[98]

Worse, personal connections between the French leadership and their Natchez counterparts failed to remedy the situation. Neither the Tattooed Serpent nor Pailloux were able to put a stop to the raids. For example, on December 16, 1722, the Apple Villagers chanted the calumet with Pailloux only to continue their depredations a few months later.[99] The concessionaires found the Tattooed Serpent's influence equally limited. The Natchez leader's numerous visits to the combatants' towns failed to stem the attacks, although he often managed to recover the stolen livestock. Dumanoir, who had been residing in New Orleans to plead his case to the Superior Council, argued that only an aggressively prosecuted war would settle the issue. In a fifteen-article petition, the concession manager recounted all of the attacks, the murder of La Rochelle, the provocations of Sergeant La Fontaine, and, finally, the tepid response of Bienville. He also wrote about an incident in which an African slave witnessed Apple Village warriors killing a steer on April 3. On another occasion, the Indians stole a horse. Once again, the Tattooed Serpent quickly arranged the animal's return, but the Indian leader could not negotiate an end to the thefts. On May 1, herdsmen found another mount with a deep wound on its cheek. A few days later, the French found a mare with similar wounds.[100] On

May 9, the Apple Villagers absconded with another horse, which they crippled.

Dumanoir's petition is particularly useful in analyzing some of the tensions within Louisiana's hierarchy. Following established bureaucratic convention, the right side of the document contained the concession director's requests divided into fifteen sections. On the left side were the marginal comments of the Superior Council. Dumanoir wrote about Pailloux and Berneval's powerlessness in the face of Natchez aggression. Both men owed their careers to Bienville's patronage. He cited numerous thefts and mutilations of horses and cattle perpetrated by the concession's indigenous neighbors. Dumanoir argued that the Apple Villagers' behavior demanded a dramatic and violent response. Aside from declaring war against the Apple Village, Dumanoir suggested that a relaxation of certain statutes would permit an influx of non-French immigrants to Natchez Country who had previously demonstrated their bravery.[101] Perhaps he was thinking of Le Page du Pratz's leadership during the autumn of 1722.[102]

Dumanoir's petition, however, provoked little in the way of concrete actions from the authorities in New Orleans. The Superior Council's running commentary offered negative responses to several of the sections. Although it recognized the enmity between Bienville and Hubert, and that the Canadian might not have wanted to see the concession succeed, it also cited the behavior of St. Catherine's inhabitants as sources of the troubles. In particular, the document cites the evidence of "a faithful witness" regarding a Native American slave named Zephyr, whom Hubert had sold to Dumanoir. According to the witness, Hubert had been accused of holding Zephyr illegally. Bienville, at the Company's expense, sent orders to have the man seized at Dumanoir's habitation without due process against either Hubert or Dumanoir. The spectacle of such "mistakes... against the persons of these *sauvages*... has conserved a mortal hatred against this habitation [St. Catherine's Concession]."[103]

The Council hesitated to act forcefully until the Apple Villagers' gestures grew more brazen. On June 15, 1723, the Indians stole three more horses. Monsieur Longrais sent some workers to look for the beasts in the Apple Village. The workers caught up with the animals as the Indians were riding them toward a French lumber camp in the cypress forests. Two warriors rode on the back of each horse "hurling out fierce cries" at the French and Africans who watched.[104]

Over the course of the summer, several ominous stories drifted into St. Catherine's Concession; most of them originated in the Grand and

Flour Villages. One of the informants reported that a Natchez spokesman had passed around the war calumet at meetings attended by the leader of the Yazoos, a nation that would later join in a general war against Louisiana. These meetings took place at the Grand Village in the presence of the Great Sun and at the Apple Village with the participation of Old Hair. Some of the speakers referred to "*les français*" as "dogs" and called for their extermination. At one point during the conferences, Old Hair gathered eighty warriors and threatened to march immediately against the French. Although the Indians did not attack, when the Sun of the Flour Village brought news of these events to St. Catherine's, such stirrings among the Native Americans terrified the Europeans.[105]

Faced with this upsurge of attacks on livestock, the settlers began to panic. The concessionaires stood little chance of defending themselves against a determined assault by Old Hair's faction since most of the Europeans living there lacked firearms. Although an all-out attack never materialized, sniping incidents continued throughout the summer. The Sun of the Flour Village, the Tattooed Serpent, and the Great Sun sounded several more alarms during these hot months. All of them proved to be groundless. The repeated warnings only served to increase the nervousness of the plantation's inhabitants.[106] The concession's tobacco went untended at the height of the growing season because it had become too dangerous to send slaves and indentured servants into the fields. Without relief, the plantation stood little chance of harvesting the crop.

In the last days of June 1723, the concession personnel reported that shots were fired at individual homes during the night. The assailants uprooted tobacco plants in the plantation's fields and also looted various homesteads. The historian Arnaud Balvay linked this raid with the rumors that the destruction of the leaf was evidence of a British plot hatched among the restive anti-Louisianan faction among the Natchez.[107]

The depredations also included animals again. Longrais wrote that in July, they injured the concession's horses by notching their ears or cutting off their tails. The slaves could not work the fields without the protection of armed guards. Although the Tattooed Serpent went to the villages of the culprits to convince them to stop their harassment of St. Catherine's, the attacks continued.[108]

The Superior Council, even after these latest incidents, hesitated to use force. It limited its response to issuing proclamations, one of which forbade "all Frenchmen" from trading "at the village of the Natchez under any pretext whatsoever without the permission of the commandant of the place, under penalty for disobedience and of imprisonment and of a greater penalty in case of repetition of the offense."[109] The next day, the Council proscribed the sale of muskets equipped with bayonets under pain of corporal punishment.[110] These latest ordinances underscored the problems wrought by unregulated trade between the two peoples, but the restrictions proved to be tardy and insufficient remedies.

At the height of these tensions, another series of events threatened to deprive the *habitants* of the assistance of the Tattooed Serpent and the pro-Louisianan faction. Worse, they threatened to destabilize the entire Lower Mississippi Valley. In late August 1723, the Natchez sent 160 men against the Tunicas to avenge the killing of some of their kinsmen. A few days later, two Choctaw warriors arrived at St. Catherine's on a reconnaissance mission. Several of the concession managers met with the Choctaws and provided them with food. According to the envoys, rumors had reached their villages that the Natchez had "destroyed all of the French."[111] The Natchez observed the Choctaws' visit from atop their vantage point on the Motte de Madame and sent word of it to the Tattooed Serpent. Their report contained an important error: the Théoloël observers mistook the travelers from the east to be Tunicas. Fortunately for the concessionaires, the Tattooed Serpent came to the plantation to ascertain whether the visitors were enemies. A small delegation from St. Catherine's confirmed the identity and nature of the Choctaws' mission. Their report satisfied the Natchez headman. While events at the Motte de Madame and among the Tunicas diverted the Théoloëls' attention, another set of actors prepared for a more forceful intervention.[112]

Bienville was aware that several of the members of the Superior Council had sent scathing reports to France regarding his rule of the colony. For several years, letters left on ships bound for France. The Canadian managed to intercept some of them before they reached the vessels. The list of their authors reads like a roll call of the key personalities of the colony. Captains Mandeville and Valdeterre, the Superior Council's registrar, and the province's engineer, Pauger, all signed notes criticizing Bienville. They complained that his administration was marked by injustice. Several accused the commandant-general of jailing colonists without due process. Others testified that Bienville seized others' private property at will. Nearly all condemned the Canadian for his abuse of Hubert, the former owner of St. Catherine's Concession. Even the demure Le Page du Pratz sent a request that Gerard Pellerin take over the settlement "to remedy the thefts and assassinations," that had caused "nearly twenty *habitants* to leave the Natchez."[113] Pierre Leblond de La

Tour registered the most scathing critique in his report to the Superior Council. He castigated the Canadian for his tardy response to the latest round of violence at St. Catherine's, and his choice of Pailloux to negotiate the peace the previous year.[114]

Among Bienville's most virulent critics, however, was Jacques de La Chaise, the *commissaire-ordonnateur* of the province. As the nephew of the Louis XIV's Jesuit confessor, his letters found their way to the desks of some of the most powerful men in France. In his role as comptroller, La Chaise was a natural nemesis of Bienville, and he wrote lengthy *mémoires* on the acting governor's harsh treatment of men like Hubert and Dumont de Montigny because they cast the Canadian in a poor light.[115] Moreover, La Chaise and several other Council members criticized Bienville's decision to present gifts to the Tattooed Serpent during the latter's visit to New Orleans during the previous November.

The day after Le Blond de La Tour's remonstrance, the commandant-general began stir. His plan was to put 150 men in the field against the Apple Villagers and their allies. Bienville gathered troops at New Orleans late in the summer of 1723. To support his campaign, the Superior Council decreed that warriors who aided the colonists in the coming expedition against the Natchez would receive the same compensation for slaves and scalps paid to those who fought against the Chickasaws, who were then at war with Louisiana.[116]

Bienville set out from the capital on September 29 with fifty-two soldiers and seventeen Canadians. Another two hundred allied warriors from the *petites nations* who lived along the Gulf coast also began to march toward Fort Rosalie.[117] On his journey up the Mississippi, the governor stopped at various Native towns to recruit more volunteers. Bienville arrived unannounced at the docks below Fort Rosalie on October 23.[118] Over the next two weeks, men from the Houmas, Tunicas, Choctaws, and other nations arrived to offer their services.

As Bienville's army assembled, the Tattooed Serpent and the Great Sun made several trips to the colonists' bivouac. He and his kinsmen undoubtedly already had word of the force growing in their midst. The Natchez leaders were well positioned to gather intelligence about the provincial army from two cabins that belonged to the Great Sun along the Mississippi. One was several miles downriver and covered the approach of vessels from the direction of New Orleans. The other lay just north of the main cluster of European homesteads near Fort Rosalie. From this vantage point, the Suns' followers could track the arrival of travelers

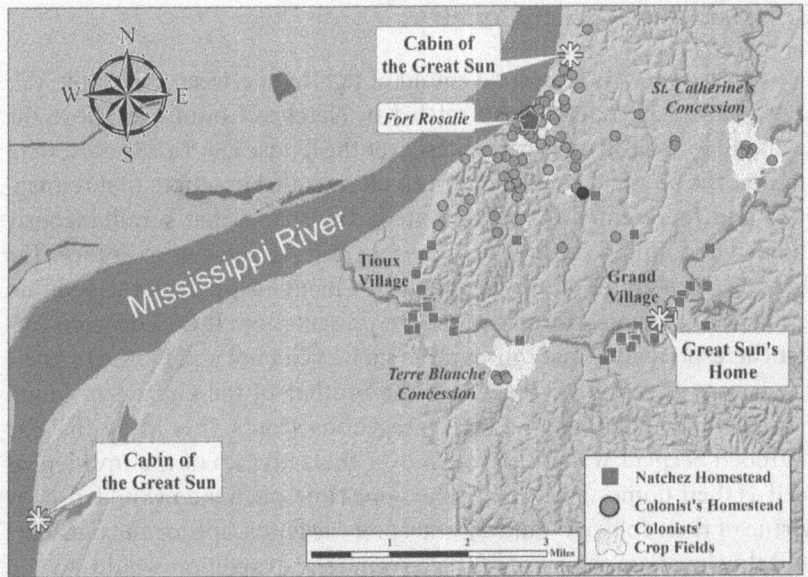

FIGURE 3.7. Cabins of the Great Sun of the Natchez.

from Illinois. These early-warning stations furnished the Tattooed Arm and his brother timely information on the size of the colonial forces.

The two Grand Village elites succeeded in diverting Bienville's wrath toward the indigenous factions that contested their authority, repeating a pattern established during the Hostage Crisis of 1716.[119] In his talks with Bienville, the Tattooed Serpent protested that the culprits behind the attacks on St. Catherine's came from the Jenzenaque, Grigra, and Apple Villages. He and the Suns who accompanied him promised Bienville that they would bring the heads of Old Hair and the "other Little Sun of the Apple Village."[120] The commandant-general agreed with their plans and said that he would spare the main towns.

Over the next several days, the Suns of the Grand Village made good on their pledges. On November 7, the Great Sun brought the head of a rebel warrior to Bienville's camp. That evening, the Tattooed Serpent arrived with the head of La Rochelle's killer. Two days later, he brought "the head of the great mutineer of the Apple [Village]." He also promised guides to help the colonists find their enemy's hiding places. Over the course of a week, the Suns showed further proof that they had eliminated three more leaders of the "mutiny." In the meantime, allied Native Americans captured several dozen inhabitants from the offending towns.[121]

Re-presenting Natchez Country

The accounts of the second round of fighting between the Apple Village and the Europeans who settled in Natchez Country disclose the evolving social and political contest over the landscape. This contest went beyond the physical control of terrain; it included practices that reimagined and represented (or re-presented), the spaces that simultaneously divided and united the People of the Sun and the subjects of France. The Tattooed Sun's offer to provide scouts for Bienville's polyglot expedition constitutes a prime example of this re-presentation. It is clear from earlier correspondence that immigrants such as Guenot and Dumenil knew the way to the Apple Village. Yet the brother of the Great Sun found reason to provide Bienville with indigenous scouts. It is likely that the Tattooed Serpent wanted to watch over the activities of the invaders as well as their domestic rivals. At the same time, such men would also, by virtue of their roles as "guides," interpret the landscape for the outsiders and thus mediate their use of the terrain. The expedition would stay on those parts of the Natchez Country that the Suns of the Grand Village chose for them. Much like the rowers provided to the La Loires for their escape at the onset of the Hostage Crisis of 1716, the Suns' guides were a means to maintain and reinforce their authority over the chiefdom during the events that were about to unfold.

Another aspect of the discourse surrounding the representation of Natchez Country involves the work of Ignace Broutin. The engineer officer had come to Louisiana from Arras, France, at the height of the great migration in 1720. Longrais's *memoir* of the 1723 war recounted Broutin's arrival in the autumn of 1723 during the corn harvest. Sometime during the remainder of the year, he drafted his massive chart of Natchez Country. The original work spanned twelve-and-half sheets of paper and measured 108 centimeters by 179 centimeters. The map indicated the locations of individual homesteads of both Native Americans and Europeans. Many of the buildings were labeled with the names of their inhabitants. It also displayed a network of footpaths that threaded between the Grand Village, the Tioux settlements, the Terre Blanche and St. Catherine's Concessions, Fort Rosalie, and the houses that lined the bluffs along the Mississippi.

Broutin produced his map at a time when French cartographers were gaining international reputations for their work. Government and church officials sponsored surveys of the kingdom's provinces and dioceses. Luminaries like Jean-Dominique Cassini, Guillaume Delisle, and Jean Baptiste Bourguignon d'Anville had made Paris the center of mapmaking and geographic publication.[122] Broutin's draftsmanship reflected this growing trend in French depictions of place and space. It also reflected the emerging discourse of spatial representation as a means to power, in Broutin's case quite explicitly. The spider's web of footpaths that he included on his chart showed a number of routes to the Grand Village and the areas beyond. His plotting of each building indicated which structures were European dwellings and which were cabins that belonged to inhabitants of the Tioux or the Grand Village.[123] The blank area of Broutin's map functioned as representation by omission. The region east of the Grand Village at the top of the chart signified the enemy country. The fact that the cartographer failed to include the Apple Village, although several Europeans like D'Artiguiette Diron, Guenot, and Dumenil knew of its whereabouts, suggests that Broutin intended the chart to serve as guide from "friendly territory" to what a later generation would call a "free-fire zone." It signified the limits of civility. Although there is no mention of this chart in the descriptions of Bienville's War, Broutin's map would have been a superb resource for the commanders of an invading army to plan an approach march. As such, it epitomized a tool of colonialism as sharp as any bayonet. It is an example of an emerging spatial discourse as a means to acquiring authority over the productive capacity of a territory.

While the Suns of the Grand Village brought in the heads of their political rivals, Bienville bided his time as more reinforcements arrived. Additional warriors from the Yazoos, Quapaws, Chacichumas, Acolapissas, Taposas, Natchitoches, and Tunicas gathered under the *fleur de lys* that fluttered above Fort Rosalie.[124] Louisiana's conflict with the Apple Village also gave the Tunicas an opportunity to avenge the previous summer's war with the Natchez.[125] A band of Choctaws under Red Shoe also arrived to assist in the impending offensive.[126]

The colonists and their Native American allies then followed up with a series of attacks during the second and third weeks of November that destroyed the Apple, Grigras, and Jenzenaque towns. In the first operation, Bienville split his forces in an attempt to surround Old Hair's camp. Lieutenant Dumont de Montigny's memoir recounted the approach march in which one column took the main cart track between Fort Rosalie and St. Catherine's Concession. The second group took one of the paths that "traversed the prairies and ravines."[127] Le Page du Pratz, who, like Dumont de Montigny, wrote his memoir two decades later, held that the Natchez thought that they were at peace with Louisiana and had not anticipated the colonists' plans.[128] The strategy failed when women working in the field detected the approach of the main force. The workers ran to a mud-walled hut from which three Natchez men fired through loopholes at the soldiers. A *habitant* named Mesplet stormed the cabin in hopes of seizing one of the women to take as a slave only to be shot dead as he pulled the cane door off its hinges. Despite the loss, the colonists quickly took the hut. They then advanced into the main part of the town to find it deserted; the inhabitants had escaped into the forests and swamps.[129]

Red Shoe and his Choctaw warriors captured four women at the Apple Village before they could flee. The prisoners revealed that the Jenzanaque village contained fifty warriors who swore to defend the place to the death. Next the combined army marched to that town with the Tunica contingent in the vanguard. They encountered a strongly built house on top of a mound. The Apple Villagers apparently had reshaped their landscape to demonstrate their authority. With drums beating, the French formed a battalion square and advanced toward the height with the Tunicas in front as skirmishers. The leader of the Tunicas reached the summit before the rest of the force and found the hut deserted. As he circled the structure, the chief caught sight of a man "the enemy called the Little Sun."[130] Both warriors took aim at each other and fired simultaneously. The Little Sun died on the spot, but not before his bullet smashed into the Tunica's musket and ricocheted into his jaw. A search of the village turned up an arms cache but none of its inhabitants as the townspeople had taken flight. The militia destroyed the food stores that they found and torched the huts. The troops and their allies then retired to Fort Rosalie and St. Catherine's Concession carrying the wounded Tunica chief with them.[131]

At this point, Bienville "thought, however, to end to this war by costing the savages more than poultry [that were the reparations he required after the last conflict] but with blood worth being spilled."[132] In a conference with the Great Sun and the Tattooed Serpent, Le Moyne dictated the terms of peace: the head of Old Hair and that of a free African who played a leading role in fomenting the attacks on the French. The Tattooed Serpent agreed to these conditions and returned with the heads of the two offenders a few days later.[133] The Great Sun's faction was quick to take advantage of French support to eliminate its rivals—Old Hair of the Apple Village, the Little Sun, and the unnamed African warrior among them. Thus, Bienville's War of 1723 put an end to a divisive element from outlying towns. The conflict also served to quell those who may have thought that the presence of the Louisianan–Native American army in the midst of Natchez Country subverted the sanctity of the ruling class. To a native observer living in one of the outer towns, the execution of the "mutineers" and the destruction of noncompliant settlements by Bienville's troops showed that the European immigrants still worked for the Grand Village's Suns.

Not all of the colonists' activities suited the Natchez hierarchy. The anonymous author of the *Punition des Natchés en 1723* provided a detailed list of the grievances presented by the Théoloël leadership. One of the most serious complaints in the document stated "that some Frenchmen were imprudent enough at the time to make insults against them despite the prohibitions that they [the colonial leaders] had made."[134] Bienville assured them that if the Natchez brought these offenses to the attention of the commandant of the fort, justice would be done. The Canadian's promise demonstrated his recognition of the Suns' status. It also demonstrated that he understood that the Natchez deference to the polity's leading family might help to quell the tensions that plagued the region. Bienville therefore pinned his hopes on the Mississippian chiefdoms' foundations of political power that had proved effective in the past. He was also careful to leave them in possession of key terrain features that generated authority. These included the temple mound and the Great Sun's mound in the Grand Village.

In return, the commandant-general extracted another concession from the Natchez: they must agree to compensate the plantation of St. Catherine's with payments of bear's oil, grain, poultry, beans, and game.[135] The People of the Sun accepted this condition since it did not stray too far from conventional Natchez patterns of food redistribution. At the close of the meeting, the assembled Suns raised their hands above their heads to show their approval. Bienville, "following their custom asked permission to depart after the Great Sun and his brother, the Tattooed Serpent."[136]

As in the Village Crisis of the previous year, the discourse that ended the third conflict demonstrated some continuity in the practices that underwrote the relationships between the colonists and the Théoloëls. The personal bond between the Tattooed Serpent and Bienville still worked to secure peace. Both men possessed the social and political capital to speak for their people. The speech performances executed by the two were beyond the capability of lower-status individuals like Guenot, Old Hair, Dumenil, or the Little Sun. Bienville's and the Tattooed Serpent's parallel status as war leaders lent further weight to the outcome.

At the same time, their association exemplified the old style of interaction with its face-to-face negotiations between men of equivalent status.

The rapport between the Tattooed Serpent and Bienville, however, masked the deepening fissures within the Natchez-Louisianan relationship. The developments that led to the hostilities marked a significant shift in the interactions between the Europeans and the Théoloëls. The location of the conflicts constituted the most obvious difference between the Hostage Crisis and the Village Crisis and Bienville's War. The last two struggles took place in the towns and inner commons between the combatants' settlements rather than on a neutral island in the Mississippi. This change of venue incited a desperation that contributed to the higher number of casualties and greater material costs of the wars. It also transformed the spaces between the groups. The Grand Village had shifted from the center of the Natchez polity to a bastion at the front of the glacis that insulated the colonial settlements from a geographic interior that the Suns were no longer able to control.

The shift in the location of the last two conflicts signified another difference: the nature of the terrain on which the two peoples met had changed. A sprawl of poorly regulated European communities had grown up around Fort Rosalie. These settlements were interspersed among Native American villages. According to Dumont de Montigny, this practice allowed the two groups to interact beyond the purview of those with sufficient authority to mediate disputes. The lieutenant introduced his account of the Village Crisis and Bienville's War by citing the Europeans' unauthorized land purchases from the Indians and from one another. These transactions resulted in unclear title to a good deal of the land around the settlements. As Dumont de Montigny wrote: "Things were in this state when the inconstancy or the malignity of the Barbarians gave rise to the events that followed."[137] Moreover, the concept of land tenure among the newcomers was radically different from that of the Théoloëls. The French believed that they held their newly acquired acreage in fee simple, in contravention to the indigenous practice of usufruct and communal tenure.

Nor were these problems limited to the strangers from overseas. The same terrain that had attracted Dumanoir and his charges attracted expansionists from the outer Natchez towns as well. The Apple Villagers sought to colonize the region west of St. Catherine's Concession. These Native American arrivistes resisted the authority of the Suns of the Grand Village. In this case, the Indians were also impudent "immigrants" who did not behave with sufficient respect toward the paramount

Natchez town. Unauthorized trade between Natchez and French villagers furthered weakened the Indians' ties to the central town.

The economics of the region changed in other ways. According to Le Page du Pratz, the Natchez's unmediated access to European goods, traded for food, disrupted the old order.[138] The hierarchy of the Grand Village had used its control of commerce with Europeans to maintain hegemony. The Apple Village stood near the trade route to the Chickasaws to the northeast. Elite males from this border town had the opportunity to acquire manufactured items that they could use to undermine the Suns' faction. Consequently, Old Hair's access to English merchants among the Chickasaws threatened the Great Sun and his family's authority. Bienville's gift to the Tattooed Serpent of 800 livres' worth of goods in November 1722 was an attempt to subsidize the Suns' prestige. It allowed the Grand Villagers to reward subordinate towns that supported them, and therefore a pro-Louisianan policy as well.

Nonetheless, the Indian leaders' prestige only went so far. The bonds between the colonists around Fort Rosalie and the Natchez had often failed under the strain. As the Suns' complaints about "insults" from the settlers and soldiers demonstrated, the Louisianans held little regard for Native American leaders. Their impertinent exploitation of the inner commons, Guenot's imprisonment of an honored man from the Apple Village, and the assault on two Natchez warriors proved that the newcomers would not take up the role of subordinate villagers in the Natchez polity. Regardless of the arrangement negotiated by the Tattooed Serpent and Bienville, keeping the peace would be difficult among such unruly immigrants.

After Bienville's War, even the most accommodating Natchez leader, the Tattooed Serpent, could no longer pretend that the French were like his own people. Once again, the increasing surveillance capabilities of the colonists played against the Natchez. Sometime after the conflict, Le Page du Pratz saw the Tattooed Serpent walking past his cabin. The Dutchman's homestead stood astride the path from the Grand Village to Fort Rosalie, which made it difficult for passersby to avoid notice. Le Page du Pratz called out to the leader and asked him why he no longer stopped to visit. During the ensuing conversation, the Tattooed Serpent expressed surprise that Le Page du Pratz had led French militia against his people. Le Page du Pratz responded: "You wound me.... Mr. Bienville was our war chief, we must obey him, as you must [obey] all of the Suns you have, you are obliged to kill or facilitate the killing of those that your brother the Great Sun orders to be killed."[139]

The Tattooed Serpent stated his opposition to the Apple Villagers' raids, and reminded his listener that he had chanted the calumet with the French the year before. He asked Le Page du Pratz:

> "Is it that the French have two hearts, a good one today and tomorrow a bad one? Why," he continued with chagrin, "why do the French come into our land? They no longer come merely to look, they have asked for our land because their land was too small, because of all of the people who were there. We have said to them that they can take the land where they would like, there is enough for them and for us, that the same sun shines on us and that we walk the same road, that we shared our food, that we helped them build their homes and clear their fields, is it not true?"[140]

The Tattooed Serpent's diatribe alluded to the old model of aggregation that had worked for the Natchez polity in the past. He also invoked the symbology of solar worship, implying that a universal moral code held for newcomers and natives alike. The Europeans, like the Indian groups who had previously migrated to the region, sought places to live from the Suns. Unlike the earlier migrant groups, the latest wave of Europeans did not respect the authority of the Suns, nor would they wait for the Tattooed Serpent and his colleagues to fulfill their promises to track down and eliminate the anti-French leaders in the Apple Village. Instead, Bienville destroyed that town and two others that had harbored Old Hair and his supporters.

During his discussion with Le Page du Pratz, the Tattooed Serpent also rejected an economic motive for allowing the French to settle among them:

> What need have we for the French? We presented them with the best of our seasons, since we deprived ourselves of a part of our corn, of our game, of the fish we caught on their behalf. What need have we of them? Is it for their muskets? Our bows and arrows were sufficient to provide us with food. Was it for their white, blue, and red blankets? We passed the coldest nights with the skins of buffalos; our women made cloaks of feathers for winter and bark cloth for summer, they were not so beautiful, but our women were more industrious and less prideful. Finally before these things arrived with the French, we lived as men who knew how to be content with what we had; instead, today we walk as slaves who do not have what they want.[141]

The Tattooed Serpent's dialogue marked a further decline in the accommodations worked out by the Natchez and their European neighbors. France's foremost advocate among the Indians had lost hope in a mutually beneficial coexistence. This decline in relations continued over the next few years as the Suns' grip on the reins of power slackened. The death of the Tattooed Serpent in 1725 and the passing of his brother, the Great Sun, in 1728, left a political vacuum in Natchez Country.[142] The Sun of the Flour Village was the only practiced male diplomat remaining. The Great Sun's nephew, the offspring of the Tattooed Arm and the perhaps the missionary St. Cosme, became the paramount chief.[143] The new leader was young and lacked experience.

A diminution in the quality of leadership soon affected the French as well. Bienville's departure for France in late 1725 left a void in the top ranks of the colony's government.[144] On August 8, 1726, the Compagnie des Indes appointed Étienne Périer to govern Louisiana. Périer came from a family of naval officers, and he had served in the Compagnie's West African slave posts. That fact that he had no experience in Native American diplomacy was of little consequence; his success in repelling an African assault on one of the Compagnie's forts in Senegal made him a fine candidate to deal forcefully with Louisiana's indigenous neighbors. Périer's conquest of a Dutch slaving post in Guinea proved his ability to deal with its European enemies.

4 / The Many Lands of Natchez Country

A modicum of tranquility descended on Natchez Country after the third conflict between the People of the Sun and the *habitants* of Louisiana. The period between 1724 and 1729 opened channels of cross-cultural exchange during which several Europeans learned more about their indigenous neighbors' society, religion, and politics. At times it appeared as if the two groups had learned to coexist. Some of the most effective means of engendering communal solidarity still worked for the Natchez. Nonetheless, pressures were at work just below the surface of the multiple landscapes that the natives and newcomers were constructing.

Bad Neighbors

As their numbers grew, the European residents of Natchez Country expanded their landholdings. After 1723, the struggles for the inner commons—those spaces between homes, fields, and gardens that were not individually owned, and the access to those parts of the environment—appeared to have died down. At least one incident, however, threatened the peace of the region about a year after the conflict. This affair bore some resemblance to the competition between the Apple Village and St. Catherine's Concession since it, too, involved unattended livestock. Lieutenant Dumont de Montigny left an account of an Indian's attack on a horse belonging to the White Earth Concession: "One day a Savage gave a blow with a *fleur de lys* [-shaped] weapon [literally: a casse-tête] to the flank of a brood mare . . . and not content to wounding it, he also cut off its tail; which the Savages of this place have regarded as a grand act of bravery and courage, as if one had taken a scalp, and by consequence the same as a declaration of war."[1] The nature of the weapon and the mark it left was particularly troublesome for the colonists who saw it. To them, the wound appeared as if an Indian had appropriated the punitive symbology of chattel slavery. It seemed as if it had come from the Code Noir, the body of laws enacted to control slaves, which contained an article that provided punishment for "thefts of . . . grain, fodder, peas, beans, or other vegetables." These laws mandated that such offenders "will be . . . beaten with a cane by the executioner of high justice and be marked [branded] by a *fleur-de-lys*."[2] It is unlikely that Native Americans knew the intricacies of French colonial law, but a person living in Natchez Country would have had many opportunities to see slaves who had received similar treatment.

The exact message the Indian intended to transmit is unclear. Was he "punishing" a beast that had "stolen" from an indigenous planting ground? Was he striking out against a creature that the colonists treated in much the same way as they treated Africans? The answers to these questions are lost, but it is clear that the *habitants* of the concession also recognized the assault as an act of belligerence. They notified Ignace Broutin, who was at this time the director of the Terre Blanche Concession. Broutin sent for the Tattooed Serpent, who quickly arrived at the scene. The Natchez leader inspected the wound and told the Frenchman that none of the people in his town possessed a weapon that left such a mark. He blamed the Tioux, a non-Natchez group subordinate to the Grand Village that lived in scattered settlements close to White Earth Concession.

Upon hearing this, Broutin summoned Bambouche, the headman of the Tioux, who was a "rascal," according to Dumont de Montigny. The Tioux headman said that his people were innocent because none of them owned a *fleur-de-lys*. He then cast the blame back upon the Natchez of the Grand Village. The charge irked the Great Sun, who, when he heard it, "brusquely responded, 'I see what is [needed] and hereby order it to be done.'"[3] Dumont de Montigny did not reveal exactly what action the statement of the headman triggered.

In the meantime, Broutin ordered a shot fired from the plantation's cannon to warn the *habitants* to prepare for another war. The blast led the Tattooed Serpent to conclude that the French were already on the march against nearby Natchez towns. He gathered the "honored men" of his nation and led them to the Terre Blanche Concession to chant the calumet with its director. After acknowledging that gesture, the Frenchman inquired, "Is it right that the concession should lose this brood mare?" The Tattooed Serpent responded, "No," and imposed a tax of one basket of corn from each household in Natchez Country, including those of the Tioux. According to Dumont de Montigny, the reparations were worth enough money "to pay an entire cavalry regiment."[4]

The incident demonstrated the accuracy that both the Europeans and the Natchez had acquired in gauging each other's intentions. The wounding of the horse was by this time a sign understood by all of the region's inhabitants. It also revealed the fact that at least one of the outlying villages continued to resist the accommodating policy of the Grand Village's Suns.

In this instance, the offense came from a group of non-Natchez living to the southwest of the Grand Village. Unlike the Apple Villagers, the Tioux lived farthest from the towns on the northeast that had contact with British traders. Therefore, commerce was probably not the motive for the Tioux since they did not have an unobstructed route to South Carolinian merchants residing among the Chickasaws. Instead, it suggests that anti-Louisianan sentiment had spread to members of a community that had supported the Tattooed Serpent when he allowed Bienville to destroy the Apple Village. With their shift away from their earlier stance, refractory towns on Natchez Country's northern and southern marchlands now flanked the concessions, European homesteads, Fort Rosalie, and the Grand Village.

Some of the old personalities and diplomatic strategies proved effective despite the Tioux's move against the colonists. It is evident that the Great Sun still retained a significant amount of political capital. His brother, the Tattooed Serpent, also wielded enough authority to organize a peace delegation in very short notice. His timely actions quashed further provocations from the Tioux. Moreover, he placated the Europeans by means of an established Mississippian practice: a corn tax. His main departure from past practice was the fact that the grain collected in this levy went to the Terre Blanche Concession rather than to the indigenous polity's main village. Furthermore, a policy of peaceful coexistence with the Europeans still enjoyed the backing of the hierarchy of the primary indigenous settlements even though that policy had become less popular among the more distant towns. The decline in those outliers' approval was most evident among the Tioux. By 1727, they had moved out of Natchez Country.[5]

The Land of the Spirits

The difficulties at Terre Blanche notwithstanding, the years following Bienville's 1723 expedition were golden times for eighteenth-century

Louisianan ethnographers. The European inhabitants who had made their homes around the Grand Village and Fort Rosalie enjoyed a period of peaceful interaction with their indigenous neighbors between 1724 and 1729. Decades later, both Le Page du Pratz and Dumont de Montigny drew upon their memories of these years when they composed their histories of the colony. The two appeared to have shared notes as they wrote some sections of their memoirs, at least until Le Page du Pratz published his in a series of articles in the *Journal Oeconomique* between 1751 and 1752. Dumont de Montigny, beaten to the punch while he was still busy writing his account, accused his erstwhile colleague of "gross inaccuracies."[6]

Nor were Dumont du Montigny and Le Page du Pratz the only colonists to leave their marks on the records of French Louisiana. Jean-Baptiste, sieur de Bienville, Étienne Périer, Pierre-François-Xavier Charlevoix, and others strove to write authoritatively about the region. Each of these men had motives to establish their expertise about Louisiana in general and Natchez Country in particular. Some, like Périer and Bienville, were driven by the need to explain away setbacks in which they played a role. Others, like De La Chaise, sought to aggrandize their positions within the colony's hierarchy. Still others simply sought recognition from France's intellectual community.[7]

A sure means to attract the attention of that community was to contribute to the emerging ethnographic discourse that was being fueled by increasingly popular travel literature. The French reading public eagerly consumed works on comparative religion such as those written by Bernard Picart and Joseph-François Lafitau. The latter was a Jesuit who had spent time in Canada as a missionary. His 1724 book, *Moeurs des sauvages amériquains: Comparées aux moeurs des premiers temps*, bore the stamp of earlier Jesuit missionaries who saw similarities between spiritual practices in East Asia, Judaism, and Christianity. Like his coreligionists, Lafitau sought to detect traces of biblical history and doctrine in Native American practices to prove that a common Abrahamic source existed for all religions. In one passage, he focused on the Natchez funeral rites based on the correspondence of Father Lemaire and other Catholic priests. Thus, Le Page du Pratz and Dumont de Montigny, who penned their memoirs in France during the 1740s and 1750s, had ample opportunities to gauge the French readership's interest in indigenous North America generated by these earlier writers. The public's appetite for accounts such as theirs became even more insatiable when the War of Austrian Succession (1740–48) underscored the strategic importance of the North American colonies. It is therefore not surprising that some of the most cited anecdotes from both authors' works involved the mourning ceremonies of the Natchez.

The burial of the Tattooed Serpent marked a moment in Natchez-Louisianan relations that secured Le Page du Pratz and Dumont de Montigny an enduring place in American ethnography. Major figures from both cultures attended the interment of the headman. Their accounts of the headman's final rites also provided vivid descriptions of Natchez spatial practices. These illustrated the means by which the landscape generated authority for the People of the Sun's leaders. The chroniclers took care to record their dialogues and, in some instances, to offer glimpses into these Native Americans' personalities. The ceremony also provided venues for elite Natchez women to speak to their neighbors in ways that highlighted their roles as intercultural diplomats.[8]

The episode recounted by the two authors began on the evening of June 1, 1725, when the Tattooed Serpent expired at home in the presence of his brother, the Great Sun, and his friend Le Page du Pratz. After the Natchez headman felt the cold body of his sibling, he stepped out of the cabin and said to the Dutchman, "He is dead." At that moment, the wife of the Tattooed Arm doused the fire inside the dwelling and let loose a mournful howl. The rest of her people, already aware of their leader's severe illness, heard her cries and echoed her lament. The wails of the People of the Sun carried from home to home across "the entire whole nation . . . and filled the neighboring woods." Off in the distance, two shots sounded to carry the news. Fires throughout Natchez Country were then extinguished to mark the commencement of five days of mourning.[9]

Even before the Tattooed Serpent's body was cold, another crisis threatened to destabilize his family's rule. Le Page du Pratz reported that the Great Sun had threatened to commit suicide if his brother failed to recover. Through the night of June 1 and the following day, anxiety over the loss of a key supporter among the Natchez wracked European army officers and concessions directors. Le Page du Pratz extracted a weak assurance from the Sun that he would not harm himself. After notifying Broutin and other important Louisianans, the Dutchman secured the aid of the Great Sun's heir apparent, who promised to give warning if the Natchez leader exhibited any self-destructive behavior.[10]

The newcomers also sought to prevent the sacrifice of the dead man's wives and servants. Dumont de Montigny, who was not present but who probably worked up his version with the help of Le Page du Pratz, claimed that as many as thirty Natchez had volunteered to die.[11] Dutisné, a commandant at Fort Rosalie who wrote an account nearly a year after the event, counted seventeen victims.[12] Although the pleas of the Europeans reduced the number of those slated for death, at least ten people followed the Tattooed Serpent to the grave. These lists of victims, though incongruous, were not without precedent; the numbers of those the Natchez sacrificed paled to insignificance when compared to the mass executions that archaeologists have uncovered at Cahokia. One burial site, dated around the twelfth century, contained two men whose bodies were richly adorned with shell beads. The tomb contained fifty-three women who had been sacrificed. One of the skeletons was that of an older women, whom one archaeologist characterized as a "matron" or a senior mate of one the two males.[13] These earlier practices bore similarities with the Natchez rites of the 1720s. During the rites for the Tattooed Serpent, two of his wives, his "lackey," pipe-bearer, doctor, and spokesman were publicly strangled and interred with the deceased Sun. One of the victims, the favorite wife of the Tattooed Serpent, took the opportunity to act as spokesperson for her people to the outsiders.

In her first recorded performance in that role, the Tattooed Serpent's mate spoke to European elites during one of the dances that took place a few days before the funeral. Besides Le Page du Pratz, Broutin and Dumanoir also heard her talk. She told them not to regret her death because she would soon join her husband in the Land of the Spirits. She told the "*chefs and nobles François*" that her husband's death "is as very regrettable for the French as it is for our Nation because he carried both in his heart, his ears were always full of the words of the French chiefs. He walked the same road as the French; and he loved them more than himself."[14]

The final phase of the rites involved the carriage of the headman's corpse to its final resting place. A close reading of Le Page du Pratz's and Dumont de Montigny's accounts reveals elements of Natchez spatial practices and the manner in which they anchored political authority to specific sites. Le Page du Pratz wrote that he and his compatriots seated themselves along the south wall of the Great Sun's home that stood atop a mound about eight to ten feet high. The Sun was inside his house so he could hear as little of the proceedings as possible. The Europeans' perch gave them a clear view from which they "could see everything, even inside the Temple, whose door faced us."[15]

The space between the Sun's cabin and the temple mound formed a plaza or "square." At the appointed hour, the "Master of Ceremonies" appeared, his entire body painted red except for his arms. He wore a headdress of red feathers and carried a red baton shaped like a cross. He led a delegation to the Great Sun's door to ask permission to begin the final rites for the Tattooed Serpent. After they had received the Sun's consent, the Master of Ceremonies proceeded to the dead man's house and let loose a mournful wail to which the people present responded in kind. The Master of Ceremonies and several of the oldest war chiefs carried a pallet of woven canes on which were placed the dead man's calumets. Next came four men who carried the Tattooed Serpent's remains on a bier slung between two poles. The bearers did not walk in a straight line; instead they traced a spiral path on the road to the temple square that covered as much ground as possible en route. Behind the retinue, a mother and father leaned against the wall of the house; in the father's arms was the lifeless body of their infant. Beneath their feet was a layer of Spanish moss, "as if they feared that they would profane the ground if they walked upon it."[16] The father tossed the dead child under the feet of the pallbearers as they passed. Once the procession passed over the little corpse, he retrieved it, caught up to the procession, and threw it under their feet again. He repeated the process until the group reached the temple mound. His sacrifice earned him and his spouse places among the ranks of the "honored people."

Seated in two rows on either side of the square were eight people who had volunteered to accompany the headman into the afterlife. It was at this point that the favorite wife of the Tattooed Serpent addressed the crowd attending the funeral. She exhorted her people's youths to "walk with the French, walk there like your father and me have walked there without deceit; talk with them as he and I have talked; do nothing contrary to the amity with the French, never tell lies about them." She turned to the "French chiefs" and told them, "Be friends always with the Natchez." She reminded them of the affection that she and her husband had shown them and admonished them to trade fairly with her people. After her speech, her relatives placed a deerskin over her head and strangled her with a rawhide cord.[17]

The name of the Tattooed Serpent's wife is lost to us, but her performances revealed several aspects of Natchez diplomacy. She had accompanied the dead leader on his missions to end the Village Crisis of 1722.[18] From the evening of the Tattooed Serpent's death until the close of the ceremonies, this high-status woman was the only Natchez who spoke directly to the assembled colonists. Although several private dialogues took place between Louisiana's elites and the Great Sun and other

FIGURE 4.1. The funeral procession of the Tattooed Serpent (from Le Page du Pratz). Museum of Natural History.

indigenous notables, only the wife of the Tattooed Serpent aimed her words at the European listeners during the public events. On her dying day, she carried out the responsibilities of her office by advocating for peace between the People of the Sun and the outsiders.[19]

The words that the wife of the Tattooed Serpent chose to convey her intentions also warrant examination. In Le Page du Pratz's accounts of the funeral, she called them "the French chiefs and nobles." At the end of her last speech, she said that she looked forward to the afterlife, a land "where finally she could eat with the French chiefs," since Natchez traditions forbade her from taking meals with foreigners.[20] Her rhetoric suggests that she recognized the parallels between her status and those of men like Dumanoir, Broutin, and Le Page du Pratz. For the wife of the Tattooed Serpent, this syncretism persisted beyond the grave. The historian Arnaud Balvay noted that her words also revealed her fears about the breakdown of intercultural relations with the passing of her husband.[21]

In Dumont de Montigny's version, his informant, most likely Le Page du Pratz, left his perch next to the Great Sun's home and walked down to the base of the mound to get a closer look.[22] He was able to see one of the priests "bless" the pills of crushed tobacco just before they were administered to those about to be sacrificed. A Sun who saw the European at the base of the hill told him, "It is good that the French stayed at the bottom of the mound and descended no further."[23] The victims swallowed the pills with a small drink. Next, their heads were covered with a deerskin, leather cords were wrapped around their necks, and teams of three men on either end of each line drew the cords tight "with all of their strength." All of the victims died with such swiftness that it was "impossible to describe."[24] Then, "the body of the Tattooed Serpent was placed in a large trench on the right side of the interior room of the Temple. His two wives were interred in the same trench. La Glorieuse, one of the Natchez's leading women, was buried on the right side of the Temple's entrance, the Chancellor [the Tattooed Serpent's spokesman], on the left. The others were carried to the Temples of their Villages and buried there. After this ceremony, according to their usage, the cabin of the deceased was burned."[25]

The Natchez burial practices described by Europeans who observed the Tattooed Serpent's interment bore resemblance to those of earlier Mississippian societies. Tombs at Cahokia contained dozens of sacrificed men, women, and children, some of whom died in extreme pain. Twentieth-century archaeologists found victims' skeletons with their hands still clenched in agony nearly a thousand years after their deaths.[26] The Natchez method of quick strangulation, which may have involved a

THE MANY LANDS OF NATCHEZ COUNTRY / 129

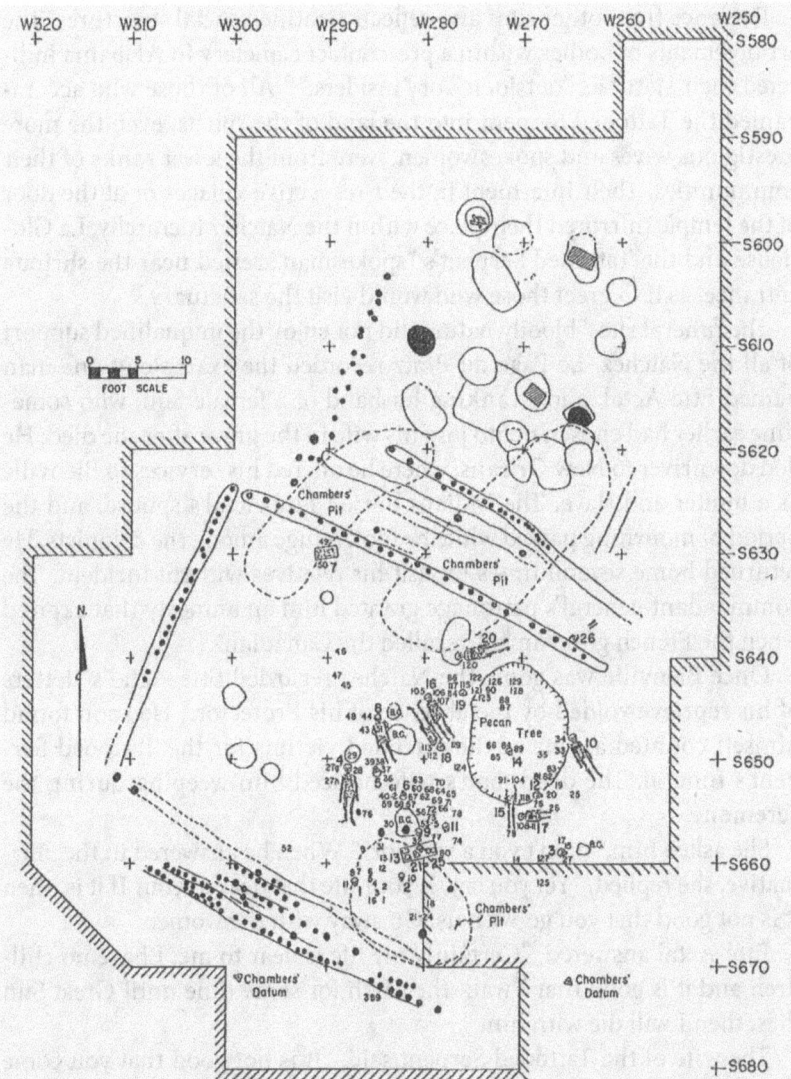

FIGURE 4.2. Plan of the historic Natchez temple on Building Level 2, Burial 1-26, Mound C. From "Archeology of the Fatherland Site: The Grand Village of the Natchez," *Anthropological Papers of the American Museum of Natural History*, vol. 51, part 1 (1965), by permission of the American Museum of Natural History.

severing of the spinal cord that caused instantaneous unconsciousness or death, was actually a relatively humane method of execution. More gruesome fates met those who died in Cahokia and elsewhere; their bodies bore the marks of blunt weapon trauma, decapitation, or stabbing.

Evidence from other sites also reflects stratified social structures. The arrangements of bodies within a pre-contact cemetery in Alabama indicated their status as "outsiders" or "insiders."[27] All of those who accompanied the Tattooed Serpent into the land of the spirits, even the more prestigious wives and spokeswomen, were from the lower ranks of their communities. Their interment in their respective villages or at the door of the temple mirrored their place within the Natchez hierarchy. La Glorieuse and the Tattooed Serpent's "spokesman" rested near the shrine's entrance, as if to greet those who would visit the sanctuary.[28]

The funeral rites' bloody nature did not enjoy the unqualified support of all the Natchez. Le Page du Pratz recorded the example of one man named Etté-Actal, a low-ranking husband of a female Sun, who sometime earlier had chosen not to join his wife in the grave after she died. He fled downriver to New Orleans, where he offered his services to Bienville as a hunter and slave. The Indians buried Etté-Actal's spouse, and the period of mourning passed while he took refuge among the colonists. He returned home several times to visit his relatives without incident. The commandant-general's patronage granted him an amnesty that expired when the French government recalled the Canadian.

Once Bienville was gone, the Natchez regarded Etté-Actal's "letters of his reprieve voided by the absence of his Protector." He soon found himself counted as one of the intended victims for the Tattooed Serpent's funeral. The dead man's wife noticed him weeping during the ceremony.

She asked him, "aren't you a warrior?" When he answered in the affirmative, she replied, "Yet you cry, is your life that dear to you? If it is, then it is not good that you go with us. Go away with the women."

Etté-Actal answered, "Certainly my life is dear to me; I have no children and it is good that I walk the earth for some time until Great Sun dies, then I will die with him."

The wife of the Tattooed Serpent said, "It is not good that you come with us and that your heart stay behind on this earth. I tell you again, take yourself away from here and do not let me see you again."

Two elderly Natchez women offered to take Etté-Actal's place among the sacrificial victims. Etté-Actal took advantage of this second reprieve. Le Page du Pratz wrote that "he became insolent and profited from the instructions that he gained from the French. He used them to dupe his Compatriots."[29]

Although Etté-Actal's experience represented aberrant behavior among the People of the Sun, the activities of another woman, the *femme chef* of the Natchez, represented a more concerted effort to change their funeral practices. According to Le Page du Pratz, some of their hierarchs were tiring of the bloodier aspects of their funerals. They had worked out a plan that involved him and some of the highest-ranking Théoloëls. One morning, sometime after the interment of the Tattooed Serpent, the Grande Soleille, or "Female Great Sun," came to call on him.

The Grande Solielle explained that the council thought it inhumane that wives should follow their husbands into the land of the spirits. In doing so, she expressed her doubts about Natchez eschatology with reasoning that resembled Catholic doctrine:

> It was an error to claim that a woman after death was still the wife of her husband in the land of the Spirits; it was the same to believe that in that land without pain there is game and all the food that one could wish for, because Spirits no longer need to eat. That error was not the smallest; since Spirits are no longer men nor women and can no longer live together and are no longer distinguished by Nationality, that if there were men and women living together and bearing children, that Spirits are immortal and in a state of youth, their number would multiply to infinity, that this was false and contrary to reason.[30]

The headwoman also divulged that the younger suns "did not have enough sense to listen to reason on this important business." Nor could the Natchez leaders count on "the female Suns to oppose this [practice] to which they consent voluntarily."[31]

She then made her proposal: she asked Le Page du Pratz to take her daughter as his wife. The Natchez hierarchs reasoned that once the Dutchman married the daughter of an important leader, the funeral sacrifices would stop. The People of the Sun would have to relent or face open war with the colonists. As the Grande Soleille said, "because you would have the protection of the French, and you have enough sense not to execute this Law."[32]

Upon hearing this, Le Page du Pratz exclaimed, "Do you take me for a 'stinkard?' because the daughters of the female Suns marry only the men of the People, and I pretended not to have the sense of what she had said to me."[33]

"She responded, no, to the contrary, it was because they wanted to extinguish this practice that I had been brought to their attention, that it was, in effect, to establish among them our [European] practice which was much better."[34]

Le Page du Pratz had cause for concern because the spouse of any Sun, male or female, followed their mate to the "Land of the Spirits." If he married the girl and she died before him, the Dutchman feared that he stood a very good chance of being strangled at her funeral. The Suns and the Grande Solielle were banking on the idea that the Europeans would prevent the sacrifice of the plantation manager as if he were a Natchez commoner.

The Female Sun might have another reason for giving her daughter to Le Page du Pratz. As the wife of the Great Sun, her life would be forfeit upon the death of her husband. She, too, would follow her mate into the land of the spirits if he died before her.

Despite her listener's reluctance to accept her offer, the Female Great Sun performed as a spokesperson for her people in her discussion with Le Page du Pratz. While her suggestion conformed to their marriage customs, it also revealed a significant departure from past practices. After a month of deliberations in which high-status women had taken part, the Suns had turned to a European to amend the custom of spousal sacrifice. In a sagacious adaptation of Catholic theology, the Natchez hierarchs employed a strategy that exemplified Richard White's "middle ground." White postulated that the "middle ground" was an intercultural space where both sides engage in an "attempt to understand the world and reasoning of the other and to assimilate enough of that reasoning to put it to their own purposes."[35] There is also the question of whether the Grande Soleille's statement constituted an instance of cultural ventriloquism on the part of Le Page du Pratz. In other passages of his memoir, he wasted few opportunities to associate indigenous spirituality with biblical stories.[36] Whatever the author's motive, the People of the Sun had apparently absorbed enough information from the missionaries and priests who lived in Natchez Country to place their system in a context that resonated with the outsider.

The role that Le Page du Pratz was to play within the Natchez polity if he married into the Suns' family is less clear. The only clue to his prospective status comes from the Female Great Sun's response to Le Page du Pratz's question about being mistaken for a "stinkard." She quickly moved on to the motives of the headmen of the Grand Village: they wanted to "extinguish" the nation's bloody funeral custom and desired French aid. The Grande Soleille's offer implied that the Suns recognized Louisiana's power and were willing for the Europeans to intervene in the Natchez order of things. Through the Grande Solielle's visit, the Suns tried to maneuver an influential colonist into a position that would benefit the Grand Village's leadership.

Their plan did not succeed, however, as Le Page du Pratz politely responded that he could not comply for religious reasons. He said that he would not marry a non-Christian, conveniently forgetting the fact that he had had a child with his Chitimacha slave. He also said that he feared that a daughter born to such a wife might become the object of some Frenchman's temporary affection.[37]

Heterotopias

These events of June 1725 also revealed fundamental aspect of the Natchez's spatial practices: the sacred nature of their ground. The Great Sun's home and mound, the temple and its mound, and the plaza or square that separated them exemplified what Michel Foucault called "heterotopias." These are sites that are "privileged or sacred or forbidden places" in which layers of meaning not immediately apparent are at work. Like all heterotopias, that of the Natchez required people for it to operate.

The Natchez square, perhaps the most prominent area in the descriptions left by the Europeans, represented an area where the other-than-human, the dead, and the living met and interacted. For the archaeologist Charles Wesson, plazas like this represented the "highly structured social positions of the upper world."[38] The Natchez square was a site that was simultaneously open and closed; accessible to those qualified to operate within it, and off-limits to those who were not.[39] During the Tattooed Serpent's funeral, sections of the plaza became charged with spiritual power. Those who tread upon it were either its officiates or its victims. The couple that had sacrificed their child as part the ritual insulated themselves from this energy with a barrier of Spanish moss.

The Europeans who watched the procession did so from the safe ground of the Great Sun's mound. When one of them walked toward the plaza to get a better view, he came close to entering this deadly zone. The comment of the Sun, "It is good that the French . . . went no further," suggested that serious consequences awaited those who took a few more steps.

The nearby Choctaws demonstrated a similar reverence for their public squares. In September 1729, the commandant-general sent Ensign Régis du Roullet to investigate their complaints about the unfair trading practices of one of Bienville's former agents. The officer journeyed to Couëchitto, one of the Choctaw's principal towns, to meet with their "Great Chief" in their town square. At the conclusion of their negotiations, three "honored men" carried him away to a prepared feast. Much like the Natchez, they protected the sacred ground of their plaza from the footsteps of an unauthorized visitor.[40]

The Creek Indians also employed public squares. They called towns important enough to have such spaces "talwas." These towns often served as political and spiritual centers for several nearby villages.[41] Buildings with religious and political purposes surrounded these spaces.[42] The Creek town square has been characterized as "a symbolic microcosm"; a place where its "sacred ground, its shelters, and the ritualized movement of males through them expressed Creek ideas about the structure of the tribal universe."[43]

The empowerment of similar terrain in Natchez Country was also related to the movement across it—in this case, of a funeral procession. The historian Thomas Tweed noted that human spirituality involves some measure of "crossing"—changes in the locations or conditions of its practitioners. He also argued that funeral rites exemplified change in both of these aspects.[44] As pallbearers crossed the plaza, they not only carried the Tattooed Serpent from his home to his grave, but they also transported him from one plane of existence to another. The circular path traced by the bearers increased the surface area consecrated by their transit. Nor were the dead man and those who would soon join him in the afterlife the only people transformed by the passage of the bier. The sacrifice of the infant that they crushed beneath its bearers' feet propelled its parents from the ranks of the commoners to that of "honored people."

In some ways, the transformative "crossing" of the funeral procession over the plaza's sacred ground resembled another sort of movement in different Natchez social practice. Dumont de Montigny described the Fête de Tonne de la valeur, a festival that took place in July immediately before the harvest. Eight days before the celebration, the townspeople cleared a route of about three-and-a-half miles from the Grand Village to the location of the *tonne* or a granary. The day before the feast, a litter was fashioned from a finely painted buffalo hide upon which the Great Sun had slept. The next morning, the headman dressed in European clothes and mounted the litter. The Natchez men formed a column of four or five ranks.[45] They lifted the Great Sun and his buffalo skin over their heads and passed him hand over hand the entire distance from the Grand Village to the granary several miles away. Dumont de Montigny reported that they did so with such speed that the officers from Fort Rosalie who were watching were unable to keep pace even though they were on horseback. The Sun, transported by this method, arrived at his destination fifteen minutes before the mounted officers.[46] Like the funeral of the Tattooed Serpent, the ritual conveyance of the leader constituted a crossing rife with spiritual significance—in this case a means to gather his people for a late-summer harvest festival that lasted six days.[47] Moreover, like the plaza between the temple and Great Sun's mound, the ground over which the two men traveled was carefully prepared and well known. The Great Sun's attire also denoted the transformative nature of the ritual. It advertised his wealth as well as his ability to negotiate with outsiders who made them.[48] This heterotopic path literally linked the homes of the celebrants with a site of production—-it united the consumers with the consumed.

The Europeans, particularly the Roman Catholics, were no strangers to sacred processions. The church historian John McManners noted that "every parish had its calendar of parades in honour of some special day, some sacred relic."[49] Ecclesiastical architects designed exterior walkways and interior passages to facilitate formal crossings over consecrated grounds. In the words of Patricia Seed, "To say the word 'ceremony' implied a parade or procession, but only in French."[50] These crossings served other purposes: "Theatrical rituals often created French possession of the New World through carefully choreographed steps by costumed participants bearing carefully chosen props, accompanied by music, and culminating in the climactic moment of cross- or standard-planting." Although the Tattooed Sun's funeral rites were more sanguine (and, so it seems, all the more riveting for the outsiders who watched them), they followed an intelligible routine. The movement of Natchez bodies, both living and dead, dressed for the occasion, symbolized their relationship to specific locales.[51]

This energizing capacity extended into a vertical as well as a horizontal plane. The march terminated at the temple, the final resting place of the Tattooed Serpent and his wives. Those who interred him inserted the power that he bore during life into the ground—where it was permanently "sedimented" into this landscape.[52]

For the Natchez, mounds framed their heterotopia. From the summits of their man-made hillocks, Natchez leaders projected their authority. The two mounds described by Dumont de Montigny were about eight to ten feet in height. These promontories, diminutive as they were, provided a vantage point over the surrounding terrain. Their physical elevation, however, was less important than the visible difference they represented in relation to the surrounding community.[53] Those who lived on or were entombed in the mounds were a group set above and apart from the rest of the village. The flat plain that made up the Grand Village extended to the far side of St. Catherine's Creek. Thus the burials raised those who commanded the respect of the Natchez peoples literally and figuratively.

In contrast to the carefully articulated landscape of the Natchez, the Europeans who lived in the area had yet to hit upon an effective system of land use. There was no gridwork of streets of a planned town or meandering lanes of a French *terroir*. Instead, a tangle of footpaths and cart tracks connected the homesteads situated between the Grand Village and Fort Rosalie. The *habitants* had not re-created the centralized towns of western Europe, nor had they adopted the "ribbon farms," the long, narrow holdings with frontage along the riverbanks like those in Canada or around New Orleans. Instead, each planter or soldier who wished to do so purchased his plots from a nearby Native American landholder. Le Page du Pratz's farm on the trail that led from the post to the Grand Village represented a prime example of a transaction between two individuals, one native, the other a newcomer. He bought a cabin and a cleared field of six arpents (approximately five acres) from a "*Naturel*."[54]

Dumont de Montigny cited these unregulated real estate transactions as a primary cause of friction between the Natchez and Louisianans. While his observations had merit, the imprecise nature of the sales led to friction between individual colonists. He was not alone in his opinions about the chaotic nature of land tenure in Natchez Country. Broutin mentioned his role in resolving these disputes in a letter to the directors of the Compagnie des Indes. To reinforce his request for an appointment as the provincial engineer, he listed among his accomplishments a survey of the *habitations* near the fort. He proposed the drafting of a cadastral map of Natchez Country to be kept in New Orleans to register future land sales, but Bienville and the Superior Council showed little interest in the project.[55]

In short, unlike their indigenous neighbors, the Europeans who lived between the Grand Village and the Mississippi failed to work out an intelligible pattern for land use. The lack of such a system would fuel the tensions that led to the Natchez War of 1729.

Other conditions in Natchez Country highlighted the Europeans' carelessness regarding their own spiritually charged spaces. Unlike those of the Natchez, the immigrants' religious heterotopias—those intersections of the sacred and the profane; the individual and the community; where questions of life and death were met and resolved—were in shambles.

To fulfill their contract with the Compagnie des Indes, the Capuchins sent Father Philibert to minister to the *habitants* and soldiers in Natchez Country. According to a letter written by Father Raphael, his superior in New Orleans, Philibert's ministry was not an easy one. The Capuchin lived in a decaying presbytery beneath the bluffs that bordered the Mississippi River. The home had once belonged to the late Father Maximin, an Augustinian priest who had served as the post cure. Part of the adjoining garden had been swept away by the river. Philibert's difficulties did not end with poor accommodations.[56]

Captain Du Tisné, who had replaced Desliettes (who had replaced Broutin) as commandant of Fort Rosalie, requisitioned the building that Father Philibert had been using as a kitchen. He was forced to say mass in a section of the presbytery without a paved floor, a roof, or windows, and could fit only twenty parishioners even though the parish's communicants numbered more than two hundred. The cemetery was also in poor shape. It lacked a wall, leaving it "exposed to all [sorts] of profanities." The *habitants* refused to bear the expense of building a proper church and complained that such undertakings were the Compagnie's responsibility. These sites provided a marked contrast to the Natchez temple, their mounds, and the homes of the Great Sun and his retinue.

There were certain areas, however, where Europeans' spatial arrangements differed radically from their otherwise shoddy constructions. Again, Dumont de Montigny, in his role as engineer, furnished glimpses of those areas. In several of his maps of Natchez Country, he depicted the neat layouts of the Terre Blanche and St. Catherine's Concessions. In the first of these two plantations, he showed the director's home, a dovecote, a kitchen, an outdoor oven, a pigsty, a paddock, and a chicken coop. Nearby he placed the guards barracks. In the upper-right corner he drew the *loge de negres* [sic], "the negroes lodges." He also included a bell beneath the dovecote that he labeled *appel des negres* (call the negroes). He drew St. Catherine's Concession with a comparable layout; a gridwork of alleys separated buildings of equal size. Dumont de Montigny did not mark the second plantation as carefully as the first, but it is safe to assume that the structures served a similar purpose.

Consequently, the best examples of European heterotopias in Natchez Country were the systematized spaces of "otherness" of the concessions' slave quarters. The layout of their precincts gave the slaveholders lines of sight that, in the words of Foucault, "eliminate the effects of imprecise distributions, the uncontrolled disappearance of individuals, their diffuse circulation, their unusable and dangerous coagulation; it was a tactic of

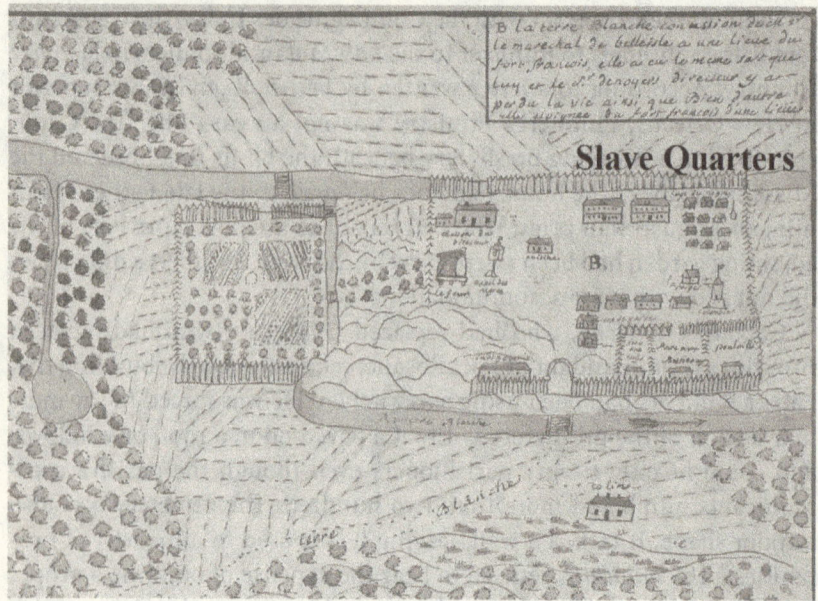

FIGURE 4.3. Terre Blanche Concession, detail from Dumont de Montigny (Archives nationales de France [Paris] Cartes et Plans, N III Louisiane 1/2).

anti-desertion, anti-vagabondage, anti-concentration." Although Foucault wrote about the heterotopias of military camps, his observations apply to the slave wards in colonial Louisiana. Moreover, they "engendered segregating spaces" within the area between the concessions, the Grand Village, and the Mississippi River that otherwise contained very diverse populations. In short, the most organized ground in the European-dominated sphere was that which was created to supervise and discipline slaves. Other terrains were little more than amorphous plots hacked out of parklands to form kitchen gardens, livestock paddocks, and tobacco fields, all presided over by a few post-in-earth huts.[57]

A People of Many Lands

Problems other than land use plagued the Europeans in Natchez Country. By 1725, the subjects of Louis XV had become rambunctious and divided, especially as they began to finally make progress toward the efficient cultivation of tobacco. A few months after the end of Bienville's War, rifts began to appear among the *habitants*. Disputes arose when the work contracts of the first wave of *engagés* expired. Large numbers of these erstwhile colonists returned to France during the mid-1720s.[58] Other former indentured workers found that their only recourse was to initiate legal proceedings to force their employers to make good on their labor agreements.

For example, in April 1724, Antoine Le Vouf filed suit in New Orleans seeking his back wages for three years of his labor at St. Catherine's Concession. He claimed that he was owed 500 livres for his efforts.[59] Later that summer, a free African named Raphael Bernard also petitioned the Superior Council to order Dumanoir to pay him. Five years earlier, Dumanoir had recruited Bernard in France to work in Louisiana, which Bernard had done with diligence. Not only had Dumanoir refused to compensate him, but he also had seized Bernard's personal effects. Eventually Raphael Bernard won a partial victory when the Superior Council ordered that his possessions be released and that Dumanoir remit 100 livres of the 1,000 livres that he owed.[60] Henry Gaspalliere lodged a similar complaint in September 1724. He requested that Dumanoir be made to pay him for his time at the concession. Moreover, he wanted to be paid in cash, not tobacco, as Dumanoir attempted to do.[61] These actions were only the vanguard of a wave of lawsuits against Dumanoir, both in his role as director of St. Catherine's Concession and for financial obligations that he had taken on personally.

Between 1724 and 1727, the Superior Council of Louisiana heard at least nine cases that dealt directly with the concession director. Roughly half concerned some action for back wages. He also faced suits by wealthier members of colonial society. Jean Baptiste Raquet demanded that Dumanoir make good on a note for 2,700 livres. In May 1724, Philippe Vincent Guenot de Trefontaine filed to recover the wages of his late brother to the tune of 3,000 livres. Pierre Guenot had been a subdirector of St. Catherine's until he was wounded at the onset of Bienville's War. After the conflict, he traveled to New Orleans, where he later succumbed to infection. A year later, the dead man's estate was still the subject of hearings.[62]

The mounting lawsuits were taking so much of Dumanoir's time that he had to move to the provincial capital. His relocation to New Orleans created even more debt for the hapless manager.[63] Antoine Brusle, a member of the Superior Council, attached Dumanoir's goods for the amount of 800 livres owed him for rent on a house in New Orleans. Despite a countersuit, Brusle obtained a favorable verdict by the end of 1724.[64]

A positive finding by the Council, however, was no guarantee of satisfaction for a suitor. One of the more poignant examples of the inability of plaintiffs to obtain compensation was the case of the former *engagé* François Gigot. In June 1725, he took Dumanoir to court for three years of unpaid wages that totaled 900 livres.[65] This must have been one of Gigot's final acts because the following month his widow repeated the request to the Superior Council. Although the Council found in her favor, the debt had not been retired as late as 1731.[66]

The suits continued to pile up on the docket. Finally, in May 1727, the Company of St. Catherine's Concession fired Dumanoir and replaced him with François de Mandeville.[67] The manager's ouster did not end his legal problems. The new director requested the seizure of Dumanoir's papers and asked for an inventory of his personal goods. Mandeville also demanded that the former director yield an enslaved African woman "who had been useful at the Concession." He also sought the return of a Native American hunter who had worked for the plantation.[68]

St. Catherine's Concession, however, remained mired in debt and litigation. In 1727, Jean Daniel Kolly decided to come and see for himself, "without rancor," the state of affairs in which he and his associates were now enmeshed. In a letter to an unnamed associate, he requested that Dumanoir be hauled back to France by a *lettre de cachet*, a preauthorized royal warrant, to answer for his management of the estates.[69] A preliminary review of the Company of St. Catherine's liabilities included 33,333 livres owed to the *engagés* with approximately 25,000 livres slated for the officers of the firm. Marcel Giraud determined that by 1731, the Company of St. Catherine's had amassed debts amounting to a half million livres owed to various creditors with another 170,000 for African slaves and provisions borrowed from the Compagnie des Indes.[70]

The other concession in Natchez Country, Terre Blanche, also faced difficulties. The tobacco production lagged when the specialized workers from Clairac returned to Europe. In 1723, Captain Berneval, acting as an agent for the Compagnie des Indes, set the price for the concession, which then passed into the hands of the Le Blanc-Belle Isle Associates.[71] The plantation was under the control of a series of managers between 1723 and 1729, among whom was the engineer Ignace Broutin. Although it, too, was the focus of some litigation, usually for borrowed supplies, Terre Blanche endured fewer legal troubles than St. Catherine's Concession.[72]

Legal matters were not the only source of division among the Europeans who lived in Natchez Country. Another rift had its roots in Louisiana's founding. Nearly all of the key individuals who took part in the reconnaissance of the Gulf Coast and Lower Mississippi Valley—the Le Moyne brothers, Iberville, Bienville, Châteauguay, and Sérigny, as well as

Le Sueur, Boisbriant, and Saint Denis—came from Canada. A significant proportion of the earlier settlers around Mobile also were Canadians.[73] The political scientist Alfred Hero argued that these North Americans struggled with appointees from France for control of the province.[74]

Yet another source of friction lurked close below the surface: religion. Louis XIV annexed lands along France's eastern frontier that contained large numbers of non-Catholics, and Louisianans felt the effects of this influx of outsiders. Protestants played a role in the province's development from its earliest days. Charles O'Neill estimated that 10 percent of the colonists were not communicants of the established church.[75] Even though Father de la Vente managed to convert some of them during his first months in Mobile in 1704, others arrived to take their place.[76] It follows that Natchez Country also had its share of "heretics." Some of its earliest and most important non-native residents, such as the Huguenot journalist Andre Penicault, were not adherents to the official religion.[77] At least one of Penicault's employers at Crozat's trading post near the Grand Village was a member of the "so-called reformed religion." Father Raphael, however, later vouched for Marc Antoine de La Loire's conversion to Catholicism.[78] Whether the other La Loire brother held to the same creed is unclear, but at least two of the Europeans among the first to live among the Natchez worshiped in different manners than the Black Robes and other clerics.

Some of Natchez Country's non-Catholic Europeans came from Languedoc, the southern part of the kingdom where Louis XIV had crushed the Protestant Camisard rebellion only a few decades earlier. Jacques de Barbazant de Pailloux, one-time commandant of Fort Rosalie, came from that region. *Commissaire-ordinateur* La Chaise, in his rush to discredit Bienville's associates, accused Pailloux of "bearing arms against the King at Cevennes," a Protestant stronghold that had resisted forced conversion in 1702.[79] The twentieth-century historian Marcel Giraud also counted him among the converts from Protestantism.[80] The tobacco workers from Clairac who staffed the Terre Blanche Concession also came from an area in southwestern France that was a Huguenot bastion. These distinctions were most likely apparent to the Native Americans; they must have noticed that some Europeans refused to join in the celebration of the Mass or other Catholic rituals.

As their heterogeneous religious practices suggest, the "French" in Louisiana were actually a mixture of various peoples. Nor was their allegiance to France or its monarch a foregone conclusion. Louis XIV had authorized his colonial project in the Lower Mississippi Valley during a period in which many of his subjects had no notion of a "French" identity. Indeed, some of those living on the eastern marches of the kingdom had only just come under his rule. As the historian David A. Bell noted: "It had not seemed particularly strange to most observers that most subjects of the French king spoke Occitan, German, Basque, Breton, Catalan, Italian, Yiddish, or distinct French dialects, rather than standard French. Such diversity was the rule, not the exception in most of Europe at the time."[81]

The paucity of records makes the search for these "foreign" elements among the *habitants* difficult. The destruction of Fort Rosalie in 1729 obliterated locally stored documents. Floods, fire, weather, and insects degraded those held in New Orleans. The task becomes even more complicated by immigrants' tendency to translate or transliterate their names to French.[82] The best evidence of non-French habitation comes from the copies of official records sent to Paris during the eighteenth century, where they were kept in good condition. These archives hold censuses taken in 1722 and 1726. Broutin's 1723 map also listed the names of some of the region's *habitants*. Father Philibert's roll of those killed in November 1729 and the sacramental registers of the survivors provide further clues. These items, along with the transcripts of the Louisiana Superior Council's meetings, reveal some of the roots of Natchez Country's European residents.

By far the largest contingent of non-French colonizers came from the Rhine Valley. Among this group, the German names of many residents of Natchez Country stand out. Two Germans, Jean Bierzel and Jean Mayeur, sailed on the *Loire* in 1720 with Dumanoir and his workforce bound for St. Catherine's Concession. Jean George Schulz *dit l'allemand* (called the German) and Pierre Schmitt, Jean Chit, and the notary Kneper were also obvious representatives of German immigration.

Other *habitants* came from lands even farther removed from the borders of France. Among them were émigrés from Bohemia that included Jean Evrard, Monsieur Stroup, and his unnamed brother-in-law. Many of these men, often accompanied by their wives and children, arrived in Louisiana during the massive wave of immigration of the early 1720s.[83]

The next major group of immigrants born in regions not controlled by Louis XV was from Switzerland. Captain Merveilleux sailed in 1720 on the *Deux Freres* with his company of Swiss workers, together with more than one hundred civilians from his homeland. Many of these men and women scattered throughout the colony after they came ashore. Nonetheless, there were several Swiss who lived at or around the fort or served in its garrison. Pierre Gaulas, for instance, hailed from Switzerland, and Michel Beau came from Bern, as did his wife.[84] One might consider Jean-Daniel Kolly and his son two of the last Swiss "immigrants" to Natchez Country. Their stay was indeed short for, a few days after they arrived, Natchez warriors killed them both while they visited Terre Blanche.

Consequently there was little in the way of national symbols around which the population of the homeland could rally, let alone those exiled to a hard life in the interior of North America. The next Bourbon to ascend to the throne after the death of Louis XIV was a child of six during the Hostage Crisis of 1716. The boy's uncle Phillip, duc d'Orleans, ruled in his stead until 1723. Social and religious solidarity were sorely lacking in Louisiana; the stresses of a new environment, disease, and war only exacerbated an already difficult situation.

Another Grand Village

Whatever differences existed among the general population, Bienville remained a lightning rod for much of the colony's discontent after his 1723 campaign. His ministrations as the chief officer of Louisiana made him a target for accusations of profiteering and favoritism. The colony's geography constituted a factor in these charges of corruption.

The province's first capital was too far up the shallow Tenasaw River to allow oceangoing vessels to off-load at the town. Although this location offered a modicum of protection from Spanish attack, ships were forced to discharge their cargoes on Dauphine Island. From there, smaller craft carried goods north to Mobile. The labyrinth of tidal creeks between the island and the town made for convenient smuggling routes to the interior.

Bienville's critics claimed that he used them to divert the king's supplies into his network of traders along the Tenasaw and Chickasawhay Rivers. An investigation conducted in February 1708 by the French-born Jean-Baptiste Martin D'Artiguiette Diron "concluded that although Bienville was far from blameless in the controversies splitting the lower Louisiana, he was the best person available to run the colony."[85] Indeed, Bienville's style of leadership exemplified "rogue colonialism," an "impulse toward experimentation [that] was local, arising from ... the practical knowledge and flexible survival strategies the colonial frontier necessitated."[86]

Despite his business acumen and local influence, Bienville continued to attract the ire of those appointed by the ministry of marine, Crozat, and the Compagnie des Indes. His run-ins with Cadillac resulted in a brief stint under house arrest. Bienville's spectacular success achieved with particularly roguish methods during the Hostage Crisis of 1716, together with the governor's irascible nature, led to Cadillac's ouster the same year. Once his nemesis departed, Bienville ruled Louisiana as commandant-general, although he longed for the power and prestige that came with the title of governor. While in charge of the colony, he put his stamp upon its landscape that persists until the present.

Bienville's decision in 1718 to locate New Orleans on a narrow strip of swampy terrain along the Mississippi constituted the Canadian's most permanent mark on the province. As Richard Campanella explained: "Had Bienville located New Orleans farther upriver (such as at Bayou Manhac or Natchez), the city would have been too inconvenient for coastal traffic and unable to answer enemy incursions. In other words: good sites, but bad situations."[87] Access to Lake Pontchartrain saved travelers from Mobile the trouble of sailing up the Mississippi against the current. The Bayou Saint Jean reduced the distance between the two bodies of water to roughly two miles.

Ironically, Bienville's choice served to undermine his influence when New Orleans became the colony's capital in 1722. The Canadian's power had been predicated on maintaining a distance between the Europeans and Native Americans of the province that could be bridged only through his meditation. Since the town stood astride what had been the "backdoor" that led to the interior, the settlement furnished a site for the surveillance of commerce entering the region from the south. Thus smuggling goods to Native communities became more difficult. The riverside location also gave the Superior Council ready access to information that drifted down from the north. Key European policy makers could hear for themselves the news of the upper reaches of the provinces without the help of Bienville's diplomatic and trading network. Once direct communications opened up, the commandant-general and his associates lost their monopoly as cultural brokers.[88]

The new capital also served as a stage for the power struggle between Bienville and the colony's government. In December 1722, Versailles appointed Jacques de La Chaise, nephew of Louis XIV's Jesuit confessor, to investigate Louisiana's finances. La Chaise took a seat on the Superior

Council and began to expand its authority. Bienville and his supporters quickly found themselves overmatched by La Chaise, who enjoyed the support of influential patrons in the *métropole*.[89] Bienville's handling of the Village Crisis of 1722, particularly his gifts to the Tattooed Serpent, and his questionable business dealings, provided La Chaise with enough ammunition to wrench the commandant-general from his office. The king recalled Bienville to France in April 1724. The Canadian turned command over to his cousin, Pierre Sidrac Dugué de Boisbriant, and departed for Lorient in April 1725.[90]

La Chaise's investigation of Bienville represented part of a broader initiative to rationalize the colony's political and economic structures. This initiative included furnishing the Superior Council with more extensive legislative powers. The Compagnie des Indes intended that these changes would protect its interest and spur growth in the province's agricultural and commercial sectors.

As a reflection of its newfound power, the Superior Council remade the New Orleans geography. It commissioned Adrien de Pauger, a French-born military engineer, to draft a municipal design for the settlement. Pauger superimposed a grid of streets that centered on a *place d'armes*, a church, and a governor's mansion. His work survives to this day as the French Quarter. Shannon Dawdy argued that his network of thoroughfares exemplified the spatial practices of a second component of "rogue colonialism": "formal and abstract planning initiatives originating in Europe that mobilized people and resources on an ambitious scale in a deliberate effort to engineer landscapes, economies, and even societies."[91] The regularity of the streets, superimposed on the flat terrain of the capital, stood in stark contrast to the chaotic web of footpaths and cart tracks that threaded through the parklands of Natchez Country.

Another crucial component of the Compagnie's plan involved the revitalization of tobacco cultivation that had stagnated despite the wild boasts of John Law. In turn, a compliant workforce was crucial to make profitable tobacco production a reality, which meant that Louisianans would need more African slaves. The new commandant would not require the diplomatic acumen of his predecessor because the colony's future would not depend so heavily on its relationships with Native Americans. Instead, it would need a leader experienced in the French Atlantic slave trade to control the province's captive workforce.

The new commandant-general, Étienne Périer, was eminently qualified for the job. Born in 1690 to a Norman seafaring family, he fought in the French navy during the War of Spanish Succession. While in command of some of the Compagnie's vessels during 1720s, he and his brother, Antoine-Alexis, helped to capture the Dutch slaving stations Arguin and Pontendick on the West African coast. He also saw action in Malabar, India.[92] During that time, he acquired the military background as well as familiarity with the Compagnie's traffic in human beings. As a result, he arrived in Louisiana with the expertise to repel European invasions, defend against attacks from indigenous peoples, and put down slave rebellions. Thus, the directors of the Compagnie des Indes could expect Périer to protect their interests in North America despite Louisiana's highly factionalized politics.

When the new commandant-general arrived in the spring of 1727, he found another rivalry already simmering between the Jesuits' Superior, Nicholas Ignatius de Beaubois, and the head of the Capuchins, Father Raphael de Luxembourg. Although the Capuchins had little experience proselytizing Native Americans, they were past masters in revitalizing religious practice in the French countryside. For more than a hundred years, they had done so through domestic missions utilizing groups of traveling priests called visitations. These clerics spent several weeks at local parishes to encourage lapsed believers to return to the Church and to educate the laity on the basics of Catholic doctrine.[93] The Capuchins' expertise with these missions held great promise for improving the morals in the notoriously amoral colony. Sin, however, was not the only barrier to their work; they faced another obstacle in the form of a coreligionist.

In 1727, a few years after they had come to Louisiana, the Capuchins found that they had to contend with Father Beaubois. The Jesuit had just returned from Paris after his high-profile tour with several headmen from the Missouri Indians.[94] Once back in the province, Beaubois began to seek a greater role for the Jesuits. He missed few opportunities to point out the Capuchins' failure to gain converts among the Amerindians of Louisiana. In turn, the Capuchin Superior Raphael resisted Beaubois's machinations because he feared that they represented the thin edge of the wedge that the Jesuits would use to take complete charge of the religious life of the colony.[95]

The tensions between the two groups escalated further when Father Beaubois aligned himself with Bienville's faction, which remained powerful even after the Canadian's departure. The Jesuit purchased Bienville's estate upriver from New Orleans to serve as a way station for the missionaries of his order. According to previous agreements between the Compagnie's director of ecclesiastical affairs, Abbé Gilles Bernard Raguet, and the Capuchin and Jesuit orders, Beaubois's ecclesiastical powers were limited and he was not to function as a parish priest.[96] Beaubois, however, ignored these restrictions by hearing the confessions of local townspeople and allowing them to attend Mass in the estate's chapel. Almost as if to add fuel to the fire, the Ursulines, an order of nuns contracted by the Compagnie to run its hospital, elected the Jesuit as their spiritual overseer without Raphael's permission.[97] Worse, Beaubois began to claim that he, not Raphael, was the vicar of the bishop of Québec. If his assertion stood, Beaubois would be the head of the Catholic Church in Louisiana.

One of the more revealing bits of evidence regarding the personalities of these clerics came from Marc Antoine Calliot, a clerk for the Compagnie des Indes. He characterized Father Raphael as a "holy man" and praised his "zeal for the advancement of the Divine Glory." Calliot contrasted the Capuchins with "the other fathers who secretly live disordered lives which is not necessary to relate. They go about dressed in lace sleeves and silk breeches, with silver shoe buckles, snuff boxes, watches, and carrying parasols."[98] Though he did not accuse Father Beaubois by name, the implication is clear. Since there were few priests in New Orleans at the time, Father Beaubois is an obvious choice for the object of Calliot's accusations.

Périer dealt with these ecclesiastical disputes without favoritism. He also took credit for the fact that the two priests had not filed lawsuits against one another.[99] Nonetheless, within a year Beaubois had fomented sufficient discord to convince his coadjutor in Paris to recall him. The troublesome priest left New Orleans in the spring of 1729.[100] The problems that plagued the Church in Louisiana, however, extended beyond the capital into Natchez Country.

Beaubois's criticism regarding the Capuchins' lack of Native American converts was not without merit. Although the order ran missions in Africa, it seemed better suited for reinvigorating Catholic practice among the peasantry of France. Raphael and his colleagues had their hands full with a similar task in Louisiana. Faced with a raucous moral climate among the colonists, Father Philibert had enough trouble ministering to his extant congregation. He had little time to find proselytes among the Natchez. Philibert's record in that area was as bleak as those of his predecessors, Fathers Maximin and St. Cosme.

Father Raphael also noted that the post commander, Captain Du Tisné, made the situation worse. The officer assigned to other tasks the only man capable of assisting Philibert during the Mass. When Raphael visited his beleaguered colleague, Du Tisné refused to allot him a seat in a boat traveling downriver for his return trip to New Orleans. This snub forced the priest and his assistant to spend an extra month in Natchez Country.

Raphael also accused Du Tisné of an "abominable crime," a euphemism for sodomy.[101] The priest cited complaints of a youth who served at the commander's earlier post in Illinois; the statements of a "young German boy"; and the corroborating testimony of Lieutenant Dumont de Montigny.[102] Though same-sex relationships were not unusual among Native Americans, these charges carried weight when leveled against European colonists. By the time Raphael wrote his letter in 1726, the Superior Council had come to the conclusion that "Du Tisné was no longer fit to command" Fort Rosalie. The members of the Council agreed that the post had "lost much without Disliettes who subdued the *Sauvages* and established tranquility among the *habitants.*"[103]

The man sent to relieve Du Tisné at Fort Rosalie was no improvement in the priest's eyes. Captain Louis Merveilleux practiced the "so-called reformed religion" and made no secret of his faith. Raphael observed that, "we have a Calvinist commandant succeeding a bad Catholic." Merveilleux, born in Switzerland as Ludwig von Wunderlich, immigrated to Louisiana in 1720 and changed his name to fit into the francophone population.[104] Raphael's 1726 report to the Compagnie's director of religious affairs mentioned several other Protestants in the province, including Louboey, commandant of Biloxi, and D'Arensbourg, the Swedish leader of the German colonists in Louisiana.[105] African slaves—arguably the largest contingent among the newcomers, stood apart from the general population in even starker terms.

A jumble of places made up Natchez Country by the mid-1720s—some organized while others were not. There was the homeland of the Théoloëls, the People of the Sun. They operated a portal to the Land of the Spirits, a unique built environment that followed the rules of a discrete spatial grammar. Around them lived a polyglot community of Europeans from several European states as well as France. Their landscape seemed to adhere to no grand scheme. The newcomers had allowed their sacred ground to deteriorate or fall into the Mississippi River. Their new central village downriver was frequently inundated. Factional strife constantly tore at New Orleans almost as if to mimic the routine destruction wrought by the Mississippi's floodwaters. The only areas that the Europeans built that followed a recognizable plan were those built to imprison captive African and Indian laborers. A military slaving society had arrived in Natchez Country. Unlike the indigenous raiders who snatched their victims and disappeared into the forests, this slaving society from overseas was there to stay.

5 / "These Are People Who Named Themselves Red Men"

On a day in the late spring of 1728, a Natchez man whom his French "owner" had named "Bontemps" mounted a scaffold in New Orleans. A free African man, Louis Congo, the colony's official executioner, placed a rope around his neck.[1] Bontemps was a thief. He had stolen a handful of silver coins. Worse, he had stolen himself; he was a slave who belonged Sieur Trudeau. Moreover, he had been convicted by the word of another enslaved Natchez held by the Capuchin Fathers who lived in the town. Bontemps's death at the hands of Congo—an Indian killed by an African on behalf of a European—illustrated the declining status of Native Americans in an increasing racialized colonial society.

The arrival of large numbers of African slaves at the farms and concessions around Fort Rosalie placed the People of the Sun in contact with a form of labor alien to their social hierarchy. Their proximity to the concessions exposed the Natchez to a discourse of racial categories that constituted the social and legal foundations for European-style chattel slavery. These experiences eventually helped these Indians to reframe the rhetoric of "race" for their own purposes. Their appropriation of the discourse became all the more vital as they became aware of the fact that the French were well on their way to including Native peoples in the same social stratum as their captive workers.[2]

Slaves

A census completed on New Year's Day 1726 listed thirty-one "*esclaves nègres*" at the Terre Blanche plantation and, at St. Catherine's Concession, twenty-five captive Africans and four "*esclaves sauvages*." A handful of other settlers held several more captive laborers, making a total of sixty-three African and seven Indian slaves in the Natchez Country.[3] By 1729, the number of African slaves had more than doubled.[4] The Europeans identified these "*esclaves nègres*" by their skin color.

The French systemized this difference with a revision of the 1685 Code Noir, or "Black Code." As the historian Jennifer Spear has noted, "the 1724 Code Noir reflected the transition from a status-based hierarchy to one rooted in race."[5] It also reflected a trend among the thinkers of the day—Le Page du Pratz included—that ascribed intellectual and moral weakness to *les nègres*.[6]

The preamble to the Code Noir of 1724 proclaimed royal authority over "The Province and Colony of Louisiana, which has been well established by a great number of our subjects who are served by *esclaves nègres* to cultivate the earth."[7] The authors of the decree made several key changes to the Code Noir of 1685. Although the first decree was far from "color-blind," its replacement focused more closely on biological characteristics. For instance, one of the old law's articles levied a fine of 2,000 pounds of sugar upon free men who had children by their slaves; it contained no reference to color. The slaves involved in the union were subject to seizure and sale, with the funds donated to colonial hospitals. The Louisiana version stated: "We forbid our white subjects [*sujets blancs*] of either sex to contract in marriage with Blacks [*Noirs*]." The revised Code allowed slaves to testify in court "only when necessary and only when a White [witness] is unavailable." Article 24 sentenced to lifelong enslavement any "free-born or freed *nègres*" who aided a runaway. This punishment replaced the earlier decree's fine of 300 pounds of sugar per day for the same offense. Thus, the Code Noir of 1724 finished a process of subjugation based on racial categories that had begun decades earlier.[8]

Viewed from a Natchez perspective, members of this African underclass received only minimal amounts of redistributed goods and few ever changed status. Even after manumission, former slaves had to refrain from "rendering harm or insult to their former masters, mistresses, or the children thereof and will be punished more severely for harming them than if it had been another person."[9] The law also prohibited Euro-African marriages, thereby eliminating among the newcomers a practice recognized by the Natchez as a means for social mobility. The Code also stripped Africans of the right to practice their faiths by requiring that their masters have them baptized and taught the tenets of Roman Catholicism.[10] These provisions deprived slaves of practices that were crucial to maintaining their former cultural identities.

By the late 1720s, the immigrants' slave regime represented a significant departure from the one that the Natchez had witnessed in the preceding decades. When Louis XIV's subjects arrived in the 1680s, their treatment of bound laborers resembled certain aspects of Native American practices.[11] La Salle's companions had acquired their slaves from other Indian groups, most notably the Quapaws and the Taensas. The Koroa slave who escaped from Henri Tonti during the group's first visit to the Natchez quickly found his way to his mother's village.[12] Tonti must have allowed the boy a good deal of personal autonomy if he slipped away so easily. On the return voyage, another Koroa slave, this one held by a Native American member of the party, saved the expedition by negotiating on their behalf with the People of the Sun.[13] The role of negotiator contrasted with the agricultural tasks routinely performed by chattel slaves in France's colony.

The Natchez's next exposure to Europeans' uncompensated laborers came in the canoes of missionaries rowed by "*donnés.*" These men had signed contracts and taken vows of service as "Secular Domestics" in the Jesuit order.[14] They worked as boatmen, guides, farmers, carpenters, and bodyguards for the Fathers. In return, they received food (which the *donnés* gathered), clothing (which they often made for themselves and the priests), and shelter (which they built for their superiors). Their reward came in the afterlife, when the *donnés* entered paradise. Natchez servants like the Tattooed Serpent's pipe-bearer performed much the same sort of work for their superiors, with much the same compensation; they, too, followed their "masters" into the "Land of the Spirits." *Donnés* could, however, annul their contracts if they wished.[15] At least one of these companions worked alongside Father St. Cosme among the Natchez during the early 1700s.[16] Another *donné* named Jacques l'Argilier attended to Jesuit Father Gravier on his journey downriver to Mobile in the winter of 1705.[17] It is likely that he stopped at the mission in Natchez Country during the trip because the Jesuit later wrote disparagingly of St. Cosme's lack of converts.[18]

Brett Rushforth has challenged more benign representations of Indian slavery in the historiography of colonial North America. He argued that the victims of enslavement by Native American often experienced extreme brutality and oppression at the hands of their captors. Nonetheless, chattel slavery, as practiced by the colonists around Fort Rosalie during the 1720s, looked quite different from the Natchez versions.[19] Moreover, by that time Europeans had enslaved some of the People of the Sun. Although the number and fate of the Apple and Jenzenaque people captured by the colonists in Bienville's War remains unknown, their lot was probably not a pleasant one. The colonists executed and scalped several prisoners. Some of the Europeans intended different uses for other detainees. At least one Louisianan died in trying to seize an Apple Villager as a slave.[20] The Choctaw leader Red Shoe captured four Jenzenaque women while fighting as an ally of Louisiana.[21] Whether the Choctaw sold them to colonists or brought them back to his homeland is uncertain. What is certain, however, is that throughout the war Europeans and their supporters took Natchez townspeople from their homes for use as unfree laborers. These earlier practices, as disturbing as they must have been to the People of the Sun, did not depart significantly from established behavior in eighteenth-century Native America.

When the first Louisianans in Natchez Country exacted labor from those whom they had captured, they followed a familiar pattern. The enslavement of prisoners of war had deep roots among indigenous communities in the region. In the words of the historian Christina Snyder: "Indians, like other peoples in early America, found themselves locked in a web of hierarchy and interdependence and saw no stark divide between slavery and freedom."[22] High-status outsiders "owned" prestigious Native American slaves. Bienville had held one of these unfortunates, a Chitimacha headman named Framboise, as an *esclave*. The commandant-general later released him and allowed him to return home.[23] Le Page du Pratz owned a female Chitimacha purchased from a *habitant* living among the Acolapissas. When she attempted to escape while the Dutchman visited the Chitimacha villages, her parents returned her to him.[24] Slaves transported from the Compagnie's posts in Senegal and Guinea suffered differently.

The records of the Superior Council contain the case concerning an African slave who had been brutalized on a farm near Fort Rosalie. Choucoura had lost two fingers on his right hand and two fingertips on his left. The man had suffered these injuries because the cords by which he was hung for his flogging were too tight and because his tormenter left him suspended on them for too long. Such was the diagnosis of Laurent Hurlot, *dit* La Sonde, the surgeon at Natchez. Hurlot signed his disposition for a suit filed by Captain Merveilleux in the autumn 1727. The captain sought compensation from his former assistant Monsieur Gaulas for damages against his "property." The proof that the plaintiff presented sheds light on the nature of chattel slavery prevalent in Natchez Country during the late 1720s.

Sometime during the end of spring 1727, Merveilleux had gone to New Orleans for medical treatment and left Gaulas, also a Swiss immigrant, to manage his estate while he was absent. Several weeks later, Choucoura ran away from Merveilleux's farm and turned up at St. Catherine's on July 15. The concession's director, Longrais, testified that Gaulas arrived and took Choucoura away in chains. Sometime between late July and early September 1727, Gaulas ordered the recaptured slave's punishment. It was after the administration of this punishment that Merveilleux discovered that his "property" had been damaged. A series of charges and countercharges between the defendant and the plaintiff soon followed.

Merveilleux contended that his subordinate was a harsh man who had severely mistreated his slave. In response, Gaulas supplied written testimony from Madame Lambermond in which the *habitante* swore that she had witnessed Choucoura refusing to obey Gaulas. She had also heard Gaulas tell Choucoura to come with him and that he "he did not have a cane and would not beat him." The slave responded with more verbal abuse and threatened to run away again.[25] Additionally, Father Philibert attested that Pierre Gaulas was an excellent employee who labored hard for the fort's commandant.[26] Gaulas also sent along the statement of Jean Sortier, a soldier in Fort Rosalie's garrison, who stated that Merveilleux had attempted to force him to bear false witness. The captain wanted Sortier to swear that Gaulas had secretly tried to give him tobacco, perhaps as an attempt to smuggle the weed out of Merveilleux's inventory or perhaps as a bribe. Whatever the facts might have been, the incident had become a contest of reputations.

During the hearings held in October 1727, Gaulas provided further evidence of his good faith. His doctor testified that he had set the former lieutenant's collarbone, which had been broken while hauling tobacco on Merveilleux's farm.[27] Gaulas then claimed that Choucoura's wounds were self-inflicted—that the African had thrust his hands into a cauldron of boiling water. Moreover, he asked for compensation for his broken collarbone, claiming that he was crippled for life.[28]

Gaulas also submitted a letter, dated June 13, 1727, from his employer that recommended severe corporal punishment for a slave he identified as "alexis" [sic]. In the letter, Merveilleux wrote that "alexis did not lack for laziness and a malicious tongue," and if he caused Gaulas any trouble, he was to have him "bound hands to a post." Gaulas was then to administer "twenty-five lashes sparing only his hands and neck, but to make sure that all the blows draw blood." Merveilleux continued, "If he does not mend his ways, whip him fifty times, and then a third round of 100 lashes and this will continue on if he disobeys you like that."[29] In his memoirs, Dumont de Montigny used the word "alexis" to denote a Natchez doctor.[30] While the identity of the man to whom Merveilleux referred will probably never be known, it is possible that he was a Natchez held as a slave by the Swiss captain. On New Year's Day 1728, the Superior Court ruled in Captain Merveilleux's favor. It ordered Gaulas to pay 200 piasters and compensate Hurlot for his services.[31] Choucoura got nothing.

Choucoura's case exemplified the declining legal and social conditions facing slaves in Natchez Country. His treatment at the hands of his Swiss captors demonstrated that terror constituted a fundamental mechanism in its rapidly developing colonial economy. It also revealed the growing concern over maroons—slaves who fled their captors and formed autonomous communities.

As Merveilleux's prescription for "alexis" suggests, Europeans had come to treat their Indian slaves in Natchez Country much like they treated their enslaved Africans. Moreover, indigenous homesteads and villages provided perfect venues from which to observe colonists dominating Africans in ways that the Indians had not seen when the outsiders were few in number and their slaves scarce. Choucoura's escape and punishment during the summer of 1727 took place within a few hundred meters of the Grand Village. It is unlikely that his plight went unnoticed by the Natchez.

A few years earlier, Hurlot, the surgeon who attended Choucoura, was directly involved in another case of abuse. On August 8, 1724, he brought suit against a cabinetmaker named Coupart from whom he had purchased a "*une petite sauvagesse*." Coupart assured Hurlot that the girl's condition was the result of a mild fever. On closer examination by the surgeon major, it became apparent that the child had been badly beaten and that it was unlikely to live. Coupart denied the charges and refused to take responsibility for the outcome of the girl's "fever." The Superior Council found for the defendant and ordered La Sonde to bear the court costs.[32] While the origin or fate of the "*petite sauvagesse*" is unclear, the cruelty she underwent probably did not escape the attention of other Native Americans. What is clear, however, that as time progressed, there were a few Natchez observers in the colonial capital with unique perspectives on the Europeans' treatment of Indian slaves.

During the late spring of 1728, the Superior Council heard the cases of two male Native American slaves, Jean Guillory and Bontemps. The records identified the latter as "a native of Natchez." Guillory, fifteen years of age, belonged to Gérard Pellerin, the manager of the Compagnie warehouse in New Orleans. Sieur Trudeau, a *habitant* who lived along the Mississippi River, claimed ownership over Bontemps. The two slaves had absconded, but not before Bontemps, a youth of eighteen, took a small purse of silver coins from Trudeau. The Council's investigation revealed that the two youths remained near the capital and that they had spent Trudeau's money on brandy purchased from a local merchant named Lemaire.[33] The officials called in Jean Baptiste, another enslaved Natchez belonging to the Capuchins, to testify. He might have been one of the Natchez boys "who had presented themselves on their own accord" to "learn to live and speak like the French" whom Father Raphael had referred to in a 1725 letter.[34] Guillory said that he knew Bontemps, and knew that Lemaire sold liquor to runaway slaves, both Indian and African, but that he did not know that the money had been stolen. The Superior Council fined Lemaire twenty livres, payable to the hospital.[35]

The interrogations of Bontemps and Guillory continued through the first two weeks of June. The slaveholders Pellerin and Trudeau gave their depositions on the seventh of the month. Pellerin reported that Guillory had run off in October of the previous year but upon capture promised to not escape again.[36] In the second week of June, Guillory spoke on his own behalf. He stated that while tending his holder's cattle, Bontemps encouraged him to run away. He said that he could no longer bear the ill-treatment he suffered at the hands of Pellerin. Bontemps's turn to speak came next. When he was asked why he had stolen Trudeau's money, he responded acerbically, "because he had none." He also testified that he had run off because Dumanoir's slaves told him that he would be hung for a thief. In a final statement, Guillory told his judges that he would await his punishment rather than return to Pellerin's custody.[37]

On the same day, June 14, 1728, the Superior Court found Bontemps guilty of desertion and of domestic theft. Guillory was found guilty of two counts of desertion. It ordered two "reputable *habitants*" to appraise the value of the two slaves so that their holders could receive compensation as per the Code Noir. After their valuation, both men were to be taken to the town square for "high justice." Bontemps was to go the gallows and be "hung and strangled" until dead. Guillory was to be whipped first and then sent to join his accomplice on the gibbet.

Bontemps's and Guillory's fates underscored the fact that Europeans not only continued to hold Native Americans as slaves, but also that they did so in a way that broke with their Gallic brethren to the north. Colonists in New France also held American Indians as slaves, but as Brett Rushforth demonstrated, the captives came from distant communities unlikely to have direct relations with the provincial government. The journeys of captives from their points of origins permitted Native groups allied to the French to reinforce their "bonds of alliance" with the colonists. Thus, for French Canadians, Indian slaves were a source of intercultural stability.[38] In contrast, Louisianans took slaves from local indigenous communities. Commandant-General Périer decried the practice in a letter to the Compagnie's religious director, Abbé Raguet. He thought that captive Native Americans "serve us very poorly or they run off to their nations or to some others nearby." He also worried that "sauvage slaves [who] mix in with our negroes can talk them into deserting."[39]

Périer's letter and the plights of Bontemps and Guillory illustrated the growing anxiety among colonists concerning small but significant communities of refugees in the swamps and forests near their settlements. Both youths, as well as the Natchez witness, knew about a local maroon "underground" where runaways could obtain food, liquor, and shelter. The historian Gwendolyn Midlo Hall traced the connections between indigenous and African maroons and their activities as a source of apprehension among the colonists. Natanapelle, a hamlet of fifteen men and one Indian woman, was reported by a man named Sansouci, a recaptured Native American.[40] Communities such as these offered sanctuary for those who left their slaveholders. They were also accused of harboring livestock rustlers and highway robbers.[41]

With the growing number of runaways and prosecutions, the Natchez could not fail to notice that the colonists perceived Indians as "racial" others, ineligible for the rights and privileges of the king's subjects. It is highly improbable that the Natchez knew about the nuances of Gallic law or the exact content of every proclamation designed to relegate them to an underclass. The Superior Council, however, provided for public readings of their decrees, making it likely that the People of the Sun heard something about them. For instance, one of the Council's edicts mandating death for those who struck their masters clearly warned, "listen well, men who are 18 or women who are 20 years old."[42]

As more newcomers poured into the region during the 1720s, the Natchez had further opportunities to learn of the Europeans' ongoing program to reduce Indians, free as well as captive, to an inferior social and legal category. The Superior Council's efforts at derogation overturned a seventeenth-century statute drafted for use in Canada. It had granted Native Americans who married the king's subjects the same liberties as those enjoyed by all Frenchmen.[43]

French officials brought the rudiments of these guidelines to North America in the early decades of the colony's existence. During their initial foray into Louisiana, officials needed to find ways to control the Native American slaves who made up a substantial portion of the population of Mobile.[44] As part of their solution, the Superior Council extended certain statutes in the Code Noir of 1685 to include Indians. The most comprehensive of these revisions was the *arrêt* of November 12, 1714. Article 23 of the 1685 Code Noir originally stated that "a slave who strikes his Master ... or his mistress ... shall be punished by death." The colony's 1714 edict spelled out the manner of execution, hanging, and then added another clause: "*sauvagesses* [sic] who strike their masters or mistresses will suffer the same penalty." The noun's feminine gender reflected the provincial leaders' preoccupation with the large number of women held by European and Canadian men. The owners of the condemned were to be compensated by the state at the rate of 150 livres per Indian and 300 livres for each African. The same decree amended the Code's Article 15, which forbade slaves to carry "offensive weapons or large staffs," by including "arrows or war-clubs."It did, however, provide exemptions for "*Sauvages* to hunt or fish on behalf of their masters or sent someplace Far away in their Service."[45] Although the Ministry of Marine took exception to the Council's circumvention of the Code, it tacitly accepted the Louisianans' addendums when it failed to quash the provisions pertaining to Indians.[46]

Within a year, Louisiana's rulers directed their attention to another set of problems: those arising from the sexual unions between French men and native women. The comptroller at Mobile, Jean-Baptiste Dubois Duclos, noted: "Although there are several examples of Indian women who have contracted such marriages especially at Illinois it is not because they have become Frenchified, if one may use that term, but it because those who have married them have themselves become almost Indians."[47] Moreover, Duclos cited skin color as a source of trouble, noting "the adulteration" that "such marriages will cause in the whiteness and purity of the blood in the children.... Experience shows every day that children that come from such marriages are of extremely dark complexion, so that in the course of time, if no Frenchmen come to Louisiana, the colony would become a colony of half-breeds who are naturally idlers, libertines and even more rascals as those of Peru, Mexico, and the other Spanish colonies give evidence."[48] In another letter, Duclos recommended that if such marriages must occur, then the wives should come from the northern nations since their women were more industrious and more "white" (*plus blanche*).[49]

Although the Natchez may have heard something about these earlier laws, at least one decree reached their ears with full force. In late December 1728, the colonial government forbade "all Frenchmen or other white Subjects of the King from contracting marriages with the Savages."[50] Native American widows of "Frenchmen" could not inherit their husbands' property. If the widows remained in European settlements, they and their offspring would receive a pension from the estate's executor. Those who returned to their own people would forgo any claims to the dead men's possessions. With the stroke of a pen, the Superior Council struck at the heart the Natchez practice of intermarriage with outsiders that preceded the earliest days of the colony. From that point, the marriage laws that previously had applied only to Africans also held for Indians, slave or free.

A development that was perhaps as disturbing was the appearance of a French sailing ship at the Tunicas a few miles downriver from Natchez Country. In fall 1728, Commandant-General Périer ordered one of the Compagnie vessels, the *La Flore*, to make its way up the Mississippi to retrieve the season's tobacco harvest waiting at the dock below Fort Rosalie.[51] Although navigational difficulties kept it from reaching that destination, it managed to pick up several thousand pounds of tobacco transported downstream by small craft.

For the People of the Sun, the journey of the *La Flore* also was ominous because it was a Compagnie slave ship. Before it approached Natchez Country, it had sailed from Lorient to the French slaving stations in Gorée in March 1728. There it picked up 400 captive souls of which 356 survived the voyage to New Orleans. The presence of a 260-ton slaving vessel—the largest craft that far north on the Mississippi River to date—must have caused some trepidation among the region's Native American population. Perhaps the next ship might bear them away in chains.[52]

By the summer of 1729, the danger posed by colonists was mounting. First, in their drive for arable land to grow tobacco, Louisianans had come to dominate the parklands between the Natchez villages. Second, their racialization of Indians overturned an established means of diplomacy and cultural exchange: marriage. The expansion of the European and African populations around Fort Rosalie gave new weight to the derogatory edicts previously issued by the Superior Council. The Natchez could now directly observe the effects of racism on enslaved Africans. It was equally apparent that many of the laws that the French employed to control the "*noirs*" were now being applied to them as "*sauvages*." Despite their efforts to maintain their former relationship with the Europeans, the People of the Sun were sliding toward the same lowly status as the African slaves, a status founded on a discourse of racial categories. It was in the midst of this growing anxiety among the Natchez that one of the least competent French officials executed one of the worst blunders in the colony's history.

Threats

According to one scholar, Périer's replacement of Merveilleux with Captain Étienne de Chépart as the executive officer of Fort Rosalie was borne of the commandant-general's desire to develop Natchez Country as an agricultural center. Yet de Chépart was no stranger to the People of the Sun. He had marched with Bienville in the 1723 campaign against the Apple Village.[53] His brief tenure at the fort began in February 1728 and lasted until he died in his vegetable garden at the hands of a Natchez "stinkard" in November 1729. The captain served long enough, however, to develop a nasty reputation among his contemporaries. Nearly all those who observed de Chépart commented on his heavy drinking and short temper. Broutin, himself a former post commander, wrote a few months after the Natchez uprising, "I do not know the reasons that made Mr. Périer support to my prejudice a drunkard and a thoughtless man like Sieur de Chépart."[54]

Dumont de Montigny harbored particular contempt for the fort's commandant. In the autumn of 1728, de Chépart ordered him arrested and thrown in the fort's guardhouse. The lieutenant wound up in jail for successfully appealing de Chépart's ruling against his landlord, Jean Rousin. The case started when Longrais, the registrar of St. Catherine's Concession, swindled Rousin in a livestock transaction. Dumont de Montigny pleaded his host's case before de Chépart, who not only ruled against Rousin, but also ordered his wife, Marie Baron Rousin, to publicly apologize to Longrais. The soldier turned advocate managed to get the Superior Council to overturn the sentence. When de Chépart read the judgment of the Council, he flew into a rage and struck Jean Rousin with his cane. When the *habitant* fought back, de Chépart put

Rousin in irons. Dumont De Montigny protested this illegal treatment of a civilian. De Chépart responded by releasing Rousin and throwing the lieutenant into the fort's guardhouse in his stead. After two months, Dumont escaped confinement and fled to New Orleans to plead his case before Périer and the Superior Council. De Chépart followed the fugitive downriver and arrived a day after his prisoner. Dumont de Montigny, however, had already convinced Commandant-General Périer and the Superior Council of the justice of his cause. The provincial government reprimanded de Chépart, but Périer returned the captain to his post.

Even Le Page du Pratz departed from his usual generosity when he admitted that he could not understand Périer's lack of discernment in reinstating the captain.[55] Yet, the unanimous contempt in which de Chépart was held actually served Périer's purposes well. Through the reappointment of de Chépart, Périer secured the cooperation of an individual utterly dependent upon his patronage.[56] The projected expansion of the tobacco industry in Natchez Country was bound to irritate the more established interests, both Native American and European. De Chépart, a man with few friends, could execute the most repugnant orders since he was not part of any of the networks of farmers, concessionaires, or native villagers that would suffer.

At the same time that the quality of the French leadership was deteriorating at Fort Rosalie, the Natchez also lost their veteran headmen. As noted earlier, the Tattooed Serpent died in 1725.[57] Three years later, the Great Sun joined him in the Land of the Spirits.[58] The son of the Tattooed Arm and a "*françois*," who may have been the missionary priest Father St. Cosme, became the primary chief of the Natchez. The new Great Sun had limited political capital to expend with the older, more experienced leaders from the outlying villages. When the military chief of the immigrants demanded ever more territory, the anticolonial faction faced little of the political opposition that they had encountered from the previous Great Sun.

Dumont de Montigny's version of events starts in the spring of 1729, when de Chépart began to make his move. It was during that season that the captain evicted an Apple Villager from his homestead and replaced him with several newly purchased African slaves. He then hired a Frenchwoman to oversee them.[59] Next, the captain aimed at a more lucrative target. Dumont de Montigny cited the Grand Village as the object of de Chépart's desire. In his 1753 book, he conflated major figures in the Indians' hierarchy: "The Tattooed Serpent was no longer the Grand Chief of the nation of the Natchez, the one who succeeded him was allied to the

Chief of the Apple Village named Old Hair, whose head the French had demanded during the last war." In this detail, Dumont de Montigny's account departed from those of his contemporaries. In his 1747 journal, Dumont de Montigny asserted that the Natchez leader with whom de Chépart argued was the offspring of the man who had been executed.[60] Equally puzzling was Dumont de Montigny's assertion that the Tattooed Serpent was the leader of the Grand Village.

It should be noted that the Dumont de Montigny was not in Natchez Country at this time. His informants for his account were likely his wife and other women who survived the uprising of November 1729. He also might have corresponded with Le Page du Pratz, who garnered his material from the Tattooed Arm, the new Great Sun's mother. Whatever discrepancies Dumont de Montigny might have included in his telling, he provided some key insights with regard to the way that de Chépart's opposite number reacted.

Dumont de Montigny described the French officer speaking through an interpreter named René Papin, who told the Indian leader that the "chief of the French, that is to say, Périer, had sent a written order that they Natchez must abandon their village because he had need of the land to erect large buildings."[61] The "Grand Chef and his Honored Men responded "that they had been there a very long time, that the Nation was in possession of the Village, and there they would stay, that the ashes of their ancestors reposed there, deposited in the Temple that they built." They also complained that "the French had never taken land by force in the past ... [and] that the French had paid with trade goods for the land that they occupied."

Dumont de Montigny wrote that de Chépart attributed his authority to letter from the commandant-general of the colony, Périer. Thus, the captain shunned responsibility for his actions. Equally important was his assertion that his orders came in writing; thereby he privileged a mode of communication that was not part of the Natchez order of things. Nonetheless, after three decades of exposure to Catholicism's sacred books, the indigenous peoples of the region must have been aware of the power that the written word held for Europeans.

Conversely, Dumont de Montigny's account highlighted an aspect of Natchez spatial practice: the People of the Sun drew their authority from the landscape itself. De Chépart's ultimatum threatened more than just the "inner commons" of Natchez Country: it jeopardized the wellsprings of its leaders' authority as well its people's connections with their past. The built environments of the Natchez were the sites that bestowed the

Great Sun with political, social, and religious powers. In the words of the archaeologist Christopher Tilley: "The architectural forms of cairn and barrow... signify a will to make ancestral powers in the land visible."[62] Through the burial of their forbearers and the rituals that they performed in specific places, aspects of Natchez authority were "sedimented" into the landscape.[63]

However, other descriptions of the dialogues between de Chépart and the leaders of the Natchez differ from Dumont de Montigny's—in some cases significantly. Le Page du Pratz wrote that de Chépart was interested in the Apple Village, which stood to the northwest of the Grand Village, and that de Chépart dealt with the leader of the Apple Village, not the Great Sun. The Apple Village leader, however, lived in the same settlement as Old Hair, the Sun whom Bienville had executed in 1723 for leading the war against St. Catherine's Concession.[64]

In Le Page du Pratz's version, de Chépart summoned the Sun of the Apple Village to come to the fort alone for their first meeting. When he arrived, the captain told Papin to tell the Natchez leader "to look for another location for his Village; that he wished to build immediately in the Apple Village, and that they must vacate their homes shortly and retire elsewhere."[65] In this account, the Sun responded, "believing that he would be heard if he spoke reasonably... that his ancestors had lived there for as many years as there were hairs in his topknot, and that it was best that they remain there still."[66] When Papin rendered the Sun's words into French, de Chépart became angry and told the Sun that within a few days he would regret not leaving his village.

The Indian leader replied: "When the French came to ask for land, they [the Natchez] said there is plenty that no person occupies, that they could take it, that the same sun shines on us all and they all walk the same path." Shaking with rage, de Chépart interrupted the Natchez and said that "he was to be obeyed without back talk." Le Page du Pratz noted that "the Commandant imagined himself, no doubt, to be speaking to a Slave which one commands with an absolute tone; but he ignored the fact that the Naturals are such enemies of slavery that they prefer death to it." Perhaps Le Page du Pratz was alluding to the cases of Guillory and his Natchez partner, Bontemps. After witnessing the captain's final outburst, the Sun of the Apple Village returned home with his composure intact.[67] To emphasize his resolve, de Chépart "had a missionary cross planted in the fields of the Grand Village."[68]

In other contemporaneous reports, the troubles between de Chépart and Native leaders take different forms. Father Le Petit, who wrote to his coadjutor seven months after the destruction of the fort, merely mentioned "some cause of dissatisfaction which the Natchez thought they had with Monsieur the Commandant."[69]

Father Charlevoix, who had access to Le Petit's letters as well as official correspondence between the colony and Paris, published his version of the events in 1744. In his three-volume *Histoire et description générale de la Nouvelle France*, the Jesuit wrote, "M. de Chepar [sic] . . . had a small quarrel with these Savages; but it seems that they carried their dissimilation so far that they persuaded him that the French had no more faithful Allies [than the Natchez]."[70]

An anonymous journal held by the Newberry Library in Chicago rendered yet another version. The journal dates from the early 1730s, most likely authored by an Irish or English trader living around Mobile. It makes no mention of the transactions between the officer and the Sun, instead focusing on the tranquility that pervaded Natchez Country until the attack on Fort Rosalie.[71]

The last reference notwithstanding, de Chépart played the role of the greedy villain in most accounts of the Franco-Natchez War. Yet these eighteenth-century authors seldom questioned the overall goal of turning Louisiana into a viable agricultural province, a goal that could be realized only at the expense of those who already occupied the land. When the newcomers controlled more of Natchez Country in a manner that put authority-generating sites at risk, the People of the Sun began to fashion a "red" identity. The encroachment of Europeans encouraged the Natchez to adapt the more "portable" discourse of racial categories to unify their disputatious villages.

Plotting Race

According to Le Page du Pratz, two further meetings took place between de Chépart and representatives of the Natchez. In the first of these, the Sun of the Apple Village carried a message from the Natchez council of elders. He informed the officer of the losses that they would sustain if they abandoned their cornfields so early in the season. De Chépart immediately rejected their protests. At the second meeting, the council embarked on a different strategy. In order to buy time for their people, Indian leaders requested that the captain allow them to stay on the land until the villagers could harvest their crops. In return for the right to stay behind until the harvest, the Natchez headmen promised payments of corn, bear's oil, and poultry.[72] The Frenchman, flush with confidence because of these concessions, ended the second meeting with a threat. If the Sun failed to deliver, de Chépart would "order him to be bound hand and foot and sent down river to New Orleans when the next galley arrived."[73] The captain's tone struck a nerve with the Native American leader. He may have recalled concession director Guenot's imprisonment of an Apple Village leader that helped to spark Bienville's War in 1723. The appearance of the slave ship *La Flore* very close to home and the ordeal of Bontemps and Guillory in the provincial capital also might have lent weight to the captain's words. After hearing them, the Sun returned to his town and called another assembly of the elders to make plans to resist the eviction.[74]

Five or six days later, the Natchez council of elders met again. The accounts of these gatherings written by Dumont de Montigny and Le Page du Pratz contained some interesting differences. According to Dumont de Montigny, the Natchez elders offered a number of plans, all of which they rejected until an all-out attack on the French was proposed.[75] In Le Page du Pratz's account, the oldest member of the council gave this speech during the meeting:

> For a long time we have perceived that the proximity of the French has done us more harm than good, we older men see this, but the young people do not see it. The merchandise of the French gives our youth pleasure, but in effect, it serves to debauch our young women and corrupt the blood of the Nation and make our women arrogant and idle. They do the same to the young men, and the married men work themselves to death to feed their family and satisfy their children. Before the French arrived in this country, we were men who knew how to be content with what we had and it satisfied us, we strode boldly on all our paths because we were our own masters; but today we grope along fearing we will find thorns, we walk as slaves, and it will not be long before we are [slaves] since the French already treat us as if we are.[76]

Le Page du Pratz was not at the meeting, of course. He probably heard about the speech from the Tattooed Arm, whom he interviewed in 1731 while she was jailed in New Orleans. Her child, the Great Sun, might have provided her with the details of the debate. The provenance of the story notwithstanding, the elder's rhetoric highlighted several disturbances in the Natchez order of things caused by the Europeans. The first and most important of these was the impact that the newcomers had on Natchez women: "to debauch our young women and corrupt the blood of the Nation and make our women arrogant and idle." The unions of European men and Indian women, arrangements common throughout colonial North America, had become a problem. For previous generations, intermarriage had worked for the Natchez by integrating migrant groups into their polity. When the Superior Council forbade "Frenchmen or other white subjects of the King from contracting marriages with 'savages,'" it derogated the People of the Sun. The proscription on widows' property rights also curtailed a crucial practice that had worked well for the frontier exchange economy of eighteenth-century Louisiana. Moreover, it removed them in a manner particularly egregious to a society whose leaders derived their status through their descent from high-status women. After the decree, the presence of the French indeed corrupted the nation, relegating the Natchez to a hereditary, biologically determined underclass.

The elder also decried the material ambitions of the wives of his countrymen. According to him, husbands had to "work themselves to death" to satisfy the demands of their spouses. His jeremiad highlighted the second set of problems: the commercialization of exchanges, which drove up the price of European goods. Harvesting more food or pelts merely increased their supply, devaluing them further. Deerskins and other forest products began to supplement foodstuffs as a trade commodity. This forced Natchez men to spend more time hunting away from their families. Their absence led to a decline in the numbers available to defend their homeland or to clear fields for planting. Moreover, the outsiders, with their livestock and European agricultural technology, were on a path to nutritional self-sufficiency. Thus, another component of the exchange economy of the region was coming under stress.

Native Americans had been working on ways to counteract the growing power of European colonists by the time de Chépart issued his threats. They were forging a racial category of their own as a diplomatic tool to build consensus among Indian peoples by capitalizing on shared biological characteristics. Elements of this emerging discourse are evident in the words of the same elder as he continued his speech before the council:

> What are we waiting for? Do we want to allow the French to multiply to a point where we are no longer in a state to oppose their efforts? What will the other nations say? We are the most spiritual of all the red Men; they will say that we have less spirit than the other People. Why wait any longer? Let us free ourselves and show that we are true men who can make due with what we have.... Let

us send the Calumet of Peace to all the other Nations in the Country, make them realize that the French were stronger in our neighborhood than elsewhere [and] make us feel that they want to enslave us, when they become strong enough, they will be stronger than all of the Nations of the Land, that it is in their interest to prevent such a tragedy; that to keep this from happening, they should join us in the destruction of all of the French, on the same day and at the same hour, that day will be the same day that the French Commandant dictated for our eviction.[77]

The Natchez elder explicitly invoked an identity that his people shared with other Native Americans when he called his people "the most spiritual [clever] of all of the red Men." The elder's speech is one of several recorded by French and English observers during the middle and late 1720s in which Indians used the color "red" to identify themselves in contrast to Europeans and Africans. The historian Nancy Shoemaker observed that "'Red' Indians quickly became standard usage in Southeastern Indian diplomacy. By the 1730s, the French in Louisiana had incorporated 'red men' into the language of intercultural exchanges. They had also adopted the term as a generic label for Indians in their official correspondences."[78]

The term had deep roots in Natchez culture. Shoemaker cited two reasons for Native Americans to call themselves "red." The first was a desire "to distinguish themselves from [Europeans'] 'black' or 'Negro' slaves." The second reason came from her recognition that the color red held special significance in Native Americans' cosmology.[79] Indeed, the Natchez had employed the term "red men" for several years before the elder made his speech. Le Page de Pratz provided a brief narrative of his conversation with his "friend, the chief guardian of the [Natchez] temple," that took place in the spring of 1725. The Dutchman asked the man what he knew of the Deluge. After some hesitation, the Indian told him "that the ancient Words taught to all of the red men that nearly all of them had perished by water, except for a very small number who had saved themselves on a high Mountain." The steward's response pleased Le Page du Pratz, who often questioned indigenous men and women for collective memories that would substantiate biblical stories. The temple guardian's reply also, more importantly, contained a reference to a common origin for the Natchez and other Native Americans based on a shared racial identity.[80]

The Dutchman recorded the idiom "red men" in another passage relating to the Natchez origin story. Again, the guardian of the temple was Le Page du Pratz's informant. The Indian spoke about the journeys of many groups of Native Americans from the West and their arrival on the banks of the Mississippi. Some of these peoples established communities on either side of the river: "Ce sont Peuples qui se nomment entr'eux *Hommes Rouges*" (These are Peoples who named themselves Red Men)."[81] The colonist confessed that he could not determine the origins of these groups because "they no longer had a Tradition as strong as the Natchez." Nancy Shoemaker suggested that Le Page du Pratz was referring to the Houmas, whose name means "red" in several Muskogean languages.[82] Le Page du Pratz's use of reflexive pronouns, mistranslated in the widely cited 1774 English-language edition, squarely identifies "red men" as a term chosen by the Indians themselves.

At almost exactly the same time that Le Page du Pratz was gathering his ethnographic data, other Frenchmen recorded the term's use by a member of one of the Petites Nations called the Taensas. In the seventeenth century, groups of Taensas had lived along the Mississippi, where La Salle encountered them south of the Arkansas River in 1682.[83] During his trip upriver in 1699, D'Iberville found them in roughly the same area, a day-and-a-half's journey north of the Natchez.[84] Father St. Cosme reported that the Taensas spoke the same language as the Natchez and shared many of their cultural practices.[85] According to Swanton, the Taensas migrated south from the mouth of the Arkansas River and, by the middle 1710s, had established a village near Mobile at Bienville's invitation.[86] They carried with them the stories of the red men that one of them related to the Capuchin Father Raphael in early 1725:

> Long ago, he said, and so long ago that the winters can no longer be counted, that is to say years, there were three men in a cave, one white, one red, and one black. The white man went out first and he took the good road that led him into a fine hunting ground. You will notice, if you please, Sir, that these poor people know of no greater happiness than that of hunting. The red man who is the Indian, for they call themselves in their language "Red Men," went out of the cave second. He went astray from the good road and took another which led him into a country where the hunting was less abundant. The black man, who is the negro, having been the third to go out, got entirely lost in a very bad country in which he did not find anything on which to live. Since that time the red man and the black man have been looking for the white man to restore them to the good road.[87]

The Taensa storyteller spoke of a category of human beings, the "red man," which had not been recorded in French documents until this point. He associated material well-being with the European "white man," who held the key to the prosperity for the other two. Most important, according to Father Raphael, a man hardly predisposed to Indian mythology, Native Americans, not Europeans, created the expression.[88]

Taken together, the Natchez and Taensa stories suggest that the appellation originated somewhere in the Lower Mississippi Valley. According to the anthropologist Marvin Jeter, the Natchez and related groups migrated into the region along a route that followed the Arkansas River.[89] That movement substantiates the Natchez stories that their people came from a homeland far to the west.[90]

Indians in other parts of the Southeast also identified themselves as red in their diplomatic exchanges. Less than a year after Father Raphael talked to the Taensas' envoy, Creek and Cherokee ambassadors met in Charles Town at a conference sponsored by the South Carolina government.[91] When the Lower Creek contingent arrived at the negotiations a month late, Long Warrior, the main Cherokee spokesman, challenged their representative Chigilee during the proceedings: "I am come from a greate way and have stayed a long while to see you and it has been by the Governor's Desire. How comes it there are so few of you here at Last? you have done a greate Deal of mischief to the white People Since the first Peace.... It is now come to this. We are all the Red People now met together. Our flesh is both alike, but now we must Talk with you."[92] Much like the Taensa leader, Long Warrior conflated Cherokee and Creek identities by invoking redness. Moreover, he contrasted their shared identity with those of the "white People." A little later in his speech, Long Warrior clarified what he meant by the latter term when he addressed Chigilee again: "Why do you go to the French & Spaniards? what do you get by it? How can you goe to so many white People? this great Town is able to supply us with everything we want, more than the French or Spaniards." For Long Warrior, other European colonists fit into a category that they had created for themselves: white. The Indians, whether they were Lower Creeks or Cherokees, fit into another grouping that they, too, had created for themselves; they were all "Red People" because their "flesh is both alike."

These simultaneous invocations of their redness by different Indians, meeting in dispersed locations and speaking before French and English colonists, demonstrated the growing importance of redness in Native American diplomacy. This also presents a conundrum. Did the

Cherokees develop their ideas of redness independently, without the influence other Indians? Nancy Shoemaker argued that this may have been the case.[93] On the other hand, perhaps Chigilee and other Lower Creeks had heard about redness on their trips to French towns, possibly at Mobile. News of this ideology may have spread north to the Cherokee villages. Long Warrior, in order to promote peaceful relations, may have been using an idiom that Chigilee had already embraced. It is also possible that the Creeks and Cherokees began to call themselves red men for one of the same reasons the Natchez did: to counteract derogation by European colonials. South Carolinian legal practices conflated the status of Africans and Indians, much like the French were doing in Louisiana in the first decades of the eighteenth century. South Carolina's Assembly differentiated between "Indians or white persons living within this Province" in its 1711 legislation regulating trade with Native Americans.[94] The next year, South Carolina made children born to enslaved Native Americans slaves for life.[95]

Several generations of anthropologists and historians have attempted to divine the reasons behind Native peoples' choice of "red" to describe themselves. It is clear that the binary mapping of "white" as a symbol for "peace chiefs," and "red" for war leaders proposed by John Swanton and others does not always work to explain the Indians' self-identification with a color associated with war.[96] The French were certainly violent enough to disqualify themselves as "peacekeeping" whites. Nancy Shoemaker suggested several origins for the term "red" that ranged from linguistic ambiguities, to totemic animals, to earthen pigments used as face and body paints. She also pointed out the plasticity of this indigenous racial category—that its meaning was by no means a fixed one.[97] Her explanations may well fit various usages arising in different communities, but Greg O'Brien's discussion of eighteenth-century Choctaw social structures lends some insight into another possible source for the Natchez elders' use of the term.

O'Brien proposed that Choctaws believed that "Choctaw women have capacity to create human life—thus they inherently commanded spiritual power." Men, however, had to acquire similar power through the shedding of blood by participating in warfare or hunting.[98] This association with blood, and therefore redness, made them whole, or "real men who lived up to their masculine ideals" as protectors of their communities.[99] To the Natchez, the Europeans were anything but whole. They arrived in the region dependent for their survival upon the largesse of the Suns. By the second decade of eighteenth century, the colonists no longer needed the support of the indigenous hierarchy, but they required the labor of Africans—"blacks"—to thrive. Perhaps, to the elders, they were "red men" because they were self-sufficient.

The Tattooed Serpent, in his dialogue with Le Page du Pratz, reminded his listener that his people's material culture had met their needs before the colonists came. He decried the corrupting influence of European goods. Sophie White has noted the increasing anxiety of both natives and newcomers regarding the unregulated exchange of material cultures, particularly clothing.[100] This flood of goods held the potential for erasing Natchez identity visually by making them appear like Europeans, and economically by making them as dependent upon the goods as "whites."

Other aspects of Natchez culture also suggest a connection between the color "red" and completeness. Menstruation and childbirth involve the shedding of blood. In the Natchez order of things, entrance into the land of the spirits also involved symbolic blood. Those who prepared the body of the Tattooed Serpent for his grave painted him red. The "master of ceremonies" who led the funeral procession was also adorned with red pigment. Many of the items with which he was buried were painted red. The nearby Choctaws allowed corpses to decompose on scaffolds and then cleaned the remaining flesh from their skeletons. Before they buried the bones, they painted the top of the skull red to symbolize the top of the head being "born" into the afterlife.[101] In these cases, the color marks both the beginning and the end of a complete life cycle. Again, the color red denoted wholeness, a quality sorely lacking on the European side of the cultural divide in Natchez Country.

Although the exact origin of Indians' self-identification with redness may never be known, within a short time after Long Warrior and the Natchez temple guardian called themselves red men, the practice spread quickly. Five years after Chigilee's meeting with Long Warrior, Alibamon Creek diplomats advised the Choctaws that "among the red men they ought to do the same thing and never again speak of making war on each other and scalping each other, and that was the way to live in peace in their houses and see their children grow up without anxiety."[102]

These uses of redness by different Native American nations constitute the earliest evidence that non-Europeans had co-opted the discourse of racial categories created in the Old World, inserted their own, and used this discourse as a means to acquire influence in intercultural negotiations. The Natchez elder's address to his countrymen, Long Warrior's harangue of his Lower Creek counterpart, the temple guardian's interviews with Le Page du Pratz, and the Taensan headman's conversation with the Capuchin priest all referred to an identity shared by the indigenous peoples of the region. The "red men" were not Europeans, nor were they African slaves, and they possessed common interests vis-à-vis the French and the English. Their rhetoric turned a set of social and political practices based on skin color, originally designed to control African laborers, against its creators. The Natchez and other nations had begun to call themselves "red men" as a means of empowerment and as a tool to protect their sovereignty in the face of European encroachment.

The Natchez experience provides a unique perspective on the formation of a red identity. Their society's political, religious, and social practices were intimately linked to the landscape of Natchez Country. While these geographically anchored practices had served certain members of the polity well—quite well in fact for the members of the Grand Village—they left other members on the margins of power. In 1722, the Apple Villagers found their attempts to settle in the parklands north of Fort Rosalie thwarted, first by the *habitants* of St. Catherine's Concession, and next by an attack from a colonial-indigenous army that enjoyed the tacit support of the Tattooed Serpent and the Great Sun. Likewise, in 1725, the Tioux found their position vis-à-vis the Terre Blanche Concession undercut by the same two men. The Tioux left Natchez Country soon after. The Natchez council of elders, no longer beholden to the powerful old Great Sun and his brother, used a red identity to keep their polity from further disintegration. By shifting from a terrain-centered source of unity to one based on a shared identity of redness, they appropriated a far more portable hegemonic practice. No longer was Natchez political power a function of proximity to sacred mounds and holy relics.

Immediately upon the close of the elder's address, the Natchez began to prepare for the attack. "The most spiritual of the red Men" held their plan in the strictest secrecy and did not reveal it even to the female Suns.[103] Dumont de Montigny noted that the Natchez gave no sign that they were getting ready to move to a new location to comply with the captain's demands: "This alone should have aroused the suspicions of de Chépart, if he had been capable of some prudence."[104]

The council's conspiratorial meeting heralded several changes in Natchez politics. From that point on, mentions of factionalism disappeared from the records. These Indians conducted themselves with a singular purpose. The People of the Sun no longer acted like an aggregation of villages under the contested leadership of a ruling clan. They were now united in their opposition to Louisiana, which had been generated over years of declining expectations that the Europeans would act according to indigenous standards of "civilized" behavior. These immigrants proved incapable of organizing the space that the Natchez gave them. They allowed their holy men to dwell in hovels. Their graveyard was in shambles. They refused to clearly mark their planting grounds. They let their animals destroy fields of corn and vegetables. The only areas that the Europeans managed well were those designated for the enslavement of their workers. Animated further by de Chépart's arrogant demands, the Natchez came together. Although their polity still consisted of numerous towns of different ethnic and linguistic backgrounds, the elders determined that the newcomers from overseas would no longer be a part of the Natchez world.

The account of the council's meeting marked another shift in the political climate of the nation. The voice of the Great Sun, whose uncle had accommodated the outsiders, went unrecorded. This silence implies that the balance of power had shifted not only from those who favored coexistence, but also from the primary leader of the Grand Village. If he spoke, either Le Page du Pratz or his informant did not think the young Sun's words worth remembering. It is also possible that he had not yet amassed the requisite social and political capital to make an impression on the elders. Alibamon Mingo, a Choctaw leader who lived during the same era, took several decades to acquire the skills and reputation required to make his voice heard in similar situations.[105]

Despite the accord reached by the men of the council, a small but significant sector of the Natchez elite refused to countenance the destruction of the Europeans among them. A handful of indigenous women, the mother of the Great Sun among them, attempted to thwart the council's plan. It may have been because of their relationships with the outsiders—part of the Natchez tradition of absorbing immigrant groups—that the men left them out of the debates. The women's unions with Europeans, rather than reinforcing the power of the Mississippian chiefdom, had disrupted its domestic equilibrium just as the elder had stated at the council. Their exclusion from this forum worked in favor of the anti-colonist faction. Events after the meeting justified the old man's fears about the corrupting influence of the newcomers; these women tried to warn the colonists, and had they succeeded, they would have undone the headmen's plans. The French had indeed made the Natchez women "arrogant."

According to Le Page du Pratz, the Great Sun's mother, the Tattooed Arm, vehemently opposed the attack. Although the plan remained a secret, the uneasiness that pervaded the Natchez villages gave her reason to suspect something was afoot. Sometime after the council meeting, she asked her son to accompany her to the Flour Village to visit a sick relative.[106] When they reached a secluded section of the path, the Tattooed Arm stopped and began to interrogate the Great Sun. She reminded him of her years of maternal care and that even though he was the son of a Frenchman, she held her own blood "more dear than that of foreigners."[107] Upon hearing her harangue, the Great Sun revealed the details of the plan to destroy the outsiders. Expressing a fear for his life, she tried to dissuade him from participating. Several times during the conversation, the Tattooed Arm referred to "red men" as a category separate from the Europeans. She told him that she was "an old woman, I do not care if it is the French or the Red Men who kill me . . . but you are dear to me. If your elders believed that it will be as easy to overcome the French as [it is to overcome] red men, they are grossly mistaken, the French have resources that red men do not."[108]

The Tattooed Arm tried several times to alert the colonists. She sent word of the impending attack to "young women who were in love with Frenchmen" but to no avail. In another instance, the Tattooed Arm stopped a soldier and told him of the plot. He went to de Chépart with the story. The commandant clapped the man in irons for cowardice. The Natchez woman later informed Sub-Lieutenant Massé, who relayed the message to the captain, only to have it dismissed as fantasy. De Chépart then ordered the officer to place himself under arrest.[109] In all, seven Frenchmen who attempted to alert the commandant were imprisoned for their efforts.[110]

De Chépart eventually investigated the reports in his own fashion. According to Broutin, "he sent the interpreter to ask the Indians to learn whether it was true that they wished to kill us. That was certainly very discreet!"[111] The Natchez, of course, denied the plot and continued to pay tribute. The elders worked this pretense of obeisance into their strategy; the Indians planned to spring their coup the next time that they visited the captain to make their payment.

November 27, the day before the uprising, was a Sunday. Jean-Daniel Kolly and his son had arrived a few days earlier on one of the galleys that Périer hoped would solve the province's riverine shipping problems. The pair had come to inspect their troubled plantation and remedy once and for all its jumbled finances. The two accompanied Captain de Chépart to Mass. After the service, Kolly mentioned the rumors of a Natchez attack. De Chépart said that he knew about these stories. St. Catherine's subdirector, Longrais, also admitted to hearing ominous reports. "They both became the laughingstock of the commander, in the presence of all the inhabitants, who all made tales about the news." De La Loire des Ursins, who had lived in Natchez Country since 1715, "knowing the *sauvages*, corroborated everything." Before he returned to his home near St. Catherine's, De La Loire armed himself with several weapons from the Compagnie warehouse.[112] In a final derisive gesture, de Chépart named Madame Desnoyers, the wife of the director of the Terre Blanche Concession, "queen of the *Sauvages*."

6 / Fallen Forts

On a late autumn evening in 1729, Marc Antoine Calliot, a clerk for the Compagnie des Indes, met his friends on the New Orleans waterfront to take a stroll along the levee. They had just attended a Te Deum to celebrate the king's recovery from a bout of illness. The ship that had brought the news of the monarch's good health also carried a consignment of trade goods. Calliot took care to acquire some of the cargo to sell for his personal profit. Before the group had gone very far, they noticed a boat traveling downriver. It was an unremarkable sight except for the speed at which the craft was being rowed. The clerk thought to himself that the little vessel's crew and passengers might make good customers for his merchandise.

When the craft made landfall, Calliot and his companions were shocked to see the condition of those it carried. Many were ragged and "nearly naked," as he put it. Others were wounded and maimed. All appeared disheveled and suffering from shock. The passengers began to talk to the crowd gathering on the riverbank. They said they had escaped down the Mississippi River and that "all was fire and blood in Natchez."[1]

Prisoners of the Suns

On November 27, 1729, a demi-galley tied up to the dock below Fort Rosalie full of merchandise for the Compagnie store. It also bore two important passengers, Jean-Daniel Kolly and his son. Kolly had traveled upriver to inspect the financial accounts of St. Catherine's Concession.[2]

They attended Mass that morning with many of the settlement's *habitants*. Still oblivious to the Natchez elders' plan, de Chépart and some of his men went to a feast at the Grand Village that night. According to Dumont de Montigny: "They were well received by the Indians and by their chief and began to drink and smoke and trade boasts together, after which they chose Indian women with whom to spend the night in debaucheries, combining the worship of Bacchus and Venus."[3] The group left at around four in the morning to return home.

Five-and-a-half hours later, de Chépart awoke to drumming of a Natchez man who had come with his compatriots to pay tribute for the privilege of remaining on their land. The hung-over captain appeared at the door of his house in his dressing gown. He smiled with satisfaction as he watched the Indians parading toward him carrying live poultry, pots of bear oil, and baskets of corn. De Chépart ordered the release of those officers and *habitants* he had imprisoned so that "they could come and see if the Indians were our enemies."[4] As the elders of the Natchez nation marched in cadence led by the Great Sun, who carried a calumet, their men filtered through gaps in the fort's palisades and took up positions around the post. Others visited acquaintances among the Europeans and borrowed muskets ostensibly to hunt game for a feast in honor of Monsieur Kolly.[5] Still more gathered around the demi-galley at the water's edge. Each man chose the nearest European as his target. When all were in their places, the Great Sun gave the signal to fire.

Father Poisson, a Jesuit normally assigned to the Arkansas Post, was on his rounds to visit the sick when a Sun threw him to the ground and severed his head with a hatchet. Du Coder, an officer from Fort St. Pierre at the Yazoos, tried to save the priest only to be felled by a musket ball.[6] Some of the Europeans fought back, however. These included a number of women who took up arms to defend their husbands or to take revenge on their killers. They soon joined the ranks of the dead.[7]

The fighting lasted four hours and cost the Natchez twelve warriors. The European casualty list stood at 145 men, 36 women, and 56 children. The deceased included Longrais, the manager of St. Catherine's and chronicler of the Second and Third Natchez Wars. Laurent Desnoyers, the director of Terre Blanche, died in front of his wife and children. Sub-Lieutenant Massé; the interpreter René Papin; and Marc Antoine de la Loire, one of the founders of Crozat's warehouse, all perished along with Captain de Chépart.[8]

Throughout the day, the *habitants* of St. Catherine's fought off several attempts by enemy forces to storm their plantation. Calliot, often prone to embellishment, wrote that sometime during these assaults, Indians cornered Jean-Daniel Kolly, who had hidden inside a barrel. There, they killed him "without resistance." His son took up his sword and defended himself admirably, killing "seven or eight" Natchez before his wounds and loss of blood rendered him vulnerable to a deathblow.[9] The Natchez broke off their attack when a rainstorm soaked their gunpowder. The downpour rendered the assailants' muskets useless, while the Europeans, sheltered inside their buildings, were able to keep their powder dry. To continue fighting at that point would have proved useless despite their numerical advantage. During the ensuing lull, a few *habitants* worked their way down to the Mississippi under the cover of darkness. They found a small boat near the demi-galley. The warriors guarding the craft had passed out from drinking. The party boarded the dugout, cast off, and drifted into the main channel to make good their escape.[10]

When the Natchez returned, they burned St. Catherine's to the ground and killed every man, woman, and child. They did not spare the plantation's livestock either. Sieur Delaye, a militiaman who served with the colonial army, surveyed the ruins of the concession several months later. According to him: "The *Sauvages* of the Apple Village distinguished themselves by committing so many crimes and such evil" from the other villages who were "less inhumane and cruel."[11] The seven-and-a-half-year rivalry between the indigenous and the immigrant settlements had been settled once and for all.

A few others slipped away to safety. Ricard, the tobacco agent for the Compagnie des Indes, had been at the docks unloading the cargo of the demi-galley when the killing started. He dove into the river and swam to a cypress forest downstream, where he hid until nightfall. Avoiding the main paths along the riverside, he came upon a cabin owned by a local potter. He found it occupied by some Yazoos who had come to Fort Rosalie with Du Coder and Father Poisson. These Indians were unaware of the events at the post. They fed Ricard, dressed his wounds, and lent him a dugout canoe. The clerk departed quickly, not stopping until he reached New Orleans.[12] One soldier escaped by hiding in a large outdoor oven located on the bluffs near the riverbank. A few other men working in the lumber camps five miles north of Fort Rosalie stole downriver after they killed the Natchez men who served them as professional hunters. A handful of African slaves absconded and made their way to the provincial capital as well.[13]

Two Frenchmen survived the battle only to become prisoners after the attacks concluded. A tailor named Lebeau was forced to mend clothes for the Natchez, while Mayeux, a drover, became the Théoloëls' carter. The latter moved the Louisianans' merchandise and military equipment, including three artillery pieces, to the two forts that the Natchez had built along the banks of St. Catherine's Creek south of the Grand Village.[14]

As a result of their coup, the Natchez also captured approximately 150 European women and children.[15] They placed them under the supervision of the Great Sun and his wife, the White Woman.[16] Some of these captive women hauled water and prepared meals in Natchez homes. Others worked as seamstresses, repairing clothing stripped from the dead.[17] Although the Natchez expected labor from their prisoners, they also appreciated the efforts of those who cooperated with them. Le Page du Pratz's Native American housekeeper was among these prisoners. The Natchez employed her in washing and mending shirts, a chore that she performed so well that they named her "Mistress of the Laundry" for the female Great Sun.[18]

The transfer of the French captives to the custody of the Great Sun and his wife demonstrated both continuity and change in Natchez practices. In one sense, it was natural that "the White Woman . . . who was regarded as the Empress of the Nation" watched over the prisoners.[19] Her standing as a member of the leading family gave her authority over the average Natchez. It is also logical that she directed the labor of the captives. This arrangement stood in contrast with other Native American communities whose fighters usually retained individual possession of the "slaves" whom they seized.[20] Thus, the White Woman's control of the European detainees reaffirmed the influence of the Great Sun's entourage.

The Europeans' imprisonment had darker sides as well. As noted above, the prisoners received no compensation. In addition, they endured physical abuse up to and including murder. Dumont de Montigny recorded that the Natchez executed Madame Massé, the widow of one of the officers who had tried to warn de Chépart, by shooting "her full of arrows at close range." He noted that,"they did the same thing to many others."[21] Calliot's journal also included descriptions of the violence inflicted on the captive European women. In March 1730, the first wave of former prisoners of the Natchez arrived in New Orleans. The clerk heard several of them tell of how they were bound to the rack to be burned only to be saved at the last minute by the wife of the Great Sun.[22]

Aside from the violence visited upon them, the European women and children found themselves under close surveillance much like their former African slaves. Dumont de Montigny depicted the homestead of the

FIGURE 6.1. Cabins of the *femme chef*, detail from Dumont de Montigny (Archives nationales de France [Paris] Cartes et Plans, N III Louisiane 1/2).

"*femme chef*" in one of his maps now held by the Archives nationales de France. He situated it between Fort Rosalie and the Terre Blanche. The settlement consists of a large structure with two smaller buildings on either side and four more to the west. Dumont de Montigny's rendering is similar to his drawings of the Europeans' slave quarters at the concessions. It appears as if the Natchez were replicating the newcomers' slave heterotopias that were designed to oversee captive workers. The Indians had reconfigured their use of space to oversee and control their prisoners.

The fact that the People of the Sun looked upon European women and children as slaves also reveals a shift away from their earlier practice of incorporating foreign elements into their nation. Charlevoix wrote that the Natchez "wanted to remove from the Women and other Slaves all hope of ever recovering their liberty."[23] Since they intended to eject the Europeans from the Lower Mississippi Valley, marriages to non-Native women would not lead to the absorption of more men who could protect or hunt for the nation. They no longer had any reason to integrate these women into their polity. This may have been a result of the Natchez elders' adoption of a red identity; they no longer wanted any more Europeans who "corrupted the blood of the nation." Regardless of their captors' motives, the enslavement of European women and children marked the end of the earlier practice of incorporating non-Natchez groups into their ranks.

Despite their rejection of their captives as candidates for adoption, the Natchez acted in other ways suggesting that they still saw some social and institutional parallels between themselves and the immigrants. For instance, the People of the Sun recognized that these captives might be able to perform in roles similar to their own female leaders. Madame Angelique Chavron Desnoyers, the widow of the director of the Terre Blanche Concession, held a position similar to that of the Tattooed Arm. She had been the wife of a "Sun" of a French village. That rank may have saved her life. She was caught in a conspiracy with her African slaves to avenge the death of her husband. The Natchez did not execute her when one of her accomplices revealed the plot.[24]

Other women, status notwithstanding, met with a different end—namely, death. Nonetheless, at least one killing indicated that the Natchez retained some of their old perceptions that the Europeans employed social and political hierarchies similar to their own. The Natchez might have killed the wife of Sub-Lieutenant Massé to eliminate the spouse of a colonial officer who held a position analogous to the wife of the late Tattooed Serpent.[25] The Indians also dispatched the widow of René Papin, the interpreter, soon after the battle. There was a more pragmatic reason for her death: she may have shared her husband's linguistic skills. If she had, Madame Papin would have been able to understand the Natchez conversations that she overheard. Worse, she would have been capable of communicating directly with the Natchez women who had opposed the elders' policies.

The other group of non-Natchez inhabitants of the region, however, fared better than these two women or the other European prisoners. The People of the Sun did not harm any of the African or Indian slaves who surrendered peaceably.[26] Father Charlevoix wrote that the Natchez treated these people the best of all their captives. He believed that they did so only because they intended to sell them to the English in Carolina.[27]

These newcomers from Africa played a significant part in the downfall of their former "masters." Sometime before the coup, the Natchez sent word of the impending attack to the Africans enslaved on the plantations by means of two drivers. These spokesmen told their fellow bondsmen that "they would be free with the Indians and that our [French] women and children would be their slaves and that they would have no need to fear the French at the other posts because they too would be massacred at the same time."[28] The Indians' strategy worked; none of the colonial records mentions slaves informing their holders of the planned assault.

Whether the Natchez cynically manipulated the slaves to their own ends can never be known with certainty. Their contacts with the captive workers before the uprising demonstrated their desire to exploit the Africans' resentment of their owners. Moreover, at least some of the African men recognized a common cause with the Natchez and fought alongside them when the French returned. Several of them served as gunners for the cannons that the Natchez captured from Fort Rosalie. Others took part in hunts to supply the nation with game.[29]

The perspectives of both the Africans and the Indians on these issues are lost. The colonial records contain little from the Natchez concerning their treatment of the Africans. They also contain nothing about the questioning the Africans must have endured after their former masters recaptured them. A few clues, however, can be gleaned from the Louisianans' accounts. Although the former slaves enjoyed some degree of personal liberty, the People of the Sun still made them work without compensation. Father Le Petit and Le Page du Pratz both wrote that they made the ex-slaves haul goods from the Compagnie magazine, the demi-galley, and the army post.[30] They also required from the Africans some of the same types of labor that they demanded from the Europeans, relegating them to a subordinate category.

Although "black" men remained inferior to "red" in the Natchez order of things, there is evidence that they had gained some power over the "whites." Calliot wrote of the treatment of Madame Desnoyers at the hands of her former slaves. The clerk wrote that he heard her say that the five Africans who manned the Natchez artillery had made her their slave and forced her to pound rice into flour for them. Desnoyers said that they also wanted to burn her to death but were prevented from doing so by the wife of the Great Sun.[31] They may have been the same men who conspired with her in a plot to strike back at her husband's killers. In the words of Dumont de Montigny, "The negro slaves became free, you might say, and the Frenchwomen, slaves."[32]

The rearrangement of status based on skin color was another indication that the manner in which the Natchez and the colonists related to each other had changed drastically. For a few months, the People of the Sun regained control of their homeland and relegated their impudent European neighbors to a servile condition. The stations of the Africans were less clear. Although they enjoyed greater autonomy, the Natchez also put them to work. In this sense, the *"noirs"* remained beneath the *hommes rouges* in the emerging racial hierarchy.

Louisiana Strikes Back

When news that "all was blood and fire at Natchz" reached Périer, he threw the resources of the colony into protecting its capital from attack. On December 5, 1729, two days after the first refugees from Fort Rosalie made their reports, Périer wrote to Paris listing the measures that he had taken to prevent further losses. He organized a militia of four companies to defend New Orleans and decreed that no Indian was to be given arms without his explicit permission. He also ordered the construction of trenches to protect the town from assault.[33] The commandant-general concluded by asking his superiors to send the colony six hundred troops from France.[34]

Périer then dispatched Captain Merveilleux and a handful of men to warn the Europeans living along the banks of the Mississippi. After sounding a tocsin, the captain was to build a fort at the village of the Tunicas and await reinforcements.[35]

Périer intended to use the Indians' town as a staging area for an assault planned for February 19, 1730, once the aid of the Choctaws was secured. On December 8, the commandant-general sent Fort Rosalie's former commandant, Ignace François Broutin, to help organize the colony's forces that were to assemble at Merveilleux's camp.[36]

Périer also took the initiative in another set of matters. On December 30, 1729, he and De La Chaise, the colony's ordinateur, froze Kolly's assests.[37] The commandant-general levied a claim of 5,000 livres owed him by the late concession owner. Within two weeks, a thorough inventory of the dead man's property on his concession at Tchapitoulas and his home in New Orleans was conducted. The lists of goods spanned several dozen pages, indicating that, whatever financial difficulties the Swiss businessman might have endured, he had managed to live in comfort. His kitchen was well-equipped and his living quarters finely furnished. Nearly one hundred books lined his library's shelves, and his chests were filled with silk and satin clothing. Kolly's plantation at Tchapitoulas ran for a mile and a half along the Mississippi and reached across the Ile d'Orléans to Lake Pontchartrain. He owned thirty-two head of cattle and horses as well as seventy-five African slaves. Although these two properties were his main plantation and his residence in the provincial capital, their contents suggest that life at St. Catherine's might also have improved since the hard days of the early 1720s. By January 23, the bulk of Kolly's goods and slaves had been auctioned off, though the registrar failed to note the total receipts of the sales.[38]

Around the time that Merveilleux and Broutin started their journeys upriver, Périer issued another command. A small Indian community known as the Chaouachas lived a few miles downriver from New Orleans. These people had never shown hostile intentions toward the colony. Moreover, their small numbers—perhaps thirty families—represented little threat to the capital. Their town, however, bordered a small European settlement that served as the staging point for shipments to St. Catherine's Concession. On December 8, 1730, Périer sent eighty African slaves armed with axes, swords, and pikes to attack the Chaouachas' village. The Africans surprised the villagers while many of the men were out fishing and hunting. The expedition killed between fifteen and thirty males and took the women and children to New Orleans as captives. When the surviving hunters and fishermen traveled to the capital to petition the commandant-general for an explanation, he refused to answer them.[39]

A few months later, Périer justified his actions to his superiors in Paris:

> Fear had so powerfully taken the upper hand that even the Chaouachas who were a nation of thirty men below New Orleans made our colonists tremble, which made me decide to have them destroyed by our negroes, which they executed with as much promptness as secrecy. This example carried out by our negro volunteers has kept the other little nations up the river in a respectful attitude. If I had been willing to use our negro volunteers I should have destroyed all these little nations which are of no use to us, and which might on the contrary cause our negroes to revolt as we see by the example of the Natchez.[40]

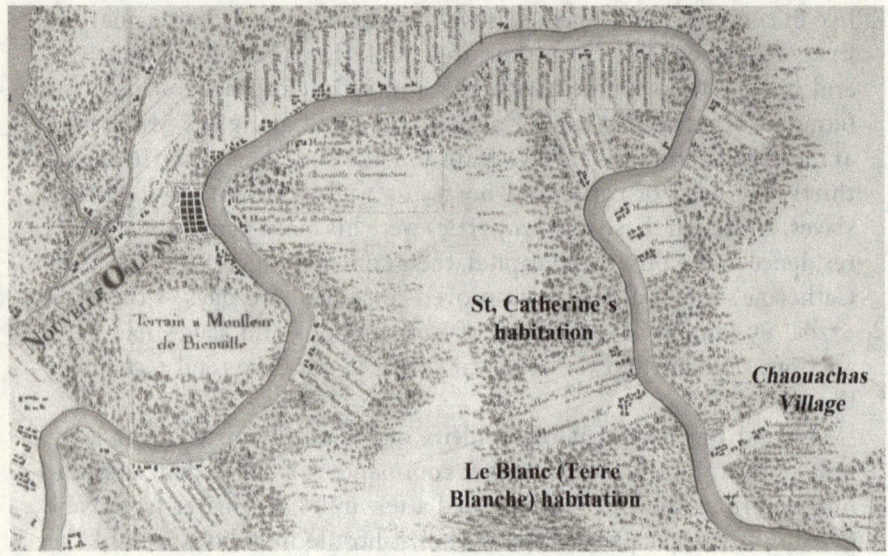

FIGURE 6.2. Concessions downriver from New Orleans showing the concessions associated with Terre Blanche (Le Blanc) and St. Catherine's Concession and the Chouauchas Village, circa 1723 (Carte Particuliére de Fleuve St. Louis, Ayers MS 30 Sheet 80, Newberry Library).

The commandant-general's decision to attack a peaceful Native American settlement foreshadowed the violence that was to mark Louisiana's relations with many of its Indian neighbors. Moreover, it revealed the anxiety over a slave revolt that plagued Europeans throughout the New World. As Africans made up an increasingly large proportion of Louisiana's non-native population, an anti-French league of "blacks" and Indians would be disastrous. In a letter that he wrote in the autumn of 1730, after the colony's government brutally suppressed a suspected slave conspiracy, Périer outlined this problem and his solution: "The greatest misfortune that could befall the colony would be a union between the Indians and the Black Slaves but happily there has been a great aversion between them, we have taken great care to maintain and augment this war."[41] Périer hoped that destruction of the Chaouachas would sow the seeds of enmity between Africans and Native Americans. The following years' events served to widen any breach between the two groups of peoples that may have existed before the commandant-general executed his scheme.

Despite his "success" in neutralizing the Chaouachas and driving a wedge between the region's two non-European populations, Périer feared that a broader coalition against Louisiana was imminent. On December 11, 1729, some Yazoos attacked Father Souel, a Jesuit missionary, on his way home from a meeting with their headman. Charlevoix provided the following reason for the attack: "Father Souel dearly loved these Barbarians; but he was impatient; he reproached them ceaselessly for falling into the infamous sin of Sodomy to which they were powerfully subjected, and it appears strongly that this was the cause of his death."[42] His slave, a recent convert to Catholicism, tried to keep the murderers from plundering the priest's home, an act for which he paid with his life. The killers took the cleric's cassock and other religious equipment.[43] The next day, Yazoo men entered Fort St. Pierre under the pretense of singing the calumet. Once inside, they pulled their weapons from beneath their robes and killed the officer and seventeen soldiers who made up the garrison. The intervention of several Koroa women from a nearby village saved five European women and four children.[44] These women may have been fulfilling the same political functions as the Tattooed Arm and her supporters. By advocating on behalf of the Europeans, they may have thought that they were preventing their peoples' men from creating an irreparable break with the outsiders. Their influence had its limits, though, since Koroa men assisted in the attack on the fort.[45]

Soon after the coup at Fort St. Pierre, a Yazoo delegation arrived at the Grand Village of the Natchez. One of the ambassadors wore the late Father Souel's black robe. He told his hosts that "his Nation had taken his word and that the outsiders who had settled among them had been massacred."[46] The Suns enticed their allies with the prospect of acquiring still more booty by making war on the colonists.[47]

While the Yazoos proffered their support, the Natchez wasted little time soliciting help from other nations in their war against Louisiana. The Natchez sent Tioux proxies to negotiate with their old enemies the Tunicas. Several incidents from the recent past caused the Natchez to deal prudently with their neighbors downriver. The first of these incidents came in 1716, when Bienville, with the Tunicas' help, captured several Suns and held them hostage. The second came in late summer of 1723, when the Natchez fought a war of retribution against the Tunicas.[48] The Tunicas took a prominent role in the destruction of the Apple and Jenzenaque Villages that same year. Bitter memories of these events made direct contact between leaders of the two nations dangerous. The Tunicas' continuing alliance with Louisiana undoubtedly increased the peril. Whatever the reason for their choice of intermediaries, the Suns stayed out of the direct negotiations. Regardless, the Tioux's delegation failed to enlist the Tunicas in the anticolonial cause.[49]

It is difficult, however, to assess the Natchez diplomatic efforts of 1729 and early 1730. Europeans generally did not record the debates that took place around the council fires of the Lower Mississippi Valley as Natchez ambassadors argued their cause. Delaye wrote about several attempts to secure more allies during the winter of that year. The Natchez sent embassies to the Houmas, who rejected their offers. The Chickasaws also refused to cooperate because they feared that the Choctaws, their long-standing foes, would use the opportunity to strike at them while their men were off fighting the colonists.[50]

Therefore, if the Natchez had been planning a pan-Indian uprising against Louisiana as several colonial officials claimed, they failed. Delaye argued against an English-inspired plot, particularly one that was supposed to have included the Choctaws when he observed that the People of the Sun "were enemies of the Choctaws for a very long time." He also noted, in regard to a widespread plot, that "the Natchez had kept this affair secret, they did not want to communicate it to any nation for fear of being betrayed."[51]

Despite the Natchez's lack of committed allies and with little evidence, Périer wrote that the Natchez had plotted their coup with the collusion of the Choctaws, who later failed to live up to their agreement.[52] Several other colonists claimed that the plot failed only because the Natchez had mistimed their assault. According to Calliot, Dumont de Montigny, and Le Page du Pratz, the Great Sun used a bundle of sticks to count down the days to the attack. Dumont de Montigny wrote that one of the Sun's children, watching his father burn one stick each day, threw a few of the counters into the fire as a lark.[53] In Le Page du Pratz's version, it was the Tattooed Arm who removed the sticks from the bundle to throw off the count.[54] In these two narratives—both written decades after the battle—the Natchez attacked the colonists several days too soon. Calliot told a similar tale in his memoir.[55] According to these sources, the Natchez mistiming caused the Choctaws to renege when they learned that the French were already on the alert due to the premature destruction of Fort Rosalie.[56] The novelist Chateaubriand built on these stories, immortalizing them in his epic *Les Natchez*. Thus, he furthered the image of Louisiana as a place of tragedy and exile that persists to this day in French popular memory.

Gordon Sayre, however, handily exploded this myth of innumeracy by pointing out that "if the Natchez and their allies could count out bundles of sticks, then they could certainly count the number of days the sticks represented."[57] Sayre also noted that none of the official reports dating from the early 1730s mentioned such a counting system.[58] The French historian Arnaud Balvay also questioned the accuracy of these stories.[59] Delaye, Broutin, and others who wrote immediately after the battles of January and February 1730 failed to make any references to errors in timing. Father Le Petit, for instance, wrote that the Natchez moved up their attack date in order to seize the trade goods on the demi-galley that carried Monsieur Kolly. Had they waited, the vessel would have continued upstream to Illinois.

There was another reason for the commandant-general to list the Choctaws among France's potential enemies. It was apparent to him that by the spring of 1730, the Choctaws were dissatisfied with the colony's failure to compensate them for fighting the Natchez. Delaye wrote of their "insolent demands" for ammunition during operations against the Natchez. The commander of the colonial forces had little choice but to turn over "200 pounds of powder, which was half of what we had."[60] Finally, as the description of the Choctaw delegation to the Natchez at the beginning of this book demonstrates, the colonists knew that their allies had contacted the Natchez only a few weeks earlier.

Périer's also characterized the Choctaws as conspirators in the Natchez scheme, perhaps to provide a ready explanation if the Indians' discontent spilled over into open warfare. The twentieth-century historian Jean Delanglez argued that Périer fabricated his pan-Indian conspiracy theory to conceal his culpability in the events that led up to the attack on Fort Rosalie.[61] The stories of a grand strategy concocted by a secret Indian coalition would have served the commandant-general's interest in covering up his role in the disintegration of the colony's relationship with the Natchez. His alleged interest in the Apple Village's land may have triggered the war.

> Gordon Sayre offered another interpretation:
>
> The existence of a Natchez "terrorist" plot was necessary for the historical emplotment of the massacre for both political and literary reasons. If the uprising had been a spontaneous act by a Natchez mob, not only might it portend more such acts of resistance to the colony, but it would be impossible to know who to blame. Likewise today, Euro-American leaders are eager to identify terrorist conspiracies and to demonize their leaders yet are highly reluctant to suppose the existence of a diffuse anti-imperialist

movement from which violent resistance might erupt without planning or warning.⁶²

Perrier's inclusion of the Choctaws in his conspiracy theory bolsters Sayre's argument for the "emplotment." Their presence in the commandant-general's communiqués, and the willingness of European audiences to accept his narrative, obscured the tensions between Louisianans and their indigenous neighbors. The motives of colonial officials notwithstanding, it is doubtful that the Choctaws wished to destroy the outsiders because they outnumbered the Louisianans more than five to one.⁶³ Had they wanted to wipe out the colony, they could have easily done so without Natchez assistance.

Father Charlevoix proposed another motive in his narrative:

> Several years before, they [the Choctaws] had wanted to destroy the Natchez and the French had prevented them, they had pretended to enter into a general conspiracy to entangle us with our Enemies, to whom we had accorded peace despite them, we were obliged to seek recourse from them while we were weak and they profited simultaneously by despoiling the Natchez and from our liberality.⁶⁴

Tales of shadowy plots aside, Périer needed to draw at least some of the Indians of the Southeast into his plans for revenge. The Choctaws were the obvious choice. Moreover, the Choctaws had several reasons to join the campaign against the Natchez. The first of these involved finishing what they had started. In the autumn of 1726, the Choctaws and Natchez fought a short but intense war. The People of the Sun lost two hundred villagers to disease because they spent most of the war behind the walls of their forts. The Choctaws' casualties were far fewer.⁶⁵ Only the mediation of D'Artiguiette Diron, the Compagnie director at Mobile, prevented the Choctaws from initiating a second war in the following year.⁶⁶

Another reason for joining the anti-Natchez coalition related to the Choctaws' desire for political primacy in the region. The Natchez had ties with the Chickasaws to the north.⁶⁷ French and Canadian officials wrote extensively about enmity between the Choctaws and the Chickasaws. Moreover, Commandant-General Périer thought that the Chickasaws were the driving force behind the Natchez uprising.⁶⁸ A Choctaw war against the People of the Sun would weaken the Chickasaws by depriving them of their allies.

Périer had already launched a diplomatic initiative to the Choctaws several months before the fall of Fort Rosalie.⁶⁹ His chief agent was a half-pay sub-lieutenant named Louis Joseph Guillaume de Régis du Roullet. He was to assure the Choctaws that New Orleans was aware of their complaints about the high costs of Compagnie goods. Régis du Roullet was also to inform them that Périer possessed the authority to remedy that situation. The commandant-general also ordered Régis to promise the Choctaws' headmen that the French would build a warehouse among them and match the prices of the British merchants.[70] He also directed his emissary to assess the military strength of the Choctaws and map the locations of their villages.[71]

Régis left New Orleans in the late summer of 1729, stopping briefly in Mobile in September. From there he started his journey up the Tombigbee River. In December 1729, still without word from his chief representative, Périer sent two more agents, Jean Paul de Le Sueur, a nephew of Bienville, and Joseph Christophe de Lusser, a Swiss officer, to secure the cooperation of the Choctaws.

While Périer's envoys traveled northeast, his troops began to gather at the Tunicas' village. After alerting the colonists living along the river, Captain Merveilleux and his six-man detachment reached the Indians' town on December 10, 1729. The presence of colonial soldiers squelched any moves toward an alliance with the Natchez if the will to join one had existed among the Tunicas. The officer quickly built a small fort in case of an attack from upstream. Ignace Broutin arrived a few days later to aid in the defense. On his way to the encampment, he delivered orders to Major Henri, chevalier de Louboëy, to bring north his garrison at Pointe Coupée. The major quickly followed with twenty-five infantrymen.[72]

In preparation for a full-scale assault, Captain Merveilleux formed a six-man reconnaissance team under the command of Sieur Mesplet, a veteran of Bienville's 1723 campaign. They were to scout the Natchez positions and report back. Mesplet also hoped to capture some prisoners that could be exchanged for those held by the Indians.[73]

The small troop quietly made their way upriver and spent an uneventful night a few miles outside of the Grand Village. Despite their stealth, Mesplet and his men found themselves surrounded by three hundred Natchez on January 25, 1730. The party sought cover in a small ravine and defended themselves as the Théoloëls called for their surrender. Navarre, a French soldier who was married to a Natchez woman and spoke their language, fired upon the assailants with a vengeance, "calling them dogs who did not deserve to live." The Natchez fired back, wounding Navarre and Mesplet. Navarre continued to shoot and hurl invectives until a second volley killed him where he stood. The rest of the survivors surrendered and were brought before the Great Sun.[74]

The Natchez leader refused to take Mesplet's word that the group had come to make peace. The Frenchman blamed the altercation on the drunken bravado of Navarre. During the parley, the Natchez gave their reasons for declaring war. They said that "it was The Commandant who had mistreated them, and for whom they had worked as slaves without having been paid, and they spoke of still many other reasons to soften and palliate their crimes."[75]

The Great Sun then called for Angelique Chaviron Desnoyers, the widow of the director of the Terre Blanche Concession, who spoke the Natchez language fluently.[76] He ordered her to draft a letter listing the conditions for release of his captives. In exchange for the prisoners' freedom, he demanded:

> two hundred muskets, two hundred barrels of powder, two thousand gun flints, two hundred knives, two hundred hatchets, two hundred pickaxes, twenty quarts of brandy, twenty casks of wine, twenty barrels of vermillion, two hundred shirts, twenty pieces of limbourg [trade cloth], twenty pieces of coats with lace on the seams, twenty hats bordered with plumes, and a hundred coats of a plainer kind.[77]

The Sun also insisted that the French turn over the chief of the Tunicas and Broutin as hostages. He sent Mesplet's drummer, a man named La Grandeur, to carry the letter to the French commander.[78]

According to Dumont de Montigny, a group of Natchez headmen held a meeting during which they asked a Frenchwoman who could speak their language her opinion about the war. They told her that they would make peace if the colonists recognized the death of de Chépart as revenge for the execution of Old Hair of the Apple Village—the headman of one French settlement for the headman of a Natchez settlement. The unnamed Frenchwoman thought the idea might work, but the records make no further mention of the plan.[79]

The Great Sun's employment of Angelique Desnoyers as a scribe and the Natchez consultation with a European woman suggests an enduring perception among the People of the Sun that they and the outsiders shared parallel social and political ranks—a mark of the old style of Natchez diplomacy. Madame Desnoyers, as the widow of a high-status European, enjoyed a status analogous to that of the Tattooed Arm. When the Great Sun employed her to write to Louboëy, she acted in a diplomatic capacity similar to that of the leader's mother. The headmen's conference with the Frenchwoman mirrored roles taken by Natchez women who had been born into lesser castes or foreign nations—she became a temporary advisor who shared the perspectives of the outsiders with whom they would have to negotiate.[80]

The Natchez soon realized that whatever parallel institutions or ranks they thought they shared with the Europeans, the colonists would not agree to their conditions. Broutin volunteered to surrender himself to the Natchez, but Périer refused to let him go.[81] When Le Grandeur failed to return with a reply, the enraged Great Sun ordered the soldiers burned on the rack. Two of the men died quickly; Mesplet lingered for several days.[82]

At the same time that the Natchez were burning Mesplet, Jean Paul Le Sueur was marching toward the Grand Village with more than five hundred Choctaw warriors. On January 27, 1730, they smashed into the unsuspecting Natchez. One chronicler wrote: "The reason that the Natchez were no longer on their guard was that they believed that the Choctaws had destroyed the lower part of this colony, they were so assured that they camped outside their forts without their munitions of war."[83] The Choctaws' assault resulted in the death of between sixty and one hundred Natchez and the capture of another fifteen to twenty. The attacking forces liberated fifty-four European women and children and seized one hundred enslaved Africans. The swiftness of the strike prevented the Indians from removing these prisoners to a more secure location. The wife of the Sun of the Flour Village had barely enough time to order the execution of three colonists to prevent them from being rescued.[84] Another group of three women, Dumont de Montigny's future wife among them, escaped from the White Woman's compound and found refuge with the Choctaws.[85]

Despite these setbacks, the Natchez had not been entirely without assistance during the battle. Périer wrote: "This defeat would have been complete if it had not been for two negroes [sic] who prevented the Choctaws from carrying off the powder and who by their resistance had given the Natchez time to enter the two forts."[86] These forts were palisaded structures a few hundred yards south of the Grand Village on either side of St. Catherine's Creek.[87]

When the People of the Sun retreated into their defensive works along with several dozen African and European hostages, chances for a quick conclusion of the war evaporated. Delaye lamented that the Choctaws' unsupported attack had deprived the colony of a decisive victory. He especially blamed Le Sueur: "Here was the sad effect of the ambition and

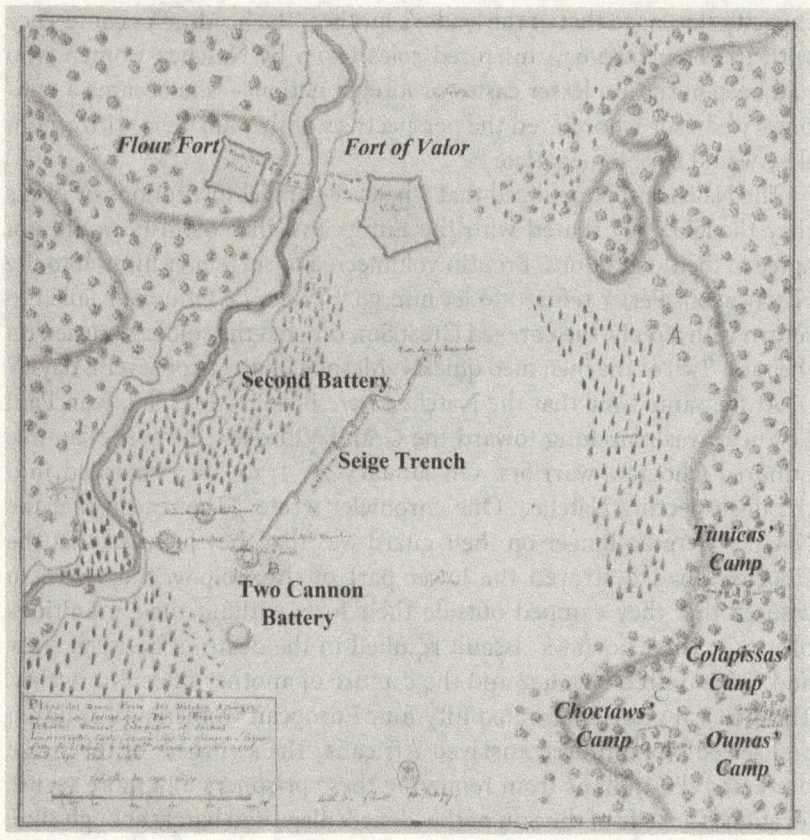

FIGURE 6.3. Natchez forts, Ignace François Broutin. (Plan des deux forts des Natchez [Indiens d'Amérique] assiégés au mois de février 1730 par les Français, Bibliothèque nationale de France, Estampes, Vd 21 [3] Fol.)

ignorance that [he] imagined that his presence alone was capable with our allies to destroy the fort made by our enemies.[88] The Choctaws looting the cabins in the Grand Village could hear the Natchez men singing their death songs inside their strongholds. They also hurled curses at the Choctaws for reneging on their commitment to unite in a war against the colony.[89]

Five days later, the colonial army stirred from their base at the Tunica Village and began to march north. Louboëy and his troops arrived at the Choctaw camp on the site of St. Catherine's Concession on February 8, 1730. It was here that Delaye surveyed the destruction wrought upon the settlement by the Apple Villagers. The colonial force consisted of two hundred men and two cannons, but they soon received several more guns: a seven-gun siege train of two- and four-pound field pieces.

The colonists set up a two-gun battery on the mound that had formerly held the temple.[90] Thus, the paramount Natchez heterotopic site, the one from which the Suns drew their power, was desecrated by their enemies. From this vantage point, the Europeans opened up on the forts at maximum range, but the barrage failed miserably.[91] The People of the Sun returned fire with three cannons they had dragged from Fort Rosalie. These did little damage because the Africans manning them lacked the training to use them effectively.[92]

The colonists began to dig an approach trench toward the Fort of Valor. The Natchez made several desperate forays to drive off the sappers. Although the Indians took the trench due to the poor leadership of the European officers, a counterattack forced them back.[93] The Louisianans continued to close in upon the fortresses. From behind their walls, the Natchez could see the Europeans setting up their batteries only a few hundred yards away. At this range, they would soon batter down the walls.

By this time hunger and disease were beginning to take their toll on the besieged. The colonists learned from a Houma woman who had recently been a Natchez prisoner "that the Natchez always had bad hearts, that from time to time they were killing our [European] women and that there was much sickness among them; that their women and their children were always crying; that their women were reproaching them for the death of the French." With time running short for the Indians, the Suns needed to find a way to parley without exposing themselves to enemy fire.

Two versions of the negotiations appear in the historical records. Both accounts reveal as much about their authors as they reflected on the events they described. According to Dumont de Montigny, Calliot, and D'Artiguiette Diron, the Suns called upon Madame Desnoyers once again.[94] They wanted her to act as their "fanimingo," representing Natchez interests to Louisiana's military decision makers. She strode across the battlefield, in the words of Dumont de Montigny, "like Pallas" [Athena].[95] Angelique Desnoyers delivered the Suns' offer: the Natchez would release all of the French women and children and remove their villages to any place the commandant would designate.[96]

Calliot, never one to miss an opportunity to tell a lurid tale, wrote that he had heard Desnoyers tell of her escape. When she returned to the Indians' forts after acting as interpreter, she noticed that she was alone with her guard, far behind the other Natchez delegates. She gestured to the man and motioned to him as if she wanted to whisper in his ear. When he came close, she stabbed him with a knife and began to run toward the colonists' positions. It was then that she felt pangs of remorse for leaving her twelve-year-old daughter in the hands of the Natchez. Nonetheless, she made it safely to the colonial army's lines.[97] D'Artiguiette Diron and Delaye also mentioned Madame Desnoyer's mission in their reports, and both wrote that the colonial officers would not let her return despite the Natchez offer to release all of the European women in exchange.[98]

Angelique Desnoyers, however, had another reason for concern. After the siege, two militiamen signed an affidavit that stated that the infant that they found on the battlefield was Angelique's son. Jacques Cantrelle, one of the signatories, swore that he witnessed Antoine Laurent Desnoyers's baptism on August 9, 1729. Cantrelle was in a unique position to know: his spouse, the town's midwife, had delivered Antoine. Angelique Desnoyers had served as ambassador for the Natchez a few months after giving birth.[99]

Despite her efforts, the Natchez did not make peace immediately. The day after Madame Desnoyers made her treks, the Choctaw leader Alibamon Mingo approached the parapets of the enemy and called out:

> Do you remember or have you ever heard it said that Indians have remained in such great numbers for two months before forts? You can judge by that our zeal and our devotion for the French. It is therefore useless for you who are only a handful of people besides our nation to persist any longer in being unwilling to surrender the women, children, and negroes whom you have to the French who are still good enough to spare you as you see after the treason that you have shown them, for if they had wished to shoot their big guns (speaking of the cannons) you would already be reduced to dust and we who will keep you blockaded here to die of hunger, until you have surrendered the women, children, and negroes who belong to the French, since we have resolved to sow here our fields and to make a village there, until you have executed what we demand of you.[100]

Alibamon Mingo might have provided incentive that the People of the Sun required. The next day they offered more favorable terms.

In their versions of the truce talks, Le Page du Pratz and Delaye listed Etté-Actal, the man who had escaped from becoming a sacrificial victim at the funeral of the Tattooed Serpent, as a primary negotiator. As Le

Page du Pratz noted, Etté-Actal had mastered the French language while serving as Bienville's hunter and used that knowledge to his advantage.[101] When the Natchez made their offer known through Madame Desnoyers, Louboëy countered that the Natchez must release all of the slaves and the slaves' children as well as all of the European captives.[102] Le Page du Pratz and Delaye wrote that Etté-Actal carried the Great Sun's promise to free his prisoners if the commander withdrew his artillery to the riverbank. The headman had one other requirement: that neither the colonists nor the Choctaws and other allies would enter the forts until the next day.[103] Delaye described Etté-Actal making several trips between the Indians' forts and the siege works to escort the Europeans and most of the Africans who had been held prisoners. The besiegers complied and pulled back their guns to the bluffs along the Mississippi.[104]

The Le Page du Pratz story took an unusual turn. He wrote that during the night of February 28, 1730, all of the Natchez, including their women, children, and some of the Africans, slipped out of their forts, crossed the Mississippi, and disappeared into the swamps. When the sun rose, the French discovered that their enemies had absconded. Le Page du Pratz intimated that Louisiana's erstwhile allies, the Choctaws and other Native American groups, had colluded to make this melodramatic getaway possible.[105] D'Artiguiette Diron's narrative contained essentially the same story, but he did not assign culpability for the Natchez escape.[106]

Delaye, however, delivered a more plausible story that once again featured Etté-Actal. In this version, the Natchez moved from their forts to the banks of the Mississippi some distance from the colonial army's camp. Over the course of two weeks, they built pirogues and sent thirty men across the river. Etté-Actal told the Louisianans that these men were leaving "to make bear oil for the French, that he wanted to give about a hundred pots to the Commandant, and about thirty pots to the officers."[107] In the Lower Mississippi Valley, bear oil was used for cooking and for its medicinal properties. It thus became a highly valued trade commodity for both natives and newcomers.[108] To further satiate their colonists, the White Woman sent cooked dishes to the officers. Apparently these ruses worked several times, because the food and excuses kept coming. According to Delaye, it was during these intervals that the Natchez slipped away to the swamps west of the river. The army failed to pursue the refugees because of the speed with which they traveled.

Worse, Louisiana's most important Indian allies refused to cooperate. The Choctaws spent the next few months negotiating over compensation for their efforts. They retained custody of a number of Africans as well as some of the colonists they had rescued in late January. They did this to ensure that the French would replenish their stocks of ammunition and pay them for missing the winter hunt—a crucial time during which they would have harvested deerskins to trade for manufactured goods. The talks between Louisianan officials and Choctaw leaders dragged on for two years. In the meantime, the Europeans still had to contend with the Natchez, who remained a potent military force despite their recent defeat.

The discrepancies between the Natchez escape accounts of Le Page du Pratz and D'Artiguiette Diron on the one hand, and Delaye on the other, reveal some key differences in their experiences and their politics. First, Delaye was an eyewitness to the events. D'Artiguiette Diron was in Mobile during the campaign while his brother Pierre was an officer in the siege trenches. Delaye vouched for Pierre D'Artaguette's bravery and character.[109] Nonetheless, D'Artiguiette Diron might have been reluctant to expose the lack of vigilance on the part of his sibling and his fellow officers. Le Page du Pratz, in New Orleans at the time of the fighting, was also far removed from the heat of battle. He wrote more than two decades later while residing in France. Le Page du Pratz had little to gain by pointing out the failures of his fellow countrymen, especially when he was attempting to highlight the importance of Louisiana to the French Empire. The Choctaws made for handy scapegoats for the Natchez escape, especially after the Choctaws' civil war that lasted from 1746 to 1750. That conflict pitted pro- and anti-Louisiana Choctaw factions against one another.[110]

Delaye, in contrast, spared little ink when it came to invectives regarding the conduct of the winter 1730 campaign. He castigated Louboëy for his slow responses. He held many of his fellow officers in contempt for their wrangling and corruption. He accused them of being more interested in "their trade in chickens, bear oil, and maize" than in fighting.[111]

His overall disdain for his colleagues notwithstanding, Delaye provided a far more direct reason for the Natchez success in eluding the colonial army. A soldier named Forban observed carrion birds circling above the Indians' forts, which made him think that they had evacuated them. When he found them empty, he reported to Louboëy. Some of the officers swarmed in to seize the goods that they found among the ruins. The worst of these, according to Delaye, was Broutin, who took pains to prevent his men from taking anything from the Terre Blanche Concession "so he could make a better prize." As Delaye recounted: "This war doesn't honor these men, whose main occupation has been to haggle and pillage from beginning to end, except for Dartaguette, Chambellan, and Mr. Louboys [sic] who appear to me very selfless, especially the first one, who has the character of a true officer."[112] With a good bit of the army bent on plunder and another part awaiting gifts of bear oil, several hundred people, including infants, the infirm, and elderly, easily slipped away over the course of two weeks.

Avaricious intentions aside, Louisiana had regained the territory that once held its most prosperous settlement, and Native American and colonial forces had driven off the most powerful indigenous group on the banks of the Mississippi River. The colony had lost several hundred settlers, several dozen slaves, and, most importantly, its diplomatic high ground with the Choctaws. Because of the mediocre performance of Louisiana troops during the 1730 campaign and the province's tardy payments to its ally, help from the Choctaws in future campaigns was uncertain.

The People of the Sun lost far more. The total casualties suffered when their forts fell went unrecorded by the Europeans, but they must have been sorely felt. The Natchez also lost their homeland, and by extension, access to those sites from which they drew their political and spiritual power. The fact that their enemies had used their holiest places as an artillery platform must have been especially painful. The subterfuge that allowed the Natchez to surprise the garrison and *habitants* at Fort Rosalie also deprived them of credibility with colonial officials. The ruses that they used in their subsequent escape across the Mississippi did little to restore it. Over the next year, Périer and his aides were hesitant to take the word of the Suns or their representatives. They frequently rejected further Natchez attempts to parley. This forced the People of the Sun into a rare position within Mississippian intercultural relations: they were faced with an implacable foe bent on their destruction.

Exile

In preparation for his next campaign, Commandant-General Périer concentrated his colonial militia in New Orleans and awaited the arrival of reinforcements from overseas. By the time the Natchez had evacuated the forts along St. Catherine's Creek, France had mobilized to aid its distant North American province. Despite the cooling of the Choctaws' ardor for war, the Tunicas continued to assist Louisiana throughout 1730 and 1731.

In March 1730, the Tunicas came to New Orleans bearing fifteen scalps and escorting two female and three juvenile prisoners, the Female Sun of the Flour Village among them. They presented the detainees to the commandant-general. During the proceedings, several former prisoners of the Natchez charged the headwoman with complicity in the deaths of three Europeans.[113] According to the witnesses, she had ordered their "heads broken" because they lacked the time to burn them alive. The commandant-general "determined that they were to die by the same torment that they had wanted for the others." Périer then acknowledged the Tunicas' gesture, pronounced sentence, and returned the Natchez women to their captors for execution.[114]

The Indians burned the headman's spouse in the Place d'armes. According to Dumont de Montigny, the female Sun "during this long and cruel agony did not come close to shedding a tear. To the contrary, she laughed at the lack of skill of her executioners who were making her suffer, speaking a thousand insults and threatening them by saying they would soon be dead when her people avenged her."[115] She cursed her tormentors, "saying that there was not a man among the Tunicas."[116] Her defiant words caused a considerable commotion among the indigenous spectators "for she suffered the same torment as a warrior with greater Courage."[117] Finally, a sergeant named Le Hoy who had once lived on the Terre Blanche Concession stepped forward and finished her off with his sword. Another *habitant* took the other Natchez woman and the three children, smashed their skulls, and threw their bodies into the flames. Thus, as the historian Sophie White has noted, the *femme chef's* killing was one means for both the Tunicas and the European survivors of the November 1729 coup to have revenge and to restore a sense of order to their world.[118]

On the other hand, the execution of the female Sun removed a key negotiator from the Natchez ranks. At the close of the Village Crisis in November 1722, her husband and the *femme chef* of the Natchez sang the calumet at St. Catherine's Concession.[119] Dumont de Montigny also noted that the Sun of the Flour Village attended the funeral of the Tattooed Serpent.[120] The headman probably brought his mate to the ceremony. The Female Sun's order to kill the Europeans demonstrated her authority over outsiders as well as the men of her community. Consequently the death of such a powerful woman served to widen the breach between the Natchez and the Tunicas. It also eliminated a person who might have been instrumental in efforts to end the fighting. After her passing, there are no records of female diplomats taking part in the Natchez subsequent attempts to negotiate with the colonists. More important, the Sun of the Flour Village became an irreconcilable enemy of both Louisiana and the Tunicas after they burned his wife.

Executing the female Sun was not the only way the Tunicas demonstrated solidarity with Louisiana. The *grand chef* of the Tunicas, Cahura-Joglio, had already converted to Catholicism.[121] On April 4, 1730, a few days after the executions, Father Raphael baptized Cahura-Juglio's son, François-Antoine, as well as the headman's wife, brother, and mother. The Tunica war chief followed suit and witnessed the baptism of his daughter, Rose Angélique, the same day.[122] Even Périer, who harbored a deep mistrust of most Native Americans, wrote: "The Tunicas, who, it can be said, were at that time the only Savage Nation truly friends of the French."[123] These Indians were to play a prominent role in Périer's latest plan to destroy the People of the Sun.

Louisiana bustled with activity during the autumn of 1730 as it prepared to attack the Natchez in their refuge west of the Mississippi. Ships had arrived at New Orleans over the summer carrying hundreds of European troops. Among them were companies of *troupes de Marine*, soldiers recruited to serve overseas under the orders of the Ministry of Marine. Each company numbered fifty men and operated outside of the regular chain of command of the French army.[124] This made them especially useful in the colonies since the commandant-generals and governors did not need to negotiate orders with regimental colonels who jealously guarded their prerogatives. The French government also sent a number of cannons and mortars—these last items were essential for siege operations. To ensure cooperation between the commandant-general and the regular troops, the Ministry of Marine appointed Périer's brother, Alexis-Antoine Périer de Salvert, as the overall military commander. Both the Natchez and the Europeans would fight the next campaign with forces led by brothers.[125] The French, however, had reassembled a pair who had defeated the Compagnie's enemies on the African littoral.

In mid-November 1730, soon after he returned to New Orleans from a conference with the Choctaws at Mobile, Périer departed with the army's vanguard as it moved to the Bayagoula's village.[126] The balance of his forces left New Orleans on December 9 and caught up five days later. The army camped for four days waiting for the civilian militia.[127]

On December 28, 1730, the troops moved on to the Red River to rendezvous with the frigate *Prince de Conti*.[128] They resumed their march five days later, accompanied by a contingent of Tunica warriors. Périer gathered reinforcements from the posts at Natchez and Natchitoches en route to the Black River. Small parties from the "Petites Nations" rounded out the force.[129] Despite the infusions of Native Americans, the army was overwhelmingly European. The expedition consisted of 192 soldiers of the *troupes de Marine* led by 20 officers. It also included 20 sailors, 190 men of the colony's troops, 164 militia, 84 Africans, and 181 Indians. Ancillary personnel brought the total to 811.[130] Their siege train included six cannons and the same number of light mortars.[131]

Périer split his men into three battalions as they searched for the Natchez. The commandant-general kept his artillery and a large detachment under his direct command during the advance.[132] On January 19, 1731, the Indian auxiliaries discovered some Natchez hunters in the bayou near the Black River. A company of *troupes de Marine* and Ouchitas returned with word that they had found the enemy's main fort.[133] Périer left Baron De Crenay with a hundred men to guard the camp while he moved his troops up the Black River.

The Tunicas acted as a screening force and maintained communications between the three battalions as they worked their way through the bayous and swamps. The thick cane breaks allowed the army to approach undetected to within musket range of the Natchez earthworks. Meanwhile, De Crenay's men broke camp and took up a position on the left of the main body of troops.[134] Before they could react, the People of the Sun were surrounded, but this time by a conventional army equipped with artillery.

On January 21, 1731, Périer sent a spokesman under a flag of truce to negotiate the return of the Africans still held by the Natchez. "They [the Natchez] fired on the flag and said to the interpreter that they do not want to talk to dogs like us.... [T]wo hours later one of our wooden mortars arrived and fired some heavy shells which fell into their huts and started fires."[135] The screams of the Natchez women and children could be heard from behind the walls after each volley. The pace of the firing took its toll on the equipment. The oversized gunpowder charges burst two of the mortars. The arrival of the last units of the siege train on January 22 replenished the French batteries, and the shelling continued for the next two days while the weather deteriorated.[136]

The bombardment eventually wore down the Natchez, who hung out a white flag at seven o'clock on the morning of January 24, 1730. They had endured three days of cannon fire. Périer recalled the preliminary negotiations:

> I said to them that he had nothing to talk to them about until they sent me the negroes who were in their fort and in their fields.

Nineteen negro men and one negro woman arrived immediately and [the Natchez reported] that the others had been killed and that six were on a hunt with some of their people. I said to the same *sauvage* that I did not want to parley about anything unless the chiefs came to our camp first.[137]

The Indian negotiator told Périer that the Great Sun's brother, a man named St. Cosme, as well as the Sun of the Flour Village intended to fight on. The Great Sun offered different terms: if Périer's army withdrew, the Natchez would never again take up arms against the French and would return to their old villages if permitted.[138] The commandant-general repeated that he would parley only if the Suns came out of their fort. Périer promised that he would let them live if they surrendered and gave them a day to think it over. He told the Natchez spokesman that if the Suns did not yield, he would resume shelling the fort, and that he would take no prisoners when he overran it.[139]

After the first Natchez diplomat withdrew, another, St. Cosme, came out to speak to Périer. He told the commandant-general that the primary instigator had died during the Choctaws' siege of 1730. Périer listened politely to the Sun's explanation and then repeated his demand that all of the Suns come out of the fort. He would hear no more and would fire upon anybody besides those headmen who emerged in an attempt to parley. Périer then threatened to reduce the Natchez defenses to cinders.[140]

St. Cosme returned to the fort and shortly reappeared with the Great Sun and the Sun of the Flour Village. Périer took the three men prisoner. The Great Sun and Périer discussed the situation later that day. The Natchez leader proclaimed his innocence, citing his lack of influence with his nation's council due to his youth and inexperience. The Great Sun blamed the leader of the Flour Village, calling him a usurper and asserting that he was responsible for the conflict. Périer listened to the headman's protest and ordered the men held in a cabin in the army's camp. The commandant-general engaged the chief of the Tunicas and a Natchez leader named the Tattooed Serpent in an unsuccessful attempt to learn more from the three. During the night, the Sun of the Flour Village escaped. Le Sueur, one of the officers assigned to guard them, threatened to blow the brains out of the other two if they tried to run.[141]

His own imprisonment and Périer's threats convinced the Great Sun to order his people to surrender. The French commander agreed not to enter the fort until all of the Natchez had evacuated it. On the morning of January 25, the White Woman led their women and children into captivity. Some of the men surrendered later that day. Roughly 450 women and children became prisoners of the Europeans. Forty-six warriors also laid down their arms.[142]

Not all of the Natchez turned themselves in; at least seventy men vowed to continue the struggle from inside the fort. Périer ordered his troops to fire upon them, but rain prevented them from doing so. The bad weather lasted through the night and soaked the gunners' powder. The dampness made it impossible for the colonists to resume their bombardment. As a result, the Natchez slipped away in the darkness and made off to the south.[143]

A different fate awaited those who had surrendered. The soldiers loaded most of their prisoners onto the demi-galley and the frigate moored in the Black River. Périer divided the rest between smaller boats for the trip to New Orleans. The next day his men set about demolishing the fort. On January 28, Périer and his convoy set sail and arrived at the capital on February 5.[144]

Since the ships in the port were too few to hold all of the prisoners, some of the Natchez women and children were locked up in the main government building. It was during this time that Le Page du Pratz spoke with the Tattooed Arm, who was imprisoned "despite all she had done to warn the French."[145] During her captivity in New Orleans, she told him her story. Le Page du Pratz included her version of events in parts of his three-volume history of Louisiana.

Périer kept his promise to the Great Sun, and none of the prisoners were executed. A few stayed behind, enslaved on European plantations along the lower reaches of the Mississippi. The commandant-general, in an act that reflected his experiences in French African slaving ports, had most of the others loaded onto a Compagnie ship bound for Saint Domingue. The 164 who survived imprisonment and the voyage—the Great Sun and the White Woman included—spent the rest of their days as slaves in the sugar fields near Cap Francis.[146]

The exile of the Natchez was not complete, though, as a powerful remnant remained free. Three bands with as many as 300 men continued to fight against Louisiana and its allies. The Sun of the Flour Village, the man who had lost his wife at the hands of the Tunicas, led the most powerful group of 140 warriors and 60 women bolstered by 20 Africans. Under his leadership, another cycle of revenge commenced.[147]

In April 1731, 120 Natchez, equal numbers of men and women, approached the Tunicas asking them to mediate with the Louisianans.

The large proportion of women appeared to underscore the group's peaceful intentions. The Natchez agreed to settle at whatever place the commandant-general designated.[148] The number of men bearing arms among them must have come as a surprise to Périer since as late as March 25, 1731, he confidently reported: "Since the river has become freed by the destruction of the Natchez, Tious, Yazoos, and Coroas . . . of these four nations not more than forty men remain who have scattered to avoid falling into the hands of the nations that I sent in pursuit of them."[149] The commandant-general agreed to the peace proposal. He ordered them to disarm and move to a site about five miles from the Tunicas. From Périer's response, it appeared that the People of the Sun had regained some diplomatic leverage.

On June 13, 1731, the Sun of the Flour Village led nearly two hundred of his people into the Tunicas' village to chant the calumet.[150] The Tunicas welcomed them on behalf of Périer. In order not to upset the women in his party, the Sun asked that his men be permitted to keep their weapons overnight.[151]

Early the next morning, the Natchez sprung upon their hosts. Cahura-Joglio was one of the first fatalities. With their leader gone, the nation's war chief rallied his men and fought for five days to eject the invaders from his town. The Tunicas lost twenty dead, twenty wounded, and eight women captured. Thirty-three Natchez combatants died, and three were taken prisoner.[152] The rest escaped, taking with them the weapons and supplies that they had seized from the Tunicas.[153]

Around the same time that the Sun of the Flour Village was fighting the Tunicas, the colonists discovered 150 Natchez in the vicinity of the Grand Village. The commandant, De Crenay, convinced thirty-seven Indians to come inside the fort. Once they were behind its walls, he ordered his soldiers to seize them. In their haste, the troopers failed to find the knives hidden among their prisoners. The captives managed to grab eight muskets, killing a sentry in the process. They then barricaded themselves in the fort's jailhouse until De Crenay trained a cannon on the building. In the ensuing bombardment, all of the Natchez died, including the women and children. Only the leader of the group survived since he had already been sent downriver to New Orleans.[154]

Afterward, many of the Natchez moved north to seek refuge with the Chickasaws. By the summer of 1731, they had constructed a village near their new hosts. When Périer demanded they be remanded, the Chickasaws replied "that they had not gone to get them to hand them over, that they know very well how to defend them."[155] Louisiana now faced six hundred Chickasaw and as many as three hundred Natchez fighters.[156] The colony responded by declaring war upon the Chickasaws in July. By this time, however, Périer had finally secured the backing of the Chickasaws' long-standing enemy, the Choctaws.[157]

The growing might of the anti-Natchez coalition did not prevent the Sun of the Flour Village and his band from harassing colonial settlements west of the Mississippi. On October 5, 1731, the Natchez tried to overrun the village of the Natchitoches and nearby Fort Jean-Baptiste. The Sun and two hundred warriors succeeded in driving the Natchitoches Indians from their riverside town and forced them to seek refuge in the colonists' fort. After rallying his allies, the commandant, Louis Juchereau de Saint Denis, counterattacked with twenty-two soldiers together with all of the Natchitoches, a band of sixteen Spaniards from nearby Texas, and 250 Caddos Indians. They swept the Natchez out of Natchitoches, killing thirty, and capturing twenty-eight men and women.[158] In his report to Périer, Saint Denis listed the "famous Flour Chief" among the dead.[159] Some of the Natchez survivors fled up the Red River to the Ouachitas, while others retreated into Chickasaw territory.[160]

After their defeat at the gates of Fort Jean-Baptiste, the People of the Sun ceased to function as an autonomous polity. Although as many as three hundred of their military-aged men remained free, they were unable to operate as a united force. Tracking down that remnant became a primary goal of Louisiana's Indian policy. As if to underscore the devastation that they had visited upon their enemies, from the death of the Sun of the Flour Village on, French records never again mentioned a Natchez leader by name. Nor did officials in Louisiana write about any further negotiations with the Natchez. The People of the Sun settled in their own villages in Chickasaw Country. In the succeeding decades, they dispersed into settlements among the Creeks and the Cherokees.[161]

Over the course of fifteen years, the diplomatic prowess of the Tattooed Serpent and his wife, the Tattooed Arm, and St. Cosme had given way to relentless warfare under the Sun of the Flour Village. From their position as the preeminent nation in the Lower Mississippi Valley that had offered shelter to bands fleeing the chaos of slave raids and warfare, the Natchez themselves had become refugees. Moreover, stripped of their homeland and its authority-generating landscape, the rubric of biological difference—race—had replaced many of the old practices that had brought them together as a people. The People of the Sun fostered internal hegemony by focusing on their identity as red men, but their initial success provoked the ire of France. That nation's quest for revenge eventually scattered them among the indigenous communities of the Southeast. The red identity, which the Natchez helped to shape, spread and took on a life of its own.

Legacies

The fates of all but two of the Natchez who were sent to Saint Domingue remain a mystery. Bienville, on his return to Louisiana to take up the post of governor, stopped at the island colony. There he met with the Great Sun and his wife. After the Canadian's cursory mention of the encounter, nothing is known of what became of the People of the Sun in their overseas exile. To date, only one vague reference to the cost of maintaining the Great Sun has surfaced and that in a secondary source without citations to eighteenth-century records. Michel Besson, an early-twentieth-century historian, noted that the Compagnie sought 1,888 livres compensation for the expenses it incurred in the maintenance of the Great Sun and his family at Cap Français.[1]

After the defeats of 1731, the Natchez who eluded capture dispersed among various indigenous communities throughout the Southeast. One group fled to the Ouchitas on the Red River, another went to the Chickasaws, and a third band attempted to return to their ancestral lands near Fort Rosalie. The Tunicas and colonial soldiers quickly captured or dispersed them.[2] Some Natchez traveled east to Charles Town. In the spring of 1734, a delegation of "Natchees" visited the capital to ask for authorization to move to South Carolina's frontier region.[3] Two years later, another group of "Natchee" Indians petitioned the colony's government for permission to settle within its borders. There they came into contact with the largest Native American group bordering the southern British colonies: the Cherokees. These American Indians called the immigrants the Ani-Ná'sti.[4] James Adair recorded Natchez villages among the Chickasaws and the Creeks some thirty years after Bienville's last campaign.[5]

Despite their small numbers, these dispersed Natchez strove to maintain their identity. During the second half of the eighteenth century, British observers noted the presence of "Notchee" towns among the Cherokees that retained unique linguistic and cultural practices.[6] In 1813, two Moravian missionaries drew a map of Creek Country that included a town called Natchez.[7]

George Stiggins, an author of Natchez and Anglo-American ancestry, wrote in the 1830s that some his mother's people lived in Alabama among the Creeks.[8] By this time, the Natchez had adopted the language of their host tribe. Stiggins noted that most of them lived in the Talladega Valley. He recorded their exile from "the seat of their ancestors" as well as their search for homes among the Cherokees and Creeks. At least some of the Suns survived the war with Louisiana. Stiggins wrote that they settled at Talladega after "the greater part of [the tribe was] headed by the royal family made a compact of assimilation with the Abekas."[9] One of their legends regarding a global flood, similar to the one heard by Le Page du Pratz, was still being told one hundred years after the destruction of Fort Rosalie.[10] When the Creeks and Cherokees moved west to Oklahoma, the People of the Sun went with them.

Other aspects of Natchez culture persisted for generations. The anthropologists James Mooney and John Swanton found that the Natchez language and customs endured through the first decade of the twentieth century.[11] During those years Natchez people continued to constitute a distinct portion of the Creek and Cherokee nations, taking part in their governance and spiritual practices.

At the dawn of the twenty-first century, there is a Notchee Town outside of Gore, Oklahoma, whose inhabitants trace their roots back to the Théoloëls. Descendants of Natchez Indians still celebrate the Deer Moon Festival at the beginning of each spring at the Grand Village near the banks of St. Catherine's Creek.[12]

The legacies of the Europeans in Natchez Country during this time period are somewhat easier to trace. Louis XV called Bienville out of retirement and appointed him governor of Louisiana. The Canadian finally attained the official rank that he had sought for more than a quarter century. Upon his return to the colony, he quickly found himself embroiled in same the hunt for the Natchez remnant that had troubled Commandant-General Périer. Bienville's single-minded pursuit of the People of the Sun drew the province into smoldering warfare that burst into heated campaigns against the Chickasaws in 1736 and again in 1739. In 1742, the aging governor requested that he be permitted to retire. The following year, the king granted him his wish, and he spent the remainder of his life in Paris, dying in March 1767. Thus, Bienville, who was present at the birth of la Louisiane, lived long enough to see it pass out of French control and into the hands of the British and Spanish Crowns.

The Périer brothers fared quite well once they returned to France. Étienne endured a brief but humiliating interval before he left Louisiana. Bienville's faction took advantage of every opportunity to publicly deride the commandant-general after news of his recall arrived in New Orleans. The new governor was not much more gracious once he disembarked.

After a brief hiatus, Étienne Périer returned to sea as second officer on the *Neptune*, which cruised his old station, the coast of Senegal, in 1734. Within three years, he was in command of his own ship, the *Griffon*, again plying the waters off the slave ports of the Company of the Indies. After taking a number of prizes and winning several battles at sea during the War of Austrian Succession, Périer was appointed vice admiral by the king in 1751. His promotion coincided with the burst of writing flowing from the pens of Le Page du Pratz and Dumont de Montigny. The former was drafting the first installments of his adventures in Louisiana for publication in one of France's most prestigious journals. Alexis-Antoine Salvert de Périer, the younger brother, also attained the rank of admiral in the French navy. Before his death in 1757, the minister of marine placed Salvert de Périer in charge of the Dêpot des cartes et plans de Marine, the naval bureau of maps and fortress architecture.[13]

During the same period that the Périers were rising through the ranks, Father Charlevoix was composing his histories of France's New World possessions. Between 1730 and 1731, he published his *Histoire de l'isle Espagnole ou de S. Domingue*. In 1742, he became the procurator for the Jesuit missions and the Ursuline convents in French North America. Two years later, with his procuracy mired in debt, he published his most famous work, *Histoire et description générale de la Nouvelle France*. In it, Charlevoix failed to mention the fracas between the Capuchin Father Raphael and his Jesuit rival, Father Beaubois. He also downplayed the events preceding the destruction of Fort Rosalie, noting only that de Chépart "had a small disagreement with the *Sauvages*."[14]

Charlevoix had cause not to alienate the kingdom's most illustrious naval personalities by criticizing the Périers. Employing materials from the naval archives, the Jesuit promulgated Étienne Périer's theory that a general Native American conspiracy behind the uprising of 1729. (He also culled a good deal of information from Father Le Petit's letters to the Jesuit headquarters on the rue de Bac.) His order had invested time and effort cultivating a constituency among France's seagoing communities. From the mid-seventeenth century, Jesuit colleges in the coastal cities included geography in the curriculum to attract the sons of merchant and naval families.[15]

The most famous of Louisiana's historians, Antoine-Simon Le Page du Pratz, returned to France in the mid-1730s with ambitions to rise in its scientific community. Unlike the Périer brothers or Father Charlevoix, few details of his life are known after his sojourn in Louisiana. Between 1751 and 1752, the *Journal Oeconomique* published a twelve-part version of his memoir of Louisiana.[16] In 1758, his three-volume *Histoire de la Louisiane* reached the reading public. As Shannon Dawdy has observed, the book was an attempt by Le Page du Pratz to gain entry into France's society of letters. His writings became the foundation for subsequent histories of French Louisiana.[17] His work coincided with the apogee of Périer's fame; the former commandant-general had attained the rank of rear admiral with a pension of 3,000 livres around the same time.

As had been the case with Charlevoix, Le Page du Pratz had little to gain from castigating the leaders of the colony. Thus, the aspiring writer gave only a passing comment regarding Périer's decision to reinstate de Chépart as commander of Fort Rosalie after the captain's abusive treatment of Dumont de Montigny. Instead, like several others who chronicled the Natchez, he placed the blame squarely on de Chépart. Le Page du Pratz went so far as to include an extensive dialogue between the captain and the Sun of the Apple Village. The Dutchman never revealed his source for that conversation, although he might have heard it from the Tattooed Arm, whom he interviewed in the winter of 1731. Whoever told him of the exchange that sparked the Franco-Natchez War, he did not hold Commandant-General Périer responsible.

The other French subject who made a name for himself with an account of Natchez Country was Lieutenant Jean-François-Benjamin Dumont de Montigny. He not only refused to hold Périer responsible for the breakdown with the colony's powerful indigenous neighbors, but he also heaped praise upon the commandant-general, a man whom he characterized as the province's "Solomon." The lieutenant had even more cause to stay on good terms with Louisiana's former leader. During the time that he was composing the draft of his journal, the Périer brothers were approaching the height of their careers. When Dumont de

Montigny published his two-volume *Mémoires historiques sur la Louisiane* in 1753, both held flag ranks in the navy.

Moreover, Dumont du Montigny was perhaps the most vulnerable of all the chroniclers. He had failed to restart his career once he returned to France, and even suffered the indignity of having the Compagnie des Indies deny him the salary it owed him for more than a decade of service. He was unable to rise above the rank of sub-lieutenant that he had held since 1717. Instead, he languished at his post at Port St. Louis near Lorient on the French Atlantic coast, hoping that his connections with Belle-Isle, his noble patron, would bring him better fortune. He also demonstrated his penchant for alienating his superiors and landed in prison again. The sub-lieutenant's decision to assign the blame for war with the Natchez to de Chépart was perhaps driven by his fear of further bad luck. In the words of Dumont de Montigny, "it was all the fault of one man, who has deprived us of these good and generous Indians," rather than an overarching colonial policy.[18]

Dumont de Montigny's other legacy actually originated with his wife. After Louboëy negotiated with the Natchez for the release of the hostages, Marie Baron Roussin, the widow of Jean Roussin, regained her freedom. The sub-lieutenant had lodged with the Roussins in 1728 while he was posted at Fort Rosalie. It was his defense of Jean during his dispute with Longrais that provoked de Chépart to clap the junior officer in irons. Marie married Dumont de Montigny on April 19, 1730, roughly two months after her liberation.[19] Her testimony about life within the Natchez forts during the siege of 1730, recorded in her husband's memoirs, constitutes the most comprehensive record of the Natchez racial strategies in operation.[20]

Hers was not the only captivity narrative, however. Several dozen women survived the ordeal and, like Marie Baron, many of them remarried soon after their arrival in New Orleans. Between February and November of 1730, at least eighteen widows took new husbands in the colonial capital. Several more took their wedding vows the following year. As Marc Antoine Calliot attested, these women brought with them more accounts of their imprisonment.[21]

Angelique Desnoyers was one of the few French women whose name and story appeared in the published accounts of the Franco-Natchez War. The perspectives of the other women and children old enough are lost. The same is true for the Africans who endured the first few months of the war. The European men who wrote the documents upon which later anthropologists and historians rely mentioned them rarely. Thus, the peoples closest to the action, the Natchez and Africans, as well as the women caught within the besieged Indian fortresses, received little attention from the authors despite the fact that they served as the primary informants for the histories. Thus, the story behind Natchez development of racial practices comes to us indirectly.

The fortunes of the Compagnie des Indes shifted radically after the destruction of Fort Rosalie.[22] On January 23, 1731, Louis XV accepted the retrocession of Louisiana, which ended nearly two decades of corporate control of the province. The Compagnie never again invested in the Lower Mississippi Valley: the Franco-Natchez War of 1729 ended any hopes that la Louisiane would blossom into a commercial export colony. Instead, the "frontier exchange economy" of the province's early days persisted into the nineteenth century. Soon after, the king replaced Périer with his predecessor, Bienville. The Compagnie turned its attention to developing its trading posts in South Asia and its slaving stations in Africa. Two of Louisiana's historians took advantage of the firm's reorientation. Marc Antoine Calliot and Dumont de Montigny took up positions on the Indian subcontinent in the 1750s. Their decisions to relocate proved unlucky for both men: the clerk drowned in a shipwreck, and the hapless sub-lieutenant perished somewhere in India in 1760.[23]

In contrast to the fleeting French commercial presence in the region, the most enduring legacy of eighteenth-century Natchez-Franco relations may well be that of its indigenous inhabitants' switch from a location-based identity to one that privileged skin color. The People of the Sun began to use redness to unite the fractious villages of their chiefdom. At first, this strategy supplemented older practices of employing sacred spaces and pathways to achieve political solidarity. The close proximity in which the Europeans, Africans, and Native Americans lived gave the Natchez perfect vantage points to observe the manner in which the disparate groups of newcomers used their skin color to achieve hegemony. Moreover, these Native Americans could see that despite their superior technologies, the Europeans could not effectively make use of the landscape—they were peoples who could not get their spatial act together. Yet they managed to control one of three major groups living in Natchez Country: the Africans. The Natchez also could see that the Europeans were about to include them in the same underclass by extending the laws that categorized "blacks" as "*sauvages*." When the Choctaw-Colonial offensive of 1730 ejected the Children of the Sun from their homeland, these older ways based on spatial practices literally lost their grounding, leaving them to turn toward a red identity to keep them together.

Father Le Petit's letters suggest that the syntax of race had already gained purchase among the Choctaws around the same time the Natchez were planning their coup. The Choctaws certainly had engaged its grammar by the time they saw the decapitated heads outside the tobacco shed at St. Catherine's Concession.[24] One Louisianan envoy, Sub-Lieutenant Louis Joseph Guillaume de Régis du Roullet, wrote about Choctaw leaders calling themselves red men as early as the autumn of 1729. In September of that year, Red Shoe, a war leader, had told him that "the words among the French as well as among the red men that the Great Chief of the Mississippi had intended to say that we wanted to embrace the talk of the English."[25] Red Shoe's employment of the term "red men" to identify American Indians resembles the use of the term by the guardian of the Natchez temple and the Taensa storyteller a few years earlier. Moreover, there was a link between Red Shoe and the People of the Sun. The war leader had captured several Natchez villagers fighting alongside colonial troops during Bienville's campaign of 1723; he may have heard about red men at that time.[26]

Red Shoe was not the only Choctaw who used the term "red men" during those years. While attending a meeting in September 1729, another headman complained to Régis that "the red men would not be duped" by the Compagnie director at Mobile when the Frenchmen refused to give the customary gifts to the leaders of Choctaw communities.[27] Another European officer, Josephe Christophe de Lusser, also on diplomatic mission to the Choctaws on behalf of the colony, met with Mingo Emita from the Scanapas' town in late February 1730 after the destruction of Fort Rosalie. The Choctaw leader told him of a rumor circulating among the villages that the "the chief of the French" had written to the "English Governor" suggesting that their two governments shut off the flow of merchandise to the Indians. According to the story, the Englishman refused and said, "Since the French wanted to abandon the red men he was going to send merchandise to the Chickasaws and to the Choctaws."[28]

On the same day, another Choctaw "peace chief" named Atachimingo told Lusser of a recent conference with the leaders of the Alibamons. These Indians spoke highly of the French because of their largesse but said that it was important "to live well with all the whites" because of the valuable items that they provided.[29] Moreover, the Alibamon leaders promulgated a discourse of unity centered upon a common identity. They told the Choctaws that "among the red men they ought to do the same thing and never again speak of making war ... and that was the way to live in peace in their houses and see their children grow up without anxiety."[30] By the spring of 1730, ideas that redness symbolized an indigenous identity had moved beyond the Taensas, Natchez, and Choctaws to the Muskogee-speaking Alibamons.

Whether the Choctaws and Alibamons borrowed redness as a source of identity from the Natchez or developed it independently remains uncertain. One thing is clear: the term gained rapid currency throughout the Southeast during the late 1720s and early 1730s. Although the Natchez cannot be identified with absolute certainty as the source of the ideology of redness in Native America, they were the first to use it in front of European observers. Le Page du Pratz dated his interview with the Natchez temple guardian to the spring of 1725, nearly a year before the Cherokees' employment of the term "red" during a conference with the Creeks in South Carolina.

The Natchez shift from a spatially grounded identity to one based on racial categories had indirect but devastating consequences for Louisiana. The colony's leaders were drawn into an exhausting quest to track down and eliminate the Natchez, a practice that led to incessant low-intensity warfare with the Chickasaws. That conflict became disruptive for the province's further development.

France soon found itself involved in another series of wars with Great Britain that would determine who would dominate the North American continent. Officers responsible for the security of the province turned to a radically different system of power-generating spatial practices. Louisiana, in its bid to retain a presence in the Mississippi basin, constructed forts at several strategic points along its waterways. The colony could no longer rely on consistent support from its Indian neighbors. Thus, by the middle of the 1700s, it counted on stone and iron to dominate key terrain features in the region and thereby generate power. The indigenous allies who once acted as a glacis for Louisiana had far more pressing issues to resolve by this time.

The Choctaws found themselves embroiled in a vicious civil war between French supporters and an anti-French faction. The struggle cost hundreds of lives and destroyed dozens of villages.[31] When the Choctaws finally emerged from the conflict in the early 1750s, they kept the Louisianans at a distance and steered a middle course between the French, the British, and the Spanish colonies. The Creeks and the Caddos followed the example of the Choctaws and also avoided entangling foreign alliances. The other Indian nations in the Southeast had suffered such catastrophic population losses that their contributions to Louisiana's cause were negligible.

When the People of the Sun abandoned Natchez Country in 1730, the time of the classic Mississippian complex chiefdoms ended. Native American groups of the Southeast still took in bands of refugees, but these became members of loose confederations rather than subordinate villages within centralized polities. While most of them still revered their landscapes, the older sacred locations such as temple mounds had lost much of their significance. The homeless Natchez who eluded the colonists helped to spread a lasting cultural practice. Choctaw, Chickasaw, Cherokee, and Creek diplomats were calling themselves red men by the beginning of the fourth decade of the eighteenth century. Before long, their British and American counterparts began using the term as well, but with less benign intentions. When the French and Indian War ended in 1763, Native American religious and political leaders often employed the concept of a shared Indian identity to unite their peoples against the British and their colonists. The racial category of "red men" had become an integral component of intercultural relations in North America, a component that was developed and refined in Natchez Country.

Notes

Abbreviations Used in the Notes

- **AM** — Archives de la marine: Naval Archives of France, Paris.
- **AN** — Archives nationales de France, Paris.
- **ANOM** — Archives nationales d'outre mer: The Colonial Archives of France, Aix-en-Provence. These are divided into subseries; the following are those that appear the most in this volume:
  - Subseries 9   St. Domingue (Haiti)
  - Subseries 11   Canada
  - Subseries 13   Louisiana

Each subseries is further broken down into volumes and folio numbers. For example, ANOM, C13A, vol. 7, 207–9v contains a dispatch in the Archives nationales d'outre mer (ANOM), from Louisiana (13A) to the Ministry of Marine, volume 7, folios 207 through 209 verso.

Several series and subseries are also cited:

- **Series A** — Royal decrees and other acts of the king.
- **Series B** — Orders, memoranda, and instructions of the king and the ministers of the Marine.
- **Series F3** — "The Moreau de St.-Méry Collection."
- **Series G1** — "Civil List."
- **ASH** — Archives du service hydrographique, Paris: A division of the Ministry of Marine responsible for producing charts and maps.
- **BN** — Bibliothèque nationale (manuscrits and cartes et plans), Paris: These include subdivisions "fr." (French) and "n.a." (new acquisitions).
- **DFC** — Dépôt des fortifications des colonies, Aix-en-Provence, France.
- **HBNAI** — *Handbook of North American Indians.* 17 vols. Washington, DC: Smithsonian Institution, 1978–2004.

HNOC	Historic New Orleans Collection, New Orleans, Louisiana.
JR	*The Jesuit Relations and Allied Documents; Travels and Explorations of the Jesuit Missionaries in New France, 1610–1791.* 73 vols. Edited by Reuben Gold Thwaites. Cleveland: Burrows Bros., 1896–1901. [The original French, Latin, and Italian texts, with English translations and notes]
MPAFD	*Mississippi Provincial Archives, French Domination.* 5 vols. Compiled and translated by Dunbar Rowland, A. G. Sanders, and Patricia Galloway. 1926–84.
NYPL	Rare Book Collection of the New York Public Library.
RSC, LSMHC	Records of the Superior Council, Louisiana State Museum Historical Center, Baton Rouge.
SME	Séminaire des missions étrangères, The Séminaire de Québec Archives, Les Musée de la civilization, Quebec.
VP	Vaudreuil Papers. Loudon Collection, Huntington Library.

Introduction

1. Lusser to Maurepas, "Journal du voyage que j'ay fait dans la nation des Chactas par ordre de Monsieur Perier a commence du 12e Janvier 1730 jusques au 23e de mars de la même année, ANOM, C13A, vol. 13, 115v–116; Father Le Petit to Father D'Avaugour, July 12, 1730, *JR*, 67:169.

2. Périer to Maurepas, March 18, 1730, ANOM, C13A, vol. 12, 23–45; Pierre-François-Xavier de Charlevoix, *Histoire et description générale de la Nouvelle France avec le Journal historique d'un voyage fait par ordre du roi dans l'Amérique Septentrionnale,* vol. 2 (Paris: Chez Nyon et Fils, 1744), 467–69; Jean-François-Benjamin Dumont de Montigny, *Mémoires historiques sur la Louisiane contenant ce qui y est arrivé de plus mémorable depuis l'année 1687,* vol. 2 (Paris: J. B. Bauche, 1753), 138–46, 319; Antoine Le Page du Pratz, *Histoire de la Louisiane, contenant la découverte de ce vaste pays; Sa description géographique; Un voyage dans les terres,* vol. 3 (Paris: Lambert, 1758), 258.

3. Andrew C. Albrecht, "Indian-French Relations at Natchez," *American Anthropologist* 48, no. 3 (1946): 321–54; Mathé Allain, *"Not Worth a Straw": French Colonial Policy and the Early Years of Louisiana* (Lafayette: Center for Louisiana Studies, 1988), 74–75, 86; Verner Winslow Crane, *The Southern Frontier, 1670–1732* (Durham: Duke University Press, 1928), 273–75; Jean Delanglez, "The French Jesuits in Lower Louisiana (1700–1763)" (PhD diss., Catholic University of America, 1935); W. J. Eccles, *The French in North America 1500–1783* (Lansing: Michigan State University Press, 1998), 185–86; Michael J. Foret, "War or Peace? Louisiana, the Choctaws, and the Chickasaws, 1733–1735," in *The French Experience in Louisiana,* ed. Glenn R. Conrad (Lafayette: Center for Louisiana Studies, 1995): 296–312; Charles Gayarré, *History of Louisiana: The French Domination* (1866; repr., Gretna, LA: Pelican, 1998), 286–315, 390–450; John Francis McDermott, *Frenchmen and French Ways in the Mississippi Valley* (Urbana: University of Illinois Press, 1969); James Pritchard, *In Search of Empire: The French in the Americas, 1670–1730* (New York: Cambridge University Press, 2004); Alan Taylor, *American Colonies* (New York: Viking, 2001), 382–91; Mason Wade, "French Indian Policies," *HBNAI,* 4:20–28 (1988).

4. Daniel H. Usner, "French Natchez Borderlands in Colonial Louisiana," in *American Indians in the Lower Mississippi Valley: Economic and Social Histories* (Lincoln: University of Nebraska Press, 1998), 16.

5. Le Page de Pratz, *Histoire de la Louisiane*, 3:87.

6. Nancy Shoemaker, "How Indians Got to Be Red," *American Historical Review* 102, no. 3 (1997); Nancy Shoemaker, *A Strange Likeness: Becoming Red and White in Eighteenth-Century North America* (Oxford and New York: Oxford University Press, 2004). See also Alden T. Vaughan, "From White Man to Redskin: Changing Anglo-American Perceptions of the American-Indian," *American Historical Review* 87, no. 4 (1982); Christina Snyder, "Conquered Enemies, Adopted Kin, and Owned People: The Creek Indians and Their Captives," *Journal of Southern History* 73, no. 2 (2007); and Christina Snyder, *Slavery in Indian Country: The Changing Face of Captivity in Early America* (Cambridge: Harvard University Press, 2010).

7. Edmund Sears Morgan, *American Slavery, American Freedom: The Ordeal of Colonial Virginia* (1975; New York: Norton, 1995).

8. Charles Gayarré, *The History of Louisiana: The French Domination* (New York: Redfield, 1854), 286–352, 397–450; Francis Parkman *La Salle and the Discovery of the Great West* (1869; Boston: Little, Brown, 1902), 304; Samuel Clemens [Mark Twain], *Life on the Mississippi* (1874; New York: Harper Brothers, 1901), 13; Alcée Fortier, *A History of Louisiana* 1:57–63, 100–102, 110–15.

9. Jean Delanglez, "Cadillac's Early Years in America," *Mid-America* 12, no. 1 (1944); "Antoine Laumet alias Cadillac, Commandant at Michilimackinac: 1694–1697 (Continued)," *Mid-America* 16, no. 3 (1945); "Antoine Laumet alias Cadillac, Commandant at Michilimackinac: 1694–1697"; "Antoine Laumet alias Cadillac, Commandant at Michilimackinac: 1694–1697 (Concluded)," *Mid-America* 16, no. 4 (1945); "The Genesis and Building of Detroit," *Mid-America* 19, no. 2 (1948); "Cadillac at Detroit," *Mid-America* 19, no. 3 (1948).

10. Jean Delanglez, "The Natchez Massacre and Governor Perrier," *Louisiana Historical Quarterly*, no. 17 (1934); "The French Jesuits in Lower Louisiana (1700–1763)" (PhD diss., Catholic University of America, 1935); "A Louisiana Poet-Historian: Dumont dit Montigny," *Mid-America* 19, no. 1 (1937).

11. Charles Edwards O'Neill, *Church and State in French Colonial Louisiana: Policy and Politics to 1732* (New Haven: Yale University Press, 1966).

12. Vaughn B. Baker, "Marcel Giraud, 1900–1994: A Memorial and a Reminiscence," *Louisiana History* 35, no. 3 (Summer 1994): 356.

13. Mathé Allain, *"Not Worth a Straw": French Colonial Policy and the Early Years of Louisiana* (Lafayette: Center for Louisiana Studies, 1988).

14. Jacob M. Price, *France and the Chesapeake: A History of the French Tobacco Monopoly, 1674–1791, and of Its Relationship to the British and American Tobacco Trades*, 2 vols. (Ann Arbor: University of Michigan Press, 1973).

15. Patricia Dillon Woods, *French-Indian Relations on the Southern Frontier, 1699–1762* (Ann Arbor: UMI Research Press, 1980); Daniel H. Usner, *Indians, Settlers, and Slaves in a Frontier Exchange Economy: The Lower Mississippi Valley before 1783* (Chapel Hill: University of North Carolina Press, 1992).

16. Kathleen Duval, *The Native Ground: Indians and Colonists in the Heart of the Continent* (Philadelphia: University of Pennsylvania Press, 2006).

17. Shannon Lee Dawdy, *Building the Devil's Empire: French Colonial New Orleans* (Chicago: University of Chicago Press, 2008).

18. James F. Barnett Jr., *The Natchez Indians: A History to 1735* (Jackson: University Press of Mississippi, 2007), xvi.

19. Arnaud Balvay, *La Révolte des Natchez* (Paris: Éditions du Félin, 2008).

20. Christopher Tilley, *A Phenomenology of Landscape: Places, Paths, and Monuments* (Providence, RI: Berg, 1994), 207.

21. Michel Foucault, "Of Other Spaces: Heterotopias," trans. Jay Miskowiec, *Architecture/Movement/Continuity* (October 1984), http://foucault.info/document/heteroTopia/foucault.heteroTopia.en.html.

22. Timothy R. Pauketat, "The Missing Persons in Mississippian Mortuaries," in *Mississippian Mortuary Practices: Beyond Hierarchy and the Representationist Perspective*, ed. Lynne P. Sullivan and Robert C. Mainfort Jr. (Gainesville: University Press of Florida, 2010), 14–30.

23. They took their name from their Sun deity, Thé. "Théoloël" can be translated as "People of the Sun" (Patricia Galloway and Jason Baird Jackson, "Natchez and Neighboring Groups," in *HBNAI*, 14:619).

24. Cameron B. Wesson, "Mississippian Sacred Landscapes: The View from Alabama," in *Mississippian Towns and Sacred Landscapes: Searching for an Architectural Grammar*, ed. R. Barry Lewis and Charles Stout (Tuscaloosa: University of Alabama Press, 1998), 95–99.

25. Daniel H. Usner, "The Frontier Exchange Economy of the Lower Mississippi Valley in the Eighteenth Century," *William and Mary Quarterly*, 3rd ser., 44, no. 2 (April 1987): 166–67.

26. Karl G. Lorenz, "The Natchez of Southwest Mississippi," in *Indians of the Greater Southeast: Historical Archaeology and Ethnohistory*, ed. Bonnie G. McEwan (Gainesville: University Press of Florida, 2000), 159; Woods, *French-Indian Relations*, 25.

27. Karl G. Lorenz, "A Re-examination of Natchez Sociopolitical Complexity: A View from the Grand Village and Beyond," *Southeastern Archaeology* 16, no. 2 (1997): 99–100, 108–9.

28. Karen Ordahl Kupperman, *Indians and English: Facing Off in Early America* (Ithaca: Cornell University Press, 2000), 39–40.

29. James Sheehan, "The Problem of Sovereignty in European History," *American Historical Review* 111, no. 1 (2006): 1–16; Max Weber, *Economy and Society: An Outline of Interpretive Sociology*, trans. Guenther Roth and Claus Wittich, vol. 2 (Los Angeles: University of California Press, 1978), 904.

30. Paul Du Ru, *The Journal of Paul Du Ru (February 1 to May 8, 1700)*, trans. Ruth Lapham Butler (Chicago: Caxton Club, 1934), 34.

31. Joseph François Lafitau, *Customs of the American Indian Compared with the Customs of Primitive Times*, trans. William N. Fenton and Elizabeth L. Moore, vol. 1 (Toronto: Champlain Society, 1974), 127, 238; Anonymous, "A Letter about Louisiana," [1718], 41; Anonymous, "Nouvelle Relation de la Louisiane," [1717], 69–71, both originally published in the *Nouvelle Mercure*, reprinted in *Le plus beau païs du monde*, ed. May Rush Gwin Waggoner (1714; repr., Lafayette: Center for Louisiana Studies, 2005); François Le Maire, "Memoir of François Le Maire," in *Le plus beau païs du monde*, ed. May Rush Gwin Waggoner (1714; repr., Lafayette: Center for Louisiana Studies, 2005), 133.

32. Dawdy, *Building the Devil's Empire*, 19.
33. Richard White, *The Middle Ground: Indians, Empires, and Republics in the Great Lakes Region, 1650–1815* (New York: Cambridge University Press, 1991), 52.
34. Ibid., 16.
35. In 1980, Patricia Dillon Woods suggested that the Théoloëls may have considered the French "a totally different race, so foreign that they could never be absorbed into the Natchez tribal structure" (see Woods, *French-Indian Relations*, 108).
36. Hal Langfur, "Moved by Terror: Frontier Violence as Cultural Exchange in Late-Colonial Brazil," *Ethnohistory* 52, no. 2 (Spring 2005): 255–89; Frederic Gleach, *Powhatan's World and Colonial Virginia: A Conflict of Cultures* (Lincoln: University of Nebraska Press, 1997), 148–58, 184.
37. Allan Greer, "Commons and Enclosures in the Colonization of North America," *American Historical Review* 117, no. 2 (April 2012): 369.
38. Winthrop Jordan, *White over Black: American Attitudes toward the Negro, 1550–1812* (Chapel Hill: University of North Carolina Press, 1968).
39. Jean-François-Benjamin Dumont de Montigny, *The Memoir of Lieutenant Dumont, 1715–1747: A Sojourner in the French Atlantic*, trans. Gordon M. Sayre, ed. Sayre and Carla Zecher (Chapel Hill: University of North Carolina Press for the Omohundro Institute of Early American History, 2012), 228, 227.
40. White, *The Middle Ground*, 53.
41. Gordon M. Sayre, "Natchez History Revisited: New Manuscript Sources from Le Page du Pratz and Dumont de Montigny," *Louisiana History* 50, no. 4 (2010): 412.
42. J. B. Harley, "Texts and Contexts in the Interpretations of Early Maps," in *The New Nature of Maps: Essays in the History of Cartography*, ed. Paul Laxton (Baltimore: Johns Hopkins University Press, 2001); J. B. Harley, "Maps, Knowledge, and Power," in *The New Nature of Maps: Essays in the History of Cartography*, ed. Paul Laxton (Baltimore: Johns Hopkins University Press, 2001). See also Christine Marie Petto, *When France Was King of Cartography: The Patronage and Production of Maps in Early Modern France*, (Lanham: Lexington, 2007), 9–14; and David Buisseret, ed., *Monarchs, Ministers, and Maps: The Emergence of Cartography as a Tool of Government in Early Modern Europe* (Chicago: University of Chicago Press,1992).
43. Tristam R. Kidder, "Mississippi Period Mound Groups and Communities in the Lower Mississippi Valley," in *Mississippian Towns and Sacred Spaces: Searching for an Architectural Grammar*, ed. R. Barry Lewis and Charles B. Stout (Tuscaloosa: University of Alabama Press, 1998), 123–50.

1 / Rising Suns

1. Pierre Le Moyne Iberville, *Iberville's Gulf Journals*, trans. Richebourg Gaillard McWilliams (Mobile: University of Alabama Press, 1981), 125–26. For Iberville's early career, see *France's Forgotten Legion: Service Records of French Military and Administrative Personnel Stationed in the Mississippi Valley and Gulf Coast Region, 1699–1769*, CD-ROM (Baton Rouge: Louisiana State University Press, 2000). For a review of Montreal's merchant community in the late 1600s, see Louise Dechêne, *Habitants et marchands de Montréal au XVII siècle* (Quebec: Boréal, 1988), 125–51, 409–11.
2. The full moon appeared on March 20, 1700, as per Erling Poulsen's online moon calendar program, www.rundetaarn.dk/ engelsk/observatorium/nymeng.html.
3. Karl G. Lorenz, "The Natchez of Southwest Mississippi," in *Indians of the Greater*

Southeast: Historical Archaeology and Ethnohistory, ed. Bonnie G. McEwan (Gainesville: University Press of Florida, 2000), 159; Patricia Dillon Woods, *French-Indian Relations on the Southern Frontier, 1699–1762* (Ann Arbor: UMI Research Press, 1980), 25. Thé was also the name of the first Great Sun who, along with White Woman, started the Natchez dynasty.

4. Iberville, *Iberville's Gulf Journal*, 126.

5. Paul Du Ru, *The Journal of Paul Du Ru (February 1 to May 8, 1700)*, trans. Ruth Lapham Butler (Chicago: Caxton Club, 1934), 34.

6. For an analysis of the similar cross-cultural recognitions at play in North American colonial projects, see Karen Ordahl Kupperman, *Indians and English: Facing Off in Early America* (Ithaca: Cornell University Press, 2000). For concepts of civilization and civilizing missions, see Michael Leroy Oberg, *Dominion and Civility: English Imperialism and Native America, 1585–1685* (Ithaca: Cornell University Press, 1999).

7. Daniel K. Richter, *Before the Revolution: America's Ancient Pasts* (Cambridge: Belknap Press of Harvard University Press, 2011).

8. For an in-depth examination of the powers of the Council, see James D. Hardy, "The Superior Council in Colonial Louisiana," in *Frenchmen and French Ways in the Mississippi Valley*, ed. John Francis McDermott (Urbana: University of Illinois Press, 1969), 87–101.

9. The thirteen *parlements* acted as courts of law that also exercised some influence on the king's legislation. The most important of these was the Parlement of Paris, from whose rulings Louisianans drew their legal practices.

10. For a review of Colbert's life, see Jean Meyer, *Colbert* (Paris: Hachette littérature générale, 1981); and Ines Murat, *Colbert*, trans. Robert Francis Cook and Jeannie Van Asselt (Charlottesville: University Press of Virginia, 1984). For Colbert's impact on French slave policy, see Mathé Allain, "Slave Policies in French Louisiana," in *The French Experience in Louisiana*, ed. Glenn R. Conrad (Lafayette: Center for Louisiana Studies, 1995), 174–82; Carl A. Brasseaux, "The Administration of Slave Regulations in French Louisiana, 1724–1766," in *The French Experience in Louisiana*, ed. Glenn R. Conrad (Lafayette: Center for Louisiana Studies, 1995), 209–25; and Thomas N. Ingersoll, "Slave Codes and Judicial Practice in New Orleans," *Law and History Review* 13, no. 1 (1995): 23–62. For a general review of the Code Noir, see William Resnick Riddell, "Le Code Noir," *Journal of Negro History* 10, no. 3 (1925): 321–29. See also Charles Gayarré, *History of Louisiana: The French Domination* (1866; repr., Gretna, LA: Pelican, 1998), 531–39. Gwendolyn Hall also wrote extensively about the French slave codes (see Gwendolyn Midlo Hall, *Africans in Colonial Louisiana: The Development of Afro-Creole Culture in the Eighteenth Century* [Baton Rouge: Louisiana State University Press, 1992]).

11. The Code Michaud regularized the office of intendant in 1629 (see G. R. R. Treasure, *Louis XIV* [New York: Longman, 2001], 69–101).

12. J. H. M. Salmon, "Venality of Office and Popular Sedition in Seventeenth-Century France: A Review of a Controversy," *Past & Present*, no. 37 (1967): 28–29.

13. The *commissaire-ordonnateur*, roughly translated as "comptroller," held a restricted commission that granted him less power than an *intendant* in the *métropole* (see Donald J. Lemieux, "Some Legal and Practical Aspects of the Office of Commissaire-Ordonnateur of French Louisiana," *Louisiana Studies* 14, no. 4 [1975]: 379–93).

14. Hardy, "The Superior Council in Colonial Louisiana," 88; Jerry A. Micelle,

"From Law Court to Local Government: Metamorphosis of the Superior Council of French Louisiana," *Louisiana History* 9, no. 2 (1968): 85–107.

15. Lemieux, "The Office of *Commissaire-Ordonnateur*," 403.

16. Rafe Blaufarb, "The Survival of the Pays D'états: The Example of Provence," *Past & Present* 209, no. 1 (2010): 83–116.

17. Paul Harsin, "La finance et l'état jusqu'au système de Law," in *Histoire économique et sociale de la France, II /1660–1789*, ed. Fernand Braudel and Ernest Labrousse (1970; Paris: Presses Universitaires de France, 1993), 267–75.

18. Collins, *From Tribes to Nation*, 292.

19. Pierre Goubert, *The Ancien Régime: French Society, 1600–1750*, trans. Steve Cox (New York: Harper and Row, 1973), 180. See also Salmon, "Venality of Office," 25–27.

20. Goubert, *The Ancien Régime*, 166.

21. Harsin, "La finance et l'état," 275.

22. Goubert, *The Ancien Régime*, 166.

23. Mathé Allain, *"Not Worth a Straw": French Colonial Policy and the Early Years of Louisiana* (Lafayette: Center for Louisiana Studies, 1988), 1–13.

24. For a discussion of Louis cooption of the French nobility, see Joseph Schumpeter, *Imperialism and Social Classes: Two Essays by Joseph Schumpeter* (New York: A. M. Kelley, 1951), 56–64. For eighteenth-century consequences of this policy, see Eric J. Hobsbawm, *The Age of Revolution 1789–1848* (New York: Signet, 1962), 22–44. For an overview of Louis's court, see John B. Wolf, *Louis XIV* (New York: Norton, 1968), 269–85. Wolf provided a concise description of the *lever, coucher*, and other daily activities that became rituals for those vying for the monarch's glance (ibid., 209–71).

25. Emmanuel Le Roy Ladurie, *The Ancien Régime: a History of France, 1610–1774* (Cambridge: Blackwell, 1996), 225.

26. Pierre Léon, "Les nouvelles élites," in *Histoire économique et sociale de la France, II /1660–1789*, ed. Fernand Braudel and Ernest Labrousse (1970; repr., Paris: Presses Universitaires de France, 1993), 610, 632–41.

27. Léon, "Les nouvelles élites," 632–33. See also Erin Michele Greenwald, "Company Towns and Tropical Baptisms: From Lorient to Louisiana on a French Atlantic Circuit" (PhD diss., Ohio State University, 2011).

28. Sara Chapman, "Patronage as Family Economy: The Role of Women in the Patron-Client Network of the Phélypeaux de Pontchartrain Family, 1670–1715," *French Historical Studies* 24, no. 1 (2001): 11–35.

29. Nicholas P. Canny, "In Search of a Better Home? European Overseas Migration, 1500–1800," in *Europeans on the Move: Studies on European Migration, 1500–1800*, ed. Canny (New York: Oxford University Press, 1994), 263–85.

30. During the 1710s and 1720s, Protestant German and Swiss settlers moved to Louisiana in contravention of the Code Noir (see "A Census of the German Villages near New Orleans," November 12, 13, and December 20, 1724, ANOM, G1, vol. 464, n.p.).

31. www.catholic-forum.com/saints/indexsnt.htm.

32. Thomas Aquinas, *Summa Theologiae: Latin Text and English Translation* (New York: McGraw-Hill, 1964), 2a2ae 81:88; Colman O'Neill, "Saints," in *New Catholic Encyclopedia* (New York: McGraw-Hill, 1967), 852–53.

33. For examples of English believers' invocation for intercession of saints for earthly benefits, see Eamon Duffy, *The Stripping of the Altars: Traditional Religion in England, c.1400–c.1580* (New Haven: Yale University Press, 1992), 169–84.

34. With one exception: a lay Catholic could administer baptism if the death of a willing unbeliever was imminent.

35. Diarmaid MacCullough, *The Reformation: A History* (New York: Penguin, 2004), 10–26.

36. James Axtell, *The Invasion Within: The Contest of Cultures in Colonial North America* (New York: Oxford University Press, 1985). For similarities among Catholic and Native American ritual and iconography, see James Taylor Carson, "Sacred Circles and Dangerous People: Native American Cosmology and the French Settlement of Louisiana," in *French Colonial Louisiana and the Atlantic World*, ed. Bradley G. Bond (Baton Rouge: Louisiana State University Press, 2005), 63–82.

37. Charles Edwards O'Neill, *Church and State in French Colonial Louisiana: Policy and Politics to 1732* (New Haven: Yale University Press, 1966), 34–37.

38. For a brief history of the Fathers of the Foreign Missions, see Louise Phelps Kellogg, *Early Narratives of the Northwest, 1634–1699* (New York: Scribner's and Sons, 1917), 337.

39. For a comprehensive, though often celebratory, assessment of the Jesuits, see Jean Delanglez, "The French Jesuits in Lower Louisiana (1700–1763)" (PhD diss., Catholic University of America, 1935).

40. John McManners, *Church and Society in Eighteenth-Century France: The Religion of the People and the Politics of Religion*, 2 vols. (New York: Oxford University Press, 1998), 2:509.

41. Deslandres, *Croire et faire croire: Les missions françaises au XVIIe siècle, 1600–1650* (Paris: Fayard, 2003), 52–59. See also Mack P. Holt, *The French Wars of Religion, 1562–1629*, 2nd ed. (New York: Cambridge University Press, 2005), 168–77.

42. Jean Delumeau, *Catholicism between Luther and Voltaire: A New View of the Counter-Reformation*, trans. Jeremy Mosier (Philadelphia: Burns and Oates, 1977), 161–63.

43. McManners, *Church and Society in Eighteenth-Century France*, 2:84–93.

44. Luca Codignola, "The Holy See and the Conversion of the Indians in French and British North America, 1486–1760," in *America in European Consciousness 1493–1750*, ed. Karen Ordahl Kupperman (Chapel Hill: University of North Carolina Press, 1995), 195–242. See also Dominique Deslandres, "Exemplo aeque ut verbo: The French Jesuits' Missionary World," in *The Jesuits: Cultures, Sciences, and the Arts, 1540–1773*, ed. John W. O'Malley et al. (Toronto: University of Toronto Press, 1999), 258–59; and Allan Greer and Kenneth Mills, "A Catholic Atlantic," in *The Atlantic in Global History*, ed. Jorge Cañizares-Esguerra and Erik R. Seeman (Upper Saddle River: Pearson, 2007), 3–19.

45. Allan Greer answers some of these questions in his study of the world of the Catholic Mohawk community of Kahnawake and the convert Catherine Tekakwitha (see Allan Greer, *Mohawk Saint: Catherine Tekakwitha and the Jesuits* [New York: Oxford University Press, 2005], 89–124).

46. These "observational 'blind-spots'" were the subject of Patricia Galloway's essay about the difficulties of using European sources to evaluate Indian social and political institutions (see Patricia K. Galloway, "The Direct Historical Approach and Early Historical Documents: The Ethnohistorian's View," in Archaeological Report No. 18, *The Protohistoric Period in the Mid-South: 1700–1700, Proceedings of the 1983 Mid-South Archaeological Conference*, ed. David H. Dye and Ronald C. Brister [Jackson: Mississippi Department of Archives and History, 1986], 14–23).

47. Joseph François Lafitau, *Customs of the American Indian Compared with the Customs of Primitive Times*, trans. William N. Fenton and Elizabeth L. Moore, vol. 1 (Toronto: Champlain Society, 1974), 127, 238.

48. Penicault, "Relation, ou annale véritable de ce qui s'est passé dans le païs de la Louisiane," manuscript, Provient du Collège des Jésuites de Clermont à Paris, n° 828, 129–30.

49. Antoine Le Page du Pratz, *Histoire de la Louisiane: Contenant la découverte de ce vaste pays; Sa description géographique; Un voyage dans les terres*, vol. 2 (Paris: Lambert, 1758), 352–53.

50. Ibid., 2:368–70.

51. Pierre-Francois-Xavier de Charlevoix, *Histoire et description générale de la Nouvelle France avec le Journal historique d'un voyage fait par ordre du roi dans l'Amérique Septentrionnale*, vol. 3 (Paris: Chez Nyon Fils, 1744), 420. An essential characteristic defining a state is the monopoly of legitimate coercion (Max Weber, *Economy and Society: An Outline of Interpretive Sociology*, ed. Guenther Roth and Claus Wittich, vol. 2 [Los Angeles: University of California Press, 1978], 903–5).

52. Charlevoix may have been taking aim at Baron Lahontan's "dialogue" with Adario, an Algonquin orator, in the latter's *Nouveaux voyages de Mr le baron de Lahontan, dans l'Amérique Septentrionale*. During an extended debate with Lahontan, Adario castigates French society for its rigid hierarchy and extols the virtues of his own classless nation. Moreover, Adario spends a good deal of time criticizing the Jesuits' efforts to convert the Indians (see Baron Louis-Armand de Lom d'Ares Lahontan, ed., *New Voyages to North American*, vol. 1 [Chicago: A. C. McClurg, 1905], 555–67).

53. B. A. Luxembourg , *Memoire sur Louisiana* (Paris: 1758), 143.

54. Goubert, *The Ancien Régime*, 82–84.

55. George R. Milner and Sissel Schroeder, "Mississippian Sociopolitical Systems," in *Great Towns and Regional Polities in the American Southwest and Southeast*, ed. Jill E. Neitzel (Albuquerque: University of New Mexico, 1991), 101–2.

56. For a detailed explanation of the Mississippian cycle, see Patricia K. Galloway, *Choctaw Genesis, 1500–1700* (Lincoln: University of Nebraska Press, 1995), 27–74. For other views of Mississippian coalescence and dispersion, see Robbie Franklyn Ethridge, *From Chicaza to Chickasaw: The European Invasion and the Transformation of the Mississippian World, 1540–1715* (Chapel Hill: University of North Carolina Press, 2010), 60–88; Timothy R. Pauketat, *Ancient Cahokia and the Mississippians* (New York: Cambridge University Press, 2004); Charles R. Cobb, "Mississippian Chiefdoms: How Complex?" *Annual Review of Anthropology* 82 (2003): 63–84; John Blitz, "Mississippian Chiefdoms and the Fusion-Fission Process," *American Antiquity* 64, no. 4 (1999): 577–92; Tristam R. Kidder, "Mississippi Period Mound Groups and Communities in the Lower Mississippi Valley," in *Mississippian Towns and Sacred Spaces: Searching for an Architectural Grammar*, ed. R. Barry Lewis and Charles B. Stout (Tuscaloosa: University of Alabama Press, 1998), 123–50; Jon Muller, *Mississippian Political Economy* (New York: Plenum, 1997); Jon Muller, "Southeastern Interaction and Integration," in *Great Towns and Regional Polities: In the Prehistoric American Southwest and Southeast*, ed. Jill E. Neitzel (Albuquerque: University of New Mexico Press, 1999),143–64; Timothy R. Pauketat and Thomas E. Emerson, *Cahokia: Domination and Ideology in the Mississippian World* (Lincoln: University of Nebraska Press, 1997); Cameron B. Wesson, "Mississippian Landscapes: The View from Alabama," in

Mississippian Towns and Sacred Spaces: Searching for an Architectural Grammar, ed. R. Barry Lewis and Charles B. Stout (Tuscaloosa: University of Alabama Press, 1998), 3–122; John F. Scarry, "The Late Prehistoric Southeast," in *The Forgotten Centuries: Indians and Europeans in the American South, 1521–1704*, ed. Charles M. Hudson and Carmen Chaves Tesser (Athens: University of Georgia Press, 1994), 17–35; and Randolph J. Widmer, "The Structure of Southeastern Chiefdoms," in *The Forgotten Centuries: Indians and Europeans in the American South, 1521–1704*, ed. Charles M. Hudson and Carmen Chaves Tesser (Athens: University of Georgia Press, 1994), 125–55.

57. Lorenz, "Natchez Sociopolitical Complexity," 98.

58. Ethridge, *From Chicaza to Chickasaw*, 5. See also Sheri Marie Shuck-Hall, "Alabama and Coushatta Diaspora and Coalescence in the Mississippian Shatter Zone," in *Mapping the Mississippian Shatter Zone: The Colonial Indian Slave Trade and Regional Instablity in the American South*, ed. Robbie Ethridge and Shuck-Hall (Lincoln: University of Nebraska Press, 2009), 250–71. For the effects of European pathogens in North America, see Alfred W. Crosby, *Ecological Imperialism: The Biological Expansion of Europe, 900–1900* (New York: Cambridge University Press, 1993), 212–17; "Virgin Soil Epidemics as a Factor in Aboriginal Depopulation," *William and Mary Quarterly* 33, no. 2 (1976): 289–99; and Jared M. Diamond, *Guns, Germs, and Steel: The Fates of Human Societies* (New York: Norton, 1999), 77–70, 210–13. For an overview of Natchez population trends, see Peter H. Wood, "The Changing Population of the Colonial South: An Overview by Race and Region, 1685–1790," in *Powhatan's Mantle: Indians in the Colonial Southeast*, ed. Gregory A. Waselkov and M. Thomas Hatley (Lincoln: University of Nebraska Press, 1989), 73–79. Paul Kelton questioned the role of disease in the decline of Indian populations in the Gulf Coast region (see Paul Kelton, "Avoiding the Smallpox Spirits: Colonial Epidemics and Southeastern Indian Survival," *Ethnohistory* 51, no. 1 [2004]: 45–72; and Paul Kelton, "The Great Southeastern Smallpox Epidemic, 1696–1700: The Region's First Major Epidemic?" in *The Transformation of the Southeastern Indians, 1540–1760*, ed. Robbie Ethridge and Charles M. Hudson [Jackson: University of Mississippi Press, 2002], 45–72).

59. Milner and Schroeder, "Mississippian Sociopolitical Systems," 104.

60. Christina Snyder, *Slavery in Indian Country: The Changing Face of Captivity in Early America* (Cambridge: Harvard University Press, 2010), 46–89; James F. Barnett, *The Natchez Indians: A History to 1735* (Jackson: University Press of Mississippi, 2007), 18.

61. Ethridge, *From Chicaza to Chickasaw*, 149–55; Barnett, *The Natchez Indians*, 28–31.

62. For the most thorough articulation of the importance of the Emerald Site in the Natchez political formation, see Lorenz, "Natchez Sociopolitical Complexity," 104–6. See also Jeffrey P. Brain, "Late Prehistoric Settlement Patterning in the Yazoo Basin and Natchez Bluffs Regions of the Lower Mississippi Valley," in *Mississippian Settlement Patterns*, ed. Bruce D. Smith (New York: Academic Press, 1978), 331–68; and John Cotter, "Stratigraphic and Area Test at the Emerald and Anna Mound Sites," *American Antiquity: A Quarterly Review of American Archaeology* 17 (1951): 18–31. Swanton surmised that the northern temple might have been the Taensas' structure, which Father Davion burned down in 1704 (Swanton, *Indian Tribes of the Lower Mississippi Valley*, 165). Father Poisson mentioned a connection between the Natchez temple and the Tunicas, who lived north of the Yazoo River at the turn of the eighteenth century (Paul du Poisson, October 3, 1727, *JR*, 67:311).

63. Ian W. Brown, "An Archaeological Study of Culture Contact and Change in the Natchez Bluffs Region," in *La Salle and His Legacy: Frenchmen and Indians in the Lower Mississippi Valley*, ed. Patricia Galloway (Jackson: University of Mississippi Press, 1982), 180.

64. Milner and Schroeder, "Mississippian Sociopolitical Systems," 104.

65. Charlevoix, *Histoire et description generale de la Nouvelle France*, 3:491.

66. Ned J. Jenkins, "Tracing the Origins of the Early Creeks, 1050–1700 CE," in *Mapping the Mississippian Shatter Zone: The Colonial Indian Slave Trade and Regional Instablity in the American South*, ed. Robbie Ethridge and Sheri Marie Shuck-Hall (Lincoln: University of Nebraska Press, 2009), 191–95.

67. Cameron B. Wesson, "Mississippian Landscapes: The View from Alabama," in *Mississippian Towns and Sacred Spaces: Searching for an Architectural Grammar*, edited by R. Lewis Barry and Charles Stout (Tuscaloosa: University of Alabama Press, 1998), 94.

68. For the various feasts in which the Great Sun's largesse plays a role, see Le Page du Pratz, *Histoire de la Louisiane*, 2:363–81. The Harvest Feast exemplified the redistributive nature of the Great Sun's office (see Jean-François-Benjamin Dumont de Montigny, *Mémoires historiques sur la Louisiane contenant ce qui y est arrivé de plus mémorable depuis l'année 1687*, vol. 1 [Paris: J. B. Bauche, 1753], 195–208).

69. Penicault, "Relation, ou annale véritable," 129–30.

70. Le Page du Pratz, *Histoire de la Louisiane*, 2:353.

71. Charlevoix, *Histoire et description generale de la Nouvelle France*, 3:420.

72. Anonymous, *Memoire sur Louisiane*, 143.

73. Snyder, *Slavery in Indian Country*, 5–6.

74. Dumont de Montigny, *Mémoires historiques sur la Louisiane*, 1:178–80; Le Page du Pratz, *Histoire de la Louisiane*, 2:393–96; Mathurin Le Petit, "Lettre au d'Avaugour, Procureur des Missions de l'Amérique Septentrionale," July 12, 1730, *JR*, 68:135; Penicault, "Relation, ou annale véritable," 131–32; Swanton, *Indian Tribes of the Lower Mississippi Valley*, 107.

75. C. W. M. Hart, "A Reconsideration of the Natchez Social Structure," *American Anthropologist* 45, no. 3 (1943): 374–86.

76. Jeffrey P. Brain, "The Natchez 'Paradox,'" *Ethnology* 10, no. 2 (1971): 215–22; George I. Quimby, "Natchez Social Structure as an Instrument of Assimilation," *American Anthropologist* 48, no. 1 (1946): 134–37; Elizabeth Tooker, "Natchez Social Organization: Fact or Anthropological Folklore?" *Ethnohistory* 10, no. 3 (1963): 359–73; Douglas White, George P. Murdock, and Richard Scaglion, "Natchez Class and Rank Reconsidered," *Ethnology* 10, no. 4 (1971): 369–88. Patricia Woods adopted Brain's hypothesis (see Woods, *French-Indian Relations on the Southern Frontier*, 26; see also Lorenz, "The Natchez of Southwest Mississippi," 152–58).

77. Vernon James Knight Jr., "Social Organization and the Evolution of Hierarchy in Southeastern Chiefdoms" *Journal of Anthropological Research* 46 (Spring 1990): 1–23; Patricia Galloway and Jason Baird Jackson, "Natchez and Neighboring Groups," in *Handbook of North American Indians: Southeast*, ed. Raymond D. Fogelson (Washington: Smithsonian Institution, 2004), 602–3.

78. Lorenz, "Natchez Sociopolitical Complexity," 98–104; Jenkins, "Origins of the Early Creeks," 191–94.

79. Lorenz, "Natchez Sociopolitical Complexity," 99.

80. Le Page du Pratz, *Histoire de la Louisiane*, 2:126–27.

81. Le Pétit, *JR*, 68:126.

82. *Les Sauvages Natchez*, BN Mss. fr., n.a., 2549, fol. 64. See also Le Petit, *JR*, 68:29–30; and Swanton, *Indian Tribes of the Lower Mississippi Valley*, 181.

83. For hopes that the Natchez would quickly convert to Catholicism, see Du Ru, *Journal of Paul Du Ru*, 29.

84. The Tattooed Arm, the mother of the last Great Sun, explained to the missionary Father St. Cosme that the Suns' claim of descent from a solar deity enhanced their authority over the commoners (see *Grand Soliel, files d'un francois en 1728*, BN Mss, fr., n.a., 2550, fols. 115–16).

85. Le Page du Pratz, *Histoire de la Louisiane*, 2:326–34. See also *Les Sauvages Natchez*, BN Mss., fr., n.a., 2549, fol. 64; and Penicault, *Fleur de Lys and Calumet*, 90–92.

86. Father Charlevoix counted three logs (see Charlevoix, *Histoire et description générale de la Nouvelle France*, 3:417).

87. Peter Nabokov and Robert Easton, *Native American Architecture* (New York: Oxford University Press, 1989), 108.

88. Anonymous, "Nouvelle relation de la Louisiane," from the *Nouvelle Mercure*, September 1717, in *Le Plus Beau Païs du Monde* (1717; repr., Lafayette: Center for Louisiana Studies, 2005), 41.

89. Joseph-François Lafitau, *Moeurs des sauvages ameriquains, comparées aux moeurs des premiers temps*, vol. 1 (Paris: Saugrain l'aîne, 1724), 120, 153–55.

90. R. Barry Lewis, Charles B. Stout, and Cameron B. Wesson, "The Design of Mississippian Towns," in *Mississippian Towns and Sacred Spaces: Searching for an Architectural Grammar*, ed. Lewis and Stout (Tuscaloosa: University of Alabama Press, 1998).

91. *Les Sauvages Natchez*, BN Mss., fr., n.a., 2549, fol. 63. See also Lafitau, *Moeurs des sauvages ameriquains*, 1:153–54; Le Page du Pratz, *Histoire de la Louisiane*, 2:118; Le Petit, *JR*, 68:126–27; and Penicault, "Relation, ou annale véritable," 132–34.

92. Le Page du Pratz, *Histoire de la Louisiane*, 1:135–36, 207–8. Le Page du Pratz recalled a Natchez doctor curing a leg ailment and an eye infection. He devoted most of the fifteenth chapter of his first volume of the *Histoire de la Louisiane* to Natchez medicine. The Jesuits Le Petit and Charlevoix regarded all Natchez healers as charlatans and described their ruses in detail (see Le Petit, *JR*, 68:151–53; and Charlevoix, *Histoire et description générale de la Nouvelle France*, 3:426–27).

93. Le Petit, *JR* 68:151. See also Patricia Galloway, "Savage Medicine: Du Pratz and Eighteenth-Century French Medical Practice," in *France in the New World: Proceedings of the 22nd Annual Meeting of the French Colonial Historical Society, 1996 Poiters, France*, ed. David Buisseret (Lansing: Michigan State University Press, 1998), 107–18.

94. Victor Fournel in *Dictionnaire alphabétique et anologique de la Langue Française: Les mots et les associations d'idées*, vol. 3 (Paris: Société du Noveau litré, 1972). See John W. Baldwin, "The Image of the Jongleur in Northern France around 1200," *Speculum* 72, no. 3 (1997).

95. For prescientific views of natural phenomena, see David D. Hall, *Worlds of Wonder, Days of Judgment: Popular Religious Belief in Early New England* (Cambridge: Harvard University Press, 1989), 7, 71–72. Hall's analysis of popular religious practice in New England provides insight into early-modern European attitudes toward unexplained illness, bad weather, crop failures, etc. For conflation of medicinal and occult

knowledge in contemporaneous New England, see John Demos, *Entertaining Satan: Witchcraft and the Culture of Early New England* (New York: Oxford University Press, 1982), 80–84. According to Demos, those known as "cunning women," those familiar with the healing properties of plants, made up a good portion of witchcraft suspects. For views of witchcraft and state prosecution in early-modern France, see Robert Mandrou, *Magistrats et sorciers en France au XVII siècle: Une analyse de psychologie historique, Civilisations et mentalités* (Paris: Plon, 1968), 75–94.

96. Henri de Tonty, "Relation de Henri de Tonty," in *Découvertes et établissements des Français dans l'Ouest et dans le Sud de l'Amérique septentrionale*, vol. 1, ed. Pierre Margry (Paris: D. Jouast, 1876), 594–95.

97. "Relation de Henri de Tonty," 599; Nicolas de La Salle, "Récit de Nicholas de La Salle," in *Découvertes et établissements des Français dans l'Ouest et dans le Sud de l'Amérique septentrionale*, vol. 1, ed. Pierre Margry (Paris: D. Jouast, 1876), 557.

98. Le Page du Pratz, *Histoire de la Louisiane*, 2:354. The new moon appeared on March 9, and the full moon appeared on March 23, 1682, as per Erling Poulsen's online moon calendar program, www.rundetaarn.dk/engelsk/observatorium/nymeng.html.

99. Le Page du Pratz, *Histoire de la Louisiane*, 2:361.

100. The Europeans who left records of the visit called the village "Natché" or "Nachié"; they called the people of the region the Coroas or Courroas (see "The Minet Relation," reprinted in Robert S. Weddle, Mary Christine Morkovsky, and Patricia Kay Galloway, *La Salle, the Mississippi, and the Gulf: Three Primary Documents* [College Station: Texas A&M University Press, 1987], 51; and "The Relation of Nicolas de La Salle," 545–70). See also "Narrative of La Salle's Voyage down the Mississippi by Father Zenobius Membré, Recollect," in *The Historical Collections of Louisiana*, vol. 4, ed. B. F. French (New York: Redfield, 1852), 172. Tonti dated the party's arrival at the village on March 22, 1682 (see "Memoir on La Salle's Discoveries, by Tonty, 1678–1690 [1693]," in Louise Phelps Kellogg, *Early Narratives of the Northwest, 1634–1699* [New York: Scribners's Sons, 1917], 301). Jeffrey Brain argued that these were the people later known as the Natchez, and that Natché was actually the Emerald Site (see Jeffrey Brain, "La Salle at the Natchez: An Archaeological and Historical Perspective," in *La Salle and His Legacy: Frenchmen and Indians in the Lower Mississippi Valley*, ed. Patricia Galloway [Jackson: University of Mississippi Press, 1982], see fig. 2.1, p. 103; 49–59).

101. "Narrative of La Salle's Voyage down the Mississippi," 173.

102. "The Relation of Nicolas de La Salle," 559; "Relation de Henri de Tonty," 604.

103. "Narrative of La Salle's Voyage Down the Mississippi," 173.

104. "The Minet Relation," 52.

105. Ibid., "Memoir on La Salle's Discoveries, by Tonty," 302.

106. "Récit de Nicholas de La Salle," 565–66; "The Minet Relation," 59.

107. "Memoir on La Salle's Discoveries, by Tonty," 313–14. Arnaud Balvay proposed that Tonti in his 1684 account might have mistaken the Natchez for the Koroas on this second visit (Balvay, *Le Révolte des Natchez*, 41). If so, Tonti knew who was who when he returned in 1690.

108. Iberville, *Iberville's Gulf Journals*, 125.

109. See John Reed Swanton, *Source Material for the Social and Ceremonial Life of the Choctaw Indians* (Washington, DC: U.S. Government Printing Office, 1931).

2 / Thefts of the Suns

1. "Le Grand Soliel des Natchés qui est le chef de la nation est batard de pere M. de S. Cosme de Canada et qui a été prêtre des missions des entrageres en Canada [a] envoyé a les Louisiane pour y être missionaire en 1699," BN Mss, fr., n.a., 2550, fol. 115, Grand Soliel, fils d'un francois en 1728.

2. Robbie Ethridge, "Creating a Shatter Zone: Indian Slave Traders and the Collapse of Southeastern Chiefdoms," in *Light on the Path: The Anthropology and History of the Southeastern Indians*, ed. Thomas J. Pluckhahn and Ethridge (Tuscaloosa: University of Alabama Press, 2006), 208–9.

3. Amedé Gosselin, Biographie du prêtre Jean-François Buisson de Saint-Cosme, missionnaire 1667–1703, SME, P12, no. 15, 25, 1–3; Céline Dupré "Buisson de Saint-Cosme, Jean François," in *Dictionary of Canadian Bibliography*, vol. 2 (1969; Toronto: University of Toronto Press: 1982).

4. John McManners, *Church and Society in Eighteenth-Century France: The Religion of the People and the Politics of Religion*, vol. 2 (New York: Oxford University Press, 1998), 523.

5. Ibid., 2:44; Jean Delanglez, "The French Jesuits in Lower Louisiana (1700–1763)" (PhD diss., Catholic University of America, 1935), 38–44.

6. Charles Edwards O'Neill, *Church and State in French Colonial Louisiana: Policy and Politics to 1732* (New Haven: Yale University Press, 1966), 32–38. The "Chinese Rites" controversy revolved around the Jesuits' willingness to permit their Chinese converts to continue to venerate their ancestors. The Fathers of the Foreign Missions stood foursquare against such practices. Pope Clement XI in 1715 resolved the issue when he forbade such rituals.

7. St. Cosme to St. Vallier, SME, R, no. 32, 6, August 1, 1701.

8. St. Cosme to Abbé Tremblay(?), December 7, 1701, SME, R, no. 33, 2–3. See also Arnaud Balvay, *La Révolte des Natchez* (Paris: Éditions du Félin, 2008), 54; and James F. Barnett Jr., *The Natchez Indians: A History to 1735* (Jackson: University of Mississippi Press, 2007).

9. James Mack Crawford, *The Mobilian Trade Language* (Knoxville: University of Tennessee Press, 1978); Kenneth H. York, "Mobilian: The Indian Lingua Franca of Colonial Louisiana," in *La Salle and His Legacy: Frenchmen and Indians in the Lower Mississippi Valley*, ed. Patricia Galloway (Jackson: University Press of Mississippi, 1982); Emanuel J. Drechsel, "An Integrated Vocabulary of Mobilian Jargon, a Native American Pidgin of the Mississippi Valley," *Anthropological Linguistics* 38 (Summer 1996): 248–354.

10. Antoine Le Page du Pratz, *Histoire de la Louisiane, Contenant la découverte de ce vaste Pays; Sa description géographique; Un voyage dans les terres*, vol. 2 (Paris: Lambert, 1758), 321.

11. St. Cosme to l'abbé Desmaizerets, April 10, 1702, SME, R, no. 35, 3.

12. St. Cosme to [Tremblay?], October 21, 1702, SME, R, no. 36, 2.

13. Ibid.

14. St. Cosme to [Tremblay?], May 4, 1704, SME, R, no. 37, 2.

15. St. Cosme to [Tremblay?], March 30, 1705, SME, R, no. 39, 1. For the effects of the Indian slave trade, see Verner Winslow Crane, *The Southern Frontier, 1670–1732* (Durham: Duke University Press, 1928), 89–96; Alan Gallay, *The Indian Slave Trade*:

The Rise of the English Empire in the American South (New Haven: Yale University Press, 2002), 101–99; Ethridge, "Creating the Shatter Zone," 206–17; and William Ramsey, *The Yamasee War: A Study of Culture, Economy, and Conflict in the Colonial South* (Lincoln: University of Nebraska Press, 2008), 34–56.

16. St. Cosme to Tremblay, January 8, 1706, SME, R, no. 40, 2. See also Balvay, *La Révolte des Natchez*, 55–56.

17. The first report of St. Cosme's murder placed the blame on the Natchez (Bienville to Minister, February 20, 1707, ANOM, C13A, vol. 2, 11). The culprits were later determined to be Chitimachas (see Jean-Baptiste Bernard de La Harpe, *The Historical Journal of the Establishment of the French in Louisiana*, trans. Joan Cain and Virginia Koenig [Lafayette: Center for Louisiana Studies, 1971], 51; and André Penicault, "Relation, ou annale véritable de ce qui s'est passé dans le païs de la Louisiane," manuscript, Provient du Collège des Jésuites de Clermont à Paris, n° 828, 102).

18. Henri Roulleaux de La Vente to (?), June 27, 1708, SME, R, no. 81, 2. See also Balvay, *Révolte des Natchez*, 58.

19. Pierre-François-Xavier de Charlevoix, *Histoire et description de la Nouvelle France et Journal d'un voyage fait par ordre du Roi dans L'amerique Septentrionalle*, vol. 2 (Paris: Chez Nyon Fils, 1744), 493–95.

20. Pierre-François-Xavier de Charlevoix, *Histoire et description de la Nouvelle France et journal d'un voyage fait par ordre du roi dans L'amerique Septentrionalle*, vol. 3 (Paris: Chez Nyon Fils, 1744), 431.

21. Antoine Le Page du Pratz, *Histoire de la Louisiane, Contenant la découverte de de vaste Pays; va Description géographique; un voyage cans les terres*, vol. 3 (Paris: Lambert, 1758), 247.

22. McManners, *Church and Society in Eighteenth-Century France*, 510.

23. Dupré, Buisson de Saint Cosme, *Dictionary of Canadian Biography*, vol. 2. Dupré included BN mss, fr., n.a., 2550, fol. 115 in the entry's bibliography but made no comment regarding its content.

24. Barnett, *The Natchez Indians*, 55–56.

25. Balvay, *La Révolte des Natchez*, 58.

26. Theda Purdue, "'A Sprightly Lover Is the Most Prevailing Missionary': Intermarriage between Europeans and Indians in the Eighteenth-Century South," in *In Light on the Path: The Anthropology and History of the Southeastern Indians*, ed. Thomas J. Pluckhahn and Robbie Franklyn Ethridge (Tuscaloosa: University of Alabama Press, 2006), 165–78.

27. Le Page du Pratz, *Histoire de la Louisiane*, 2:403. See also Gordon Sayre, *The Indian Chief as Tragic Hero: Native Resistance and the Literatures of America, from Moctezuma to Tecumseh* (Chapel Hill: University of North Carolina Press, 2005), 216.

28. Jacques Gravier, "Relation ou journal du voyage en 1700 depuis le Pays des Illinois Jusqu'a l'Embouchure du Fleuve Mississipi," February 16, 1701, *JR*, 65:133.

29. Ibid., 65:142–43.

30. Sauvole to Minister, August 4, 1701, ANOM, C13A, vol. 1, 318.

31. For a comprehensive treatment of the war, see John A. Lynn, *The Wars of Louis XIV, 1667–1714* (New York: Longman, 1999), 266–360.

32. Penicault, "Relation, ou annale véritable," 118–40.

33. For the Choctaws' comments about the French in Mobile, see Bienville to Pontchartrain, February 20, 1707, *MPAFD*, 3:40. For the quartering of troops among the

Indians, see D'Artaguette to Pontchartrain, June 20, 1710, *MPAFD*, 2:55. (The various spellings of the name D'Artiguiette Diron are regularized to that form in the chapter text. In the notes, however, the spellings used in the source materials are used.) For the threat of attack, see Bienville to Pontchartrain, February 25, 1708, *MPAFD*, 3:111–16.

34. Marcel Giraud, *A History of French Louisiana, The Reign of Louis XIV*, vol. 1, *1698–1715*, trans. Joseph C. Lambert (Baton Rouge: Louisiana State University Press, 1974), 249–302; Patricia Dillon Woods, *French-Indian Relations on the Southern Frontier, 1699–1762* (Ann Arbor: UMI Research Press, 1980), 33–38.

35. Pontchartrain to Dautin, September 2, 1698 AM, B2, vol. 136, fols. 159–160v; Thomas Nairne, *Nairne's Muskhogean Journals: The 1708 Expedition to the Mississippi River* (Jackson: University of Mississippi Press, 1988), 4; Thomas Nairne to the Lords Proprietors, July 10, 1708, in *Records in the British Public Records Office Relating to South Carolina 1701–1710*, ed. A. S. Salley (Columbia: Historical Commission of South Carolina, 1947), 193–202. See also Crane, *The Southern Frontier*, 89–96; and Giraud, *A History of French Louisiana: The Reign of Louis XIV*, 1:80–101. For a more recent discussion of Nairne's travels among the Creeks, see Joshua Piker, *Okfuskee: A Creek Indian Town in Colonial America* (Cambridge: Harvard University Press, 2004), 15–19.

36. Bienville to Pontchartrain, October 12, 1708, *MPAFD*, 2:40.

37. For the Indian slave trade, see Crane, *The Southern Frontier*, 47–70; and Robbie Franklyn Ethridge, *From Chicaza to Chickasaw: The European Invasion and Transformation of the Mississippian World* (Chapel Hill: University of North Carolina Press, 2010), 194–220. For Carolinian slave raiding policies, see L. H. Roper, *Conceiving Carolina: Proprietors, Planters, and Plots* (New York: Palgrave, 2004), 117–33. For the destruction of the Timucuan Chiefdoms, see John H. Hann, *Apalachee: The Land between Two Rivers* (Gainesville: University of Florida Press, 1988), 264–83; and John E. Worth, *The Timucuan Chiefdoms of Spanish Florida*, vol. 2, *Resistance and Destruction* (Gainesville: University of Florida Press, 1998), 117–46.

38. James B. Collins, *The State in Early Modern France*, 2nd ed. (New York: Cambridge University Press, 2009), 199–215; William Doyle, *Old Regime France* (New York: Oxford University Press, 2001), 27.

39. Jacob M. Price, *France and the Chesapeake: A History of the French Tobacco Monopoly, 1674–1791, and of Its Relationship to the British and American Tobacco Trades*, vol. 2 (Ann Arbor: University of Michigan Press, 1973), 17–19.

40. Ibid., 2:57.

41. Giraud, *A History of French Louisiana: The Reign of Louis XIV*, 1:290–300; Price, *France and the Chesapeake*, 1:201; Céline Vidal, "French Louisiana in the Age of the Companies, 1712–1731," in *Constructing Early Modern Empires: Proprietary Adventures in the Atlantic World*, ed. L. H. Roper and Bertrand Van Ruymbeke (Boston: Brill, 2007), 139–40.

42. Vidal, "French Louisiana in the Age of the Companies," 141.

43. Louis XIV to La Mothe, May 13, 1710, *MPAFD*, 3:143; Giraud, *A History of French Louisiana: The Reign of Louis XIV*, 1:189. For Cadillac's career at the Detroit post, see Jean Delanglez, "The Genesis and Building of Detroit," *Mid-America* 19, no. 2 (1948): 75–104; and Jean Delanglez, "Cadillac at Detroit," *Mid-America* 19, no. 3 (1948):152–76.

44. Cadillac to Pontchartrain, October 26, 1713, *MPAFD*, 2:167–68.

45. O'Neill, *The Church and State in French Colonial Louisiana*, 78–102.

46. Vidal, "French Louisiana in the Age of the Companies," 142–43.
47. Du Clos to Pontchartrain, October 9, 1713, *MPAFD*, 2:94.
48. Giraud, *A History of French Louisiana: The Reign of Louis XIV*, 1:303–12.
49. Crozat, 1713, "Mémoire sur la Louisiane," ANOM, C13A, vol. 3, 367–69.
50. Louis XIV to Cadillac, December 27, 1714, ANOM, C13A, vol. 3, 684.
51. For the founding of the Natchez post, see Giraud, *A History of French Louisiana: The Reign of Louis XIV*, 1:305–6.
52. Ned J. Jenkins, "Tracing the Origins of the Early Creeks, 1050–1700 CE," in *Mapping the Mississippian Shatter Zone: The Colonial Indian Slave Trade and Regional Instability in the American South*, ed. Robbie Ethridge and Sheri M. Shuck-Hall (Lincoln: University of Nebraska Press, 2009), 192.
53. Karl G. Lorenz, "A Re-examination of Natchez Sociopolitical Complexity: A View from the Grand Village, *Southeastern Archaeology* 16, no. 2 (1997): 101–2.
54. John E. Worth, "Spanish Missions and the Persistence of Chiefly Power," in *The Transformation of the Southeastern Indians, 1540–1760*, ed. Robbie Ethridge and Charles M. Hudson (Jackson: University of Mississippi Press, 2002), 21–83.
55. Worth argues that archaeological evidence supports the persistence of precontact social patterns into the late eighteenth century among the Creeks (see John E. Worth, "Bridging Prehistory and History in the Southeast: Evaluating the Utility of the Acculturation Concept," in *Light on the Path: The Anthropology and History of the Southeastern Indians*, ed. Thomas J. Pluckhahn and Robbie Franklyn Ethridge [Tuscaloosa: University of Alabama Press, 2006], 196–206).
56. Penicault placed the post at or near the Grand Village (see Penicault, "Relation, ou annale véritable," 248).
57. For a full listing of grave goods, see Robert S. Neitzel, *Archeology of the Fatherland Site: The Grand Village of the Natchez*, Archaeological Report No. 28 (Jackson: Mississippi Department of Archives and History, 1997), 40–45, 50–51. For further analyses of Natchez archaeology, see Ian W. Brown, "Historic Indians of the Lower Mississippi Valley: An Archaeologist's View," in *Towns and Temples along the Mississippi*, ed. David H. Dye and Cheryl Ann Cox (Tuscaloosa: University of Alabama Press, 1990), 176–93; and James A. Brown, "Archaeology Confronts History at the Natchez Temple," *Southeastern Archaeology* 9, no. 1 (1990): 1–10. See also Andrew C. Albrecht, "Indian-French Relations at Natchez," *American Anthropologist* 48, no. 3 (1946): 321–54; and Jon Muller, *Mississippian Political Economy* (New York: Plenum, 1997), 63–69.
58. Lorenz, "A Re-examination of Natchez Sociopolitical Complexity," 103.
59. Karl G. Lorenz, "The Natchez of Southwest Mississippi," in *Indians of the Greater Southeast: Historical Archaeology and Ethnohistory*, ed. Bonnie G. McEwan (Gainesville: University Press of Florida, 2000), 163–73; "A Re-examination of Natchez Sociopolitical Complexity," 103–7. Lorenz's work responds to Ian W. Brown's suggestion that adopted villages like the Grigras should yield different artifacts than "native" Natchez towns (see Ian W. Brown, "An Archaeological Study of Culture Contact and Change in the Natchez Bluffs Region," in *La Salle and His Legacy: Frenchmen and Indians in the Lower Mississippi Valley*, ed. Patricia Galloway [Jackson: University of Mississippi Press, 1982], 49–59).
60. For a review of France's diplomatic strategy during the negotiations at the close of the war, see Dale Miquelon, "Envisioning the French Empire: Utrecht, 1711–1713," *French Historical Studies* 24, no. 4 (2001): 653–77.

61. Bienville to Minister, September 1, 1715, ANOM, C13A, vol. 3, 786.

62. For Hughes's plans for colonizing the Mississippi, see Crane, *The Southern Frontier*, 100–108. For Bienville's perceptions of the Yamasee War and for Hughes's capture, see Bienville to Pontchartrain, June 15, 1715, *MPAFD*, 3:181–82. See also Giraud, *A History of French Louisiana: The Reign of Louis XIV*, 1:326–38: Barnett, *The Natchez Indians*, 60; and Balvay, *La Révolte des Natchez*, 66.

63. Bienville to Minister, January 20, 1716, ANOM, C13A, vol. 4, 775. Cadillac left for Illinois without leaving instructions for Bienville, the king's lieutenant and second-in-command, and without revealing his destination (see Bienville to Pontchartrain, June 15, 1715, *MPAFD*, 3:181).

64. The "lieutenant of the king," was an officer appointed as the second-in-command to the governor of a post. This was a royal commission that put Bienville in charge of the military affairs of the colony (see Christopher Duffy, *Fire and Stone: The Science of Fortress Warfare, 1660–1860* [1975; Edison: Castle, 2006], 87).

65. For the initial orders for the expedition, see Cadillac to Bienville, January 5, 1716, ANOM, F, vol. 3, 24. For problems with supplies and manpower, see Marcel Giraud, *A History of French Louisiana: Years of Transition, 1715–1717*, trans. Brian Pearce, vol. 2 (Baton Rouge: Louisiana State University Press, 1974), 79; Bienville to Minister, January 20, 1716, ANOM, C13A, vol. 4, X; Jean-Baptiste Bernard de La Harpe, *The Historical Journal of the Establishment of the French in Louisiana*, trans. Joan Cain and Virginia Koenig (Lafayette: Center for Louisiana Studies, 1971), 66. For reports of desertion, see Minutes of the Superior Council, January 23, 1716, *MPAFD*, 2:212.

66. Instructions de Lamothe Cadillac, gouveneur à Bienville, commandant de Rosalie, January 5, 1716, ANOM, F3, vol. 24, 73. Bienville suspected that the governor wanted the expedition to fail because he refused to marry Cadillac's daughter (Bienville to Minister, January 20, 1716, ANOM, C13A, vol. 4, 775).

67. Penicault, "Relation, ou annale véritable," 242–46.

68. Ibid., 244.

69. Ibid., 246–50.

70. Ibid., 253–54; ANOM, C13A, vol. 4, 785–87.

71. [Chavanne de Richebourg?], "Memoire en la forme de ce qui est passé dans la premiere Expedition que Mr. Bienville fit aux Natchez en 1716," ANOM, C13A, vol. 4, 787; Penicault, "Relation, ou annale véritable de," 255–57. Penicault put the number of Natchez warriors at "more than 1,200 men."

72. Penicault, "Relation, ou annale véritable," 255–56; La Harpe, *The Historical Journal*, 68.

73. "Memoire en forme de journal," ANOM, C13A, vol. 4, 788; "Punition des Sauvages Natchez en 1716 et Etablissent d'un fort français chez eux," BN Mss, fr., n.a., 2549, fol. 42.

74. Ibid.

75. "Memoire en forme de journal," ANOM, C13A, vol. 4, 790; "Punition des Sauvages Natchez en 1716," BN Mss, fr., n.a., 2549, fol. 42.

76. Memoire en forme de journal," ANOM, C13A, vol. 4, 790–91; La Harpe, *The Historical Journal*, 68–69.

77. Memoire présenté à Lamothe Cadillac, gouveneur, par de Richebourg . . . avec observations de Lamothe Cadillac, May 10, 1716, ANOM, F3, fols. 76v–77; Memoire

en forme de journal..., ANOM, C13A, vol. 4, 793; Penicault, "Relation, ou annale véritable," 258–59; La Harpe, *The Historical Journal*, 69–70.

78. Bienville demanded the entire head in order to identify the deceased by their tattoos.

79. Penicault and other French observers referred to this town as the White Earth Village (*terre blanche*) (Penicault, "Relation, ou annale véritable," 259; Punition des Sauvages Natchez en 1716," BN Mss, fr., n.a., 2549, fol. 45). Karl G. Lorenz argued that the White Earth Village and the White Apple Village were different names for the same town (see Lorenz, "The Natchez of Southwest Mississippi," 161).

80. "Punition des Sauvages Natchez en 1716," BN Mss, fr., n.a., 2549, fols. 43–44.

81. Penicault, "Relation, ou annale véritable," 260. La Harpe reported that the head belonged to a man who offered to die in the place of the Sun of the White Earth (La Harpe, *The Historical Journal*, 69).

82. Balvay, *La Révolte des Natchez*, 77.

83. "Memoire en forme de journal," ANOM, C13A, vol. 4, 796.

84. Ibid., vol. 4, 797.

85. Ibid., vol. 4, 798–99; "Punition des Sauvages Natchez en 1716," BN Mss, fr., n.a., 2549, fol. 45. The French text uses the term *les noyers*, or "the Walnuts." Swanton suggested that Jenzenaques and Walnut Villagers were the same people (see John Reed Swanton, *Indian Tribes of the Lower Mississippi Valley and the Adjacent Coast of the Gulf of Mexico* [Washington, DC: U.S. Government Printing Office, 1911], 47–48).

86. "Memoire en forme de journal," ANOM, C13A, vol. 4, 799.

87. Ibid., vol. 4, 800; "Punition des Sauvages Natchez en 1716" BN Mss, fr., n.a., 2549, fol. 46.

88. "Memoire en forme de journal," ANOM, C13A, vol. 4, 802; "Punition des Sauvages Natchez en 1716," BN Mss, fr., n.a., 2549, fol. 46.

89. "Memoire en forme de journal," ANOM, C13A, vol. 4, 802.

90. Ibid., vol. 4, fol. 804; "Punition des Sauvages Natchez en 1716," BN Mss, fr., n.a., 2549, fols. 46–47.

91. Swanton, *Indian Tribes of the Lower Mississippi Valley*, 193.

92. "Tu nous defais d'un mechant homme." "Memoire en forme de journal," ANOM, C13A, vol. 4, 804.

93. Giraud, *A History of French Louisiana: The Reign of Louis XIV*, 1:77.

94. Patricia Galloway argues that much of what Le Page du Pratz knew about Natchez kinship and social practices came from his Chitimacha slave informant (Patricia Galloway and Jason Baird Jackson, "Natchez and Neighboring Groups," in *HBNAI*, 14:603).

95. Duffy, *Fire and Stone*, 87. Pierre Le Moyne died from yellow fever in Havana in 1706 while organizing an invasion of Carolina (Jay Higginbotham, *Old Mobile: Fort Louis de la Louisiane, 1702–1711* [Mobile: Museum of the City of Mobile, 1977], 284–85). Charles Le Moyne, Bienville, and Iberville's father had twelve sons and two daughters (see Jean Jacques Lefebvre, "Charles Le Moyne de Longueuil et Châteauguay," *The Dictionary of Canadian Biography*, vol. 1 [Toronto: University of Toronto Press, 1970]).

96. Anonymous, *Memoire sur Louisiana*, 143, NYPL.

97. Christine Snyder, *Slavery in Indian Country: The Changing Face of Captivity in Early America* (Cambridge: Harvard University Press, 2010), 7.

98. Ibid., 4–5.

99. The study of Native American slavery has expanded enormously over the past decade, and the following is by no means an exhaustive list: Carl J. Ekberg, *Stealing Indian Women: Native Slavery in the Illinois Country* (Urbana: University of Illinois Press, 2007); Alan Gallay, *The Indian Slave Trade*; Brett Rushforth, "'A Little Flesh We Offer You': The Origins of Indian Slavery in New France," *William and Mary Quarterly* 60, no. 4 (2003); Brett Rushforth, "Slavery, the Fox Wars, and the Limits of Alliance," *William and Mary Quarterly* 63, no. 1 (2006); Christina Snyder, "Conquered Enemies, Adopted Kin, and Owned People: The Creek Indians and Their Captives," *Journal of Southern History* 73, no. 2 (2007); Fay A. Yarbrough, *Race and the Cherokee Nation: Sovereignty in the Nineteenth Century* (Philadelphia: University of Pennsylvania Press, 2008).

100. Anonymous, *Memoire sur Louisiana*, 43, NYPL. See also Pierre-Francois-Xavier de Charlevoix, *Histoire et description générale de la Nouvelle France*, 3:420; "Grand Soliel, files d'un francois en 1728," BN Mss, fr., n.a., 2550, fol. 116.

101. Higginbotham, *Old Mobile*, 359.

102. Paul du Poisson aux Akensas, October 3, 1727, *JR*, 67: 299.

103. Penicault, "Relation, ou annale véritable," 261–63.

104. Louis XIV to D'Artaguette, June 30, 1707, *MPAFD*, 3:61; Pontchartrain to Boisbriant, June 30, 1707, *MPAFD*, 3:72; Abstract of Testimony against Bienville, taken by D'Artaguette February 24–28, 1708, *MPAFD*, 3:78–110; Higginbotham, *Old Mobile*, 315–39.

105. Cadillac to Pontchartrain, October 26, 1713, *MPAFD*, 2:167–68.

106. La Harpe, *The Historical Journal*, 63.

107. Le Page du Pratz, *Histoire de la Louisiane*, 2:280.

108. Lorenz, "A Re-examination of Natchez Sociopolitical Complexity," 106.

109. Le Page du Pratz, *Histoire de la Louisiane*, 2:355–60.

110. For a detailed examination of the ritual use of war clubs, see Wayne William Van Horne, "The War Club: Weapon and Symbol in Southeastern Indian Societies" (PhD diss., University of Georgia, 1993).

111. Marshall Sahlins wrote extensively on a similar convergence of indigenous religious/cultural reenactments and the timing of a European leader's appearance. In the late 1770s, Captain Cook arrived in Hawaii at the same time its inhabitants were celebrating the festival commemorating the appearance of their deity *Lono*. The Hawaiians welcomed the Englishman with great ceremony. When Cook unexpectedly returned to the islands a few weeks later, he disturbed the calendar cycle, and the Hawaiians redressed the imbalance by killing him (see Marshall David Sahlins, *How "Natives" Think: About Captain Cook, for Example* [Chicago: University of Chicago Press, 1995], 17–83).

112. Richard White's formulation of European and Indian accommodation in cases of murder works well in this instance (see Richard White, *The Middle Ground: Indians, Empires and Republics in the Great Lakes Region, 1650–1815* [Cambridge: Cambridge University Press, 1991], 76–82; see also Patricia K. Galloway, "The Barthelemy Murders: Bienville's Establishment of the Lex Talonis as a Principle of Indian Diplomacy," *Proceedings of the Eighth Meeting of the French Colonial Historical Society* [1985]: 91–103). For a contrasting view of Native American justice, see Cornelius Jaenen, *Friend and Foe: Aspects of French-Amerindian Cultural Contact in the Sixteenth and Seventeenth Centuries* (New York: Columbia University Press, 1976), 97.

113. "Memoire en forme de journal," ANOM, C13A, vol. 4, 800.

114. The French took special notice of the elaborate funerary rites of the Natchez. Swanton compiled and translated accounts of these rites (see Swanton, *Indian Tribes of the Lower Mississippi Valley*, 138–57). These accounts included Penicault, "Relation, ou annale véritable," 134–40 (Swanton used Margry's version of Penicault's "Relation"), as well as observations by Le Page du Pratz, Dumont de Montigny, Fathers Gravier, Charlevoix, and Le Petit. See also Patricia Galloway and Jason Baird Jackson, "Natchez and Neighboring Groups," in *HBNAI*, 15:606–7.

115. Le Page du Pratz, *Histoire de la Louisiane*, 2:418–19. See also Father Le Petit, *JR*, 68:142–51.

116. Cadillac and Du Clos to Minister, July 15, 1716, AM, B, vol. 19, 419v.

117. Mémoire présenté à Lamothe Cadillac, gouverneur, par de Richebourg, dépêché par de Bienville des Tonicas avec observations de Lamothe Cadillac, 1716, ANOM, F3, vol. 24, 74–79v.

118. Bienville to Cadillac, June 23, 1716, ANOM, C13A, vol. 4, 693–94v.

119. Crozat, "Memoire sur la Louisiane," January 11, 1717, ANOM, C13A, vol. 5, 231v.

120. Price, *France and the Chesapeake*, 205–7.

121. Vidal, "French Louisiana in the Age of the Companies," 145.

122. Marcel Giraud, "La Compagnie d'Occident, 1717–1718," *Revue Historique* 226, no. 3 (1961): 23–56; *Lettres patentes*, August 26, 1717, ANOM, A, vol. 22, 69–71; see also Allain, *"Not Worth a Straw,"* 64–67.

123. Balvay, "La Révolte des Natchez," 77.

3 / Impudent Immigrants

1. Daryl Dee, *Expansion and Crisis in Louis XIV's France: Franche-Comté and Absolute Monarchy, 1674–1715* (Rochester, NY: University of Rochester Press, 2009), 22, 64–65.

2. Jacob M. Price, *France and the Chesapeake: A History of the French Tobacco Monopoly, 1674–1791, and of Its Relationship to the British and American Tobacco Trades*, vol. 1 (Ann Arbor: University of Michigan Press, 1973), 92–96.

3. Philip P. Boucher, *France and the American Tropics: Tropics of Discontent?* (Baltimore: Johns Hopkins University Press, 2007), 243.

4. Ibid.; Price, *France and the Chesapeake*, 1:160–61.

5. James Breck Perkins, *France under Louis XV* (New York: Houghton Mifflin, 1897), 49–53.

6. Emmanuel Le Roy Ladurie, *The Ancien Régime: A History of France, 1610–1774* (Cambridge, MA: Blackwell, 1996), 206, 288.

7. Price, *France and the Chesapeake*, 1:209–11.

8. Ibid., 1:302.

9. James B. Collins, *The State in Early Modern France*, 2nd ed. (New York: Cambridge University Press, 2009), 223–25.

10. Marcel Giraud, "La Compagnie d'Occident, 1717–1718," *Revue Historique* 226, no. 3 (1961): 23–56.

11. Collins, *The State in Early Modern France*, 224–28.

12. Arnaud Balvay, *La Révolte des Natchez* (Paris: Éditions du Félin, 2008), 79.

13. Charles Poor Kindleberger, *A Financial History of Western Europe*, 2nd ed. (New York: Oxford University Press, 1993), 100.

14. Ibid., 99.

15. Collins, *The State in Early Modern France*, 228.

16. Historians' views of Law's "system" and its collapse vary. The most comprehensive account remains Marcel Giraud's *Histoire de la Louisiane française*, vol. 3, *L'époque de John Law* (Paris: Presses Universitaires de France, 1966), 1–100. Charles Gayarré castigated the Scot as a "stock-jobber" who carried out a confidence scheme on a grand scale (see Charles Gayarré, *History of Louisiana: The French Domination* [1866; repr., Gretna, LA.: Pelican, 1998], 193–203). See also Mathé Allain, *"Not Worth a Straw": French Colonial Policy and the Early Years of Louisiana* (Lafayette: Center for Louisiana Studies, 1988), 67–68; and Patricia Dillon Woods, *French-Indian Relations on the Southern Frontier, 1699–1762* (Ann Arbor: UMI Research Press, 1980), 62. For Law's ouster, see Le Roy Ladurie, *The Ancien Régime*, 294.

17. Kindleberger, *A Financial History of Western Europe*, 100.

18. Gilles Havard and Cécile Vidal, *Histoire de l'amérique française* (Paris: Flammarion, 2006), 225.

19. For France's emigration policies during this era, see Carl A. Brasseaux, "The Image of Louisiana and the Failure of Voluntary French Emigration, 1683–1731," in *The French Experience in Louisiana*, ed. Glenn R. Conrad (Lafayette: Center for Louisiana Studies, 1995), 153–62; Glenn R. Conrad, "Emigration Forcée: A French Attempt to Populate Louisiana, 1716–1720," in *The French Experience in Louisiana*, ed. Conrad (Lafayette: Center for Louisiana Studies, 1995), 125–35. For the recruitment of women, see Allain, *"Not Worth a Straw,"* 83–87. For the transport of convicts, see James D. Hardy, "The Transportation of Convicts to Colonial Louisiana," in *The French Experience in Louisiana*, ed. Glenn R. Conrad (Lafayette: Center for Louisiana Studies, 1995). For Prévost's novel, see Antoine François Prévost, *Histoire du chevalier des Grieux et de Manon Lescaut* (1731; Paris: A. Perche, 1920). For popular images of Louisiana, see Pierre H. Boulle, "Some Eighteenth-Century French Views on Louisiana," in *Frenchmen and French Ways in the Mississippi Valley*, ed. John Francis McDermott (Urbana: University of Illinois Press, 1969), 15–27.

20. "Memoir de l'etat Actuel ou est la colonie de la Louisiane pour juger de ce que l'on peut en espérer," undated, 1721, ANOM, C13, C, vol. 1, 319-331v. The census is on fols. 319-20v.

21. Glenn R. Conrad, ed., *Immigration and War: Louisiana 1718–1721: From Memoir of Charles Le Gac*, trans. Conrad (Lafayette: University of Southwestern Louisiana, 1970), 11.

22. Jean François Benjamin Dumont de Montigny, *Mémoires historiques sur la Louisiane contenant ce qui y est arrivé de plus mémorable depuis l'année 1687*, vol. 2 (Paris: J. B. Bauche, 1753), 42.

23. Hubert to the Council, no date [1717–18?], *MPAFD*, 2:232.

24. Hubert to the Council, October 26, 1717, *MPAFD*, 2:244.

25. Marcel Giraud, *Histoire de la louisiane française*, vol. 4, *La Louisiane après le système de Law* (Paris: Presses Universitaires de France, 1974), 260–62.

26. Ibid., 4:369.

27. André Penicault, "Relation, ou annale véritable de ce qui s'est passé dans le païs de la Louisiane," manuscript, Provient du Collège des Jésuites de Clermont à Paris, n° 828, 350–51.

28. Antoine Le Page du Pratz, *Histoire de la Louisiane, Contenant la découverte de*

vaste Pays; Sa Description géographique; Un voyage cans les terres, vol. 1 (Paris: Lambert, 1758), 118, 125–26; Giraud, *La Louisiane après le système de Law*, 368.

29. Jean-François Benjamin Dumont de Montigny, *Regards sur le monde atlantique, 1717–1747* (Sillery: Septentrion, 2008), 150–51.

30. Penicault, "Relation, ou annale veritable," 353. See also James F. Barnett Jr., *The Natchez Indians: A History to 1735* (Jackson: University of Mississippi Press, 2007), 81. See also Arnaud Balvay, *La Révolte des Natchez* (Paris: Éditions du Félin, 2008), 83.

31. Extrait de la lettre que M. Faucon Dumanoir . . . a Ecrite aux Intéressés de ladite Colonie, July 18, 1721, ANOM, G1, vol. 465, n.p.

32. Penicault, "Relation, ou annale véritable," 354; La Chaise to the Directors of the Company of the Indies, September 6, 1723, *MPAFD*, 2:340.

33. La Loire to [Minister?], March 21, 1721, Hubert Papers, 1738 fHu, James Ford Bell Library, University of Minnesota, 5.

34. Le Page du Pratz, *Histoire de la Louisiane*, 1:125–26; Penicault, "Relation, ou annale véritable," 351; Giraud, *La Louisiane après le système de Law*, 265–69.

35. Extrait de l'acte de Societé, September 4, 1719, ANOM, G1, vol. 465, n.p.; Giraud, *L'époque de John Law*, 187–89.

36. Extrait de l'acte de Société entre la Cie des Indes et les associés en la Concession de Ste. Catherine, September 4, 1719, ANOM, G1, vol. 465, n.p.; Deucher to the Directors, February 6, 1720, ANOM, G1, vol. 465, n.p. See also Antoine Le Page du Pratz, *Histoire de la Louisiane*, 1:173.

37. Engagement du sieur Dumanoir, December 29, 1719, ANOM, G1, vol. 465, n.p.; Procuration de Kolly et Deucher au Sieur Faucon Dumanoir, December 29, 1719, ANOM, G1, vol. 465, n.p.

38. Etat des Passagers embarqués sur "La Loire" pour la Concession de Sainte-Catherine, August 20, 1720, ANOM, G1, vol. 464, n.p.

39. Extrait de la lettre que M. Faucon Dumanoir, July 18, 1721, ANOM, G1, vol. 465, n.p.

40. Pierre-Francois-Xavier de Charlevoix, *Histoire et description générale de la Nouvelle France avec le Journal historique d'un voyage fait par ordre du Roi*, vol. 3 (Paris: Chez Pierre-François Giffart, 1744), 415.

41. Etat de ce qui est dû par la Colonie de S$^{te.}$ Catherine, 'AN T66$^{1-2}$, doc. 28, pièces 1–5; Giraud, *La Louisiane après le système de Law*, 104.

42. Etat des ouviers qui Sont actuellement a la Colonie de S$^{te.}$ Catherine, September 1722, AN T66$^{1-2}$, doc. 28.

43. Longrais, June 15, 1723, "Journal des principaux événements de la guerre des Natchez et de la campagne de M. de Bienville contre cette nation, December 10, 1723, ANOM, C13A, vol. 7, 302.

44. Virginia DeJohn Anderson, *Creatures of Empire: How Domestic Animals Transformed Early America* (New York: Oxford University Press, 2004). For free-range husbandry, see 111; for competition with Native American environments, see 185–95.

45. Henri Lefebvre, *The Production of Space*, trans. Donald Nicholson Smith, (1974; Cambridge, MA: Blackwell, 1991), 38.

46. Samuel Wilson Jr., "Ignace Francois Broutin," in *Frenchmen and French Ways in the Mississippi Valley*, ed. John Francis McDermott (Urbana: University of Illinois Press, 1969), 236–37.

47. For a discussion of the textuality of maps, see J. B. Harley, "Silences and Secrecy:

The Hidden Agenda of Cartography in Early Modern Europe," *Imago Mundi* 40 (1988): 57–76. For a more recent treatment of maps as texts, see Martin Brückner, *The Geographic Revolution in Early America: Maps, Literacy, and National Identity* (Chapel Hill: University of North Carolina Press, 2006),13–44.

48. Karl G. Lorenz, "The Natchez of Southwest Mississippi," in *Indians of the Greater Southeast: Historical Archaeology and Ethnohistory*, ed. Bonnie G. McEwan (Gainesville: University Press of Florida, 2000), 163–73.

49. Requête présentée par Faucon Dumanoir au Conseil Supérieur au sujet de la Concession de la Ste. Catherine, May 20, 1723, article 2, ANOM, G1, vol. 465, n.p.

50. Frederic Gleach, *Powhatan's World and Colonial Virginia: A Conflict of Cultures* (Lincoln: University of Nebraska Press, 1997), 148–58, 184.

51. Preuve du premier attentat des Natchez, March 9, 1722, ANOM, G1, vol. 465, n.p.

52. Dumanoir, Preuve du premier attentat des Natchez contre la Concession de St. Catherine, March 9, 1722, ANOM, G1, vol. 465, n.p. See also La Harpe, *The Historical Journal*, 157. For Berneval's career, see Carl Brasseaux, ed., *France's Forgotten Legion: Service Records of French Military and Administrative personnel Stationed in the Mississippi Valley and Gulf Coast Region, 1699–1769* (Baton Rouge: Louisiana State University Press, 2000), CD-ROM.

53. Louis Auguste de La Loire de Flaucourt, "Relation de la guerre des Sauvages Natchez," September 6, 1723, ANOM, DFC, vol. 31, 1.

54. Ibid., 1–2. See also Giraud, *La Louisiane après le système de Law*, 289–91; Barnett, *The Natchez Indians*, 84–85; and Balvay, *La Révolte des Natchez*, 98.

55. Le Page du Pratz, *Histoire de la Louisiane*, 1:180–81.

56. Swanton, Woods, and Barnett, *The Natchez Indians*, 85.

57. "Relation des hostilités commises par les Natchez contre la Concession de St. Catherine," November 4, 1722, ANOM, G1, vol. 465, n.p. The following individuals signed this report: Broutin, Casseneuve, Le Page du Pratz, Papin, Hardy de Villeneuve, Lorenso, Bingant, Dufaur, de La Loire de Flaucourt, Guenot, Jacque Blouvin, and Malo. See also the Journal de Diron D'Artaguette, October 26, 1722, ANOM, B, vol. 2, 187; Jean-François-Benjamin Dumont de Montigny, *Mémoires historiques sur la Louisiane contenant ce qui y est arrivé de plus mémorable depuis l'année 1687*, vol. 2 (Paris: J. B. Bauche, 1753), 95–96; and Le Page du Pratz, *Histoire de la Louisiane*, 1:182.

58. "Requête présentée par Faucon Dumanoir au Conseil Supérieur au sujet de la Concession de St. Catherine," May 20, 1723, ANOM, G1, vol. 465, n.p.

59. Timothy R. Pauketat, *Cahokia: Ancient America's Great City on the Mississippi* (New York: Penguin, 2009), 128–30.

60. Lorenz, "The Natchez of Southwest Mississippi," 163–71.

61. De La Loire, "Relation de la Guerre . . . ," June 6, 1723, ANOM, DFC, vol. 31, 3. Dumont wrote that La Rochelle was a soldier who lived off base from the fort (see Dumont de Montigny, *Mémoires historiques sur la Louisiane*, 2:95).

62. Allan Greer, "Commons and Enclosures in the Colonization of North America," *American Historical Review* 117, no 2 (April 2012): 369.

63. "Relation des hostilités commises par les Natchez," November 4, 1722, ANOM, G1, vol. 465, n.p.

64. Ibid.

65. De La Loire, "Relation de la Guerre . . . ," June 6, 1723, ANOM, DFC, vol. 31, 4.

66. "Relation des hostilités commises par les Natchez," ANOM, G1, vol. 465, n.p.; Journal de Diron D'Artaguette, October 28, 1722, ANOM, 13B, vol. 2, 87.

67. Journal de Diron D'Artaguette, October 28, 1722, ANOM, 13B, vol. 2, 87; Le Page du Pratz, *Histoire de la Louisiane*, 1:183.

68. "Relation des hostilités commises par les Natchez," ANOM, G1, vol. 465, n.p.

69. Ibid.

70. William Cronon, *Changes in the Land: Indians, Colonists, and the Ecology of New England* (New York: Hill and Wang, 1983), 128–30; Jill Lepore, *The Name of War: King Philip's War and the Origins of American Identity* (New York: Knopf, 1998), 72, 78–79; James Hart Merrell, *The Indians' New World: Catawbas and Their Neighbors from European Contact through the Era of Removal* (New York: Norton, 1989), 174–75.

71. Daniel H. Usner, *Indians, Settlers, and Slaves in a Frontier Exchange Economy: The Lower Mississippi Valley before 1783* (Durham: University of North Carolina Press, 1992), 181–89; "French-Natchez Borderlands in Colonial Louisiana," in *American Indians in the Lower Mississippi Valley: Social and Economic Histories* (Lincoln: University of Nebraska Press, 1998), 24; "Relation des hostilités commises par les Natchez," November 4, 1722, ANOM, G1, vol. 465, n.p.

72. For problems with unfenced Indian planting grounds, see Patricia Seed, *Ceremonies of Possession in Europe's Conquest of the New World, 1492–1640* (New York: Cambridge University Press, 1995), 16–40; and Anderson, *Creatures of Empire*, 37.

73. Anderson, *Creatures of Empire*, 224–26.

74. E. P. Thompson, "The Moral Economy of the English Crowd in the Eighteenth Century," *Past & Present*, no. 50 (February 1971): 76–136.

75. Douglas Hay, "Poaching and the Game Laws on Cannock Chase," in *Albion's Fatal Tree: Crime and Society in Eighteenth-Century England* (New York: Pantheon, 1975), 189–254.

76. "Relation des hostilités commises par les Natchez," November 4, 1722, ANOM, G1, vol. 465, n.p.

77. Lepore, *The Name of War*, 96; Anderson, *Creatures of Empire*, 199.

78. Christina Snyder, *Slavery in Indian Country: The Changing Face of Captivity in Early America* (Cambridge: Harvard University Press, 2011), 6.

79. Hal Langfur, "Moved by Terror: Frontier Violence as Cultural Exchange in Late-Colonial Brazil," *Ethnohistory* 52, no. 2 (2005): 266.

80. The enumeration of slaves at the plantation can be found in the Census of St. Catherine's Concession, June 19, 1723, ANOM, G1, vol. 464, n.p.

81. De La Loire, "Relation de la guerre . . . ," ANOM, DFC, vol. 31, 5.

82. "Relation des hostilités commises par les Natchez," ANOM, G1, vol. 465, n.p.

83. De La Loire, "Relation de la guerre . . . ," ANOM, DFC, vol. 31, 6–7.

84. Ibid., 10–14.

85. Ibid.

86. "Relation des hostilités commises par les Natchez," ANOM, G1, vol. 465, n.p.

87. De La Loire, "Relation de la guerre . . . ," ANOM, DFC, vol. 31, 13–14.

88. "Relation des hostilités commises par les Natchez," November 4, 1722; "Requête préséntée par Faucon Dumanoir," May 20, 1723, Journal de Diron D'Artaguette, October 26, 1722; Le Page du Pratz, *Histoire de la Louisiane*, 1:184–85. See also La Harpe, *The Historical Journal*, 157.

89. "Relation des hostilités commises par les Natchez," November 4, 1722, ANOM, G1, vol. 465, n.p.

90. Charlevoix, *Histoire et description générale de la Nouvelle France*, 2:420. The Jesuit spent only a few days around Christmas 1721. Perhaps he did not see enough during his short stay to make an accurate assessment of Natchez politics. There is other evidence in archaeological data that women shared power with men in other Mississippian chiefdoms (see Charles R. Cobb, "Mississippian Chiefdoms: How Complex?" *Annual Review of Anthropology* 82 [2003]: 63–84).

91. De La Loire, "Relation de la guerre . . . , ANOM, DFC, vol. 31, 4–5.

92. Journal de Diron D'Artaguette, October 29, October 31, 1722, ANOM, B2, 187–88.

93. De La Tour to the Directors of the Company, February 22, 1723, ANOM, C13A, vol. 7, 207.

94. De La Chaise to the Directors of the Company, January 6, 1723, ANOM, C13A, vol. 7, 300–301v.; Barnett, *The Natchez Indians*, 88–89.

95. De La Tour to the Directors of the Company, February 22, 1723, ANOM, C13A, vol. 7, 206–7v.

96. Woods suggested that relatives of Old Hair died at the hands of the French during the 1716 war (see Woods, *French-Indian Relations*, 74, 76).

97. "Relation des hostilités commises par les Natchez," November 4, 1722, ANOM, G1, vol. 465, n.p.

98. Longrais to Dumanoir, May 11, 1723, ANOM, G1, vol. 465, n.p.

99. Longrais, June 15, 1723, "Journal des principaux événements de la guerre des Natchez et de la campagne de M. de Bienville contre cette nation, December 10, 1723, ANOM, C13A, vol. 7, 303v–4. See also Dumont de Montigny, *Mémoires historiques sur la Louisiane*, 2:98–99.

100. Requête présentée par Faucon Dumanoir, May 20, 1723, ANOM, G1, vol. 465, n.p.

101. Ibid.

102. Ibid.

103. Ibid.

104. Longrais, June 15, 1723, "Journal des principaux événements de la guerre des Natchez," ANOM, C13A, vol. 7, 302v.

105. Ibid., vol. 7, 303v–4. See also Dumont de Montigny, *Mémoires historiques sur la Louisiane*, 2:98–99.

106. Longrais, December 10, 1723, "Journal des principaux événements de la guerre des Natchez," ANOM, C13A, vol. 7, 304–4v. The Council's decree reflects a preoccupation with the Fontaine incident of November 1722.

107. Arnaud Balvay, "The French and the Natchez: A Failed Encounter," in *French and Indians in the Heart of North America, 1630–1815*, ed. Robert Englebert and Guillaume Teasdale (East Lansing: University of Michigan Press, 2013), Kindle edition, loc. 4004 of 5533.

108. Longrais, December 19, 1723, "Journal des principaux événements de la guerre des Natchez," ANOM, C13A, vol. 7, 304v–6v.

109. Decrees of the Superior Council, June 21, 1723, *MPAFD*, 2:292; Arrêt du Conseil Superieur, C A23, vol. 23, 41.

110. Decrees of the Superior Council, June 22, 1723, *MPAFD*, 2:292.

111. Longrais, December 10, 1723, "Journal des principaux événements de la guerre des Natchez," ANOM, C13A, vol. 7, 309.
112. Ibid.
113. Hubert Papers, John Ford Bell Library, 1738 fHu. For Le Page du Pratz's quote, see p. 2.
114. Leblond de La Tour to Superior Council, August 5, 1723, *MPAFD*, 3:363–65.
115. La Chaise to the Directors, September 6, 1723, *MPAFD*, 2:337–38, 340.
116. Deliberations of the Superior Council, September 18, 1723, ANOM, C13A, vol. 7, 143–43v.
117. "Punition des Natchés en 1723," BN, Mss fr., n.a., 2550, 3.
118. Le Page du Pratz, *Histoire de la Louisiane*, 1:198–99; Woods, *French-Indian Relations*, 76. See also Dumont de Montigny, *Mémoires historiques sur la Louisiane*, 2:102; "Punition des Natchés en 1723," 3.
119. Longrais, December 10, 1723, "Journal des principaux événements de la guerre des Natchez," ANOM, C13A, vol. 7, 310v.
120. "Punition des Natchés en 1723," 3–4.
121. Longrais, December 10, 1723, "Journal des principaux événements de la guerre des Natchez," ANOM, C13A, vol. 7, 311; "Punition des Natchés en 1723," 6–7.
122. Christine Marie Petto, *When France Was King of Cartography: The Patronage and Production of Maps in Early Modern France* (Lanham, MD: Lexington, 2007); Josef W. Konvitz, *Cartography in France, 1660–1848: Science, Engineering, and Statecraft* (Chicago: University of Chicago Press, 1987).
123. For a discussion of the textuality of maps, see J. B. Harley, "Silences and Secrecy, 57–76. For a more recent treatment of maps as texts, see Brückner, *The Geographic Revolution in Early America*, 13–44.
124. Minutes of the Council of War assembled on the order of M. de Bienville, January 7, 1724, ANOM, C13A, vol. 7, 173v.
125. Longrais, December 10, 1723, "Journal des principaux événements de la guerre des Natchez," ANOM, C13A, vol. 7, 309.
126. Dumont de Montigny, *Mémoires historiques sur la Louisiane*, 2:108–9.
127. Ibid., 2:101.
128. Le Page du Pratz, *Histoire de la Louisiane*, 1:198.
129. Ibid., 1:198–99.
130. See "Punition des Natchés en 1723," 3; and Dumont de Montigny, *Mémoires historiques sur la Louisiane*, 2:110–12.
131. Ibid., 2:110.
132. Ibid., 2:111–12.
133. Ibid., 2:112–13.
134. "Punition des Natchés en 1723," 8.
135. Both Native Americans and Europeans employed bear's oil for many uses, including as a cooking fat (see Le Page du Pratz, *Histoire de la Louisiane*, 1:89; and Usner, *Indians, Settlers, and Slaves*, 36, 100).
136. "Punition des Natchés en 1723," 8.
137. Dumont de Montigny, *Mémoires historiques sur la Louisiane*, 2:94.
138. Le Page du Pratz, *Histoire de la Louisiane*, 1:179.
139. Ibid., 1:203.
140. Ibid., 1:202–4.

141. Ibid., 1:204.

142. "The Great Sun of the Natchés who is the chief of the nation is the bastard of Father M. de S. Cosme of Canada" (Grand Soleil, fil d'un François en 1728, BN Mss, fr., n.a., 2550, p. 115). According to Le Page du Pratz, the Tattooed Arm maintained that a Frenchmen had sired the new Great Sun. He did not, however, identify St. Cosme as the father (see Le Page du Pratz, *Histoire de la Louisiane*, 3:247).

143. Ibid., 3:243.

144. See also Woods, "French-Indian Relations," 70–71.

4 / The Many Lands of Natchez Country

1. Jean-François-Benjamin Dumont de Montigny, *Mémoires historiques sur la Louisiane contenant ce qui y est arrivé de plus mémorable depuis l'année 1687*, vol. 2 (Paris: J. B. Bauche, 1753), 118.

2. Code Noir ou recueil d'edits, declarations et arrets Concernant la Discipline & Commerces des Esclaves Négres des Isles de l'Amérique française, 1724, in *Recueil d'edits, declarations et arrests de sa majesté concernant l'administration de la Justice et Police des Colonies françaises de l'Amérique, & les Engagés* (Paris: Chez les Librairies Associez, 1744), 93.

3. Dumont de Montigny, *Mémoires historiques sur la Louisiane*, 2:119.

4. Ibid., 2:120–22.

5. Dumont de Montigny boarded in the home of the Rousseaus, who had purchased the land from a Tioux "whose nation had abandoned their village and move elsewhere" (Jean-François-Benjamin Dumont de Montigny, *Regards sur le monde Atlantique, 1715–1717* [Sillery: Septentrion, 2008, 224).

6. Shannon Lee Dawdy, "Enlightenment from the Ground: Le Page Du Pratz's *Histoire de la Louisiane*," *French Colonial History* 3 (2003): 19, 21. See also Gordon M. Sayre, "Natchez Ethnohistory Revisited: New Manuscript Sources from Le Page du Pratz and Dumont de Montigny," *Louisiana History* 1, no. 4 (Fall 2009): 420–23.

7. Dawdy, "Enlightenment from the Ground," 20–23. For question of authority within a discourse, see Michel Foucault, *History of Sexuality, Vol. 1: An Introduction*, trans. Robert Hurley (New York: Vintage, 1978), 97–102.

8. James F. Barnett Jr., *The Natchez Indians: A History to 1735* (Jackson: University of Mississippi Press, 2007), 95–98; Arnaud Balvay, *La Révolte des Natchez* (Paris: Félin, 2008), 123–27. Swanton translated most of Dumont de Montigny and Le Page du Pratz's account: John R. Swanton, *Indian Tribes of the Lower Mississippi Valley and Adjacent Coast of the Gulf of Mexico* (1911; repr., Mineola, NY: Dover, 1998), 144–57.

9. Le Page du Pratz, *Histoire de la Louisiane, Countenant la découverte de ce vaste pays*, vol. 3 (Paris: Bure l'aine, 1758), 30–31.

10. Ibid., 3:33–35.

11. Jean-François-Benjamin Dumont de Montigny, *Mémoires historiques sur la Louisiane*, vol. 2 (Paris: J. B. Bauche, 1753), 224–25.

12. Dutisné [to the Directors], March 1726, ANOM, C13C, vol. 4, 23.

13. Timothy R. Pauketat, *Cahokia: Ancient America's Great City on the Mississippi* (New York: Penguin, 2009), 71–78.

14. Le Page du Pratz, *Histoire de la Louisiane*, 3:37–39.

15. Ibid., 3:53

16. Ibid., 3:55. See also Dumont de Montigny, *Mémoires historiques sur la Louisiane*, 1:234; Dutisné [to the Directors], March 1726, ANOM, C13C, vol. 4, 23.

17. Le Page du Pratz, *Histoire de la Louisiane*, 3:51–52; Dumont de Montigny, *Mémoires historiques sur la Louisiane*, 1:208–39.

18. "Relation des hostilités commises par les Natchez," November 4, 1722, ANOM, G1, vol. 465, n.p.

19. Le Page du Pratz, *Histoire de la Lousiane*, 3:52.

20. Ibid.

21. Balvay, *La Révolte des Natchez*, 126–27.

22. Gordon Sayre discounted the possibility that Le Page du Pratz was Dumont de Montigny's informant (Sayre, "Natchez Ethnohistory Revisited," 427).

23. Dumont de Montigny, *Mémoires historiques sur la Louisiane*, 1:234–35.

24. Le Page du Pratz, *Histoire de la Louisiane*, 3:57.

25. Ibid.

26. Timothy R. Pauketat, "The Missing Persons in Mississippian Mortuary Practices," in *Mississippian Mortuary Practices: Beyond Hierarchy and the Representative Perspective*, ed. Lynne P. Sullivan and Robert C. Mainfort Jr. (Gainesville: University of Florida Press, 2010), 25; Pauketat, *Cahokia*, 77.

27. Jon Bernard Marcoux, "The Materialization of Status and Social Structure at Kroger's Island Cemetery, Alabama," in *Mississippian Mortuary Practices: Beyond Hierarchy and the Representative Perspective*, ed. Lynne P. Sullivan and Robert C. Mainfort Jr. (Gainesville: University of Florida Press, 2010), 146–48.

28. Pauketat, *Cahokia*, 132–33.

29. Ibid., 47–48.

30. Le Page du Pratz, *Histoire de la Louisiane*, 2:401–2.

31. Ibid., 2:402.

32. Ibid.

33. Ibid., 2:403.

34. Ibid.

35. Richard White, *The Middle Ground: Indians, Empires, and Republics in the Great Lakes Region, 1650–1815* (New York: Cambridge University Press, 1992), 53.

36. Dawdy, "Enlightenment from the Ground," 26.

37. Le Page du Pratz, *Histoire de la Louisiane*, 2:403–5.

38. Charles B. Wesson, "Mississippian Sacred Landscapes: The View from Alabama," in *Mississippian Towns and Sacred Landscapes: Searching for an Architectural Grammar*, ed. R. Barry Lewis and Charles Stout (Tuscaloosa: University of Alabama Press, 1998), 112.

39. Michel Foucault, "Of Other Spaces: Heterotopias," trans. Jay Miskowiec, *Architecture/Movement/Continuity* (October 1984), http://foucault.info/document/heteroTopia/foucault.heteroTopia.en.html.

40. Régis du Roullet to Maurepas, "Journal du voige que jay fait dans La nation des Chactas Lanné 1729, ANOM, C13A, vol. 12, 72v–73v.

41. Joshua Piker, *Okfuskee: A Creek Town in Colonial America* (Cambridge: Harvard University Press, 2003), 9.

42. Robert Paullet, *An Empire of Small Places: Mapping the Southeastern Anglo-Indian Trade, 1732–1795* (Athens: University of Georgia Press, 2012), 93.

43. Peter Nabokov and Robert Easton, *Native American Architecture* (New York: Oxford University Press, 1989), 111.

44. Thomas A. Tweed, *Crossing and Dwelling: A Theory of Religion* (Cambridge: Harvard University Press, 2006), 152. See also Christopher Tilley, *A Phenomenology of Landscape: Places, Paths, and Monuments* (Providence, RI: Berg, 1994), 28, 31.

45. For the Natchez adoption of European clothing, see Sophie White, *Wild Frenchmen and Frenchified Indians: Material Culture and Race in Colonial Louisiana* (Philadelphia: University of Pennsylvania Press, 2012), 205, 209.

46. Dumont de Montigny, *Mémoires historiques sur la Louisiane*, 1:195–98.

47. Sayre, "Natchez History Revisited," 426–28.

48. Sophie White, "Massacre, Mardi Gras, and Torture in Early New Orleans," *William and Mary Quarterly* 70, no. 3 (July 2013): 507–9.

49. John McManners, *Church and Society in Eighteenth-Century France*, vol. 2, *The Religion of the People and the Politics of Religion* (New York: Oxford University Press, 1998), 119. See also John Harper, *The Forms and Orders of Western Liturgy from the Tenth to the Eighteenth Century: A Historical Introduction and Guide for Students and Musicians* (New York: Oxford University Press, 1991), 127–29.

50. Patricia Seed, *Ceremonies of Possession in Europe's Conquest of the New World, 1492–1640* (New York: Cambridge University Press, 1995), 49.

51. Ibid., 67.

52. Tilley, *Phenomenology of Landscape*, 207.

53. R. Barry Lewis, Charles Stout, and Cameron B. Wesson, "The Design of Mississippian Towns," in *Mississippian Towns and Sacred Landscapes: Searching for an Architectural Grammar*, ed. Lewis and Stout (Tuscaloosa: University of Alabama Press, 1998), 17.

54. Le Page du Pratz, *Histoire de la Louisiane*, 1:126–28.

55. Broutin to the Directors, ANOM, C13A, vol. 8, 4v–5.

56. Ibid., 49v.

57. Michel Foucault, *Discipline and Punish: The Birth of the Prison*, trans. Alan Sheridan (New York: Vintage, 1995), 143. See also Michel Foucault, "Of Other Spaces"; and Gilles-Antoine Langlois, *Des Villes pour la Louisiane française: Théorie et pratique de l'urbanistique colonials au 18e siècle* (Paris: L'Harmattan, 2003), 97.

58. Marcel Giraud, *A History of French Louisiana*, vol. 5, *The Company of the Indies, 1723–1731*, trans. Brian Pearce (Baton Rouge: Louisiana State University Press, 1987), 160.

59. Le Vouf v. Ceard, April 4, and 22, 1724, RSC, LSMHC.

60. Bernard v. Dumanoir, July 7, 1724, September 20, 1724, RSC, LSMHC.

61. Gaspalliere v. Dumanoir, September 9, 1724, RSC, LSMHC.

62. Hearing on effects of Guenot, August 8, 1724, RSC, LSMHC.

63. Raquet v. Dumanoir, September 11, 1724, RSC, LSMHC.

64. Brusle v. Dumanoir, September 20, 24; December 20, 1724, RSC, LSMHC.

65. Gigot v. Dumanoir, June 25, 1725, RSC, LSMHC.

66. Widow Gigot v. Dumanoir, July 16, 1725, RSC, LSMHC, "Records of the Superior Council," *Louisiana Historical Quarterly* 2, no. 3 (October 1919): 339.

67. Giraud, *A History of French Louisiana*, 5:167. Superior Council, May 5, 1727, RSC, LSMHC.

68. Mandeville v. Dumanoir, October 31, 1727, RSC, LSMHC. See also Giraud, *A History of French Louisiana*, 5:167.

69. Kolly to ?, August 19, 1728, AN T66$^{1-2}$, document 27. See also Giraud, *A History of French Louisiana*, 5:149.
70. Giraud, *A History of French Louisiana*, 5:166.
71. Marcel Giraud, *Histoire de la Louisiane française*, vol. 4, *La Louisiane après le système de Law (1721–1723)* (Paris: Presses Universitaires de France, 1974), 267–68.
72. Belcourt v. Desfointaine, [Director of Terre Blanche Concession], January 1, 1724, LSC, LHSM. See also Giraud, *Histoire de la Louisiane française*, 4:119; Giraud, *A History of French Louisiana*, 5:170.
73. Alfred Oliver Hero Jr., *Louisiana and Quebec: Bilateral Relations and Comparative Sociopolitical Evolution, 1673–1993* (New York: University Press of America, 1995), 75.
74. Hero, *Louisiana and Quebec*, 1–68. See also Marcel Giraud, *A History of French Louisiana*, vol. 1, *The Reign of Louis XIV, 1698–1715*, trans. Joseph C. Lambert (Baton Rouge: Louisiana State University Press, 1974), 107–31.
75. O'Neill, *Church and State in French Louisiana*, 95; Jay Higginbotham, *Old Mobile: Fort Louis de la Louisiane* (Mobile: Museum of the City of Mobile, 1977), 180.
76. De la Vente to [Brisacier], June 25, 1704, SME lettres 75, fol. 3.
77. Hero, *Louisiana and Quebec*, 65–66.
78. Raphael affidavit, April 19, 1727, RSC, LSMHC.
79. O'Neill, *Church and State in French Louisiana*, 95.
80. Giraud, *A History of French Louisiana*, 2:100.
81. David A. Bell, *The Cult of Nation in France: Inventing Nationalism, 1680–1800* (Cambridge: Harvard University Press, 2001), 15.
82. Recensement des habitants . . . par M. Diron, January 2, 1722, ANOM, G1, vol. 464, n.p.; La Chaise, "Recensement general des habitions et habitants de la colonne de La Louisiane," January 1, 1726, ANOM, G1, vol. 464, n.p.; Philibert, "Estat des personnes du Poste des Natchez qui ont été Massacrés le 28 November, 1729," ANOM, C13A, vol. 12, 57–58.
83. Philibert, "Estat des personnes du Poste des Natchez qui ont été Massacrés le 28 November, 1729," ANOM, C13A, vol. 12, 57–58; Giraud, *History of French Louisiana*, 5:134.
84. Longrais affidavit, July 20, 1727, RSC, LSMHC.
85. Shannon Lee Dawdy, *Building the Devil's Empire: French Colonial New Orleans* (Chicago: University of Chicago Press, 2008), 5. See also Langlois, *Des villes pour la Louisiane*, 146.
86. Lee Dawdy, *Building the Devil's Empire*, 5.
87. Richard Campanella, *Bienville's Dilemma: A Historical Geography of New Orleans* (Lafayette: University of Louisiana Press, 2008), 113.
88. Jerry A. Micelle, "From Law Court to Local Government: Metamorphosis of the Superior Council of French Louisiana," *Louisiana History* 9, no. 2 (1968): 100–103. A few decades later, Sir William Johnson played a similar role in the New York borderlands (see Alan Taylor, *The Divided Ground: Indians, Settlers, and the Northern Borderlands of the American Revolution* [New York: Vintage, 2006], 42).
89. Bienville to the Duke of Orleans, August 23, 1725, *MPAFD*, 3:494; Giraud, *A History of French Louisiana*, 5:32–37.
90. "Jacques de la Chaise," in *France's Forgotten Legion: Service Records of French*

Military and Administrative personnel Stationed in the Mississippi Valley and Gulf Coast Region, 1699–1769 (CD-ROM) (Baton Rouge: Louisiana State University Press).

91. Dawdy, *Building the Devil's Empire*, 5; see also ibid., 63–74, for Pauger's attempts to shape New Orleans into a colonial capital.

92. Michel Vergé-Franceschi, *Les officiers généraux de la marine Royale (1715–1774)* (PhD diss., Paris IV–Sorbonne) (Paris: Librarie de L'inde editeur, 1990), 263; Gwendolyn Midlo Hall, *Africans in Colonial Louisiana: The Development of Afro-Creole Culture in the Eighteenth Century* (Baton Rouge: Louisiana State University Press, 1992), 31; Giraud, *A History of French Louisiana*, 5:53–54.

93. McManners, *Church and Society*, 2:84.

94. Charles Edward O'Neill, *Church and State in French Colonial Louisiana: Policy and Politics to 1732* (New Haven: Yale University Press, 1966), 157.

95. "Traite avec les R. P. Jesuites," 1726, ANOM, B, vol. 43, 584–92.

96. La Chaise to Raguet, December 28, 1728, ANOM, 13A, vol. 11, 171v.

97. Ibid., 196.

98. Marc Antoine Calliot, "Relation du Voyage de la Louisiane ou Nouvelle France fait par le Sr. Caillot en l'annee 1730," Ms. 2005.11, Historic New Orleans Collection, 104–5.

99. Jean Delanglez, "The French Jesuits in Lower Louisiana (1700–1763)" (PhD diss., Catholic University of America, 1935), 220–30.

100. Raphael to Raguet, December 28, 1726, ANOM, C13A, vol. 10, 49–50. See also Giraud, *A History of French Louisiana*, 5:393–94.

101. Raphael to Raguet, December 28, 1726, ANOM, C13A, vol. 10, 50.

102. Ibid., vol. 10, 51.

103. Minutes of the Superior Council, April 23, 1725, ANOM, C13A, vol. 9, 127. See also Giraud, *A History of French Louisiana*, 5:394.

104. O'Neill, *Church and State in French Louisiana*, 274.

105. La Chaise to the Directors of the Company, September 6, 1723, ANOM, C13A, vol. 7, 22. See also Balvay, *Révolte des Natchez*, 116–17.

5 / "These Are People Who Named Themselves Red Men"

1. Shannon Lee Dawdy, "The Burden of Louis Congo and the Evolution of Savagery in Colonial Louisiana," in *Discipline and the Other Body: Correction, Corporeality, Colonialism*, edited by Stephen Pierce and Anupama Rao (Durham, NC: Duke University Press, 2006), 61–71.

2. Nancy Shoemaker discussed the European appellations "white" and "black" and suggested that the Indians used red as a response to the newcomers' binary classifications (see Nancy Shoemaker, "How Indians Got to Be Red," *American Historical Review* 102, no. 3 [1997]: 625–27, 629). Shoemaker's work informed a good deal of my discussion of race and the construction of redness.

3. De La Chaise, recensement général des habitants de la Louisiane, ANOM, G1, vol. 464, n.p.

4. No census survives from 1729. Africans recaptured by the French and their allies included one hundred recovered in February 1730 (Dumont de Montigny, *Mémoires historiques sur la Louisiane*, 2:181; Le Page du Pratz, *Histoire de la Louisiane*, 2:284–85), with twenty more taken from the Natchez in 1731 (Périer to the Minister, March 25, 1731, ANOM, C13A, vol. 13, 38). Others remained unaccounted for.

5. Jennifer M. Spear, *Race, Sex, and Social Order in Early New Orleans* (Baltimore: Johns Hopkins University Press, 2009), 53.

6. For Le Page du Pratz's conceptualization of African "inferiority," see chapter 25, "Negroes, on choosing Negroes; their illnesses and the manner of treating them for cures; the manner in which to govern them," in Le Page du Pratz, *Histoire de la Louisiane*, 1:333. Patricia K. Galloway, "Rhetoric of Difference: Le Page du Pratz on African Slave Management in Eighteenth-Century Louisiana," *French Colonial History* 3 (2003): 1–16. Guillaume Aubert observes that the French used the term "blood" (*sang*) to denote inherited biological characteristics (see Aubert, "'The Blood of France': Race and Purity of Blood in the French Atlantic World," *WMQ* 61, no. 3 [2004]: 439–78; and Jennifer M. Spear, "Colonial Intimacies: Legislating Sex in French Louisiana," *WMQ* 60, no. 1 [2003]: 75–98).

7. *Code Noir, ou edit du roi servant de réglement pour le gouvernement et l'administration de la justice, police, discipline, et le commerce des esclaves nègres dans la province et colonie de la Louisiane*, March 1724, ANOM, A, vol. 22, fol. 119. For an overview of the Code Noir and its implementation in Louisiana, see Carl A. Brasseaux, "The Administration of Slave Regulations in French Louisiana, 1724–1766," in *The French Experience in Louisiana*, ed. Glenn R. Conrad (Lafayette: Center for Louisiana Studies, 1995); Thomas N. Ingersoll, "Slave Codes and Judicial Practice in New Orleans," *Law and History Review* 13, no. 1 (1995): 23–62; and William Resnick Riddell, "Le Code Noir," *Journal of Negro History* 10, no. 3 (1925): 321–29. See also Patricia Dillon Woods, "The French and the Natchez Indians in Louisiana: 1700–1731," in *The French Experience in Louisiana*, ed. Glenn R. Conrad (Lafayette: Center for Louisiana Studies, 1995), 278–95. For a review of the early years of slavery in the French colony, see Hall, *Africans in Colonial Louisiana*, 97–118; Daniel H. Usner, "From African Captivity to American Slavery: The Introduction of Black Laborers to Colonial Louisiana," in *The French Experience in Louisiana*, ed. Glenn R. Conrad (Lafayette: Center for Louisiana Studies, 1995), 183–200.

8. The thirteenth article limited the testimony of slaves (see *Code Noir*, Article 13, fols. 120v–121. Article 24, fol. 123).

9. Ibid., Article 6, fol. 120.

10. Ibid., Article 2.

11. For an overview of Native American slavery and the Indian slave trade, see Robbie Ethridge, "Creating the Shatterzone: Indian Slave Traders and the Collapse of the Southeastern Chiefdoms," in *Light on the Path: The Anthropology and History of the Southeastern Indians*, ed. Thomas J. Pluckhahn and Ethridge (Tuscaloosa: University of Alabama Press, 2006), 206–17; Alan Gallay, *The Indian Slave Trade: The Rise of the English Empire in the American South, 1670–1717* (New Haven: Yale University Press, 2002); Almon Wheeler Lauber, *Indian Slavery in Colonial Times within the Present Limits of the United States* (New York: Columbia University Press, 1913); Brett Rushforth, "'A Little Flesh We Offer You': The Origins of Indian Slavery in New France," *WMQ* 60, no. 4 (2003); Brett Rushforth, "Slavery, the Fox Wars, and the Limits of Alliance," *WMQ* 63, no. 1 (2006): 53–80; Brett Rushforth, *Bonds of Alliance: Indigenous and Atlantic Slaveries* (Chapel Hill: University of North Carolina for the Omohundro Institute of Early American History and Culture, 2012); Christina Snyder, *Slavery in Indian Country: The Changing Face of Captivity in Early America* (Cambridge: Harvard University Press, 2010); and Stanford Winston, "Indian Slavery in the Carolina Region," *Journal of Negro History* 19, no. 4 (1934): 431–40.

12. "Relation de Henri de Tonty," in *Découvertes et établissements des Français dans l'ouest et dans le Sud de l'Amérique septentrionale*, vol. 1, ed. Pierre Margry (Paris: D. Jouast, 1876), 604; "Relation de Henri de Tonty," 599, "Récit de Nicholas de La Salle" in *Découvertes et établissements des Français dans l'ouest et dans le sud de L'Amérique septentrionale*, vol. 1, ed. Pierre Margry (Paris: D. Jouast, 1876), 559.

13. "Récit de Nicholas de La Salle," 565–66; "The Minet Relation," in Robert S. Weddle, Mary Christine Morkovsky, and Patricia Kay Galloway, *La Salle, the Mississippi, and the Gulf: Three Primary Documents*, (College Station: Texas A&M University Press, 1987), 59.

14. Father Jerome Lalament, May 22, 1642, "Mémoire touchant les Domestiques," *JR*, 21 293–301.

15. Jean Delanglez, "The French Jesuits in Lower Louisiana (1700–1763)" (PhD diss., Catholic University of America, 1935), 150–51.

16. Ibid., 34.

17. Jean Mermet aux Cascaskias, Lettre aux Jésuites du Canada, March 2, 1706, *JR*, 66:63; Jay Higginbotham, *Old Mobile*, 253–54.

18. Jacques Gravier, Lettre sur les Affaires de la Louisiane, Fort St. Louis de la Louisiane, February 23, 1708, *JR*, 66:129.

19. Rushforth, *Bonds of Alliance*, 51–71.

20. Dumont de Montigny, *Mémoires historiques sur la Louisiane*, 2:106.

21. Ibid., 2:109.

22. Snyder, *Slavery in Indian Country*, 7.

23. Paul du Poisson [Father Poisson] aux Akensas, October 3, 1727, *JR*, 67:293.

24. Le Page du Pratz, *Histoire de la Louisiane*, 1:82–83, 114.

25. Testimony of Madame Lambermond, September 20, 1727, RSC, LSMHC.

26. Testimony of Father Philibert, September 21, 1727, RSC, LSMHC.

27. Testimony of hospital surgeons Alexandre and Pauyadon Delatour, October 22, 1727, RSC, LSMHC.

28. Gualas to Superior Council, October 21, 1727, RSC, LSMHC.

29. Merveilleux to Gaulas, June 18, 1727, RSC, LSMHC.

30. Dumont de Montigny, *Regards sur le monde atlantique*, 364.

31. For other reviews of the Gaulas case, see Spear, *Race, Sex, and Social Order in Early New Orleans*, 72–73; and Hall, *Africans in Colonial Louisiana*, 150.

32. La Sonde v. Coupart, August 11–14, 1724; September 14, 1724, RSC, LSMHC.

33. Interrogation of Guillory and Bontemps, May 31, 1728, RSC, LSMHC.

34. Raphael to Raguet, September 25, 1725, MPAFD, 2:509.

35. Interrogation of Jean Baptiste, June 2, 1728, RSC, LSMHC; Decree of the Superior Council against Lemaire, June 5, 1728, LSMHC.

36. Deposition of Pellerin and Trudeau, June 7, 1728, RSC, LSMHC.

37. Interrogation of Bontemps and Guillory, June 18, 1728, RSC, LSMHC.

38. Rushforth, *Bonds of Alliance*, 118–19; 156–58.

39. Pérrier to Abbé Raguet, May 12, 1728, ANOM, C13A, vol. 11, 7–7v.

40. Interrogation of Sansouci, March 31, 1727, RSC, LSMHC.

41. Hall, *Africans in Colonial Louisiana*, 97–100.

42. Regulations of the Superior Council, November 12, 1714, ANOM, A, vol. 23, 5.

43. Acte pour l'établissement de la Compagnie des Cent Associés pour le Commerce du Canada, contenant les articles accordés à la dite Compagnie par M. Le

Cardinal de Richelieu, le 29 Avril 1627, transcribed in *Edits, ordonnances royaux, et arrêts du Conseil d'Etat du Roi concernant le Canada*, vol. 1 (Quebec, 1854), 10.

44. In 1708, 80 Native American slaves and 279 Europeans lived in Mobile (Census of Mobile, August 8, 1708, *MPAFD*, 2:31).

45. Regulation of the Superior Council, November 12, 1714, ANOM, A, vol. 23, 5-6.

46. One side note left by a government official in Paris read: "This regulation no longer remains, the Code Noir has the power to police slaves" (Regulations of the Superior Council, November 12, 1714, ANOM, A, vol. 23, 5).

47. Duclos to Pontchartrain, December 25, 1715, *MPAFD*, 2:205.

48. Ibid.

49. Minutes of the Council, September 1, 1716, *MPAFD*, vol. 2:218.

50. Arrêt du Conseil Supérieur de la Louisiane concernant le marriage des Français avec les sauvagesses, December 18, 1728, ANOM, A, vol. 23, 103.

51. Périer to Minister, April 1, 1729, ANOM, C13A, vol. 12, 16v-17. Marcel Giraud, *A History of French Louisiana*, vol. 5, *The Compagnie of the Indies, 1723-1731*, trans. Brian Pearce (Baton Rouge: Louisiana State University Press, 1991), 341.

52. Hall, *Africans in Colonial Louisiana*, 390-91; Jacobs, *France and the Chesapeake*, 1:320-22.

53. Liste de officiers qui y ont participé, du 2 juin au 10 decembre 1723, ANOM, C13A, vol. 7, 315.

54. Broutin to the Company August 7, 1730, *MPAFD*, 1:126.

55. Le Page du Pratz, *Histoire de la Louisiane*, 3:230.

56. Jean-François-Benjamin Dumont de Montigny, *Regards sur le monde Atlantique*, 220-24; Dumont de Montigny, *Mémoires historiques sur la Louisiane*, 2: 126-28; Le Page du Pratz, *Histoire de la Louisiane*, 3:231.

57. Dumont de Montigny, *Mémoires historiques sur la Louisiane*, 1:221-40; Le Page du Pratz, *Histoire de la Louisiane*, 3:43-60.

58. Dumont de Montigny, *Mémoires historiques sur la Louisiane*, 1:180, 240-43.

59. Ibid., 2:129.

60. Jean-François-Benjamin Dumont de Montigny, *Regards sur le monde atlantique*, 235.

61. Ibid.

62. Christopher Tilly, *A Phenomenology of Landscape: Places, Paths, and Monuments* (Providence, RI: Berg, 1994), 204.

63. Ibid., 207.

64. Dumont de Montigny, *Mémoires historiques sur la Louisiane*, 2:129; Le Page du Pratz, *Histoire de la Louisiane*, 3:232-33. For disputes between the two colonists over their versions of Louisiana history, see Sayre, "Plotting the Natchez Massacre," 381-413.

65. Le Page du Pratz, *Histoire de la Louisiane*, 3:232.

66. Ibid., 3:233.

67. Ibid., 3:233-34.

68. Jean-François-Benjamin Dumont de Montigny *The Memoir of Lieutenant Dumont: A Sojourner in the French Atlantic*, trans. Gordon M. Sayre, ed. Sayre and Carla Zecher (Chapel Hill: University of North Carolina Press for the Omohundro Institute of Early American Culture and History, 2012), 227.

69. Father Le Petit to Father d'Avaugour, July 12, 1730, *JR*, 68:163.

70. Pierre-François-Xavier de Charlevoix, *Histoire et description générale de la Nouvelle France avec le Journal historique d'un voyage fait par ordre du roi dans L'amerique septentrionnale*, vol. 2, (Paris: Chez Nyon et Fils, 1744), 466.

71. Anonymous, "Relation de la Louisiane" [ca. 1735], MS 530, Ayer Collection, Newberry Library, Chicago.

72. Le Page du Pratz, *Histoire de la Louisiane*, 3:234.

73. Dumont de Montigny collapsed all three encounters into one meeting (see Dumont de Montigny *Mémoires historiques sur la Louisiane*, 2:133; see also Diron to Minister, February 10, 1730, ANOM, C, 13A, vol. 12, 362v).

74. The accounts of de Chépart's negotiations came from Dumont de Montigny, *Mémoires historiques sur la Louisiane*, 2:128–34; Le Page du Pratz, *Histoire de la Louisiane*, 3:230–33.

75. Dumont de Montigny, *Mémoires historiques sur la Louisiane*, 2:133–35; Le Page du Pratz, *Histoire de la Louisiane*, 3:236–37.

76. Le Page du Pratz, *Histoire de la Louisiane*, 3:238–39.

77. Ibid., 239–40. Dumont de Montigny's account mentions Natchez embassies to their neighbors (see Dumont de Montigny, *Mémoires historiques sur la Louisiane*, 2:135). See also Jon Muller, *Mississippian Political Economy* (New York: Plenum Press, 1997), 64–68; Shoemaker, *A Strange Likeness*, 130–34; and Shoemaker, "How Indians Got to Be Red," 625–44.

78. Shoemaker, "How the Indians Got to Be Red," 628.

79. Ibid., 629.

80. Le Page du Pratz, *Histoire de la Louisiane*, 3:27.

81. Ibid., 3:87.

82. Shoemaker, *A Strange Likeness*, 132. See also Jack Campisis, "Houmas" in *HBNAI*, 14:632–41.

83. "Récit de Nicholas de La Salle," 556.

84. Pierre Le Moyne D'Iberville, *Iberville's Gulf Journal*, trans. Richebourg Gaillard McWilliams (Mobile: University of Alabama Press, 1981), 72.

85. Letter of St. Cosme, August 1, 1701, quoted in Swanton, *Indian Tribes of the Lower Mississippi Valley*, 22. See also Galloway and Jackson, "Natchez and Neighboring Groups," *HBNAI*, 14:598, 600; Marvin D. Jeter, "From Prehistory through Protohistory to Ethnohistory in and near the Northern Lower Mississippi Valley," in *The Transformation of the Southeastern Indians, 1540–1760*, ed. Robbie Ethridge and Charles M. Hudson (Jackson: University of Mississippi Press, 2002), 206–13.

86. Bienville to Pontchartrain, June 15, 1715, *MPAFD*, 3:183.

87. Father Raphael to Abbé Raguet, May 15, 1725, *MPAFD*, 2:485–86.

88. For another discussion of "redness" in English-Native American diplomacy, see Alden T. Vaughan, "From White Man to Redskin: Changing Anglo-American Perceptions of the American-Indian," *American Historical Review* 87, no. 4 (1982): 917–53.

89. Marvin D. Jeter, "Tunicans West of the Mississippi: A Summary of Early Historic and Archaeology Evidence," in Archaeological Report No. 18, *The Protohistoric Period in the Mid-South: 1700–1700*, ed. David H. Dye and Ronald C. Brister (Jackson: Mississippi Department of Archives and History, 1986).

90. Le Page du Pratz, *Histoire de la Louisiane*, 3:27.

91. For the background to these negotiations, see Verner W. Crane, *The Southern Frontier, 1760–1732* (Durham, NC: Duke University Press, 1928), 268–70; Stephen J.

Oatis, *A Colonial Complex: South Carolina's Frontiers in the Era of the Yamasee War, 1680–1730* (Lincoln: University of Nebraska Press, 2004), 252–55.

92. "At a Conference of the Headmen of the Cherokees and the Lower Creeks in the Presence of Both Houses of the assembly, January 26, 1726," British Public Records Office, Colonial Office, 5: Original Correspondence, American and West Indies, vol. 387, fol. 137.

93. Shoemaker gave a detailed analysis of the Cherokees' role in developing the term (Shoemaker, "How Indians Got to Be Red," 639–43).

94. Thomas Cooper, ed., *The Statutes at Large of South Carolina*, vol. 2 (1837; Columbia: A. S. Johnston, 1970), 357.

95. A. Leon Higginbotham, *In the Matter of Color: Race and the American Legal Process, the Colonial Period* (New York: Oxford University Press, 1978), 169; Alden T. Vaughan, "From White Man to Redskin," 935.

96. John Swanton, *Source Material for the Social and Ceremonial Life of the Choctaw Indians* (Washington, DC: U.S. Government Printing Office, 1931), 20, 78–79, 122, 164. See also James Taylor Carson, *Searching for the Bright Path: The Mississippi Choctaws from Prehistory to Removal* (Lincoln: University of Nebraska Press, 1999), 15.

97. Shoemaker, "How Indians Got to be Red," 641, 643.

98. Greg O'Brien, *Choctaws in a Revolutionary Age, 1750–1830* (Lincoln: University of Nebraska Press, 2002), xxiv, 1–12.

99. Greg O'Brien, personal e-mail correspondence, June 12, 2013.

100. Sophie White, *Wild Frenchmen and Frenchified Indians: Material Culture and Race in Colonial Louisiana* (Philadelphia: University of Pennsylvania Press, 2013), 222–25.

101. Patricia Galloway, "Dual Organization Reconsidered: Eighteenth-Century Choctaw Chiefs and the Exploration of Social Design Space," in *Practicing Ethnohistory: Mining Archives, Hearing Testimony, Constructing Narrative* (Lincoln: University of Nebraska Press, 2006), 363–64.

102. Lusser to Maurepas, February 21, 1730, *MPAFD*, 1:92–93.

103. Le Page du Pratz, *Histoire de la Louisiane*, 3:242.

104. Dumont de Montigny, *Mémoires historiques sur la Louisiane*, 2:136.

105. Patricia K. Galloway, "Four Ages of Alibamon Mingo, Fl. 1700–1766," *Journal of Mississippi History* 65, no. 4 (2003): 320–42.

106. Le Page du Pratz, *Histoire de la Louisiane*, 3:246.

107. Le Page du Pratz did not identify the father of the Great Sun except to say that he had been dead for some time (ibid., 3:247).

108. Ibid., 3:249.

109. Dumont de Montigny, *Mémoires historiques sur la Louisiane*, 2:139; Le Page du Pratz, *Histoire de la Louisiane*, 3:151–54.

110. Périer to Maurepas, March 18, 1730, *MPAFD*, 1:62; Broutin to the Company, August 7, 1730, *MPAFD*, 1:127–28; Dumont de Montigny, *Mémoires historiques sur la Louisiane*, 2:137, 139–40; Le Page du Pratz, *Histoire de la Louisiane*, 3:254.

111. Broutin to the Company, August 7, 1730, *MPAFD*, 1:128; Périer to Maurepas, March 18, 1730, *MPAFD*, 1:62.

112. Delaye, June 1, 1730, "Relation du Massacre des Francais aux Natchez, 1729," ANOM, DFC, vol. 38, 1.

6 / Fallen Forts

1. Marc Antoine Calliot, "Relation du Voyage de la Louisiane ou Nouvelle France fait par le Sr. Caillot en l'annee 1730" Ms. 2005.11, p. 143, Historic New Orleans Collection. See also Arnaud Balvay, *Le Révolte des Natchez* (Paris: Éditions du Felin, 2008), 133.

2. *Extrait de l'acte de Société entre la Cie des Indes et les associés en la Concession de Ste. Catherine*, September 4, 1719, ANOM, G1, vol. 465, n.p.; Lettre au Père d'Avaugour, Procureur des Missions de l'Amérique Septentrionale de Mathurin le Petit [Fr. Le Petit], Nouvelle Orleans, July 12, 1730, *JR*, 68:166; Charlevoix, *Histoire et description générale de la Nouvelle France*, 2:467; Jean-François-Benjamin Dumont de Montigny, "L'Etablissement de la Province de la Louisiane, poème composé de 1728 à 1742," *Société des Américanistes* 23, no. 2 (1931): 275–440; Jean François Benjamin Dumont de Montigny, *Mémoires historiques sur la Louisiane contenant ce qui y est arrivé de plus mémorable depuis l'année 1687*, vol. 2 (Paris: J. B. Bauche, 1753), 137.

3. Dumont de Montigny, *The Memoir of Lieutenant Dumont, 1715–1747: A Sojourner in the French Atlantic*, trans. Gordon M. Sayre, ed. Sayre and Carla Zecher (Chapel Hill: University of North Carolina Press for the Omohundro Institute of Early American History and Culture, 2012), 231. See also Antoine Le Page du Pratz, *Histoire de la Louisiane, Contenant la découverte de ce vaste pays; Sa description géographique; Un voyage dans les terres*, vol. 3 (Paris: Lambert, 1758), 254.

4. Dumont de Montigny, *The Memoir of Lieutenant Dumont*, 232. For two twenty-first-century versions of the attacks in Natchez Country, see James F. Barnett Jr., *The Natchez Indians: A History to 1735* (Jackson: University of Mississippi Press, 2007), 103–6; and Arnaud Balvay, *La Révolt des Natchez* (Paris: Éditions du Félin, 2008), 129–33.

5. Charlevoix, *Histoire et description générale de la Nouvelle France*, 2:466; Dumont de Montigny, *The Memoir of Lieutenant Dumont*, 232. See also Delaye, "Relation du Massacre des François des Natchez," ANOM, DFC, Louisiane, vol. 38, 4.

6. Le Petit to D'Avaugour, *JR*, 68:166; Dumont de Montigny, *Mémoires historiques sur la Louisiane*, 2:146–47; Le Page du Pratz, *Histoire de la Louisiane*, 2:257.

7. Le Page du Pratz counted a Euro-African population of seven hundred at Natchez (see Le Page du Pratz, *Histoire de la Louisiane*, 3:258).

8. For the Natchez's losses, see Périer to Maurepas, March 18, 1730, *MPAFD*, 1:62 *Etat des personnes tuées au massacre des Natchez*, December 13, 1737; Broutin to the Company, August 7, 1730, *MPAFD*, 1:127–28; Woods, *French-Indian Relations*, 96.

9. Calliot, "Relation du Voyage de la Louisiane," Ms. 2005.11, fol. 148, Historic New Orleans Collection.

10. Dumont de Montigny, *Mémoires historiques sur la Louisiane*, 2:148.

11. Delaye, "Relation du Massacre, ANOM, DFC, Louisiane, vol. 38, 5. See also Balvay, *La Révolt des Natchez*, 131.

12. Dumont de Montigny, *Mémoires historiques sur la Louisiane*, 2:149–50.

13. Charlevoix, *Histoire et description générale de la Nouvelle France*, 2:469; Dumont de Montigny, *Mémoires historiques sur la Louisiane*, 2:150–53; Le Page du Pratz, *Histoire de la Louisiane*, 3:258.

14. Delaye, "Relation du Massacre," ANOM, DFC, Louisiane, vol. 38, 26; Dumont de Montigny, *Mémoires historiques sur la Louisiane*, 2:154–55.

15. Charlevoix, *Histoire et description générale de la Nouvelle France*, 2:467.

16. Dumont de Montigny, *Mémoires historiques sur la Louisiane*, 2:154; Le Page du Pratz, *Histoire de la Louisiane*, 3:261.

17. Le Page du Pratz, *Histoire de la Louisiane*, 3:260–61; Le Petit to D'Avaugour, *JR*, 68:169.

18. Le Page du Pratz, *Histoire de la Louisiane*, 3:261.

19. Dumont de Montigny, *Mémoires historiques sur la Louisiane*, 2:154.

20. Rushforth, *Bonds of Alliance*, 17–72.

21. Dumont de Montigny, *The Memoir of Lieutenant Dumont*, 241.

22. Calliot, "Relation du Voyage," 165.

23. Charlevoix, *Histoire et description générale de la Nouvelle France*, 2:468–69.

24. Le Petit to D'Avaugour, *JR*, 68:171.

25. Dumont de Montigny, *Mémoires historiques sur la Louisiane*, 2:153–54.

26. Le Petit to D'Avaugour, *JR*, 68:166; Charlevoix, *Histoire et description générale de la Nouvelle France*, 2:468. See also Gwendolyn Midlo Hall, *Africans in Colonial Louisiana: The Development of Afro-Creole Culture in the Eighteenth Century* (Baton Rouge: Louisiana State University Press, 1992), 97–106; and Daniel H. Usner, *Indians, Settlers, and Slaves in a Frontier Exchange Economy: The Lower Mississippi Valley before 1783* (Durham: University of North Carolina Press, 1992), 72–76.

27. Charlevoix, *Histoire et description générale de la Nouvelle France*, 2:467–68.

28. Ibid.

29. Dumont de Montigny, *Regards sur le monde atlantique*, 254; Calliot, "Relation du Voyage," 166; Delaye, "Relation du Massacre," ANOM, DFC, Louisiane, vol. 38, 25. See also Hall, *Africans in Colonial Louisiana*, 100.

30. Le Petit to D'Avaugour, *JR*, 68:167; Le Page du Pratz, *Histoire de la Louisiane*, 3:260.

31. Calliot, "Relation du Voyage," 166.

32. Dumont de Montigny, *The Memoir of Lieutenant Dumont*, 240.

33. Le Petit to D'Avaugour, *JR*, 68:137.

34. Périer to the Minister, December 5, 1729, ANOM, C13A, vol. 12, 34.

35. Ibid., vol. 12, 33–35v. See also Charlevoix, *Histoire et description générale de la Nouvelle France*, 2:89; Delaye, "Relation du Massacre," ANOM, DFC, Louisiane, vol. 38, 25.

36. Périer to Minister, March 18, 1730, ANOM, C13A, vol. 12, 48v; Le Page du Pratz, *Histoire de la Louisiane*, 2:265–68.

37. Périer and De La Chaise vs. Kolly, December 30, 1729, RSC, LSMHC.

38. Succession of Sieur Kolly, January 9, 1730, RSC, LSMHC.

39. "Coup de François sur les Sauvages Tchiwachas 8 decembre," BN MSS. fr., n.a., 2551, p. 25.

40. Périer to Minister, March 18, 1730, *MPAFD*, 1:64.

41. Périer to Minister, October 22, 1731, ANOM, C13A, vol. 13, 87v. For an appraisal of an anti-French coalition, see Daniel H. Usner, *Indians, Settlers, and Slaves*, 72–75. For the alleged African slave uprising of 1731, see Patricia K. Galloway, "Rhetoric of Difference: Le Page du Pratz on African Slave Management in Eighteenth-Century Louisiana," *French Colonial History* 3 (2003): 1–16; and Hall, *Africans in Colonial Louisiana*, 99–112.

42. Charlevoix, *Histoire et description générale de France*, 2:470.

43. Le Petit to D'Avaugour, July 12, 1730, *JR*, 68:175. For another account, see Diron to Minister, February 9, 1730, ANOM, C13A, vol. 12, 363v. Aside from this charge, Charlevoix's account is the same as Father Le Petit's version of this incident. See also Le Page du Pratz, *Histoire de la Louisiane*, 2:264.

44. Lusser to Maurepas, "A Journal..." January 12, 1730, to March 23, 1730, *MPAFD*, 1:99.

45. Le Petit to D'Avaugour, July 12, 1730, *JR*, 68:175; Delaye, "Relation du Massacre," 64.

46. Le Petit to D'Avaugour, July 12, 1730, *JR*, 68:175. My translation; Reuben Gold Thwaites's rendition is an inexact paraphrase.

47. Delaye, "Relation du Massacre," ANOM, DFC, Louisiane, vol. 38, 64.

48. "Longrais's Relation of the War," September 1, 1723, ANOM, C13A, vol. 7, 308v–9.

49. Diron to Maurepas, March 20, 1730, *MPAFD*, 1:77; Delaye, "Relation du Massacre," ANOM, DFC, Louisiane, vol. 38, 51–52.

50. Delaye, "Relation du Massacre," ANOM, DFC, Louisiane, vol. 38, 65.

51. Ibid., 66–67.

52. Marcel Giraud, relying exclusively on Périer's correspondence, ruled out British instigation. He argued that the Natchez had been deluded by Chickasaw representatives, who were the force behind the rising (Marcel Giraud, *A History of French Louisiana*, vol. 5, *The Company of the Indies, 1723–1731*, trans. Brian Pearce [Baton Rouge: Louisiana State University Press, 1974], 401–3).

53. Le Page du Pratz, *Histoire de la Louisiane*, 3:241; Dumont de Montigny, "L'etablissement de la province de la Louisiane," 323–24.

54. Le Page du Pratz, *Histoire de la Louisiane*, 3:253.

55. Calliot, "Relation du Voyage," 153.

56. Gordon Sayre, *The Indian Chief as Tragic Hero: Native Resistance and the Literatures of America, from Moctezuma to Tecumseh* (Chapel Hill: University of North Carolina Press, 2005), 237.

57. Gordon Sayre, *The Indian Chief as Tragic Hero*, 237. See also François-René de Chateaubriand, "Les Natchez," in *Romans et Poésies diverses* (1826; rpt., Paris: Furne, Jouvet et Cie, 1876), 442–55. For a more recent fictionalized installment of the Natchez plot, see Michel Peyramaure, *Louisiana* (Paris: Presses de la Cité, 1996), 549. A twenty-first-century website hosted by the French Ministry of Culture and Communication opens with an extended quote from Chateaubriand's novel *Atala* (1802) characterizing Louisiana as "a new Eden," and then proceeds to correct the persistent myth of the Mississippi as a lost paradise (see *La Louisiane française, 1682–1803*, www.louisiane. culture.fr/fr/index.html).

58. Gordon Sayre, *The Indian Chief as Tragic Hero*, 237.

59. Balvay, *La Révolte des Natchez*, 153–54.

60. Delaye, "Relation du Massacre," ANOM, DFC, Louisiane, vol. 38, 49, 52–53.

61. Jean Delanglez, "The Natchez Massacre and Commandant-general Perrier," *Louisiana Historical Quarterly* 17 (1934).

62. Sayre, *The Indian Chief as Tragic Hero*, 234. See also Gordon M. Sayre, "Plotting the Natchez Massacre: Le Page du Pratz, Dumont de Montigny, Chateaubriand," *Early American Literature* 37, no. 3 (2002): 392.

63. Peter H. Wood, "The Changing Population of the Colonial South: An Overview

by Race and Region, 1685-1790," in *Powhatan's Mantle: Indians in the Colonial Southeast*, ed. Gregory A. Waselkov and M. Thomas Hatley (Lincoln: University of Nebraska Press, 1989), 39, 70.

64. Charlevoix, *Histoire et description générale de la Nouvelle France*, 2:475. See also Diron to Minister, February 9, 1730, ANOM, C13A, vol. 12, 364v.

65. Boisbriant to the Directors, January 12, 1727, ANOM, C13A, vol. 10, 251.

66. Diron d'Artaguette to Maurepas, October 17, 1729, *MPAFD*, 4:24-25.

67. For the Choctaw-Chickasaw rivalry, see Robert A. Brightman and Pamela S. Wallace, "Chickasaw," in *HBNAI*, 14:491; Crane, *The Southern Frontier*, 45-46; 67-70; Robbie Ethridge, "Creating the Shatterzone: Indian Slave Traders and the Collapse of the Southeastern Chiefdoms," in *Light on the Path: The Anthropology and History of the Southeastern Indians*, ed. Thomas J. Pluckhahn and Ethridge (Tuscaloosa: University of Alabama Press, 2006), 213-17; Patricia K. Galloway, *Choctaw Genesis, 1500-1700* (Lincoln: University of Nebraska Press, 1995), 182-99; "Henri de Tonti du village des Chacta 1702: The Beginning of the French Alliance," in *La Salle and His Legacy: Frenchmen and Indians in the Lower Mississippi Valley*, ed. Patricia Galloway (Jackson: University of Mississippi Press, 1982), 146-75; Patricia Galloway and Clara Sue Kidwell, "Choctaw in the East," in *HBNAI*, 14:511-12; Jay Higginbotham, "Henri de Tonti's Mission to the Chickasaw, 1702," *Louisiana History* 19, no. 3 (1978): 258-96; Usner, *Indians, Settlers, and Slaves*, 18-19; Richard White, *The Roots of Dependency: Subsistence, Environment, and Social Change among the Choctaws, Pawnees, and Navajos* (Lincoln: University of Nebraska Press, 1983), 9; and Woods, *French-Indian Relations on the Southern Frontier*, 1-22, 45-64.

68. Périer to Maurepas, April 10, 1730, *MPAFD*, 1:117.

69. Périer and la Chaise to the Directors of the Company of the Indies, January, 30, 1729, *MPAFD*, 2:610.

70. Périer to Régis du Roullet, undated, *MPAFD*, 1:18.

71. Périer to Régis du Roullet, August 21, 1729, *MPAFD*, 1:17-20.

72. Périer to Minister, March 18, 1730, *MPAFD*, 1:66; Le Petit to D'Avaugour, July 12, 1730, *JR*, 68:189. Diron accused Louboëy of procrastination (see Diron to Maurepas, March 20, 1730, *MPAFD*, 1:77). Broutin also criticized the arrangements he found in the village as well as the fortitude of the commander: "Mr. Merveilleux was quite unwilling to leave the village on account of the Tunica Indians, where we did not have a drop of water stored up and almost no bread" (see Broutin to the Company, August 7, 1730, *MPAFD*, 1:131).

73. Delaye, "Relation du Massacre," ANOM, DFC, Louisiane, vol. 38, 18.

74. Dumont de Montigny, *Mémoires historiques sur la Louisiane*, 2:175; Le Page du Pratz, *Histoire de la Louisiane*, 2:268, 277; Delaye, "Relation du Massacre," ANOM, DFC, Louisiane, vol. 38, 20-21.

75. Delaye, "Relation du Massacre," ANOM, DFC, Louisiane, vol. 38, 20-21.

76. Calliot, "Relation du Voyage," 165.

77. Le Petit to D'Avaugour, July 12, 1730, *JR*, 68:191; for Madame Desnoyers's roles, see Dumont de Montigny, *Regards sur le monde atlantique*, 251.

78. Diron to Minister, March 20, 1730, *MPAFD*, 1:78; Le Petit to D'Avaugour, July 12, 1730, *JR*, 68:191; Dumont de Montigny, *Mémoires historiques sur la Louisiane*, 2:175-80.

79. Dumont de Montigny, *Mémoires historiques sur la Louisiane*, 2:180-82.

80. Le Page du Pratz's Chitimacha slave woman acted in a similar manner by providing the Dutchman with access to the Natchez and Chitimacha hierarchy (see Galloway and Jackson, "Natchez and Neighboring Groups," in *HBNAI*, 14:603).

81. See Broutin to the Company, August 7, 1730, *MPAFD*, 1:131–32; and Périer to Minister, March 18, 1730, *MPAFD*, 1:68.

82. Diron to Minister, March 20, 1730, *MPAFD*, 1:78; Charlevoix, *Histoire et description generale de la Nouvelle France*, 2:479; Dumont de Montigny, *Mémoires historiques sur la Louisiane*, 2:178; Le Page du Pratz, *Histoire de la Louisiane*, 2:280; Delaye, "Relation du Massacre," ANOM, DFC, Louisiane, vol. 38, 26.

83. Anonymous, "Relation of the Last of Attack of the French on the Natchez, January 1731," ASH 67, no. 16, n.p.

84. Dumont de Montigny, *Mémoires historiques sur la Louisiane*, 2:181; Le Page du Pratz, *Histoire de la Louisiane*, 2:284–85. See also Calliot, "Relation du Voyage," fol. 170.

85. Dumont de Montigny, *The Memoir of Lieutenant Dumont*, 244.

86. For Périer's comments, see Périer to Maurepas, March 18, 1730, *MPAFD*, 1:68. For other accounts of the attack, see Diron to Minister, February 9, 1730, ANOM, C13A, vol. 12, 368; Diron to Maurepas, March 20, 1730; *MPAFD*, 1:78; Delaye, "Relation du Massacre," ANOM, DFC, Louisiane, vol. 38, 24; "Relation of the Last of Attack of the French on the Natchez, January 1731," ASH 67, no. 16, n.p.

87. For the development of Native American fortifications in the Southeast during the eighteenth century, see Wayne E. Lee, "Fortify, Fight, or Flee: Tuscarora and Cherokee Defensive Warfare and Military Culture Adaptation," *Journal of Military History* 68, no. 3 (2004): 713–70. For a broader analysis, see David E. Jones, *Native North American Armor, Shields, and Fortifications* (Austin: University of Texas Press, 2004).

88. Delaye, "Relation du Massacre," ANOM, DFC, Louisiane, vol. 38, 25.

89. Le Petit to D'Avaugour, July 12, 1730, *JR*, 68:191; Périer to Maurepas, March 18, 1730, *MPAFD*, 1:73.

90. Diron D'Artaguette to Maurepas, March 20, 1730, *MPAFD*, 1:78; Périer to Minister, March 18, 1730, *MPAFD*, 1:68; Charlevoix, *Histoire et description generale de la Nouvelle France*, 3:480; Le Page du Pratz, *Histoire de la Louisiane*, 2:287.

91. Diron D'Artaguette to Maurepas, March 20, 1730, *MPAFD*, 1:78; Broutin to the Company, August 7, 1730, 134–35.

92. Dumont de Montigny, *Mémoires historiques sur la Louisiane*, 2:185; Le Page du Pratz, *Histoire de la Louisiane*, 2:287–88.

93. Father Le Petit, July 12, 1730, *JR*, 68:195; Diron D'Artaguette to Maurepas, March 20, 1730, *MPAFD*, 1:78–79.

94. Ibid., 79; Dumont de Montigny, *Mémoires historiques sur la Louisiane*, 2:188.

95. Dumont du Montigny, *Regards sur le monde atlantique*, 256.

96. See Dumont de Montigny, *Mémoires historiques sur la Louisiane*, 2:188–89.

97. Calliot, "Relation du Voyage," 165.

98. Ibid.; Diron to Minister, March 20, 1730, *MPAFD*, 1:79; Delaye, "Relation du Massacre," 34.

99. *Sacramental Records of the Diocese of New Orleans, Saint Louis Cathedral, Baptisms, Marriages, and Funerals*, vol. A, Book 2, 1731–1733, 89, no date.

100. Diron to Minister, March 20, 1730, *MPAFD*, 1:79–80.

101. Le Page du Pratz, *Histoire de la Louisiane*, 3:47–48; 2:291.
102. Ibid., 2:290–91.
103. Diron to Minister, March 20, 1730, *MPAFD*, 1:80; Le Page du Pratz, *Histoire de la Louisiane*, 2:291–93.
104. Delaye, "Relation du Massacre," ANOM, DFC, Louisiane, vol. 38, 50.
105. Broutin to the Company, August 7, 1730, *MPAFD*, 1:135–36; Périer to Minister, March 18, 1730, *MPAFD*, 1:70; Charlevoix, *Histoire et description générale de la Nouvelle France*, 2:482; Dumont de Montigny, *Mémoires historiques sur la Louisiane*, 2:190; Le Page du Pratz, *Histoire de la Louisiane*, 2:292.
106. Diron to Minister, March 20, 1730, *MPAFD*, 1:80; Le Page du Pratz, *Histoire de la Louisiane*, 2:293.
107. Delaye, "Relation du Massacre," 56.
108. Daniel Usner, *Indians Slaves and Settlers*, 206.
109. Delaye, "Relation du Massacre," 57.
110. For a detailed account of the Choctaw Civil War, see Patricia K. Galloway, "Choctaw Factionalism and Civil War, 1746–1750," in *Practicing Ethnohistory: Mining Archives, Hearing Testimony, Constructing Narrative* (Lincoln: University of Nebraska Press, 2006), 259–91.
111. Delaye, "Relation du Massacre,"12, 17.
112. Ibid., 57. I would like to thank Anne-Marie Libério for her help translating this passage.
113. Calliot, "Relation du Voyage," 165.
114. Extracts of letters from Périer to Minister, April to August 1730, ANOM, C13A, vol. 12, 308; Dumont de Montigny, *Mémoires historiques sur la Louisiane*, 2:195–97; Le Page du Pratz, *Histoire de la Louisiane*, 2:301.
115. Dumont de Montigny, *Mémoires historiques sur la Louisiane*, 2:197.
116. Femme brulé au Poteau en 1730 à la Nouvelle Orleans, BN Mss., fr., n.a., 2551, fol. 53. See also Calliot, "Relation du Voyage," 169–70.
117. Femme brulé au Poteau en 1730 à la Nouvelle Orleans, BN Mss., fr., n.a., 2551, fol. 53.
118. Sophie White, "Massacre, Mardi Gras, and Torture in Early New Orleans" *William and Mary Quarterly* 70, no 3 (July 2013): 521–38.
119. Relation des hostilités commises par les Natchez, November 4, 1722, ANOM, G1, vol. 465, n.p.
120. Dumont de Montigny, *Mémoires historiques sur la Louisiane*, 1:218.
121. Jeffrey Brain, George Roth, and William J. De Reuse, "Tunica, Biloxi, and Ofo," in *HBNAI*, 14:587–88.
122. Registre des Baptesmes de la Paroisse de la Nouvelle Orleans, 1730, ANOM, C1, vol. 41, 111.
123. Extracts of letters from Périer to Minister, April to August, 1730, ANOM, C13A, vol. 12, 308.
124. Eighteenth-century European regiments were regarded as the property of their colonels, who controlled every aspect of the unit's pay, dress, discipline, equipment, as well as appointment of field grade officers (see John A. Lynn, *The Wars of Louis XIV, 1667–1714* [New York: Longman, 1999], 45–104; William Hardy McNeill, *The Pursuit of Power: Technology, Armed Force, and Society since A.D. 1000* [Chicago: University of Chicago Press, 1982], 117–84; and Christopher Duffy, *The Military*

Experience in the Age of Reason [Hertfordshire: Cumberland House, 1987]). For details on the organization of the *troupes de marine,* see W. J. Eccles, "The Social, Economic, and Political Significance of the Military Establishment in New France," in *Essays on New France* (Toronto: Oxford University Press, 1987), 110–24. For further information on the composition France's troops in Louisiana, see Khalil Saadani, "Colonialisme et stratégie: Le Rôle des Forces Militaires en Louisiane, 1731–1743," in *France in the New World: Proceedings of the 22nd Annual Meeting of the French Colonial Historical Society* (1996), 203–24.

125. Périer to the Minister, March 25, 1731, ANOM, C13A, vol. 13, 35.

126. Woods, *French-Indian Relations on the Southern Frontier,* 103.

127. Périer to the Minister, March 25, 1731, ANOM, C13A, vol. 13, 35–36.

128. Ibid.

129. Ibid.

130. Attaque du fort des Natchez par les François en janvier 1731, BN Mss, fr., n.a.,2551, fol. 111. See also Charlevoix, *Histoire et description générale de la Nouvelle France,* 2:488.

131. Ibid.

132. Périer to the Minister, March 25, 1731, ANOM, C13A, vol. 13, 35; Charlevoix, *Histoire et description générale de la Nouvelle France,* 2:490; Dumont de Montigny, *Mémoires historiques sur la Louisiane,* 2:205; Le Page du Pratz, *Histoire de la Louisiane,* 2:321.

133. Dumont de Montigny, "L'etablissement de la province de la Louisiane," 327.

134. Périer to the Minister, March 25, 1731, ANOM, C13A, vol. 13, 37; Charlevoix, *Histoire et description generale de la Nouvelle France,* 2:490–91; Dumont de Montigny, *Mémoires historiques sur la Louisiane,* 2:205–7; Le Page du Pratz, *Histoire de la Louisiane,* 2:321.

135. "Relation de la derniere attaque des Natchez faite par les françois en 1731," January 1731, ASH 67, no. 16, n.p.

136. Périer to the Minister, March 25, 1731, ANOM, C13A, vol. 13, 38.

137. Ibid., vol. 13, 40. The anonymous account in the Archives de Sociétié Hydrographique counted forty Natchez and twenty Negroes out on the hunt (Relation de la derniere attaque des Natchez faite par les françois en 1731," January 1731, ASH 67, no. 16, n.p.

138. Périer to the Minister, March 25, 1731, ANOM, C13A, vol. 13, 40. In his description of the funeral of the Tattooed Serpent, Dumont De Montigny mentioned St. Cosme as one of the offspring of the Tattooed Arm (see Dumont de Montigny, *Mémoires historiques sur la Louisiane.* 1:229).

139. Charlevoix, *Histoire et description générale de la Nouvelle France,* 2:491.

140. Ibid., 491–92.

141. Charlevoix, *Histoire et description générale de la nouvelle France,* 2:492–93.

142. Périer to the Minister, March 25, 1731, ANOM, C13A, vol. 13, 40; Relation of the Last of Attack of the French on the Natchez, January 1731, ASH 67, no. 16, n.p.; Charlevoix, *Histoire et description générale de la Nouvelle France,* 2:493–94.

143. Charlevoix, *Histoire et description générale de la Nouvelle France,* 2:498.

144. Périer to the Minister, March 25, 1731, ANOM, C13A, vol. 13, 41; Charlevoix, *Histoire et description générale de la Nouvelle France,* 2:494–95.

145. Le Page du Pratz, *Histoire de la Louisiane,* 3:327.

146. M. Lancelot to Minister, March 1731, BN Mss, fr., n.a., 2610, fols. 63–64v; Attaque du fort des Natchez par les François en janvier 1731, BN Mss fr. n.a., 2551, fol. 113; Charlevoix, *Histoire et description générale de la Nouvelle France*, 2:496–97; Dumont de Montigny, *Mémoires historiques sur la Louisiane*, 2:208.

147. ANOM, Cartes et Plans, vol. 67, 15.

148. Périer to Minister, December 10, 1731, ANOM, C13, vol. 14, 151.

149. Périer to Maurepas, March 25, 1731, *MPAFD*, 4:73.

150. Perier to Minister, October 22, 1731, ANOM, C13A, vol. 13, 85–86.

151. Diron to Minister, June 24, 1731, ANOM, C13A, vol. 13, 147v.

152. "The Natchez Attack on the Tunicas," BN mss., n.a. 2551, fol. 135; Périer to Minister, December 10, 1731, ANOM, C13A, vol. 14, 151v.; Beauchamp to Maurepas, November 5, 1731, *MPAFD*, 6:79.

153. Diron d'Artaguette to Maurepas, June 24, 1731, *MPAFD*, 4:77.

154. Beauchamp to Maurepas, November 5, 1731, *MPAFD*, 4:80; Périer to Minister, December 10, 1731, ANOM, C13A, vol. 14, 152.

155. Diron d'Artaguette to Maurepas, June 24, 1731, *MPAFD*, 4:77.

156. Beauchamp to Maurepas, November 5, 1731, *MPAFD*, 4:8.

157. Beaudouin to Salmon, November 23, 1732, *MPAFD*, 4:159; Memoir of the King to Bienville, February 4, 1732, *MPAFD*, 3:552.

158. St. Denis to Salmon, November 2, 1731, ANOM, C13A, vol. 13, 163.

159. Perier to Minister, October 22, 1731, ANOM, C13A, vol. 13, 91–93; Anonymous memoir entitled *Defaite des Natchez Prés du poste des Natchitoches*, BN Mss, fr., n.a., 2551, p. 107; Périer to Minister, December 1, 1731, ANOM, C13A, vol. 14, 152–52v.

160. St. Denis to Salmon, November 2, 1731, ANOM, C13A, vol. 13, 163.

161. James Adair, *The History of the American Indians*, ed. Kathryn E. Holland Braund (Tuscaloosa: University of Alabama Press, 2005), 272, 355–58; Patricia Galloway and Jason Baird Jackson, "Natchez and Neighboring Groups," in *HBNAI*, vol. 14, 610–11; John Reed Swanton, *The Indians of the Southeastern United States* (Washington, DC: U.S. Government Printing Office, 1946), 250–57.

Legacies

1. Maurice Besson, "Les Deniers Natchez: Épisode de la colonisation de la Louisiane en 1730," *Revue de l'histoire des colonies française*, no. 16 (1923): 120.

2. Périer to Minister, December 1, 1731, ANOM, C13, vol. 14, 152–52v; Bienville to Maurepas, May 18, 1733, *MPAFD*, 3:622. See also Louboëy to Maurepas May 20, 1733, *MPAFD*, 1:215.

3. *South Carolina Gazette*, April 27, 1734; Verner Winslow Crane, *The Southern Frontier, 1670–1732* (Durham, NC: Duke University Press, 1928), 275.

4. James Mooney, "End of the Natchez," *American Anthropologist* 1, no. 3 (1899): 510–21.

5. James Adair, *The History of the American Indians*, ed. Kathryn E. Holland Braund (Tuscaloosa: University of Alabama Press, 2005), 273, 355.

6. Patricia K. Galloway and Jason B. Jackson, "Natchez and Neighboring Groups," *HBNAI*, 14: 610; John Reed Swanton, "Ethnological Position of the Natchez Indians," *American Anthropologist* 9, no. 3 (1907): 513–28; and *Indian Tribes of the Lower Mississippi Valley and the Adjacent Coast of the Gulf of Mexico* (Washington, DC: Government Printing Office, 1911), 251–52.

7. Johann Christian Burckard and Karsten Peterson, *Partners in the Lord's Work: The Diary of Two Moravian Missionaries in Creek Indian Country*, trans. Carl Mauelshagen and Gerald Davis (Atlanta: Georgia State College, 1969), 11–12.

8. George Stiggins, *Creek Indian History: A Historical Narrative of the Genealogy, Traditions, and Downfall of the Ispocoga or Creek Indian Tribe of Indians* (Birmingham, AL: Birmingham Public Library Press, 1989), 37.

9. Ibid., 41.

10. Ibid., 42–44.

11. Mooney, "End of the Natchez," 510–21; Swanton, *Indian Tribes of the Lower Mississippi Valley*, 255–57.

12. www.natcheznation.gq.nu.

13. Michel Vergé-Franceschi, "Les officers généraux de la marine Royale (1715–1774), Origens, conditions, services (Paris: Librairie de l'Inde Editeur, 1990), 263–71.

14. Pierre François-Xavier de Charlevoix, *Histoire et description générale de la Nouvelle France, avec le Journal historique d'un voyage fait par ordre du roi dans l'Amérique Septentrionale*, vol. 2 (Pierre-François Giffart, 1744), 466.

15. Steven J. Harris, "Mapping Jesuit Science: The Role of Travel in the Geography of Knowledge," in *The Jesuits: Cultures, Sciences, and the Arts, 1540–1773*, edited by John W. O'Malley, Gauvin Bailey Bailey, Harris, and T. Frank Kennedy (Toronto: University of Toronto Press, 1999), 258–71.

16. Shannon Lee Dawdy, "Enlightenment from the Ground: Le Page du Pratz's *Histoire de la Louisiane*," *French Colonial History* 3 (2003): 22; Gordon M. Sayre, "A Newly Discovered Manuscript Map by Antoine-Simon Le Page du Pratz," *French Colonial History* 11 (2010): 27.

17. Dawdy, "Enlightenment from the Ground," 17–34.

18. Jean-Françoise-Benjamin Dumont de Montigny, *The Memoir of Lieutenant Dumont, 1715–1747*, trans. Gordon M. Sayre; ed. Sayre and Carla Zecher (Chapel Hill: University of North Carolina Press for the Omohundro Institute for Early American History and Culture, 2012), 396.

19. Marriage of Dumont de Montigny and Marie Baron, April 19, 1730, No. 354, *New Orleans Diocesan Sacramental Records*, Diocese of New Orleans, Louisiana.

20. See Gordon M. Sayre's introductory remarks in Dumont de Montigny, *The Memoir of Lieutenant Dumont*, 36–37.

21. Marc Antoine Calliot, "Relation du voyage de la Louisiane ou Nouvelle France fait par le Sr. Caillot en l'annee 1730," Ms. 2005.11, pp. 164–66, Historic New Orleans Collection.

22. Royal Decree, ANOM, C13A, vol. 13, 247–47v.

23. Gordon Sayre, introduction to *The Memoir of Lieutenant Dumont*, 50.

24. Father Le Petit to Father D'Avaugour, July 12, 1730, *JR*, 67:169.

25. Régis, "Journal du voyage que j'ay fait dans La nation des Chactas, L'année 1729," ANOM, C13A, vol. 12, 79.

26. Antoine Le Page du Pratz, *Histoire de la Louisiane, Contenant la découverte de ce vaste pays; Sa description géographique; Un voyage dans les terres*, vol. 1 (Paris, Lambert, 1758), 102.

27. Règis du Roullet to Maurepas, 1729, ANOM, C13, vol. 12, 82v.

28. Josephe Christophe de Lusser, "Journal du voyage que j'ay fait dans la Nation des Chactas, ANOM, C13A, vol. 12, 110.

29. Ibid., vol. 12, 111.

30. Ibid.

31. Patricia K. Galloway, "Choctaw Factionalism and Civil War, 1746–1750," in *The Choctaw before Removal*, ed. Carolyn Keller Reeves (Jackson: University of Mississippi Press, 1985), 120–56.

Bibliography

Unpublished Primary Sources

Archdiocese of New Orleans Sacramental Records. Archives of the Archdiocese of New Orleans, New Orleans, Louisiana.

Archives de la Marine. French Naval Archives, held at the Archives nationales, Paris.

Archives de la Marine, Service hydrographiques. Archives of the French Navy's cartography section, held at the Archives nationales, Hotel Soubise, Paris.

Archives nationales d'outre mer. French Colonial Archives, Series A, F, G, 9A, 13A, 13B, 13C; Archives nationales d'outre mer, Aix-en-Provence, France, and the Center for Louisiana Studies, the University of Southwest Louisiana, Lafayette, microfilm collections.

Archives of the Seminaire du Quebec (Seminaire des Missiones Étrangeres). Archives of the Seminary of the Foreign Missions. Complexe muséal du Musée de la civilization à Québec, Québec, Canada.

Bibliothèque nationale. Manuscript collections of the French National Library, Site Richelieu, Paris.

British Public Records Office, Colonial Office, CO 5. Original Correspondence, American and West Indies, no. 387, on microfilm at the Huntington Library, San Marino, California.

Calliot MSS. Marc Antoine Caillot, "Relation du Voyage de la Louisiane ou Nouv. France fait par le Sr. Calliot en l'Année 1730." Historic New Orleans Collection, 2005.0011.

O'Neill, Father Charles. Papers. Jesuit Archives, Loyola University New Orleans, New Orleans, Louisiana.

Penicaut [Penicault], André Joseph. "Relation, ou annale véritable de ce qui s'est passé dans le païs de la Louisiane pendant vingt-deux années consecutifes, depuis le commencement de l'établissement des François dans le païs, par Mr d'Hyberville et Mr le comte de Sugère, en 1699, continué jusqu'en 1721." Manuscript. Provient du Collège des Jésuites de Clermont à Paris, n° 828.

Records of the Superior Council of Louisiana. Louisiana State Museum Historical Center, New Orleans.

Vaudreuil Papers. Loudon Collection, Huntington Library, San Marino, California.

Published Primary Sources

Adair, James. *The History of the American Indians.* Edited by Kathryn E. Holland Braund. Tuscaloosa: University of Alabama Press, 2005.

Anonymous. *Memoire sur Louisiane.* Recueil B. A. Luxembourg. Paris, 1758. Rare Book Collection, New York Public Library.

Anonymous. "Nouvelle relation de la Louisiane." From the *Nouvelle Mercure*, in *Le plus beau païs du monde*, 35–47. 1717. Reprint, Lafayette: Center for Louisiana Studies, 2005.

Aquinas, Thomas. *Summa Theologiae: Latin Text and English Translation.* New York: Blackfriars; McGraw-Hill, 1964.

Boucher, Pierre. *Histoire veritable et naturelle des moeurs et productions du pays de la Nouvelle France: Vulgairement dite le Canada.* Paris: Florentin Lambert, 1664.

Charlevoix, Pierre-François-Xavier de. *Histoire et description générale de la Nouvelle France avec le Journal historique d'un voyage fait par ordre du roi dans L'amérique septentrionale.* Vol. 2. Paris: Chez Nyon et Fils, 1744.

———. *Histoire et description générale de la Nouvelle France avec le Journal historique d'un voyage fait par ordre du roi dans L'amérique septentrionale.* Vol. 3. Paris: Chez Nyon Fils, 1744.

———. *History and General Description of New France.* Translated by John Gilmary Shea. Vol. 6. Chicago: Loyola University Press, 1962.

Chicken, George. "Colonel Chicken's Journal to the Cherokees, 1725." In *Travels in the American Colonies*, edited by Newton D. Mereness, 93–172. New York: Macmillan, 1916.

Conrad, Glen R., *Immigration and War: Louisiana 1718–1721: From Memoir of Charles Le Gac.* Translated by Conrad. Lafayette: University of Southwestern Louisiana, 1970.

Cooper, Thomas, ed. *The Statutes at Large of South Carolina.* Vol. 2. 1837. Columbia: A. S. Johnston, 1970.

D'Iberville, Pierre Le Moyne. *Iberville's Gulf Journal.* Translated by Richebourg Gaillard McWilliams. Mobile: University of Alabama Press, 1981.

Du Ru, Paul. *The Journal of Paul Du Ru (February 1 to May 8, 1700).* Translated by Ruth Lapham Butler. Chicago: Caxton Club, 1934.

Dumont de Montigny, Jean-François-Benjamin. "L'etablissement de la province de la Louisiane, poème composé de 1728 À 1742." *Sociéte des Américanistes* 23, no. 2 (1931): 275–440.

———. *The Memoir of Lieutenant Dumont, 1715–1747.* Translated by Gordon M. Sayre. Edited by Sayre and Carla Zecher. Chapel Hill: University of North Carolina Press for the Omohundro Institute for Early American History and Culture, 2012.

———. *Mémoires historiques sur la Louisiane contenant ce qui y est arrivé de plus mémorable depuis l'année 1687.* 2 vols. Paris: J. B. Bauche, 1753.

———. *Regards sur le monde atlantique, 1717–1747.* Sillery: Septentrion, 2008.

Edits, ordonnances royaux, declarations et arrêts du Conseil d'Etat du roi concernant le Canada. Edited by W. B. Lindsay. Quebec: E. R. Fréchette, 1854.

Kellogg, Louise Phelps. *Early Narratives of the Northwest, 1634–1699.* New York: Scribner's Sons, 1917.

La Harpe, Jean-Baptiste Bernard de. *The Historical Journal of the Establishment of the French in Louisiana.* Translated by Joan Cain and Virginia Koenig. Lafayette: Center for Louisiana Studies, 1971.

Lafitau, Joseph-Franõcois. *Moeurs des sauvages Amériquains: Comparées aux moeurs des premiers Temps.* Vol. 1. Paris: Saugrain l'aîne, 1724.

Lahontan, Baron Louis-Armand de Lom d'Ares, ed. *New Voyages to North American.* Vol. 1. Chicago: A. C. McClurg, 1905.

Le Page du Pratz, Antoine. *Histoire de la Louisiane, Contenant la découverte de ce vaste pays; Sa description géographique; Un voyage dans les terres.* 3 vols. Paris: Lambert, 1758.

Lindsay, W. B., ed. *Edits, ordonnances royaux, declarations et arrêts du Conseil D'etat du roi concernant le Canada.* Quebec: E. R. Fréchette, 1854.

Mississippi Provincial Archives—French Dominion. 5 vols. Collected, edited, and translated by Dunbar Rowland, A. G. Sanders, and Patricia Galloway. Jackson: Department of Archives and History, 1927–84.

Nairne, Thomas. *Nairne's Muskhogean Journals: The 1708 Expedition to the Mississippi River.* Jackson: University of Mississippi Press, 1988.

Phelps, Dawson, ed. and trans. "Narrative of the Hostilities Committed by the Natchez against the Concession of St. Catherine's," *Journal of Mississippi History* 7, no. 1 (1945): 3–10.

Saint-Simon, Louis de Rouvroy, and Henri Jean Victor de Rouvroy Saint-Simon. *Mémoires complets et authentiques du Duc de Saint-Simon sur le siècle de Louis XIV et la régence.* Paris: A. Sautelet et cie [etc.], 1829.

Salley, A. S, ed. *Records in the British Public Records Office Relating to South Carolina 1701–1710.* Columbia: Historical Commission of South Carolina, 1947.

Stiggins, George. *Creek Indian History: A Historical Narrative of the Genealogy, Traditions, and Downfall of the Ispocoga or Creek Indian Tribe of Indians.* Birmingham, AL: Birmingham Public Library Press, 1989.

Thwaites, Reuben Gold. *The Jesuit Relations and Allied Documents; Travels and Explorations of the Jesuit Missionaries in New France, 1610-1791*. 73 vols. Cleveland: Burrows Bros., 1896-1901.

Secondary Sources

Albrecht, Andrew C. "Indian-French Relations at Natchez." *American Anthropologist* 48, no. 3 (1946): 321-54.

Allain, Mathé. *"Not Worth a Straw": French Colonial Policy and the Early Years of Louisiana*. Lafayette: Center for Louisiana Studies, 1988.

———. "Slave Policies in French Louisiana." In *The French Experience in Louisiana*, edited by Glenn R. Conrad, 174-82. Lafayette: Center for Louisiana Studies, 1995.

Atkinson, James R. *Splendid Land, Splendid People: The Chickasaw Indians to Removal*. Tuscaloosa: University of Alabama Press, 2004.

Aubert, Guillaume. "'The Blood of France': Race and Purity of Blood in the French Atlantic World." *William and Mary Quarterly* 61, no. 3 (2004): 439-78.

———. "'Français, Negres et sauvages': Constructing Race in Colonial Louisiana (France)." PhD diss., Tulane University, 2002.

Axtell, James. *Beyond 1492: Encounters in Colonial North America*. New York: Oxford University Press, 1992.

———. *The Invasion Within: The Contest of Cultures in Colonial North America*. New York: Oxford University Press, 1985.

Baker, Vaughn B. "Marcel Giraud, 1900-1994: A Memorial and a Reminiscence," *Louisiana History: Journal of the Louisiana Historical Association* 35, no. 3 (Summer 1994): 355-60.

Baldwin, John W. "The Image of the *Jongleur* in Northern France around 1200." *Speculum* 72, no. 3 (1997).

Balvay, Arnaud. "The French and the Natchez: A Failed Encounter." In *French and Indians in the Heart of North America, 1630-1815*, edited by Robert Englebert and Guillaume Teasdale. East Lansing: University of Michigan Press, 2013. Kindle edition.

———. *La Révolte des Natchez*. Paris: Éditions du Félin, 2008.

Barnett, James F., Jr. *The Natchez Indians: A History to 1735*. Jackson: University Press of Mississippi, 2007.

Bell, David A. *The Cult of Nation in France: Inventing Nationalism, 1680-1800*. Cambridge: Harvard University Press, 2001.

Berlin, Ira. *Many Thousands Gone: The First Two Centuries of Slavery in North America*. Cambridge: Belknap Press of Harvard University Press, 1998.

Besson, Maurice. "Les Deniers Natchez: Épisode de la colonisation de la Louisiane en 1730." *Revue de l'histoire des colonies française* 16 (1923): 120.

Blitz, John. "Mississippian Chiefdoms and the Fusion-Fission Process." *American Antiquity* 64, no. 4 (1999): 577-92.

Black, Patti Jo. *Art in Mississippi, 1720–1980*. Jackson: Mississippi Historical Society, 1998.
Blaufarb, Rafe. "The Survival of the Pays D'états: The Example of Provence." *Past & Present* 209, no. 1 (November 1, 2010): 83–116.
Boucher, Philip P. *France and the American Tropics: Tropics of Discontent?* Baltimore: Johns Hopkins University Press, 2007.
Boulle, Pierre H. "Some Eighteenth-Century French Views on Louisiana." In *Frenchmen and French Ways in the Mississippi Valley*, edited by John Francis McDermott, 15–27. Urbana: University of Illinois Press, 1969.
Brain, Jeffrey P. "Late Prehistoric Settlement Patterning in the Yazoo Basin and Natchez Bluffs Regions of the Lower Mississippi Valley." In *Mississippian Settlement Patterns*, edited by Bruce D. Smith, 331–68. New York: Academic Press, 1978.
———. "The Natchez 'Paradox.'" *Ethnology* 10, no. 2 (1971): 215–22.
Brasseaux, Carl A. "The Administration of Slave Regulations in French Louisiana, 1724–1766." In *The French Experience in Louisiana*, edited by Glenn R. Conrad, 209–25. Lafayette: Center for Louisiana Studies, 1995.
———. *France's Forgotten Legion: Service Records of French Military and Administrative Personnel Stationed in the Mississippi Valley and Gulf Coast Region, 1699–1769*. CD-ROM. Baton Rouge: Louisiana State University Press.
———. "The Image of Louisiana and the Failure of Voluntary French Emigration 1683–1731." In *The French Experience in Louisiana*, edited by Glenn R. Conrad. Lafayette: Center for Louisiana Studies, 1995.
Braudel, Fernand. *Civilization and Capitalism, 15th–18th Century*. 3 vols. Berkeley: University of California Press, 1992.
Braudel, Fernand, and Ernest Labrousse. *Histoire économique et sociale de la France, 1660–1789*. 1970. Reprint, Paris: Presses Universitaires de France, 1993.
Braund, Kathryn E. Holland. *Deerskins & Duffels: The Creek Indian Trade with Anglo-America, 1685–1815*. Lincoln: University of Nebraska Press, 1993.
Brown, Ian W. "An Archaeological Study of Culture Contact and Change in the Natchez Bluffs Region." In *La Salle and His Legacy: Frenchmen and Indians in the Lower Mississippi Valley*, edited by Patricia Galloway, 176–89. Jackson: University of Mississippi Press, 1982.
———. "Historic Indians of the Lower Mississippi Valley: An Archaeologist's View." In *Towns and Temples along the Mississippi*, edited by David H. Dye and Cheryl Ann Cox, 227–38. Tuscaloosa: University of Alabama Press, 1990.
Brown, James A. "Archaeology Confronts History at the Natchez Temple." *Southeastern Archaeology* 9, no. 1 (1990): 1–10.
Brown, Kathleen M. *Good Wives, Nasty Wenches, and Anxious Patriarchs: Gender, Race and Power in Colonial Virginia*. Chapel Hill: University of North Carolina Press, 1996.
———. "Native Americans and Early Modern Concepts of Race." In *Empire*

and Others: British Encounters with Indigenous Peoples, 1600–1850, edited by Martin Dauton and Rick Halpern, 79–98. Philadelphia: University of Pennsylvania Press, 1999.

Brückner, Martin. *The Cartographic Revolution in Early America: Maps, Literacy, and National Identity.* Chapel Hill: University of North Carolina Press for the Omohundro Institute of Early American History and Culture, 2006.

Buisseret, David, ed. *Monarchs, Ministers, and Maps: The Emergence of Cartography as a Tool of Government in Early Modern Europe.* Chicago: University of Chicago Press, 1992.

Burckard, Johann Christian, and Karsten Peterson. *Partners in the Lord's Work: The Diary of Two Moravian Missionaries in Creek Indian Country.* Translated by Carl Mauelshagen and Gerald Davis. Atlanta: Georgia State College, 1969.

Calloway, Colin G. *The American Revolution in Indian Country: Crisis and Diversity in Native American Communities.* New York: Cambridge University Press, 1995.

Campanella, Richard. *Bienville's Dilemma: A Historical Geography of New Orleans.* Lafayette: University of Louisiana Press, 2008.

Canny, Nicholas P. "In Search of a Better Home? European Overseas Migration, 1500–1800." In *Europeans on the Move: Studies on European Migration, 1500–1800*, edited by Canny, 263–85. New York: Oxford University Press, 1994.

Carson, James Taylor. "Ethnography and the Native American Past." *Ethnohistory* 49, no. 4 (2002): 769–88.

———. "Sacred Circles and Dangerous People: Native American Cosmology and the French Settlement of Louisiana." In *French Colonial Louisiana and the Atlantic World*, edited by Bradley G. Bond, 63–82. Baton Rouge: Louisiana State University Press, 2005.

———. *Searching for the Bright Path: The Mississippi Choctaws from Prehistory to Removal.* Lincoln: University of Nebraska Press, 1999.

Chaplin, Joyce E. *Subject Matter: Technology, the Body, and Science on the Anglo-American Frontier, 1500–1676.* Cambridge: Harvard University Press, 2001.

Chapman, Sara. "Patronage as Family Economy: The Role of Women in the Patron-Client Network of the Phélypeaux De Pontchartrain Family, 1670–1715." *French Historical Studies* 24, no. 11–35 (2001): 11–35.

Clemens, Samuel [Mark Twain]. *Life on the Mississippi.* 1874. Reprint, New York: Harper Brothers, 1901.

Clute, Janet R. "Faunal Remains from Old Mobile." *Historical Archaeology* 36, no. 1 (2002): 129–34.

Chocquette, Leslie. "Proprietorships in French North America." In *Constructing Early Modern Empires: Proprietary Ventures in the Atlantic World*, edited by L. H. Roper and Bertrand Van Ruymbeke, 117–31. Boston: Brill, 2007.

Cobb, Charles R. "Mississippian Chiefdoms: How Complex?" *Annual Review of Anthropology* 82 (2003): 63–84.

Codignola, Luca. "The Holy See and the Conversion of the Indians in French and British North America, 1486–1760." In *America in European Consciousness 1493–1750*, edited by Karen Ordahl Kupperman, 195–242. Chapel Hill: University of North Carolina Press, 1995.
Collins, James B. *From Tribes to Nation: The Making of France 500–1799*. Fort Worth, TX: Wadsworth, 2002.
———. *The State in Early Modern France*. 2nd ed. New York: Cambridge University Press, 2009.
Conrad, Glenn R. "*Emigration Forcée*: A French Attempt to Populate Louisiana 1716–1720." In *The French Experience in Louisiana*, edited by Conrad, 125–35. Lafayette: Center for Louisiana Studies, 1995.
———. *Immigration and War: Louisiana 1718–1721: From Memoir of Charles Le Gac*. Translated by Conrad. Lafayette: University of Southwestern Louisiana, 1970.
Cotter, John. "Stratigraphic and Area Test at the Emerald and Anna Mound Sites." *American Antiquity: A Quarterly Review of American Archaeology* 17 (1951): 18–31.
Crane, Verner Winslow. *The Southern Frontier, 1670–1732*. Durham, NC: Duke University Press, 1928.
Crawford, James Mack. *The Mobilian Trade Language*. Knoxville: University of Tennessee Press, 1978.
Cronon, William. *Changes in the Land: Indians, Colonists, and the Ecology of New England*. New York: Hill and Wang, 1983.
Crosby, Alfred W. *Ecological Imperialism: The Biological Expansion of Europe, 900–1900*. New York: Cambridge University Press, 1993.
———. "Virgin Soil Epidemics as a Factor in Aboriginal Depopulation." *William and Mary Quarterly* 33, no. 2 (1976): 289–99.
Davis, David Brion. "Constructing Race: A Reflection." *William and Mary Quarterly* 54, no. 1 (1997).
Dawdy, Shannon Lee. *Building the Devil's Empire: French Colonial New Orleans*. Chicago: University of Chicago Press, 2008.
———. "The Burden of Louis Congo and the Evolution of Savagery in Colonial Louisiana." In *Discipline and the Other Body: Correction, Corporeality, Colonialism*, edited by Steven Pierce and Anupama Rao, 61–90. Durham, NC: Duke University Press, 2006.
———. "Enlightenment from the Ground: Le Page du Pratz's *Histoire de la Louisiane*." *French Colonial History* 3 (2003): 17–33.
Dechêne, Louise. *Habitants et marchands de Montréal au XVII siècle essai*. Montreal: Boréal, 1988.
Dee, Daryl. *Expansion and Crisis in Louis XIV's France: Franche-Comté and Absolute Monarchy, 1674–1715*. Rochester, NY: University of Rochester Press, 2009.
Delanglez, Jean. "Antoine Laumet alias Cadillac, Commandant at Michilimackinac: 1694–1697." *Mid-America* 16, no. 2 (1945): 108–32.

———. "Antoine Laumet alias Cadillac, Commandant at Michilimackinac: 1694–1697 (Concluded)." *Mid-America* 16, no. 4 (1945): 232–56.

———. "Antoine Laumet alias Cadillac, Commandant at Michilimackinac: 1694–1697 (Continued)." *Mid-America* 16, no. 3 (1945): 188–216.

———. "Cadillac's Early Years in America." *Mid-America* 16, no. 1 (1944): 3–39.

———. "The French Jesuits in Lower Louisiana (1700–1763)." PhD diss., Catholic University of America, 1935.

———. "A Louisiana Poet-Historian: Dumont *dit* Montigny." *Mid-America* 19, no. 1 (1937): 31–49.

———. "The Natchez Massacre and Governor Perrier." *Louisiana Historical Quarterly* 17 (1934): 631–41.

Delumeau, Jean. *Catholicism between Luther and Voltaire: A New View of the Counter-Reformation*. Translated by Jeremy Mosier. Philadelphia: Burns and Oates, 1977.

Demos, John. *Entertaining Satan: Witchcraft and the Culture of Early New England*. New York: Oxford University Press, 1982.

Deslandres, Dominique. *Croire et faire croire: Les missions Françaises au XVIIe siècle, 1600–1650*. Paris: Fayard, 2003.

———. "Exemplo aeque ut verbo: The French Jesuits' Missionary World." In *The Jesuits: Cultures, Sciences, and the Arts, 1540–1773*, edited by John W. O'Malley, Gauvin Bailey Bailey, Steven J. Harris, and T. Frank Kennedy, 258–71. Toronto: University of Toronto Press, 1999.

Diamond, Jared M. *Guns, Germs, and Steel: The Fates of Human Societies*. New York: Norton, 1999.

Dickason, Olive Patricia. "The Concept of *L'homme Sauvage* and Early French Colonialism in the Americas." *Revue Française d'Histoire d'Outre-Mer* 64, no. 234 (1977): 5–32.

———. *The Myth of the Savage: And the Beginnings of French Colonialism in the Americas*. Edmonton: University of Alberta Press, 1984.

Drechsel, Emanuel J. "An Integrated Vocabulary of Mobilian Jargon, a Native American Pidgin of the Mississippi Valley." *Anthropological Linguistics* 38 (Summer 1996): 248–354.

Duffy, Christopher. *Fire and Stone: The Science of Fortress Warfare, 1660–1860*. 1975. Edison: Castle Books, 2006.

Duffy, Eamon. *The Stripping of the Altars: Traditional Religion in England, C.1400–C.1580*. New Haven: Yale University Press, 1992.

Duval, Kathleen. *The Native Ground: Indians and Colonists in the Heart of the Continent*. Philadelphia: University of Pennsylvania Press, 2006.

Eccles, W. J. *The French in North America 1500–1783*. Lansing: Michigan State University Press, 1998.

Edmunds, R. David, and Joseph L. Peyser. *The Fox Wars: The Mesquakie Challenge to New France*. Norman: University of Oklahoma Press, 1993.

Ethridge, Robbie. "Creating the Shatterzone: Indian Slave Traders and the Collapse of the Southeastern Chiefdoms." In *Light on the Path: The Anthropology and History of the Southeastern Indians*, edited by Thomas J. Pluckhahn and Ethridge, 206–17. Tuscaloosa: University of Alabama Press, 2006.

———. *From Chicaza to Chickasaw: The European Invasion and the Transformation of the Mississippian World, 1540–1715*. Chapel Hill: University of North Carolina Press, 2010.

Ferguson, R. Brian, and Neil L. Whitehead. "The Violent Edge of Empire." In *War in the Tribal Zone: Expanding States and Indigenous Warfare*, edited by Ferguson and Whitehead, 1–30. Santa Fe: School of American Research, 1999.

Fischer, J. R. "Solutions for the Natchez Paradox." *Ethnology* 3, no 1 (1964): 53–65.

Foret, Michael J. "War or Peace? Louisiana, the Choctaws, and the Chickasaws, 1733–1735." In *The French Experience in Louisiana*, edited by Glenn R. Conrad, 296–312. Lafayette: Center for Louisiana Studies, 1995.

Foucault, Michel. *History of Sexuality, Vol. 1: An Introduction*. Translated by Robert Hurley. New York: Vintage, 1978.

———. "Of Other Spaces: Heterotopias." Translated by Jay Miskowiec. *Architecture /Movement/Continuity* (October 1984). http://foucault.info/document/heteroTopia/foucault.heteroTopia.en.html.

Fournel Victor. *Dictionnaire alphabétique et anologique de la Langue Française: Les mots et les associations d'idées*. Vol. 3. Paris: Société du Noveau litré, 1972.

Gallay, Alan. *The Indian Slave Trade: The Rise of the English Empire in the American South, 1670–1717*. New Haven: Yale University Press, 2002.

Galloway, Patricia K. "'The Chief Who Is Your Father': Choctaw and French Views of Diplomatic Relation." In *Powhatan's Mantle: Indians in the Colonial Southeast*, edited by Peter H. Wood, Gregory A. Waselkov, and M. Thomas Hatley, 254–78. Lincoln: University of Nebraska Press, 1989.

———. *Choctaw Genesis, 1500–1700*. Lincoln: University of Nebraska Press, 1995.

———. "The Direct Historical Approach and Early Historical Documents: The Ethnohistorian's View." In Archaeological Report No. 18, *The Protohistoric Period in the Mid-South: 1700–1700, Proceedings of the 1983 Mid-South Archaeological Conference*, edited by David H. Dye and Ronald C. Brister, 14–24. Jackson: Mississippi Department of Archives and History, 1986.

———. "Four Ages of Alibamon Mingo, Fl. 1700–1766." *Journal of Mississippi History* 65, no. 4 (2003): 320–42.

———."Henri De Tonti Du Village Des Chacta 1702: The Beginning of the French Alliance." In *La Salle and His Legacy: Frenchmen and Indians in the Lower Mississippi Valley*, edited by Galloway, 146–75. Jackson: University of Mississippi Press, 1982.

———. "Louisiana Post Letters: Missing Evidence for Indian Diplomacy." In

The French Experience in Louisiana, edited by Glenn R. Conrad. Lafayette: Center for Louisiana Studies, 1995.

———. "Ougoula Tchetoka, Ackia, and Bienville's First Chickasaw War: Whose Strategy and Tactics?" *Journal of Chickasaw History* 2, no. 1 (1996): 3–10.

———. "Rhetoric of Difference: Le Page Du Pratz on African Slave Management in Eighteenth-Century Louisiana." *French Colonial History* 3 (2003): 1–16.

———. "Savage Medicine: Du Pratz and Eighteenth-Century French Medical Practice." In *France in the New World: Proceedings of the 22nd Annual Meeting of the French Colonial Historical Society, 1996 Poiters, France*, edited by David Buisseret, 107–18. Lansing: Michigan State University Press, 1998.

———. "'So Many Little Republics': British Negotiations with the Choctaw Confederacy." *Ethnohistory* 41 (1994): 513–38.

Galloway, Patricia, and Jason Baird Jackson. "Natchez and Neighboring Groups." In *Handbook of North American Indians: Southeast*, edited by Raymond D. Fogelson, 598–615. Washington, DC: Smithsonian Institution, 2004.

Gayarré, Charles. *History of Louisiana: The French Domination*. 1866. Reprint, Gretna, LA: Pelican, 1998.

Giraud, Marcel. "La Compagnie D'occident, 1717–1718." *Revue Historique* 226, no. 3 (1961): 23–56.

———. *Histoire de la Louisiane française*. Vol. 4, *La Louisiane après le système de Law (1721–1723)*. Paris: Presses Universitaires de France, 1974.

———. *A History of French Louisiana*. Vol. 5, *The Company of the Indies, 1723–1731*. Translated by Brian Pearce. Baton Rouge: Louisiana State University Press, 1974.

———. *A History of French Louisiana*. Vol. 1, *The Reign of Louis XIV, 1698–1715*. Translated by Joseph C. Lambert. 1953. Baton Rouge: Louisiana State University Press, 1974.

———. *A History of French Louisiana*. Vol. 2, *Years of Transition, 1715–1717*. Translated by Brian Pearce. 1966. Baton Rouge: Louisiana State University Press, 1974.

Gleach, Frederic. *Powhatan's World and Colonial Virginia: A Conflict of Cultures*. Lincoln: University of Nebraska Press, 1997.

Goubert, Pierre. *The Ancien Régime: French Society, 1600–1750*. Translated by Steve Cox. New York: Harper and Row, 1973.

Green, F. C. *Eighteenth-Century France*. Toronto: J. M. Dent, 1929.

Greenwald, Erin Michele. "Company Towns and Tropical Baptisms: From Lorient to Louisiana on a French Atlantic Circuit." PhD diss., Ohio State University, 2011.

Greer, Allan. "Commons and Enclosures in the Colonization of North America." *American Historical Review* 117, no. 2 (April 2012): 365–86.

———. *Mohawk Saint: Catherine Tekakwitha and the Jesuits*. New York: Oxford University Press, 2005.

Greer, Allan, and Kenneth Mills. "A Catholic Atlantic." In *The Atlantic in Global History*, edited by Jorge Cañizares-Esguerra and Erik R. Seeman, 3–19. Upper Saddle River: Pearson, 2007.

Hall, David D. *Worlds of Wonder, Days of Judgment: Popular Religious Belief in Early New England*. Cambridge: Harvard University Press, 1989.

Hall, Gwendolyn Midlo. *Africans in Colonial Louisiana: The Development of Afro-Creole Culture in the Eighteenth Century*. Baton Rouge: Louisiana State University Press, 1992.

Hardy, James D. "The Superior Council in Colonial Louisiana." In *Frenchmen and French Ways in the Mississippi Valley*, edited by John Francis McDermott, 87–101. Urbana: University of Illinois Press, 1969.

———. "The Transportation of Convicts to Colonial Louisiana." In *The French Experience in Louisiana*, edited by Glenn R. Conrad, 115–22. Lafayette: Center for Louisiana Studies, 1995.

Harley, J. B. "Maps, Knowledge, and Power." In *The New Nature of Maps: Essays in the History of Cartography*, edited by Paul Laxton, 51–82. Baltimore: Johns Hopkins University Press, 2001.

———. "Silences and Secrecy: The Hidden Agenda of Cartography in Early Modern Europe." *Imago Mundi* 40 (1988): 57–76.

———. "Texts and Contexts in the Interpretations of Early Maps." In *The New Nature of Maps: Essays in the History of Cartography*, edited by Paul Laxton, 33–50. Baltimore: Johns Hopkins University Press, 2001.

Harris, Steven J. "Mapping Jesuit Science: The Role of Travel in the Geography of Knowledge." In *The Jesuits: Cultures, Sciences, and the Arts, 1540–1773*, edited by John W. O'Malley, Gauvin Bailey Bailey, Harris, and T. Frank Kennedy, 258–71. Toronto: University of Toronto Press, 1999.

Hart, C. W. M. "A Reconsideration of the Natchez Social Structure." *American Anthropologist* 45, no. 3 (1943): 374–86.

Hauck, Philomena. *Bienville: Father of Louisiana*. Lafayette: Center for Louisiana Studies, 1998.

Hay, Douglas. "Poaching and the Game Laws on Cannock Chase." In *Albion's Fatal Tree: Crime and Society in Eighteenth-Century England*. New York: Pantheon, 1975.

Higginbotham, A. Leon. *In the Matter of Color: Race and the American Legal Process, the Colonial Period*. New York: Oxford University Press, 1978.

Higginbotham, Jay. *Old Mobile: Fort Louis De La Louisiane, 1702–1711*. Mobile: Museum of the City of Mobile, 1977.

Hobsbawm, Eric. J. *The Age of Revolution 1789–1848*. New York: Signet, 1962.

Holt, Mack P. *The French Wars of Religion, 1562–1629*. 2nd ed. New York: Cambridge University Press, 2005.

Ingersoll, Thomas N. "Slave Codes and Judicial Practice in New Orleans." *Law and History Review* 13, no. 1 (1995): 23–62.

Jaenen, Cornelius. *Friend and Foe: Aspects of French-Amerindian Cultural Con-*

tact in the Sixteenth and Seventeenth Centuries. Toronto: McClelland and Stewart, 1976.

Jenkins, Ned J. "Tracing the Origins of the Early Creeks, 1050–1700 CE." In *Mapping the Mississippian Shatter Zone: The Colonial Indian Slave Trade and Regional Instability in the American South*, edited by Robbie Ethridge and Sheri Marie Shuck-Hall, 188–249. Lincoln: University of Nebraska Press, 2009.

Jeter, Marvin D. "From Prehistory through Protohistory to Ethnohistory in and near the Northern Lower Mississippi Valley." In *The Transformation of the Southeastern Indians, 1540–1760*, edited by Robbie Ethridge and Charles M. Hudson, 177–223. Jackson: University of Mississippi Press, 2002.

———. "Tunicans West of the Mississippi: A Summary of Early Historic and Archaeology Evidence." In Archaeological Report No. 18, *The Protohistoric Period in the Mid-South: 1700–1700, Proceedings of the 1983 Mid-South Archaeological Conference*, edited by David H. Dye and Ronald C. Brister. Jackson: Mississippi Department of Archives and History, 1986.

Jordan, Winthrop P. *White over Black: American Attitudes toward the Negro 1550–1812*. Chapel Hill: University of North Carolina Press, 1968.

Kellogg, Louise Phelps. *The French Régime in Wisconsin and the Northwest*. Madison: State Historical Society of Wisconsin, 1925.

Kelton, Paul. "Avoiding the Smallpox Spirits: Colonial Epidemics and Southeastern Indian Survival." *Ethnohistory* 51, no. 1 (2004): 45–72.

———. "The Great Southeastern Smallpox Epidemic, 1696–1700: The Region's First Major Epidemic?" In *The Transformation of the Southeastern Indians, 1540–1760*, edited by Robbie Ethridge and Charles M. Hudson, 45–72. Jackson: University of Mississippi Press, 2002.

Kilman, Grady W. "Slavery and Agriculture in Louisiana: 1699–1731." In *The French Experience in Louisiana*, edited by Glenn R. Conrad, 201–8. Lafayette: Center for Louisiana Studies, 1995.

Kindleberger, Charles Poor. *A Financial History of Western Europe*. 2nd ed. New York: Oxford University Press, 1993.

Konvitz, Josef W. *Cartography in France, 1660–1848: Science, Engineering, and Statecraft*. Chicago: University of Chicago Press, 1987.

Kulikoff, Allan, and Omohundro Institute of Early American History and Culture. *Tobacco and Slaves: The Development of Southern Cultures in the Chesapeake, 1680–1800*. Chapel Hill: University of North Carolina Press for the Omohundro Institute of Early American History and Culture, 1986.

Kupperman, Karen Ordahl. *Indians and English: Facing Off in Early America*. Ithaca: Cornell University Press, 2000.

———. *Settling with the Indians: The Meeting of English and Indian Cultures in America, 1580–1640*. Totowa, NJ: Rowman and Littlefield, 1980.

Langfur, Hal. "Moved by Terror: Frontier Violence as Cultural Exchange in Late-Colonial Brazil." *Ethnohistory* 52, no. 2 (2005): 255–89.

Langlois, Gilles-Antoine. *Des villes pour la Louisiane française: Théorie et pratique de l'urbanistique colonials au 18e siècle*. Paris: L'Harmattan, 2003.

Lauber, Almon Wheeler. *Indian Slavery in Colonial Times within the Present Limits of the United States*. New York: Columbia University Press, 1913.

Le Roy Ladurie, Emmanuel. *The Ancien Régime: A History of France, 1610–1774*. Cambridge, MA: Blackwell, 1996.

———. *Saint-Simon and the Court of Louis XIV*. Translated by Jean-François Fitou. Chicago: University of Chicago Press, 2001.

Lefebvre, Henri. *The Production of Space*. Translated by Donald Nicholson Smith. 1974. Cambridge, MA: Blackwell, 1991.

Lefebvre, Jean Jacques. "Charles Le Moyne de Longueuil et Châteauguay." In *The Dictionary of Canadian Biography*, vol. 1. Toronto: University of Toronto Press, 1970.

Léon, Pierre. "Les nouvelles élites." In *Histoire économique et sociale de la France*, vol. 2, *1660–1789*, edited by Fernand Braudel and Ernest Labrousse. 1970. Reprint, Paris: Presses Universitaires de France, 1993.

Lepore, Jill. *The Name of War: King Philip's War and the Origins of American Identity*. New York: Knopf, 1998.

Lewis, R. Barry, Charles B. Stout, and Cameron B. Wesson. "The Design of Mississippian Towns." In *Mississippian Towns and Sacred Spaces: Searching for an Architectural Grammar*, edited by Lewis and Stout, 1–21. Tuscaloosa: University of Alabama Press, 1998.

Libby, David J. *Slavery and Frontier Mississippi, 1720–1835*. Jackson: University Press of Mississippi, 2004.

Lemieux, Donald J. "Some Legal and Practical Aspects of the Office of Commissaire-Ordonnateur of French Louisiana." *Louisiana Studies* 14, no. 4 (1975): 379–93.

Lorenz, Karl G. "The Natchez of Southwest Mississippi." In *Indians of the Greater Southeast: Historical Archaeology and Ethnohistory*, edited by Bonnie G. McEwan, 142–77. Gainesville: University Press of Florida, 2000.

———. "A Re-examination of Natchez Sociopolitical Complexity: A View from the Grand Village and Beyond." *Southeastern Archaeology* 16, no. 2 (1997): 97–112.

MacCullough, Diarmaid. *The Reformation: A History*. New York: Penguin, 2004.

Mandrou, Robert. *Magistrats et sorciers en France au XVII siècle: Une analyse de psychologie historique, civilisations et mentalités*. [Paris]: Plon, 1968.

Marcoux, Jon Bernard. "The Materialization of Status and Social Structure at Kroger's Island Cemetery, Alabama." In *Mississippian Mortuary Practices: Beyond Hierarchy and the Representative Perspective*, edited by Lynne P. Sullivan and Robert C. Mainfort Jr. Gainesville: University Press of Florida, 2010.

McDermott, John Francis, and Southern Illinois University at Edwardsville.

Frenchmen and French Ways in the Mississippi Valley. Urbana: University of Illinois Press, 1969.

McManners, John. *Church and Society in Eighteenth-Century France: The Religion of the People and the Politics of Religion*. 2 vols. New York: Oxford University Press, 1998.

Merrell, James Hart. *The Indians' New World: Catawbas and Their Neighbors from European Contact through the Era of Removal*. New York: Norton, 1989.

———. "Some Thoughts on Colonial Historians and American Indians." *William and Mary Quarterly* 46, no. 1 (1989): 94–119.

Mettam, Roger. "The French Nobility, 1610–1715." In *The European Nobilities in the Seventeenth and Eighteenth Centuries*, 114–41. New York: Longman House, 1995.

Meyer, Jean. *Colbert*. [Paris]: Hachette littérature générale, 1981.

Micelle, Jerry A. "From Law Court to Local Government: Metamorphosis of the Superior Council of French Louisiana." *Louisiana History* 9, no. 2 (1968): 85–107.

Miller, Nancy M. *The Commerce of Louisiana during the French Regime, 1699–1763*. New York: Longmans, Green, 1916.

Milner, George R., and Sissel Schroeder. "Mississippian Sociopolitical Systems." In *Great Towns and Regional Polities in the American Southwest and Southeast*, edited by Jill E. Neitzel, 101–2. Albuquerque: University of New Mexico, 1991.

Moogk, Peter J. "Manon's Fellow Exiles: Emigration from France to North America before 1763." In *Europeans on the Move: Studies on European Migration, 1500–1800*, edited by Nicholas P. Canny, 236–60. New York: Oxford University Press, 1994.

———. *La Nouvelle France: The Making of French Canada—A Cultural History*. Lansing: Michigan State University Press, 2000.

Mooney, James. "End of the Natchez." *American Anthropologist* 1, no. 3 (1899): 510–21.

Morgan, Edmund Sears. *American Slavery, American Freedom: The Ordeal of Colonial Virginia*. New York: Norton, 1995.

Morgan, Jennifer. "'Some Could Suck over Their Shoulder': Male Travelers, Female Bodies, and the Gendering of Racial Ideology, 1500–1700." *William and Mary Quarterly* 64, no. 1 (1996): 167–92.

Morgan, Philip D. *Slave Counterpoint: Black Culture in the Eighteenth-Century Chesapeake and Lowcountry*. Chapel Hill: University of North Carolina Press for the Omohundro Institute of Early American History and Culture, 1998.

Muller, Jon. *Mississippian Political Economy*. New York: Plenum, 1997.

Murat, Ines. *Colbert*. Translated by Robert Francis Cook and Jeannie Van Asselt. Charlottesville: University Press of Virginia, 1984.

Nabokov, Peter, and Robert Easton. *Native American Architecture*. New York: Oxford University Press, 1989.

Neitzel, Robert S. *Archeology of the Fatherland Site: The Grand Village of the Natchez*. Archaeological Report No. 28. Jackson: Mississippi Department of Archives and History, 1997.

O'Brien, Greg. *Choctaws in a Revolutionary Age*. Edited by Michael D. Green and Theda Perdue. Lincoln: University of Nebraska Press, 2002.

O'Neill, Charles Edward. *Church and State in French Colonial Louisiana: Policy and Politics to 1732*. New Haven: Yale University Press, 1966.

O'Neill, Colman. "Saints." In *New Catholic Encyclopedia*. New York: McGraw-Hill, 1967.

Parkman, Francis. *The Jesuits in North America in the Seventeenth Century*. 1867. Reprint, New York: Penguin, 1983.

———. *La Salle and the Discovery of the Great West*. Reprint, Boston: Little, Brown, 1902.

Pauketat, Timothy R. *Cahokia: Ancient America's Great City on the Mississippi*. New York: Penguin, 2009.

———. "The Missing Persons in Mississippian Mortuary." In *Mississippian Mortuary Practices: Beyond Hierarchy and the Representative Perspective*, edited by Lynne P. Sullivan and Robert C. Mainfort Jr. Gainesville: University Press of Florida, 2010.

Paulett, Robert. *An Empire of Small Places: Mapping the Southeastern Anglo-Indian Trade, 1732–1795*. Athens: University of Georgia Press, 2012.

Perkins, James Breck. *France under Louis XV*. New York: Houghton Mifflin, 1897.

Petto, Christine Marie. *When France Was King of Cartography: The Patronage and Production of Maps in Early Modern France*. Lanham, MD: Lexington, 2007.

Peyramaure, Michel. *Louisiana*. Paris: Presses de la Cité, 1996.

Piker, Joshua. "Colonists and Creeks: Rethinking the Pre-Revolutionary Southern Backcountry." *Journal of Southern History* 70, no. 3 (2004): 503–40.

———. *Okfuskee: A Creek Indian Town in Colonial America*. Cambridge: Harvard University Press, 2004.

Power, Susan C. *Early Art of the Southeastern Indians: Feathered Serpents & Winged Beings*. Athens: University of Georgia Press, 2004.

Price, Jacob M. *France and the Chesapeake: A History of the French Tobacco Monopoly, 1674–1791, and of Its Relationship to the British and American Tobacco Trades*. 2 vols. Ann Arbor: University of Michigan Press, 1973.

Pritchard, James. *In Search of Empire: The French in the Americas, 1670–1730*. New York: Cambridge University Press, 2004.

Prévost, Antoine François. *Histoire du Chevalier des Grieux et de Manon Lescaut*. 1731. Reprint, Paris: A. Perche, 1920.

Purdue, Theda. "'A Sprightly Lover Is the Most Prevailing Missionary': Intermarriage between Europeans and Indians in the Eighteenth-Century South." In *In Light on the Path: The Anthropology and History of the South-*

eastern Indians, edited by Thomas J. Pluckhahn and Robbie Franklyn Ethridge, 165–78. Tuscaloosa: University of Alabama Press, 2006.

Quimby, George. I. "Natchez Social Structure as an Instrument of Assimilation." *American Anthropologist* 48, no. 1 (1946): 134–37.

Reid, John Phillip. *A Law of Blood: The Primitive Law of the Cherokee Nation.* New York: New York University Press, 1970.

Richter, Daniel K. *Facing East from Indian Country: A Native History of Early America.* Cambridge: Harvard University Press, 2001.

———. *The Ordeal of the Longhouse: Change and Persistence on the Iroquois Frontier, 1609–1720.* Chapel Hill: University of North Carolina Press: 1984.

Riddell, William Resnick. "Le Code Noir." *Journal of Negro History* 10, no. 3 (1925): 321–29.

Roper, L. H. *Conceiving Carolina: Proprietors, Planters, and Plots.* New York: Palgrave, 2004.

Rushforth, Brett. *Bonds of Alliance: Indigenous & Atlantic Slaveries in New France.* Chapel Hill: University of North Carolina Press for the Omohundro Institute for Early American History and Culture, 2012.

———."'A Little Flesh We Offer You': The Origins of Indian Slavery in New France." *William and Mary Quarterly* 60, no. 4 (2003).

———."Slavery, the Fox Wars, and the Limits of Alliance." *William and Mary Quarterly* 63, no. 1 (2006): 53–80.

Saadani, Khalil. "Colonialisme et stratégie: Le rôle des forces militaires en Louisiane, 1731–1743." In *France in the New World: Proceedings of the 22nd Annual Meeting of the French Colonial Historical Society*, edited by David Buisseret. East Lansing: University of Michigan Press, (1998): 203–24.

———. "Gift Exchange between French and Native Americans in Louisiana." In *French Colonial Louisiana and the Atlantic World*, edited by Bradley G. Bond, 43–64. Baton Rouge: Louisiana State University Press, 2005.

Sahlins, Marshall David. *How "Natives" Think: About Captain Cook, for Example.* Chicago: University of Chicago Press, 1995.

Salmon, J.H.M. "Venality of Office and Popular Sedition in Seventeenth-Century France: A Review of a Controversy." *Past & Present*, no. 37 (1967): 21–43.

Saunt, Claudio. *A New Order of Things: Property, Power, and the Transformation of the Creek Indians, 1733–1816.* New York: Cambridge University Press, 1999.

Sayre, Gordon M. *The Indian Chief as Tragic Hero: Native Resistance and the Literatures of America, from Moctezuma to Tecumseh.* Chapel Hill: University of North Carolina Press, 2005.

———. "Natchez History Revisited: New Manuscript Sources from Le Page du Pratz and Dumont de Montigny." *Louisiana History* 50, no. 4 (2010): 407–36.

———. "Plotting the Natchez Massacre: Le Page Du Pratz, Dumont De Montigny, Chateaubriand." *Early American Literature* 37, no. 3 (2002): 381–413.

———. *Les Sauvages Américains: Representations of Native Americans in French* and *English Colonial Literature*. Chapel Hill: University of North Carolina Press, 1997.

Scarry, John F. "The Late Prehistoric Southeast." In *The Forgotten Centuries: Indians and Europeans in the American South, 1521–1704*, edited by Charles M. Hudson and Carmen Chaves Tesser, 17–35. Athens: University of Georgia Press, 1994.

Schumpeter, Joseph. *Imperialism and Social Classes, Two Essays by Joseph Schumpeter*. New York: A. M. Kelley: 1951.

Seed, Patricia. *Ceremonies of Possession in Europe's Conquest of the New World, 1492–1640*. Cambridge and New York: Cambridge University Press, 1995.

Sheehan, James. "The Problem of Sovereignty in European History." *American Historical Review* 111, no. 1 (2006): 1–16.

Shoemaker, Nancy. "How Indians Got to Be Red." *American Historical Review* 102, no. 3 (1997): 625–44.

———. *A Strange Likeness: Becoming Red and White in Eighteenth-Century North America*. Oxford and New York: Oxford University Press, 2004.

Shorter, George W., Jr. "Status and Trade at Port Dauphin." *Historical Archaeology* 36, no. 1 (2002): 135–42.

Shuck-Hall, Sheri Marie. "Alabama and Coushatta Diaspora and Coalescence in the Mississippian Shatter Zone." In *Mapping the Mississippian Shatter Zone: The Colonial Indian Slave Trade and Regional Instability in the American South*, edited by Robbie Ethridge and Shuck-Hall, 250–71. Lincoln: University of Nebraska Press, 2009.

Silverman, David J. "Indians, Missionaries, and Religious Translation: Creating Wampanoag Christianity in Seventeenth-Century Martha's Vineyard." *William and Mary Quarterly* 62, no. 2 (2005): 141–74.

Smith, Adam T. *The Political Landscape: Constellations of Authority in Early Complex Polities*. Berkeley: University of California Press, 2003.

Smith, Marvin T. "Aboriginal Population Movements in the Postcontact Southeast." In *The Transformation of the Southeastern Indians, 1540–1760*, edited by Robbie Ethridge and Charles M. Hudson, 3–20. Jackson: University of Mississippi Press, 2002.

Snyder, Christina. "Conquered Enemies, Adopted Kin, and Owned People: The Creek Indians and their Captives." *Journal of Southern History* 73, no. 2 (May 2007): 255–58.

———. *Slavery in Indian Country: The Changing Face of Captivity in Early America*. Cambridge: Harvard University Press, 2010.

Soja, Edward W. *Postmetropolis: Critical Studies of Cities and Regions*. Malden, MA: Blackwell, 2000.

Spear, Jennifer M. "Colonial Intimacies: Legislating Sex in French Louisiana." *William and Mary Quarterly* 60, no. 1 (2003): 75–98.

———. *Race, Sex, and Social Order in Early New Orleans*. Baltimore: Johns Hopkins University Press, 2009.

Stein, Robert Louis. *The French Slave Trade in the Eighteenth Century: An Old Regime Business*. Madison: University of Wisconsin Press, 1979.
Swanton, John Reed. "Ethnological Position of the Natchez Indians." *American Anthropologist* 9, no. 3 (1907): 513–28.
———. *Indian Tribes of the Lower Mississippi Valley and the Adjacent Coast of the Gulf of Mexico*. Washington, DC: U.S. Government Printing Office, 1911.
———. *Source Material for the Social and Ceremonial Life of the Choctaw Indians*. Washington: U.S. Government Print Office, 1931.
Taylor, Alan. *American Colonies*. New York: Viking, 2001.
Thompson, E. P. "The Moral Economy of the English Crowd in the Eighteenth Century." *Past & Present*, no. 50 (February 1971): 76–136.
Tilley, Christopher. *A Phenomenology of Landscape: Places, Paths, and Monuments*. Providence, RI: Berg, 1994.
Tooker, Elizabeth. "Natchez Social Organization: Fact or Anthropological Folklore?" *Ethnohistory* 10, no. 3 (1963): 359–73.
Treasure, G. R. R. *Louis XIV*. New York: Longman, 2001.
Trigger, Bruce G. "The French Presence in Huronia: The Structure of Franco-Huron Relations in the First Half of the Seventeenth Century." *Canadian Historical Review* 49, no. 2 (1968): 107–41.
———. "The Jesuits and the Fur Trade." *Ethnohistory* 12, no. 1 (1965): 30–53.
———. *Natives and Newcomers: Canada's "Heroic Age" Reconsidered*. Kingston: McGill-Queen's University Press, 1985.
Usner, Daniel H. *American Indians in the Lower Mississippi Valley: Social and Economic Histories*. Lincoln: University of Nebraska Press, 1998.
———. "From African Captivity to American Slavery: The Introduction of Black Laborers to Colonial Louisiana." In *The French Experience in Louisiana*, edited by Glenn R. Conrad, 183–200. Lafayette: Center for Louisiana Studies, 1995.
———. "The Frontier Exchange Economy of the Lower Mississippi Valley in the Eighteenth Century." *William and Mary Quarterly*, 3rd ser., 44, no. 2 (April 1987): 165–92.
———. *Indians, Settlers, and Slaves in a Frontier Exchange Economy: The Lower Mississippi Valley before 1783*. Durham: University of North Carolina Press, 1992.
Van Horne, Wayne William. "The War Club: Weapon and Symbol in Southeastern Indian Societies." PhD diss., University of Georgia, 1993.
Vaughan, Alden T. "From White Man to Redskin: Changing Anglo-American Perceptions of the American-Indian." *American Historical Review* 87, no. 4 (1982): 917–53.
Vergé-Franceschi, Michel. "Les officiers généraux de la marine Royale (1715–1774)." PhD diss., Paris IV–Sorbonne. Paris: Librarie de L'inde editeur, 1990.
Vidal, Cécile. "French Louisiana in the Age of Companies, 1712–1731." In *Constructing Early Modern Empires: Proprietary Ventures in the Atlantic World*,

edited by L. H. Roper and Bertrand Van Ruymbeke, 133–61. Boston: Brill, 2007.
Wade, Mason. "French Indian Policies." In *The History of Indian-White Relations*, edited by Wilcomb Washburn. Washington, DC: Smithsonian Institution, 1988.
Weber, Max. *Economy and Society: An Outline of Interpretive Sociology*. Translated by Guenther Roth and Claus Wittich. Vol. 2. Los Angeles: University of California Press, 1978.
Wesson, Cameron B. "Mississippian Sacred Landscapes: The View from Alabama." In *Mississippian Towns and Sacred Landscapes: Searching for an Architectural Grammar*, edited by R. Barry Lewis and Charles Stout, 95–99. Tuscaloosa: University of Alabama Press, 1998.
White, Douglas, George P. Murdock, and Richard Scaglion. "Natchez Class and Rank Reconsidered." *Ethnology* 10, no. 4 (1971): 369–88.
White, Richard. *The Middle Ground: Indians, Empires and Republics in the Great Lakes Region, 1650–1815*. Cambridge: Cambridge University Press, 1991.
———. *The Roots of Dependency: Subsistence, Environment, and Social Change among the Choctaws, Pawnees, and Navajos*. Lincoln: University of Nebraska Press, 1983.
White, Sophie. "Massacre, Mardi Gras, and Torture in Early New Orleans. *William and Mary Quarterly* 70, no 3 (July 2013): 497–53.
———. *Wild Frenchmen and Frenchified Indians: Material Culture and Race in Colonial Louisiana*. Philadelphia: University of Pennsylvania Press, 2012.
Widmer, Randolph J. "The Structure of Southeastern Chiefdoms." In *The Forgotten Centuries: Indians and Europeans in the American South, 1521–1704*, edited by Charles M. Hudson and Carmen Chaves Tesser, 125–55. Athens: University of Georgia Press, 1994.
Winston, Stanford. "Indian Slavery in the Carolina Region." *Journal of Negro History* 19, no. 4 (1934): 431–40.
Wolf, John B. *Louis XIV*. New York: Norton, 1968.
Wood, Peter H. "The Changing Population of the Colonial South: An Overview by Race and Region, 1685–1790." In *Powhatan's Mantle: Indians in the Colonial Southeast*, edited by Gregory A. Waselkov and M. Thomas Hatley, 34–103. Lincoln: University of Nebraska Press, 1989.
Woods, Patricia Dillon. "The French and the Natchez Indians in Louisiana: 1700–1731." In *The French Experience in Louisiana*, edited by Glenn R. Conrad, 278–95. Lafayette: Center for Louisiana Studies, 1995.
———. *French-Indian Relations on the Southern Frontier, 1699–1762*. Ann Arbor: UMI Research Press, 1980.
Worth, John E. "Spanish Missions and the Persistence of Chiefly Power." In *The Transformation of the Southeastern Indians, 1540–1760*, edited by Robbie Ethridge and Charles M. Hudson, 21–83. Jackson: University of Mississippi Press, 2002.

———. *The Timucuan Chiefdoms of Spanish Florida*. 2 vols. Vol. 2, *Resistance and Destruction*. Gainesville: University Press of Florida, 1998.

Wright J. Leitch, Jr. *The Only Land They Knew: The Tragic Story of the American Indians of the Old South*. New York: Macmillan, 1981.

York, Kenneth H. "Mobilian: The Indian Lingua Franca of Colonial Louisiana." In *La Salle and His Legacy: Frenchmen and Indians in the Lower Mississippi Valley*, edited by Patricia Galloway, 139–45. Jackson: University Press of Mississippi, 1982.

Zitomersky, Joseph. *French Americans–Native Americans in Eighteenth-Century French Colonial Louisiana: The Population Geography of the Illinois Indians, 1670s–1760s: The Form and Function of French-Native Settlement Relations in Eighteenth Century Louisiana*. Lund: Lund University Press, 1994.

Index

Africans, 7–12, 93, 148; attack Chaouachas, 183; brutalized, 152–54, 155; Code Noir, 150–51, 157, 249n6; conversions, 151, 185; enslaved, 9, 71, 149–58; Franco-Natchez War, 191, 193, 195–96, 200, 202; free Africans, 114, 139, 149; increased numbers in Louisiana, 145, 149–50, 159, 184, 254n7; intermarriage forbidden, 150, 158; Natchez racial hierarchy, 166, 167, 181–82, 211–12; noted by Natchez, 121, 152, 154, 166; played off against Indians, 183–84; religious practices, 29; slave conspiracies, 156, 180; sided with Natchez, 114, 181, 191, 193, 195, 200–201, 260n137; South Carolina, 169; status different from Indian slaves, 101, 150–52; St. Catherine's Concession, 79, 86, 107, 150; Village Crisis of 1722, 97, 98, 101

Alahofléchia (Natchez Sun), 66, 75

Alibamon Indians, 213–14

Alibamon Mingo, 172, 194

Apple Village of the Natchez, 10, 122, 152; access to Chickasaw traders, 93; Bienville's War, 106, 108, 110, 111–14, 116–17, 185, 190; Franco-Natchez War, 159–63, 171, 177, 192; Natchez Hostage Crisis of 1716, 64; opposition to Great Sun, 34–35, 93, 116–17; relocation near St. Catherine's Concession, 78, 84, 88–90, 116; rivalry with Grand Village, 97, 105; Village Crisis of 1722, 79, 84, 93–10, 102–3; White Earth Village, 235n79

artillery, 99, 121; Franco-Natchez War, 178, 181, 193–95, 197, 199–202

axes, 183, 190; symbols of chiefly authority, 35, 97

Balvay, Arnaud, 5, 65, 108, 128, 187; Bienville-Cadillac rivalry, 77–78; Law's schemes, 81; younger Great Sun's paternity, 48–49

Barnett, James F., Jr., Natchez politics, 4–5; Great Sun's paternity, 49

Baron Roussin, Marie, 159, 191; historical informant, 211–12; marriage to Dumont de Montigny, 211

Bearded One (*le Barbu*, Natchez Sun), 62, 64, 66, 69, 74; execution, 68, 75

bear oil, 115, 163, 176, 195, 197, 243n135

Beaubois, Nicholas Ignace de, 49, 209; disputes with Capuchin Order, 146–47

Berneval, Captain, 94–95, 99, 102–4, 107, 140; wife, 95

Bienville, Jean-Baptiste Le Moyne, sieur de, 8–11, 59, 130, 136; alleged corruption, 11, 71, 109–10, 133, 141, 143–44; Bienville's War, 106–12, 122, 162, 213;

286 / INDEX

de facto governor, 71, 144; diplomatic skills, 9, 11, 70, 74–77, 104–5, 111, 114–15, 144; disputes with Cadillac, 55–56, 70–71, 73, 77, 144; disputes with Hubert, 83–85; disputes with Superior Council, 109–10, 141, 144–45; early career in Louisiana, 53–54, 167; ethnographic observations, 123; family ties, 36, 69–70, 140–41, 189; Natchez Hostage Crisis of 1716, 60, 61, 62–68, 235n78; New Orleans, 144–45; official governor, 207–9; parallels with Tattooed Serpent, 68–71, 140; recalled to France, 145; slave holder, 70–71, 152; Village Crisis of 1722, 94, 104–6

Bienville's War (1723), 111–19, 152, 162; Apple Village, 113–14, 122, 164; contrasts with Hostage Crisis of 1716 and Village Crisis of 1722, 116–19; Jenzanaques, 113; Great Sun's cooperation, 113; preliminaries, 110–12

black racial category, 2, 166–67, 248n2; defined by Code Noir, 10, 150; in Natchez racial hierarchy, 166, 170, 181, 184–85, 212; Taensas origin story, 167–68

Bohemian colonists, 8, 142

Bontemps (enslaved Natchez man), 149, 162, 164; trial and execution, 155–56

Broutin, Ignace, 136, 173; cartographer, 93, 98, 112–13, 142; commander of Fort Rosalie, 137, 159; director of Terre Blanche Concession, 121, 124, 140; Franco-Natchez War, 182, 183, 189, 190, 191, 196, 257n72; Tattooed Serpent's funeral, 125, 128

Cadillac, Antoine de la Mothe, sieur de la, 21, 59; appointed governor, 55; disputes with Bienville, 55–56, 70–72, 77–78; Natchez Hostage Crisis of 1716, 60–63; Natchez recalled to France, 77; outside colonial kinship network, 70

Calliot, Marc Antoine, 147, 175; account of Franco-Natchez War, 175, 176, 181, 186, 193–94, 211–12; later career, 212; Natchez enslaved European captives, 178–79

calumet, 61, 84; Natchez Hostage Crisis of 1716, 60, 63–67, 68, 75–76; Franco-Natchez War, 166, 176, 185, 203; political authority, 40, 43, 58–59, 97, 115; Village Crisis, 88, 102–4, 108, 118, 198

Canadians, 7, 13, 71; competition with French-born, 21, 141; Indians slaves, 110, 156–57; Natchez Hostage Crisis of 1716, 60, 64, 72

Capuchin Order, 27–28, 137; conflicts with Jesuits in Louisiana, 146–47, 209; missions in France 146; slaveholders, 149, 155

cartography: in colonial projects, 13, 91–93, 112–13; regulatory aspects, 137, 155, 209. *See also* spatial practices

Cahura-Juglio (Tunica leader), 114, 190, 199, 201, 203

censuses of Natchez Country, 12, 142, 168, 248n4

Chackchiumas Indians, 84, 105

Charlevoix, Pierre-François-Xavier, 3; ethnographic observations, 31–32, 36, 104, 123; Franco-Natchez War, 163, 178–79, 185; Great Sun's paternity, 48–50; later career, 209–10; pan-Indian conspiracy, 188; visit to Natchez Country, 86–87, 242n90

Chateaubriand, François-René de, 3, 5, 186

Cherokee Indians, 168–69, 204, 213; sheltered Natchez refugees, 204, 207–08

Chickasaw Indians, 41, 84, 105, 120; English merchants, 58–59, 72, 117, 122; English allies, 54, 74; Franco-Natchez War, 186, 188; slave raiders, 33, 48, 54; sheltered Natchez refugees, 203–4, 208–9, 214, 215

Chitimacha Indians, 48, 64–65, 71, 235, 231n17; Le Page du Pratz's slave, 133, 152

Choctaw Indians, 32, 53, 105; Bienville's War, 109, 110, 152; Choctaw Civil War, 214; Choctaw-Natchez War (1726), 188; diplomacy, 1, 84, 187, 199, 204; Franco-Natchez War, 182, 186, 189, 191–97, 201; leaders, 54, 113–14, 172, 196; pan-Indian conspiracy, 188; plazas, 133–34; red racial category, 169–70, 213–15

Choucoura (African slave), 152–54

Clairac tobacco workers, 85, 86, 140; possible Protestants, 141

Code Noir (1685, 1724), 10, 19, 150; excluded non-Catholics from colonies, 19, 223n30; punishments codified, 121, 155; revisions, 157. *See also* Africans

Colbert, Jean-Baptiste, 19, 23–24
colonists' documents: contexts of production, 12, 163, 209–12
commissaire-ordonnateur, 20, 56, 110, 222n13; Hubert, 83; La Chaise, 159
Compagnie des Indes, 86, 95, 175; African slaving stations, 10, 146, 152, 158, 199, 211; commerce in Louisiana, 85, 87, 97, 140, 145, 175, 181, 188, 189; governed Louisiana, 119, 136, 140, 144–46; Law's schemes, 81–82; retroceded Louisiana, 212; sponsorship of missionaries, 27, 137, 146–48, 156
complex chiefdoms, 10, 94; coalescence and dispersal, 32–35, 100; coopted by Spanish, 57; diffuse political authority, 2; human sacrifice, 124–25, 128–29; Natchez complex chiefdom, 2, 6, 43, 52, 65, 74, 215
Creek Indians, 54, 57; plazas, 134; red racial category, 168–69, 213–14; sheltered Natchez refugees, 204, 207–08
Crozat, Antoine, 4, 7, 24, 144; Louisiana monopoly concession, 54–56, 58, 59–60, 67, 72; ordered Fort Rosalie built, 56, 60; retroceded colony, 77, 80, 82

D'Artiguette Diron, Jean-Baptiste Martin, 104, 143; Bienville's War, 113; Choctaw-Natchez War (1726), 188; Franco-Natchez War, 193–95, 196; spellings, 231n33
D'Artiguette, Pierre, 196–97
Dauphin Island, 83; smuggling route, 143
Davion, Antoine, 52, 62–63, 226n62
Dawdy, Shannon, 4, 8, 62, 145, 210. *See also* rogue colonialism
decapitation, 1, 65, 129
de Chépart, Etienne, 3; alcoholism, 159, 176; commander of Fort Rosalie, 159; death, 1, 176, 198; disputes with colonists, 159–60; ignored warnings, 173–74, 178; instigator of Franco-Natchez War, 10–11, 161–64, 165, 172, 209–10; seized Natchez land, 160; tribute from Natchez, 163–64, 176
Deer Moon Festival, 15, 41, 226; relation to Natchez Hostage Crisis of 1716, 73–74
Delangez, Jean, 3; pan-Indian conspiracy, 187

Delaye, Jean sieur, 177; Franco-Natchez War, 186, 187, 191–93, 194–95, 196–97
Desnoyers, Angelique Chavron, 174, 180, 181; historical informant, 211–12; husband Laurent Desnoyers, 176; negotiator, 190–91, 193–95; remarried, 211–12
D'Iberville, Pierre le Moyne, sieur de, 53, 167; Bienville's brother, 8, 36, 69–70, 140–41, 235n95; Natchez Country, 15–16, 30, 32
du Clos, Jean-Baptiste du Bois, 56, 157–58
Dumanoir, Jean-Baptiste Fauçon, sieur, 105, 125, 128, 155; Bienville's War, 106–7, 116; founding St. Catherine's, 86; legal problems, 87, 138–40; ouster, 140; Village Crisis, 93–95
Dumont de Montigny, François-Benjamin, 3, 83, 148; Bienville's War, 113, 116; cartographer, 91, 93, 137, 180; de Chépart's encounter with Suns, 160–62, 176; ethnographic observations, 120–25, 128, 134–36, 154; Franco-Natchez War, 164, 171, 178, 190, 191, 193, 198; Indian innumeracy, 186; jailed by de Chépart, 159–60; later career, 209–12; Natchez racial hierarchy, 181; perceptions of Bienville, 110
Du Ru, (Father), 15–16
Du Tisné, Captain, 104, 125, 137, 147–48

Emerald Site, 33–35, 56, 229n100
English colonists, 163; Indian slave trade, 48; influence in Natchez Country, 52, 62, 66, 73, 93, 108, 117, 181, 204, 213; military rivals, 53–54; trade rivals, 53–60, 189
Etté-Actal, 130–31, 194–95
European: alternative to "French," 13–14

fanimingo, 193
Fatherland Site, 58
femme chef: acculturating outsiders, 50–51; Franco-Natchez War, 179, 198; relations with St. Cosme, 45, 48–51, 52; Village Crisis of 1722, 103–4. *See also* St. Cosme, Jean-François de Buisson de; White Woman; women: diplomatic roles: Natchez
Flour Village, 173; diplomacy, 79, 99–100, 102–5; Village Crisis of 1722, 106; Franco-Natchez War, 199–203

Flour Village, Sun, 108, 119; attacked Tunicas, 202; death, 203; Franco-Natchez War, 199, 201–3; wife, 191, 198. *See also* women: diplomatic roles
forced emigration, 25, 81–83
Fort Jean-Baptiste. *See* Natchitoches
Fort Rosalie, 1, 2, 9, 27, 86; Bienville's War, 110, 112–14; de Chépart command, 159, 176, 210; commanders, 11, 77, 94, 125, 137, 148; founded, 56, 60, 67, 76; Franco-Natchez War, 1, 177, 181–82, 208, 212; Village Crisis of 1722, 95–96, 97, 99, 102–5
Fort St. Pierre, 176; destroyed by Yazoos, 185
Foucault, Michel, 6, 133, 137–38. *See also* heterotopias
France: military practices, 114, 199–200, 234n64; nobility, 18, 20–24, 41; political factionalism, 20; political institutions, 225; social ranks, 223n13, 225n52
Franco-Natchez War (1729–31), 1; Black River Campaign, 4, 199–202; de Chépart's demands for land, 160–63; Chickasaw Indians, 186, 188; Choctaw Indians, 182, 186, 189, 191–97, 201; costs, 197, 212–15; French reinforcements, 197–99; Natchez escapes, 194–97, 202; Natchez forts, 178, 191–95; Natchez preparations, 164; Natchez racial hierarchy, 181; Natchez reasons for war, 190; Natchez surrender and captivity, 202–3; Natchez treatment of African slaves, 180–82; Natchez treatment of captured colonists, 177–78, 180; negotiations, 190–91, 193–97, 200–202; New Orleans, 175, 177–78; sieges, 193–96, 199–202; Yazoos, 176–77, 185, 203
frontier exchange economy, 4, 7, 212; colonists' self-sufficiency, 88–90, 105, 118; destabilizing effects on Natchez, 165
fur trade, 55; impact on Indian polities, 57; impact on Natchez society, 117–19; 164–65

Galloway, Patricia, K., 32–33, 37, 224n46
Geographic Information Systems (GIS), 13
German-born colonists, 8, 13, 22, 142, 148, 223n30
Giraud, Marcel, 4, 140, 141

Gorée, 158
Grand Village (of the Natchez), 4, 5, 7, 9, 12, 208; Bienville's War, 111, 113, 115–16; Franco-Natchez War, 160–62, 176, 185, 189, 202; Natchez Hostage Crisis of 1716, 60–61, 62, 64, 67, 75; political center, 15–16, 30–33, 37, 52, 58, 133; pro-Louisianan, 65, 72, 105, 117, 121–22; religious center, 43, 56, 134; rival villages, 38, 59, 71–74, 85, 171; spatial practices, 112–13, 136, 171; temple plaza, 35, 133–36; Village Crisis of 1722, 98, 107–8
Gravier, Jacques, 51–52, 151
Great Sun, elder, 15–16; authority challenged, 35, 60, 62–63, 65, 117; Bienville' hostage, 64–68; Bienville's War, 108, 110–12, 114; death, 11, 119, 160; diplomacy, 84, 115, 121; Natchez Hostage Crisis of 1716, 61–62, 77; redistributive practices, 72, 93; similarities to Le Moynes, 69–70; slave holder, 70–72; surveillance of Mississippi River, 110–11; Tattooed Serpent's funeral, 124–26; wife, 104, 131–33
Great Sun (political office), 15–16; descriptions of "absolute" authority, 5, 8, 30–32, 36, 38; divine origin, 50–51, 73; French goods reinforce influence, 58; La Salle's visit, 41–43; limited political authority, 29, 35, 38, 58–59; religious duties, 35, 39–40, 52, 73, 134–35; similarities to Louis XIV, 16–17, 43; succession, 39, 50–51, 69
Great Sun, younger, 1, 164; ascension, 160; enslaved, 202, 208; Franco-Natchez War, 173, 176, 186, 190–95, 200–202; French father, 45, 48–51, 160, 244 (*see also* St. Cosme; Tattooed Arm); politically weak, 35, 171–72, 201
Greer, Alan. *See* inner commons
Grigras Indians, 31, 58, 66, 103, 113, 233n59
Guenot de Tréfontaine, Pierre, 87; death and estate, 139; Village Crisis of 1722, 96–97, 103–4, 107, 117, 187

heterotopias, 6; Catholic versions, 135–37; generated authority, 135, 179, 193, 197; movement through, 134–35;

surveillance, 136; temple mound and plaza, 35–36, 128–29; 133–36; transformative power, 134. See *also* Foucault, Michel
Houma Indians, 110, 167, 193
Hubert, Marc-Antoine, 83; disputes with Bienville, 83–85, 107, 110; plantation in Natchez Country, 84, 89
Hughes, Price, 59–60

Illinois, 27, 46, 53, 54, 63, 175, 187
Indian innumeracy, 186–87
Indian slavery, 41–42; brutalized by colonists, 154–55; English role, 48, 53, 58; Franco-Natchez War, 162, 164; held by Bienville, 130; held by Louisianans, 70, 79, 84, 88, 107, 133, 149–57, 202; held by Natchez, 32, 36, 70–71; indigenous slave raiders, 45, 48, 54, 57–58, 93, 204; Natchez Hostage Crisis of 1716, 66, 70–71; Natchez perceptions, 118, 162, 164–66, 180; Saint Domingue, 202; South Carolina, 169; varieties of status, 32, 36, 101, 151–52
inner commons, 9, 11; Bienville's War, 116–17, 120; Franco-Natchez War, 161; Village Crisis of 1722, 98–99
intendants, 18–21, 23, 71, 222n11
intercultural marriage, 172, 180, 189; deleterious effects on Natchez, 172; forbidden for Africans, 150; forbidden by Superior Council, 156–57, 164–65; means of acculturation, 37, 45, 132
interpreters, 41, 64, 193, 200. See *also* Papin, René

Jenzenaque Indians, 58, 73, 93, 152, 185, 235n85; anti-Louisianan, 66, 97, 111, 113
Jesuits (Society of Jesus), 3, 15, 28, 176, 185; Chinese Rites controversy, 27, 46, 230n6; *donnes*, 151; ethnographic observations, 30, 32, 38, 51–52, 123, 163; North American missions, 46–47, 209–10; political influence, 49, 110, 144; rivalry with Capuchin Order, 49, 146–47; rivalry with SME, 46, 146. See *also* Beaubois, Nicholas Ignace de; Charlevoix, Pierre-François-Xavier; Le Petit, Mathurin
jongleurs, 40

kinship, 4; in Europe, 16, 18, 24; in Louisiana, 23, 25; Natchez, 35, 36, 65, 69, 235n94
Kolly, Jean-Daniel, 85–86; arrival at Fort Rosalie, 173, 175; death, 177; estate seized, 182–83; feasted at Grand Village, 176; traveled to Louisiana, 140; Swiss origins, 85, 143
Koroa Indians, 33, 41–42, 47; Franco-Natchez War, 185; in Natchez Country, 58, 71, 151, 239n107

La Chaise, Jacques de, 110; *commissaire-ordinateur*, 144–45; seized Kolly's estate, 182
Lafitau, Joseph-François, 123
La Flore (slave ship), 158, 164
La Fontaine, Sergeant. 95, 106, 242n106
La Loire de Flaucourt, Louis August de, 56, 61–62, 95
La Loire des Ursins, Marc Antoine de, 56, 59, 61–62, 84, 174, 176; converted from Protestantism, 141
La Loires' warehouse, 61, 72, 9
La Rochelle (colonist), 97, 98, 106, 111, 240n61
La Salle, René-Robert Cavelier, sieur de, 3, 7, 16, 151; in Natchez Country, 36, 42–43, 69
Law, John, 80; financial schemes, 80–82, 238n16; impact on Louisiana, 82–83, 145
Le Bouteux, Jean Baptiste Michel, 88, 89, 90, 97
Le Moyne family, 8, 235n95; nepotism in Louisiana, 23, 140–42; resembled Natchez kinship patterns, 69–70
Le Page du Pratz, Antoine, 3; arrival in Louisiana, 84, 85; Bienville's War, 113, 117; de Chépart's activities, 160, 162–64; Chitimacha slave, 133, 152, 178, 258; ethnographic observations, 30–31, 123–24, 166–67, 202, 210–11, 258n80; Franco-Natchez War, 172, 178, 181, 186, 194–96; friendship with Tattooed Serpent, 117–19; Great Sun's paternity, 49; Indian innumeracy, 186; later career, 209–10, 214; Natchez language speaker, 47; Natchez religion, 38, 73–74, 131–33, 208; red racial category, 166–72; slavery, 36, 150; Tattooed Serpent's funeral,

124–31; Village Crisis of 1722, 95–96, 99–100, 103, 104
Le Petit, Mathurin, 38; ethnographic observations, 40, 213, 228n92; Franco-Natchez War, 162–63, 181, 187, 210
Le Sueur, Jean-Paul de, 141, 189, 191, 201
Little Sun, 64–68, 69, 74–75, 115; death, 114
livestock, 88–90, 98, 100, 106–8, 172; targeted by Natchez, 93–94, 120, 165, 177
Longrais, Martin des, 99, 103–4, 107–8; death, 176; imprisonment of Dumont de Montigny, 159; Franco-Natchez War, 173; memorial on Village Crisis of 1722, 112, 211
Louboey, Henri, chevalier de, 189–90, 192, 195, 196, 211, 257n72; Protestant 148
Louis XIII, 18
Louis XIV, 17–20, 46; limited authority: 18, 21, 54, 79, 80; political hegemony, 17–18, 43, 141; similarities with Great Sun, 16, 35–36; wars of, 22, 52. *See also* War of Spanish Succession
Louis XV, 80, 143
Louisiana, 2; colonists' marital practices, 24, 211–12; Crozat's monopoly, 54–56, 58, 59–60, 67, 72; early years, 53; economic and strategic potential, 9, 15, 55, 81, 96, 214; European immigrants, 38; factionalism, 20, 55–56, 70–71, 143; missions, 27–28, 46; political institutions, 18, 20, 23, 77, 94, 136, 222; slavery, 138, 145, 150, 184
Lusser, Josephe-Christophe, de, 213

Massé, Sub-Lieutenant, 173, 176; wife, 178, 180
Merveilleux, François-Louis de: Choucoura case, 152–54; commander of Fort Rosalie, 148, 159; Franco-Natchez War, 182, 188–89, 257n72; Protestantism, 148; Swiss origins, 142–43
Mesplet, sieur, 189–91
"middle ground," 8, 11–12, 75, 132, 236n112
ministry of marine (French naval and colonial administration), 24, 56, 71, 157, 199
Mississippi River, 12, 42, 52, 66; gateway to Natchez Country, 56, 91, 112; link to Illinois, 61, 72, 144, 182; missions, 27
Mobile, 53–54; colonial capital, 17, 43, 59, 60–62; smuggling route, 143, 144

Mobilian trade language, 47
Motte de Madame, 60, 89, 93, 98, 109

Nairne, Thomas, 54
Natchez Country, 7–8, 13; African immigrants, 29; cartographic representations, 87–92, 112, 136; cultural and ethnic diversity, 78, 121; dimensions, 11, 47, 51; empowering landscape, 6, 124, 133–35, 161, 204; European immigrants, 2, 9, 44, 53, 85–89, 107; inner commons, 9, 11, 98–99, 116–17, 120, 161; missions, 27; Native American immigrants, 32, 58; racial categories, 5, 178; settlement patterns, 11, 145, 148
Natchez Hostage Crisis of 1716, 60–68, 94; Bienville's role, 63–68; Great Sun supported Louisiana, 61–62; Natchez peace terms, 67, 76; reinforced perceptions of similarity, 68–72; Tunicas, 62. *See also* Bearded One; La Loire de Flaucourt, Louis August de; La Loire des Ursins, Marc Antoine de; Penicault, André
Natchez Indians, 1; absorption of Europeans discontinued, 179–80; absorption of outsiders, 9, 50–51, 98; cosmology, 38–39, 50, 125, 131, 222n3; council of elders, 39, 163–64, 171–73, 176, 180; dispersal, 202–4, 207–8; ethnonyms, 15, 220n23; enslaved by colonists, 149, 154–56; female leaders, 45, 48–49, 126–28, 131–33, 172–73; festivals, 41, 134–35; fortresses, 178, 191, 199–202; French colonists possible adoptees, 41–42, 50, 52; French popular memory, 3, 5, 256n57; funeral rites, 124–31, 170; human sacrifice, 125, 128, 133–34; language, 47; marital practices, 36–38; medicine, 40, 228n92; in Oklahoma, 208; origin stories, 166–67; political hierarchy, 8, 30–32; politically reunified as red men, 11, 170–71, 205; priesthood, 40–41; redistributive practices, 7, 32–35, 52, 56–57, 93, 115, 117; slaveholders, 36, 70–71; social ranks, 1, 36–37, 70–71, 131–33; social status derogated by colonial law, 156–9, 165; spatial practices, 6, 11, 38, 125; surrender and captivity, 201–3; temple, 33, 35, 39–40, 125–30; 161, 226n62 (*see*

also Grand Village; heterotopias); war with Tunicas (1723), 109. *See also* Apple Village; Bienville's War; Flour Village; Flour Village Sun; Franco-Natchez War; Great Sun, elder; Great Sun (political office); Great Sun, younger; Jenzenaque Village; Natchez Hostage Crisis of 1716; red racial category; Tattooed Arm; Tattooed Serpent; Tioux Indians; Village Crisis of 1722

Natchez Paradox, 37–38

Natchitoches (colonial settlement), 113; attacked by Natchez, 203

New Orleans, 10, 139, 160; Franco-Natchez War, 175, 181; named colonial capital, 49, 144

noblesse de robe, 21–24. *See also* venal offices

non-French colonists, 140–43

Old Hair, 94, 102–3, 105, 115; death, 114, 190. *See also* Apple Village; Bienville's War; Village Crisis of 1722

O'Neill, Charles, 3–4, 55, 141

Orléans, Philippe duc d', 80, 143

Oyelape (Sun of Apple Village), 64, 65, 67, 74–75, 88

Pailloux, Jacques Barbazant de, 67, 104–6; Protestant, 140

pan-Indian conspiracy, 3, 186–88

Papin, René (interpreter), 161–62, 173, 176; wife, 180

parallels between Natchez and Louisianan colonists, 7, 16; "absolutism," 43; ascensions through marriages, 24, 50; deities, 29–30, 42–43; factional strife, 71; female diplomats, 48–49, 125–26, 131–33, 180, 190–92; heterotopias, 35–36, 135; medicine, 40; moral codes, 38, 118; Natchez Hostage Crisis of 1716, 68–76; origin stories, 38–39, 166–67; political hierarchy, 8, 31, 63, 115, 128; reciprocal killings, 65–66, 75; religious practices, 16, 25–29, 38–41, 123–24, 151; slaveholding, 70–71; social practices, 32, 76–77, 151; spatial practices, 6, 35, 179; Village Crisis of 1722, 101, 104

parlements, 18, 20, 23, 222n9

Penicault, André, 56; ethnographic observations, 30, 36, 69; Natchez Hostage Crisis of 1716, 61–62; 65; Protestant, 141

People of the Sun. *See* Natchez Indians: ethnonyms

Périer de Salvert, Alexis-Antoine, 199, 209

Perier, Étienne, 5, 10, 158; alliance with Choctaws, 188–89; appointed commandant-general, 119; appointment of de Chépart, 159; early career, 145–46; Franco-Natchez War, 161, 182, 191, 197–204, 208; journalist, 123; Kolly's estate, 182; later career, 209; pan-Indian conspiracy, 186–88; reinstatement of de Chépart, 159–60; responses to factionalism, 147. *See also* Franco-Natchez War

petites nations, 110, 167, 200

Pontchartrain, Louis Phélypeaux, comte de, 24, 46, 56, 59, 71, 77

Powhatan Indians, 8, 9, 94

Protestants, 28, 141, 148; excluded from colonies, 19, 222n30

Quapaw Indians (Arkansas), 84, 113, 151

Raphael de Luxembourg, 137, 139, 141, 199; disputes with Beaubois, 49, 146–49, 209; ethnographic observations, 167–68

red racial category, 1–3, 5, 13, 205, 252; alternative to spatially-generated identity, 11, 162–63, 171, 197, 205; contrasted with other categories, 166–67, 173, 181; Cherokees, 168–69; Choctaws, 213; Creeks, 168–69, 213; Deer Moon festival, 73–74; dissemination, 167–71, 215; metaphor for completeness, 169–70; Natchez formation of, 165–71, 173; Taensas origin story, 167–68; Tattooed Serpent's funeral, 126. *See also* Shoemaker, Nancy

Red Shoe, 113–14, 152, 213. *See also* Bienville's War

Régis du Roullet, Louis Joseph Guillaume, 133, 189, 213

Richebourg, Chavagne de, 68–69, 76, 77

rogue colonialism, 4, 8, 143–45. *See also* Dawdy, Shannon

Roman Catholicism, 6; Africans converted, 151, 185; Chinese Rites controversy, 27–28, 46, 230n6; cosmology, 25–26,

38, 42, 131–32, 228–29; domestic missions, 27–28, 146; missions in Louisiana, 44, 50–51, 146–48, 199; moral codes, 38; priesthood and rites, 26–27, 42, 135. *See also* Capuchins; heterotopias; Jesuits

Rushforth, Brett, 151–52; Indian slaves, 156

Saint Domingue, 80, 85, 202, 207

Sayre, Gordon M., 12, 245n22; Indian innumeracy, 186; pan-Indian conspiracy, 187–88

Second Natchez War. *See* Village Crisis of 1722

Seven Years' War ([1754] 1756–1763), 96

Shoemaker, Nancy, 2, 166–7, 169, 248n2. *See also* red racial category

slave codes, 10. *See also* Code Noir

Snyder, Christina, 36, 70, 101, 152

Société des Missions Étrangères (SME), 27, 46. *See also* St. Cosme, Jean-François de Buisson de

Society of Jesus. *See* Jesuits

South Carolina, 168; contact with Natchez, 53, 54; Indian slave trade, 59; racial categories, 168–69, 214; sheltered Natchez refugees, 207; trade rival of Louisiana, 57, 59, 81

spatial practices, 5, 7, 11; Bienville's War, 110–11, 116; built environments, 35; colonists', 90, 137–38, 212, 214; European cartographic representations, 88, 91, 112–13, 137, 179; land tenure, 116; Natchez practices, 110–11, 125, 133, 145, 163, 204; urban planning, 145; Village Crisis of 1722, 93. *See also* cartography; heterotopias; Natchez Indians: temple

St. Catherine's Concession, 1, 159, 171; acquired by Kolly, 85; Bienville's War, 103–6, 108; food production, 89–90; founding, 84; Franco-Natchez War, 176–77, 192, 198; legal troubles, 138–40; parallels with Natchez villages, 84–85; poor financial conditions, 86–87, 105–6; relations with Natchez, 88, 115–16; spatial practices, 137; tobacco production, 91, 105; Village Crisis of 1722, 79, 93–102, 106–7, 164

St. Catherine's Creek, 33, 56, 84–85, 136, 178, 191

St. Cosme, Jean-François de Buisson de, 45–52; difficulties at Natchez mission, 46–48; ethnographic observations, 48; father of younger Great Sun, 45, 49–51, 244n142; murdered by Chitimachas, 48, 64–65, 231n17

St. Cosme (Natchez leader), 201–2

Sun King. *See* Louis XIV

Superior Council of Louisiana, 18, 20, 94, 136; Bienville's War, 106–10; Bontemp's trial, 155–56; Choucoura case, 152–54; disputes with Bienville, 109–10, 144–45; edicts regarding Native Americans' legal and social statuses, 10, 156–59, 165; responses to Village Crisis of 1722, 94, 106–7; ruling on de Chépart, 159–60; rulings regarding St. Catherine's Concession, 138–40

Swanton, John, 36–37, 68, 167, 169, 208, 226n62

Swiss-born colonists, 8, 13, 142–43, 153–54, 189

Taensas, 151, 226n62; red racial category, 167–68, 214

Tattooed Arm, 49, 104, 186; advocate for peace, 172–73, 180, 185, 190; cross-cultural informant, 164–65, 202, 204, 210

Tattooed Serpent, 8, 36, 145; association with Bienville, 69–75, 115–16; Bienville's hostage, 64–68; Bienville's War, 106, 108–12, 114, 171; death, 119, 124, 160; diplomacy, 121–23; funeral, 124–35; Le Page du Pratz, 117–19; redness, 170; Village Crisis of 1722, 104–5; wife, 103, 125–26, 195

Tattooed Serpent (Natchez leader of same name), 201–2

tax farms, 20; 54, 81

Terre Blanche Concession, 143, 150, 171, 174, 190, 235n79; conflicts with Tioux, 120–23; founding, 85–86, 174; Franco-Natchez War, 176, 184, 190, 196, 198; sold to Le Blanc-Belle Isle Associates, 140; spatial practices, 112, 137–38. *See also* Broutin, Ignace; Desnoyers, Angelique Chavron; Tioux Indians

Thé (Natchez solar deity), 15, 38–39

Théoloëls. *See* Natchez Indians: ethnonyms

Third Natchez War. *See* Bienville's War

Tioux Indians, 102, 105, 184, 185–86; abandoned Natchez Country, 123, 171, 244n5; arrived in Natchez Country, 58; disputes with Terre Blanche Concession, 120–23; language, 33; location, 113

tobacco, 4, 10, 108; competition with Virginian tobacco, 80; cultivation expanded, 5, 158, 160; French domestic market, 54–55, 80–81; Louisianan, 86, 91, 105, 138–39, 145; Natchez uses, 40, 128

tobacco workers, 12, 81, 140–41

Tonti, Henri, 41–42, 151, 229n100

Tunicas, 33, 51, 158, 226n62; Bienville's War, 109–10, 113, 114; Franco-Natchez War, 182, 185–86, 189–90, 197–203; Natchez Hostage Crisis of 1716, 62–64; war with Natchez (1723), 109

Usner, Daniel H., 2. *See also* frontier exchange economy

venal offices, 20–21, 24

Versailles, 18, 21–22; coopted French nobility, 23

Village Crisis of 1722, 93; attacks on St. Catherine's Concession, 93–99; diplomacy, 79, 102–3. *See also* Dumanoir, Jean-Baptiste Fauçon, sieur

villages: complex chiefdoms, 32, 38; primary social unit, 8, 17, 24–25, 73–74, 100, 171, 215

violence, 1, 5, 10, means of intercultural communications, 9; Village Crisis of 1722: 94–97, 100–102

voyageurs, 54; Natchez Hostage Crisis of 1716, 64–72, 75, 78

War of Austrian Succession (1740–1748), 123, 209

War of Spanish Succession (1702–1713), 52–54, 59, 79, 145

White Earth Village, 65, 66, 69, 73, 75. *See also* Apple Village

white racial category, 2; Code Noir, 150; intermarriage with Indians forbidden, 157–59, 165; Taensas origin story, 167–68

White, Richard. *See* "middle ground"

White, Sophie, 170

White Woman (female Sun), 8, 39, 42, 201–2, 221n3; diplomacy, 104, 195; supervision of captured Europeans, 178, 191. *See also* femme chef

widows of Franco-Natchez War, 211

Woebegon, Lake, 44

women: agents of acculturation, 45, 50–51, 258n80; diplomatic roles: colonists, 190–91, 193–95; diplomatic roles: Natchez, 103–4, 164–65, 185, 198–99; means of social ascent, 24. *See also* Desnoyers, Angelique Chavron; fanimingo; femme chef; Tattooed Arm; White Woman

Wood, Patricia Dillon, 4

Yazoo Indians, 59, 84, 108, 113; Franco-Natchez War, 176–77, 185, 203

Early American Places

On Slavery's Border: Missouri's Small Slaveholding Households, 1815–1865
by Diane Mutti Burke

Sounds American: National Identity and the Music Cultures of the Lower Mississippi River Valley, 1800–1860
by Ann Ostendorf

The Year of the Lash: Free People of Color in Cuba and the Nineteenth-Century Atlantic World
by Michele Reid-Vazquez

Ordinary Lives in the Early Caribbean: Religion, Colonial Competition, and the Politics of Profit
by Kirsten Block

Creolization and Contraband: Curaçao in the Early Modern Atlantic World
by Linda M. Rupert

An Empire of Small Places: Mapping the Southeastern Anglo-Indian Trade, 1732–1795
by Robert Paulett

Everyday Life in the Early English Caribbean: Irish, Africas, and the Construction of Difference
by Jenny Shaw

Natchez Country: Indians, Colonists, and the Landscapes of Race in French Louisiana
by George Edward Milne

Slavery, Childhood, and Abolition in Jamaica, 1788–1838
by Colleen A. Vasconcellos

Privateers of the Americas: Spanish American Privateering from the United States in the Early Republic
by David Head

Charleston and the Emergence of Middle-Class Culture in the Revolutionary Era
by Jennifer L. Goloboy

Anglo-Native Virginia: Trade, Conversion, and Indian Slavery in the Old Dominion, 1646–1722
by Kristalyn Marie Shefveland

Slavery on the Periphery: The Kansas-Missouri Border in the Antebellum and Civil War Eras
by Kristen Epps

In the Shadow of Dred Scott: St. Louis Freedom Suits and the Legal Culture of Slavery in Antebellum America
by Kelly M. Kennington

Brothers and Friends: Kinship in Early America
by Natalie R. Inman

George Washington's Washington: Visions for the National Capital in the Early American Republic
by Adam Costanzo

Borderless Empire: Dutch Guiana in the Atlantic World, 1750–1800
by Brian Hoonhout

Complexion of Empire in Natchez: Race and Slavery in the Mississippi Borderlands
by Christian Pinnen

Toward Cherokee Removal: Land, Violence, and the White Man's Chance
by Adam J. Pratt

A Weary Land: Slavery on the Ground in Arkansas
by Kelly Houston Jones

Generations of Freedom: Gender, Movement, and Violence in Natchez, 1779–1865
by Nik Ribianszky

www.ingramcontent.com/pod-product-compliance
Lightning Source LLC
Chambersburg PA
CBHW010502270825
31736CB00007B/283